Eagles Rampant Rising

Eagles Rampant Rising
Two Lives of American Fighter Pilots During the First World War

The Way of the Eagle
Charles J. Biddle

Quentin Roosevelt a Sketch With Letters
Edited by Kermit Roosevelt

Eagles Rampant Rising
Two Lives of American Fighter Pilots During the First World War
The Way of the Eagle
by Charles J. Biddle
and
Quentin Roosevelt a Sketch With Letters
Edited by Kermit Roosevelt

First published under the titles
The Way of the Eagle
and
Quentin Roosevelt a Sketch With Letters

FIRST EDITION

Leonaur is an imprint
of Oakpast Ltd

Copyright in this form © 2013 Oakpast Ltd

ISBN: 978-1-78282-203-5 (hardcover)
ISBN: 978-1-78282-204-2 (softcover)

http://www.leonaur.com

Publisher's Notes
The views expressed in this book are not necessarily
those of the publisher.

Contents

The Way of the Eagle   7
Quentin Roosevelt a Sketch With Letters   221

The Way of the Eagle

"I THEREFORE STOOD THERE WITH MY POSIES LIKE SOME JUNE BRIDE, LOOKING AS SELF-CONSCIOUS AS I FELT."

Contents

Foreword	13
In the Schools	17
Escadrille N. 73	43
Escadrille Lafayette	116
13th Aero Squadron, A. E. F.	165
4th Pursuit Group, A. E. F.	212

To
OLIVER MOULTON CHADWICK
KILLED IN ACTION. AUGUST 14, 1917

Foreword

In order that anyone who may chance to read this book of letters may better understand the detailed descriptions of fights in the air which it contains, certain fundamental facts of a more or less technical nature should be at all times kept clearly in mind.

As everyone knows, there are many different types of aeroplanes specially adapted to as many different uses. Among these there are three distinct classes which cannot be confused without resulting in an almost complete failure to appreciate the tactics of air fighting.

These three classes are: first, the small single-seater fighting plane known to the French as an "*avion de chasse*," to the English as a "scout," and to the American Air Service as a "pursuit machine." Next comes the larger type used for the taking of photographs and gathering of information, the regulation of artillery fire, liaison work with the infantry, and the dropping of bombs from high altitudes during the daytime. This type usually carries two, sometimes three, men. Finally we have the great multi-motored bomber equipped with two, three or four engines and carrying a crew of from two to eight men.

The pursuit plane is the smallest and fastest of all flying machines and has almost always carried but one man. Typical of this type are the French Spad and Nieuport, the English S. E. 5 and Sopwith Camel, and for the Germans the Albatross, the Pfalz, and the Fokker. The United States produced no machines of this type and our pursuit squadrons were entirely equipped with French Spads and Nieuports. The speed of these machines varies from 100 to almost 135 miles per hour. Their function is purely to fight and by fighting to create an area in which it will be reasonably safe for their own larger machines to work and by attacking the larger machines of the enemy, to prevent them from accomplishing their missions. They are also used for attacking roads, etc., from a low altitude with small bombs and machine-gun fire, known in the Air Service as "strafing."

Speaking generally the pursuit machine is armed with one or two machine-guns which are bolted fast in front of the pilot above the motor and which cannot be moved in any direction. The guns fire only straight ahead through the revolving blades of the propeller and the machine is totally unprotected in the rear, relying for its safety upon its speed and ability to manoeuvre quickly. Above the guns is mounted a sight which is lined up with them and then bolted fast. To shoot it is therefore necessary for the pilot to aim his whole plane by manoeuvring it with his controls and when he has in this way brought his sights to bear upon his enemy, he fires by pressing triggers which are attached to his control stick and connected with the guns by means of wires.

There is no mystery about a machine-gun firing through a propeller without hitting the blades. Nearly every one understands the principle by which the valves of a gasoline motor are timed so as to open and close at a given point in the revolution of the engine. In the same way a machine-gun may be timed to shoot. On the end of the cam shaft of the motor is placed an additional cam. Next to this is a rod connected with the breech block of the gun. When the gun is not being fired the rod is held away from the cam by a spring. Pressing the trigger brings the two into contact and each time that the cam revolves it strikes the rod which in turn trips the hammer of the gun and causes it to fire. The cam is regulated so that it comes in contact with the rod just as each blade has passed the muzzle of the gun which can therefore fire at this time only. The engine revolves at least 1000 turns per minute and as there are two chances for. the gun to fire for each revolution, this would allow the gun to fire 2000 shots per minute.

The rate of fire of a machine-gun varies from about 400 to 1000 shots per minute according to the type of gun and the way in which it is rigged. The gun therefore has many more opportunities to fire between the blades of the propeller than its rate of fire will permit it to make use of. Consequently the gun can work at full speed regardless of ordinary variations in the number of revolutions of the engine. The second type of plane is nearly always a two-seater although some three-seaters were also used for this work. Their purpose is to gain information, take pictures and so forth but not to fight unless attacked and forced to defend themselves. Examples of the two-seater type are the English De Havilands and R. E. 8, the French Breguet and Salmson, the American Liberty, which is a copy of the English De Haviland 4, and the German Rumpler and Halberstadt. In this class of machine the pilot has one or two fixed guns shooting straight ahead as in the single-seater.

In addition to this, however, the observer, who sits in a cockpit behind the pilot, is armed with one or two movable machine-guns mounted on a swivel. He can fire these guns in any direction except in those angles which are blinded by the wings, body, and tail portions of his own machine. The two-seater, called a *"biplace"* by the French, being larger and slower than the single-seater and therefore incapable of being so quickly handled, would be at the latter's mercy were it not for the protection afforded by its movable guns. The pilot of a two-seater has comparatively little opportunity to use his guns and they can be rather easily avoided by the single-seater. It is the fire from the observer's guns which the pursuit machine must guard against in attacking a two-seater. This he usually does by approaching either from the front or by seeking to get into a position behind and below so as to shield himself by keeping behind the body and tail planes of his enemy. The observer cannot of course shoot through his own machine without risk of bringing himself down.

The third class is much the largest and slowest of all, constructed with a view to carrying great weights. It is protected both fore and aft by movable machine-guns, but its size, slow speed, and inability to climb to high altitudes, make it very vulnerable to attack both by anti-aircraft fire from the ground and by enemy pursuit machines. It was therefore used, at least on the western front, almost exclusively for night bombing. Examples of this type are the English Handley-Page, the Italian Caproni and the German Gotha. The United States at the end of the war had not gotten any night bombers on the front.

The distances at which fighting is carried on in the air is not nearly so great as is generally supposed. Almost all successful combats were fought at ranges less than 300 feet and again the majority of these at between 200 feet and 30 feet. There were of course many instances of planes being brought down at longer ranges but these were the exception. The speed of machines is so great and the angles so changeable as to be almost impossible to calculate with anything approaching accuracy. The only sure shot is that at almost point-blank range where the question of how far one must shoot ahead of a moving mark in order to hit it is greatly simplified.

This difficulty in shooting explains why so much air fighting is often carried on with so little result. In addition to this, although an aeroplane seems to present a large target, the vital spots which must be hit in order to bring it down are in reality very small. The men and the vitals of the machinery take up but a small fraction of the machine and the parts where they are not may be riddled without apparent effect.

These letters were written to members of the author's family without thought of publication and the author is still very much in doubt as to whether they should be published. They have been printed almost exactly as they were written except for the omission of some personal names and of the more private matters. In addition to this, accounts of a number of combats have been omitted which, owing to their similarity to other fights described, it was feared might become tedious. A few descriptions and criticisms have been inserted which the author would have written at the same time as the rest of the letters had it not been for lack of time and the censorship regulations. Names of places have also been added.

Charles J. Biddle.

Philadelphia, Pa., March 25, 1919.

THE PIN OF A FRENCH
MILITARY PILOT

CHAPTER 1

In the Schools

Avord, France, April 15, 1917.

My application for permission to enlist in the French Foreign Legion, Aviation Section, went in on March 24th. It takes several weeks for this to go through however and it was not until last Tuesday that Dr. X—— notified me that I had been accepted. The next day I went to a dingy recruiting office near the Invalides and was examined by the French doctors. The office reminded me very much of an old print of an ancient police station from Dickens. A dark little place with barred windows adorned with numerous cobwebs, on each side of the main room a rough bench, and in the corner a huge old-fashioned barrel stove. The examination was not severe, none of that business of shooting pistols off unexpectedly that we used to hear was part of an aviator's preliminary examination. There were a number of men being examined for the infantry of the Foreign Legion at the same time.

We all stripped to our bare skins, negroes, Frenchmen, another American and myself, and some gentlemen at whose nationality one could only guess. One of the latter who spoke a little English was much perturbed because he forgot and signed his real name. He had all his papers made up in an alias and then got excited at the last minute. The officer in charge noticed the mistake but laughed and passed it over. They are used to such things in the Legion. Of course the Aviation Division of "*La Légion Étrangère*" is entirely separate from the infantry so far as our seeing anything of the latter is concerned. On Thursday I went to the Invalides, enlisted, and received my orders, which were to proceed to the aviation school at Avord the following morning. This I did, arriving here Friday afternoon and here I am.

This school is a most extremely interesting place and more enormous than anything one who had not seen it could possibly imagine.

The aviation fields and hangars literally stretch for miles and I can hardly guess how many machines there are here. I should say about six hundred. At the Curtiss school at Newport News there were about fifteen. This is the largest school in France, but there are many other very large ones scattered all over the country. Any morning or afternoon when the weather permits, the machines look like the crows flying home to roost from the marshes on the Delaware.

I started work on Saturday morning in the beginners' class. The machines are known as "Penguins" and are Bleriot monoplanes with small engines and their wings cut down so that they cannot fly. They are rather difficult to handle and are designed to teach the men to steer straight. At first you go sideways and twist around in every direction except the one in which you wish to go. After you catch on to them however you go tripping along over the ground at some 35 or 40 miles an hour. When you graduate from this class you go to another called "*Rouleurs*." These are Bleriots which will fly but the pupils are not allowed to take them off the ground. I will write you all about the various steps as I go along.

At all events it will probably be from one to two months before I get off the ground and six before I get to the front, so there is nothing to worry about just yet. In this school a pupil is so thoroughly trained in the rudiments that by the time he is ready to fly he is capable of doing so with the least possible danger. The French machines are beautifully made, nothing that we have so far in America can compare with them.

You would laugh to see your cute little son dressed up in the blue uniform of a French *poilu*. The government gives us everything from the skin out and the committee for the Franco-American Flying Corps provides us with a really good uniform. I have just ordered mine from the tailor. I am going to take some pictures with my Kodak and will send them to you as soon as they are finished. We live in a barracks, about twenty men in a room, and eat in a great mess shack. There are about three thousand men in the camp counting mechanics and quantities of *annamites*. These latter act as servants, make roads and do the dirty work generally. They come from Indo-China, and look much like Chinese. They all shellac their teeth until they are coal black which gives their faces a most extraordinary expression.

The food is wholesome enough although extremely rough, nothing like as good as the U. S. Army gets. There are canteens where we buy things to help out and we receive 200 *francs* a month from the

Franco-American Committee for this purpose. I am therefore not exactly living in luxury but am getting so fat and healthy you won't know me when I come home.

P. S. I enclose two notes, one for one *franc* and the other for 50 *centimes*. They are part of my first pay as a soldier of France and I thought that you or mother might care to keep them. We get one *franc* 25 *centimes* per day which is 5 times what the infantry gets.

Avord, May 3, 1917.

On May 1 a new schedule went into effect here and we now get up at 4 a. m., work until 9 a. m., lunch at 10, supper at 5 p. m., back to work at 5.30 and do not quit until dark which is about 9 p. m. Remember that under our daylight saving plan the clocks are all one hour ahead, so this really means getting up at 3 a. m. You can see that this does not leave much time for sleep, but as we are off all during the heat of the day, we make it up then. The reason for these peculiar hours is of course because during the heat of the day the air becomes full of holes or "*remous*" as the French call them, which are very unpleasant affairs for an "*éleve pilote.*"[1] Although we have been having beautiful weather for the past ten days, only about half of them have been good for flying, owing to too much wind. May is however supposed to be the best month of the year here for our work, so we should make good progress. I have just been promoted with the rest of my class from the Penguins to the "*Rouleurs*," and shall probably remain in this class for three weeks. The object of the *Rouleurs* is to teach the pupil to steer a straight course and to get a correct "*ligne de vol.*"[2] The machine will fly but we are not allowed to leave the ground. It will therefore be some time yet before I begin to do any actual flying.

Avord, May 15th, 1917.

Since my last letter I have passed through the "*Rouleur*" class and am now in the "*Décolleur*". In the latter class we use the same machine as in the "*Rouleur*" but are allowed to fly it a little. We start by going up three feet, flying along a short distance and then shutting off the motor and allowing the machine to settle back on the ground. By degrees we take the machine higher and higher in straight flights up and down a big field. After a while we will be sent on to another class where we fly a little higher and make regular sure enough landings. All these flights are straight, the machine being brought to the ground

---

1. Student pilot.
2. Line of flight.

at each end of the field and turned by hand. In this way the pupil in a sense teaches himself to fly and the instructor merely stands on the ground with the rest of the class and tells you what to do before you start. The monitor does not go up with the pupil as a general rule until after he has obtained his military license on the Bleriot machine and begins to learn to drive a Nieuport.

The training for the pilots of the large machines such as Caudrons and Farmans is somewhat different but I hope not to have anything to do with these types. The schooling for a pilot of the small fast scout or *"chasse"* machines as the French call them is usually the training on the Bleriot monoplanes. The chasse machines are more difficult to drive than the bigger planes, and if a man proves inapt in the Bleriot School he is "radiated" to a Caudron or a Farman and after completing his training on these types is sent to the front as a pilot of one of the larger planes which do such work as picture taking, the regulation of artillery fire and bomb dropping. This is of course very interesting work but I should much prefer to be in the chasse, which appeals to me more than the other.

As I said before I am now in the *Décolleur* class and am just beginning to fly. So far I have not been higher than the remarkable altitude of six feet.

Avord, May 24th, 1917.

The last page of this letter has been written on the above date and at Avord. I came back last Saturday the 19th, and have really not had a moment to do anything but work, eat and sleep since that time. About a week ago, almost the whole school closed up due to a lack of oil and everyone went away on permission. My particular class had gone away the week before and so when our one week's permission was up we had to come back although there was but little prospect of our being able to work. It so happens, however, that there is enough oil for the few men who are here to work with, and as there are plenty of machines and monitors I have been able to fly to my heart's content. No standing around waiting for someone else to get through. Since last Saturday I have had twice as much time flying as in all the rest of my sojourn here put together, and it is now real flying.

Yesterday I was up for two hours and a half and an hour and a half this morning. The flying is all by yourself of course under this system. This morning I got up a little over two hundred metres.[3] The country

---

3. A metre is, roughly speaking, a yard, more exactly 39 and 3/8 inches.

is beautiful in its spring plumage and with the ranges of hills on the horizon, presents a wonderful picture from the air. You get no feeling of dizziness and one is so thoroughly familiarized with the machines before being allowed to leave the ground that when one does go up one feels capable of handling one's plane.

Even after we are allowed to fly we are kept making straight lines up and down a big field at low altitudes for several days before we do any cruising about the country. Since Saturday I have passed through four classes so you can see that we are moving right along. It goes without saying that this is infinitely better than the first of the training and I certainly am enjoying it. There is nothing scary about it so far and the work is very interesting and no end of sport. I would, however, rather shoot ducks!!!!

Avord, May 30th, 1917.

Since writing to mother last week I have finished up all the work preliminary to the tests for my military brevet and have started in on the latter. The last two things the *élève* does before beginning his final tests, are a serpentine and a spiral from seven or eight hundred metres with motor shut off, to a given landing place. These manoeuvres are simply what their name implies and are methods of losing height without gaining distance, *i.e.*, to land on a spot under you. Yesterday morning I did the first of the tests for my brevet, consisting of two short trips to a nearby village, a landing there and return. This is very easy, the round trip being only about sixty kilometres. The first time I flew at a height of 1000 metres. From this height you can see for miles and it is quite easy to follow a map, as streams, roads, woods, and other landmarks stand out very clearly. By the time I made my second trip a good many low clouds had come up. I had just about reached the top of them at 800 metres when my motor commenced to go badly so that I could not climb any higher.

As I had still about twenty-five minutes to stay up in order to fill in the necessary hour, which one must remain in the air on these trips, I had to spend it dodging about among the clouds. They are very unpleasant things to get in in a Bleriot and when we go through them at all we pick a hole. Yesterday there was plenty of room in between them so that it was easy to see the ground, but when you looked off in the distance they seemed solid and resemble a huge snow field more than anything else. It is quite a novel experience flying around above the clouds but I do not think it will take long to get used to it. The trouble with them is that they shut out the view and the going around the edges is very rough and bumpy.

One thing that bothers me a little is that the machine-gun instruction and practice has been much reduced. The reason for this seems to be in order to save time in turning out pilots, but to my mind it is very poor economy. I know enough about shooting to know how hard it is to hit a moving mark. Many of the men here know nothing about shooting and think that all you have to do is to shoot straight at what you want to hit, which is of course the surest way to miss it. There is a machine-gun school near Bordeaux where the men used to go. A friend of mine named Chadwick who has just finished here and gone to this school, got there by putting in a special request on the ground that he did not know one end of the gun from another. I have had no black marks here so far and if I go through without any, I am going to put in a similar request. In this business it seems to me it is as important to know how to shoot as to fly.

Avord, June 4th, 1917.

To supplement my last letter to father and tell you what I have been doing lately in the flying line, I have been very busy taking my tests for my military brevet which I completed successfully on June 2. They consisted of two triangles of 225 kilometres each. The route lay from Avord to two other towns the names of which I shall not give in order not to irritate our friend the censor.[4] A landing is required at each of these towns, where you have your papers signed and take on gasoline and oil. We are furnished with an excellent map and there is really no difficulty at all in following one's route. The country lies before you like a reproduction of your map and from 1200 metres you can make out with ease such landmarks as rivers, canals, woods, ponds and roads, and cities show up while you are still miles away from them.

I found 1200 or 1300 metres a very satisfactory height as you are then high enough to get a good comprehensive view of the country and to have time in which to pick out a suitable landing place in case anything goes wrong with your motor and you have to land. At the same time you are low enough to be able to distinguish the detail of things below you and thus to better identify places on your map. Another thing we must do is to ascend to an altitude of 2000 metres and remain above that height for an hour, and I have already written

---

4. Chateauroux and Romorantin.

to father about the "*petit voyage*" tests.

On June first I started off on my first triangle and as the weather was good and my motor ran well, I had no trouble at all. On the last leg of the trip I thought I would work in my altitude so let her climb right on up. By the time I reached the camp I was up 2000 metres, but to be on the safe side went on up to 2400 which is about as high as a Bleriot of the kind I had will go, without forcing the motor too much. It took me 45 minutes to reach 2000 metres and this is very good for the type of machine I had. The new Spad biplanes in use at the front will do the same thing in six or seven minutes. It is not so very different at this height than at a thousand metres, except that the details begin to fade a little and the country looks even more like a map. June first was warm on the ground but at 2400 metres your breath looked like a lot of smoke and it was quite cold.

After I had been up there cruising around for almost an hour over the camp and had only ten more minutes to stay, my motor suddenly stopped as though it had run out of gasoline. There was nothing for it but to start down and I was very much disgusted as it meant I should have to do the altitude over again. As soon as I started for the ground I began regulating my gas, etc., to try and find out what was wrong and as luck would have it, got the motor going again by the time I reached 2200 metres. After that she went all right until I finally came down, but the next day she quit on me completely when I was half way through my second triangle. That day the clouds and mist were so low that you could not fly, at the particular time that I had my trouble, at an altitude of more than 450 metres. This is entirely too low to be comfortable as it gives you little time to pick out a landing place if you are forced to come down, and makes it necessary to fly around woods and country where a landing cannot be made.

When my motor started to go bad I picked out a fine field, but when I reached 300 metres the engine improved and I thought it was going to come to life again as it had the day before. I therefore decided to go on for a few minutes and when I had gotten just far enough to miss the good field, she died suddenly and irretrievably. On one side of me was a large woods and on the other a small stream and country so cut up with hills, hedges and trees that it was impossible to land. In the middle was what appeared to be a very good narrow field full of wild flowers, but I was suspicious of it on account of the stream along the edge. However, a marsh is better than a woods any day and there was nothing else to do but take a try at it.

When I got low to the ground I saw that it was soft and fully expected to turn over when my wheels hit the mud. The only chance in such a situation is to put the tail down first and let the machine lose all the speed possible before the wheels hit the ground. This I did and to my delight she only ran about fifteen feet on the ground and stopped right side up.

The grass was eighteen inches high and water slopped up over your shoes when you walked. My wheels were six inches in the mud and you should have seen the mud and water fly when I hit. The inevitable crowd of French peasants soon began to arrive and I took some pictures of the machine with the gang of onlookers standing around it. The trouble was soon located in a couple of broken spark plugs. These I replaced from my tool kit and with the help of some peasants pushed the machine to dryer ground. I instructed the most intelligent looking man how to turn over the propeller so as to start the motor and at the same time not have it come around and take his head off. The ground was still pretty soft and it was quite a job to get enough speed to lift the machine off the ground. When I did get going, it was the middle of the day, quite windy and the heat waves and holes in the air were pretty bad. The ride to my next stopping place was the roughest I have yet experienced, but was not enough so to be dangerous and really made the trip more fun.

The sensation reminded me more of a canoe on the river on a very rough day than anything else. My experience in canoes has I think helped me more than anything else to get the feel of an aeroplane and to be able to know just how far I can let one go without being afraid that it is going to turn over. In the Nieuports and Spads, once you are a sufficient distance from the ground, you can let them fall sideways, turn upside down or do any old thing and then right them again. As a matter of fact they really right themselves most of the time, but a Bleriot monoplane is a different proposition and once she upsets with you, the jig is often up.

The remainder of my test was uneventful and I am now a breveted military "*pilote aviateur*" and am ranked as a corporal. To all appearances I am the same sweet young thing except that I now have wings on my collar and my "*ensigne*" has two wings on it instead of one. When I get to Paris I may have a picture taken in uniform and send it to you if they don't soak me too much for it. By the way, I have no wings on my back yet!

From what I have told you of a Bleriot you may be glad to know

"ATTERRISSAGE SUR LE DOS.
A Spad single-seater as it should not be landed.
July, 1917. Plessis-Belleville, France,

AUTHOR'S BLERIOT MONOPLANE TRAINING-PLANE AFTER
FORCED LANDING, JUNE 2, 1917.

that I have now finished with them and tonight start work in the Nieuport School here. The average time in the Nieuport School is about two weeks and is spent in learning how to do ordinary flying and landings in this type of plane. They are biplanes and entirely different from the Bleriot monoplane, being much more stable but also a great deal heavier and faster. The Bleriots which we used only make something between fifty and sixty miles an hour while the Nieuport goes nearer one hundred. The former is however as I have said, a wonderful training machine and the way you can smash them up without hurting yourself, is nothing short of marvellous. I have myself seen students charge headfirst into the ground at full speed from a height of fifty feet, completely wreck the machine and yet step out of it without a scratch.

It was not at all uncommon in the Bleriot School for a man to fall a hundred metres and sometimes more and come off with a few cuts and bruises. Wrecking machines by bad landings is the commonest thing in the world and the average must be at least two a day. This is a minimum estimate and I have seen five or six wrecks lined up at the side of the field to be taken to the shops as the result of a single day's work. Yet in all the time I have been here there has not been a single fatal accident in the Bleriot School nor a single bone broken. Some few men have been pretty badly bruised up so that they had to sojourn in the hospital for a couple of weeks but that is about all. The reason for this is that the Bleriots are very light and just strong enough to take up the shock, at the same time going to pieces and letting the pilot down easy. He is protected on every side by some part of the machine and when belted in, is just as though he were suspended in the middle of a lot of shock absorbers.

This system of self-instruction is only used in the Bleriot School and when a man completes the course he should have pretty well acquired the feel of an aeroplane. It is a very expensive method and one that no private school could afford to follow unless indemnified by the pupils. In every case that I know of, however, the accident has been the fault of the pupil and due either to his not following instructions, losing his head, or to rank stupidity.

Barring the one case of having your motor go back on you when you are over country where it is very difficult to land, there is no reason at all why a man of reasonable ability who is accustomed to out of door sports, should smash if he keeps his wits about him. Many of the men hardly give their work a thought except when they are actually in a machine and do not seem to appreciate how much there is to learn. I am trying to spend all my spare time studying French so as to be able to take the instruction in better, and in reading up books on planes and motors and how and why they work. This is the reason that I am pressed for time and cannot write a great deal but it seems to me only common sense and your own salvation to do so.

The one case I mentioned of a motor going bad when you have no safe place on which to make a landing, should really never occur in school as you can always pick a good route to the places you are sent and if you fly high enough, should have no difficulty in effecting a landing. A man hardly ever goes through his triangles without having his motor "*panne*"[5] with him at least once and I really think the authorities want this to happen so as to see how the student will take care of himself. The reason for the motors failing is that we use a type of engine in most of the Bleriots which is much inferior to those used at the front and is no longer in service there.

Avord, June 5, 1917.

Julian Biddle arrived here on Saturday and has started in in the Caudron School instead of the Bleriot as I did. The training in the Caudron is not a system of self-instruction but you begin by flying right away in a double command machine with a monitor. Julian chose this method because he thinks it is quicker, which is probably true, but I doubt if it is as good. It is the same system as that used at Newport News and the machines are much larger and more stable than the Bleriots. Yesterday when I was writing to you I was sitting in a hay-rick at an old farm about three miles from the school and Julian was in the straw nearby. I first went to this place ten days ago with Oliver Chadwick and have spent many pleasant hours there since. Chadwick was in my class at the Harvard Law School and is an exceptionally fine fellow. He was also probably the most skilful American pilot here, but I am sorry to say that he left several days ago and is now at the school of "*perfectionnement*" and acrobatics at Pau.

I shall follow him there in a couple of weeks as soon as I have finished the Nieuport School. I hope we get in the same unit as we get along very well together and he is a first class man in every way. It is very nice also to have Julian here and there are several other good fellows whom I know that are expected shortly. I hope we can continue to get men of this type in the organisation.

---

5. Break down.

The farm I spoke of is just a typical French peasant place where a nice old man and his wife live with their two grandchildren, a very lively pair of boys. The "family" also includes two girls and a young fellow who work about the farm, look after the sheep, cook, etc. You can get quantities of delicious fresh milk, eggs, and cottage cheese at a ridiculously cheap price. Nearby is a great big hay-rick where I sit and write and do a good deal of sleeping. As we get up at 3.30 a. m. and cannot get to bed before 10.30, it is absolutely necessary to get some sleep during the day and I find the quiet of this place a great relief. The walk to and back from the farm also provides a bit of exercise.

I think that probably the most important thing in this business is perfect physical condition and I have been taking care of myself as I never have before. You said in your last letter that Bishop Brent was so impressed with the moral conditions over here. They are not good I must admit, according to our standards, but then you must remember that French ideas on these things are entirely different from ours even among the best people. They are brought up to an entirely different standard and the worth while ones live up to their own ideals although at the same time doing things that we would not approve of. It seems to me that if a man lives up to his own standards of what is right, that that is about all you can expect of him. The man who deserves condemnation is the one who has standards or should have them but is not man enough to live up to them.

You asked me in one of your letters if I had ever heard of the place where your little French "orphan" lives with his mother. I don't know for sure but should say at a guess that it was somewhere in heaven. I never before heard of an orphan living with a parent but will try to look him up if I ever get near his abode.

Avord, June 13, 1917.

After my long letter to mother of last week, there is not so much news to tell you. For eight days after I was transferred to the Nieuport school, I did nothing but warm a bench and wait until I could get a chance to fly. Three days ago it came, and so far, I have found no difficulty in driving a Nieuport after my training on the Bleriot. The Nieuport is much steadier and gives you a feeling of perfect safety. You can look all about you without thinking much of the flying of the machine and the sensation in volplaning down to a landing is much the same as that you get in coming down in a good elevator so far as stability is concerned; without any of the queer feeling in your stomach that an elevator gives you. As to smashes and injuries, as I think I told you before, I have yet to see a case where the trouble was not caused either by the student getting rattled and not using his head, or by doing something contrary to instructions.

The Nieuport lands much faster than the Bleriot and although easier to do ordinary simple flying in, is harder to fly and land really well. The machine of this type in use at the front has a plane area of only 15 metres. The wings are so small you hardly see how they lift the weight. The reason of course is the high speed.

You speak in your letter about not being rash. Taking chances to no purpose is of course foolish, but in a game of this kind one must act on the judgment of a second and snap and dash are, I think, essential to success. The nature of the work makes necessary what to many people would seem rashness. In order to attain real skill a military aviator does many things that he would not do for the fun of it if he were learning to be a peaceful pilot. You of course know what I mean and we both know that there is a great difference between this sort of thing and mere foolhardy rashness.

War is of course largely a matter of chances, but in aviation it is a good rule, I think, never to take a chance just for the sport of the thing when there is nothing to be gained by succeeding, and above all, never do a stunt, etc., in a machine not intended for that kind of work. This is the way many splendid flyers are killed and the way O——— met his end. A new student here who was at P——— at the time and picked up O———'s remains, told me today that he was killed because he attempted to loop the loop in a machine which had been weakened by the many rough landings made in it by students. One of the other men had remarked the same morning that O——— would kill himself if he did not stop doing stunts in that machine. It is the same way here, there are hundreds of machines perfectly safe for the ordinary straight flying that you are supposed to do, which would not be expected to stand the acrobatic work such as is done in the machines used at Pau.

Avord, June 21, 1917.

Am still here at Avord and owing to a couple of slight mishaps it will probably be three or four days more before I have finished up and am on my way to Pau. This Nieuport school is not as easy as it is cracked up to be and the landing of this type of machine has proved the most difficult thing for me so far. The machines are heavy and fast and land in a totally different fashion from the Bleriots on which

NIEUPORT TRAINING-PLANE ON ITS NOSE.
Accident caused by a wheel being broken by a rough landing, Avord, France, June, 1917. A monument to the author's skill or rather lack of it.

we received our preliminary training. If you do not get them on the ground properly, you are very likely to bounce, then a wheel breaks when you come down again, the axle sticks in the ground and the old boat turns turtle. Four or five days ago I made a rough landing and in doing so must have bent one of the wheels. I stopped the machine and then started to roll along the ground from the landing place to the starting point. After I had gone about fifty yards, a wheel suddenly caved in and the machine stood on its nose, breaking the propeller but that was all. As we are of course belted in, all I had to do was to unfasten the belt and slide out. I then proceeded to take a picture of the machine as she stood on her nose, a pretty monument to my prowess. When they are done, I will send you one. This accident was due to my not having sense enough to stop and see if everything was all right after I had made the landing.

After that everything went all right for a couple of days when I made another rough landing, the wheels gave way and the next thing I knew the machine turned a summersault and lit in the middle of its back. As you are already on the ground when you perform these stunts you cannot very well hurt yourself, but not so the machine.

Mine was pretty well bunged up this time, while nothing at all happened to me except a pair of barked shins where I kicked the front of the gas tank. I should say that at least sixty *per cent*, of the pupils in the Nieuport School have the same thing happen to them before they learn and the daily average of "*capotages*"[6] as the French call them, must certainly be five machines out of about thirty on the field. I should, however, by using my head, have been one of those to go through without a smash, especially after completing what is supposed to be the hardest part of the training, the Bleriot School, without difficulty.

Yesterday I made ten trips by myself again and think I now have it. My difficulty was caused by trying to cut the landings too fine for a beginner and should have been avoided by the exercise of a little intelligence.

I am glad my troubles came here rather than at Pau, for on what we do there, will depend largely what kind of a machine we get later on and I am of course anxious to get the best.

Pau. June 30, 1917.

The only thing I have done here so far in the way of flying, is

---

6. Capsizings.

some vertical spirals, but in the course of these I did some acrobatic stunts by mistake. In the vertical spirals you are instructed to tip your machine over sideways to an angle of about 75 or 80 degrees and then by pulling up on your elevating planes (which by reason of the vertical position of the machine, then operate in the same way as the rudder when the machine is in its normal position *i.e.* as a horizontal control) to execute a close spiral. In doing this the machine follows a course much like a grain of shot would if you put it in a bottle and caused it to run round the side by moving the bottle rapidly in a circle. The first time I tried this everything went all right, but the next time, I pulled my elevating planes too soon before the machine had tipped up enough. The result was that the elevating planes were still performing their normal functions and instead of doing a spiral, I did something which resembled an irregular loop the loop. When the machine got up on her end and started to go over backwards and sideways, it naturally did not take me long to guess that something was wrong.

When you get mixed up in a Nieuport, all you have to do is to put your controls in the centre and the machine soon begins to dive head first for mother earth. It is then a very simple matter to pull her up straight again. I simply followed instructions and did this and the machine came out without the slightest difficulty. Started in again on my spiral and did the same trick over again, not realising what I was doing wrong. After that I flew along straight for a minute until I had time to work out what was wrong and then did my spiral all right and have done a number of others since. It gives you a great deal of confidence and makes flying much more pleasant, to find that you can do this kind of thing so easily.

One is of course always careful not to try any unusual manoeuvres unless one is so high that a fall of a couple of hundred metres more or less will not make any difference. Provided you are high enough you do not care much what the machine does and it is a great comfort to begin to get the feeling that no matter what happens you can come out right side up. There is nothing the matter with my heart I guess, as I purposely came down three thousand metres in five minutes the other day and did not feel it at all.

Plessis-Belleville. July 13, 1917.

I reached Plessis-Belleville last Sunday and am now going in to Paris for the big celebration tomorrow on Bastille Day. There is to be another grand parade of all the allied troops like the one last year, but this year we hear that there will also be an American contingent. Both Chadwick and I were offered the chance of flying from Plessis to Paris tomorrow and circling over the city at the time of the parade as a part of the performance, but as we had both received a permission to go and see the parade, etc., from the ground, we declined the chance to fly. I have seen Paris from the Eiffel Tower and it would not be much fun simply flying over high in formation and then flying back to Plessis again. There is much more of interest to see on the ground.

Plessis-Belleville is one of the great French distributing stations for pilots going to the front. We are sent here for some further training which usually occupies about two weeks. I have not had much further trouble since my smash at Avord and was declared available and ready for the front after three days at Plessis. Chadwick and I are the next two pilots on the list and we shall therefore probably be off to the front in three or four days. I had hoped to remain longer at Plessis and get in some more practice, but I am glad to get through in one way as it will enable me to go in the same *escadrille*[7] as Oliver Chadwick. He is the best man I know in the organisation and we get along very well together. We asked to be put in the same squadron as it would be rather lonely for one American to be by himself in a French *escadrille*. To what *escadrille* we shall be sent and to what section of the front, we do not as yet know. The captain at Plessis said he would put us together and we also hope to be able to get M—— with us.

You will probably be surprised that I am going to the front so soon. It is sooner than I had expected but I am glad of the opportunity to fight with the French, before we are transferred to the U. S. forces, which I think will be soon.

Plessis-Belleville. July 15, 1917.

At last I have a little while in which to write you something about what I have been doing lately. I am not now really at Plessis, but am sitting in the garden of an inn in the town of Ermenonville which is about six or seven kilometres from Plessis. Chadwick and I strolled over here for lunch and have been writing some letters ever since. The town is chiefly famous as the place where Jean Jacques Rousseau died and is buried. Also there are several fine *châteaux* nearby and a wonderful big old estate called the "*Domaine de Chalis.*" There is the ruin of a beautiful old castle on it and the place is now kept as a museum by the "*Institut de France.*" I would like to know something of its history,

---

7. Squadron.

but have not been able to discover anything as yet. The grounds are very beautiful and have the most complete system of artificial ponds and lakes. They are now so old that you would never know that they were artificial, were it not for the way in which they are connected up at different levels. Chadwick and I took a long walk through the place the other day.

I have spent considerable time in walking about the country in the various places where I have been. Physical health is of course of prime importance in this business and I think the time is well spent. I have also spent a good deal of time in another way which I do not think nearly as profitable, namely, in keeping a diary. I bought a good sized one as soon as I arrived and have kept it faithfully ever since. I think a diary in which one merely puts down in outline what one does each day, is very tiresome both for the keeper and anyone who might afterwards look at it. There should certainly be included some thoughts on various topics as they arise, but to keep such a diary which is at all complete, involves the expenditure of a great deal of time, and also a great deal of repetition of what I write home to you in my letters. It seems to me that it will be better to write more letters home, and if they are fairly complete and you save them, they will serve the purpose of a diary. From this day henceforth therefore, no more diary. When I get to the front and am flying every day, I shall have even less spare time than I have now and I prefer to spend it learning how to get the Boche. I would like to make myself proficient enough to warm up a few of Kaiser Bill's aviators without having them do the same to me. Better a live aviator with a whole skin than a dead one with a complete diary.

Pau was great fun and a most delightful place. You will soon have the postals I sent which will show you what the country is like better than I could describe it. One afternoon just before I left, I was up 2800 metres with two other machines, doing some *"vol de groupe"*[8] work. Down below there was a haze which allowed you to see the ground under you very well, but which in the distance appeared solid. We were just at the top of the haze and the air above was as clear as crystal and freezing cold. Fifty kilometres away rose the towering snow covered peaks of the Pyrenees, but they appeared very close in the clear thin air. The haze completely hid all the lower portions of the mountains and as this haze in the distance very much resembles water, it seemed exactly as though one was in a boat looking at a chain

---

8. Formation flying.

of rocky islands rising out of a winter sea. A very fine sight, but as one is within 50 metres of several other machines in *vol de groupe*, and as it is necessary to maintain that relative position, one has not a great deal of time to be gaping at the scenery. This kind of work is good fun and of course very important, as machines no longer go out alone at the front except in the case of a few very skilful and experienced pilots.

The flying is generally in groups of four or five, the reason being both for the protection of the hunters and to make surer of the hunted. The idea seems to be to try to find one machine by itself or to manoeuvre one of a group until it is out of touch with its fellows, and then the whole gang jumps on the one unfortunate "*isolé.*"[9] Hardly seems a square deal, but after all, the aim is to put as many of the other fellow's machines out of business as possible. The *vol de groupe* work at Pau was done on Nieuports of a type now in use at the front, having 15 sq. metres of wing surface, 110 H. P. motor and making a little better than 100 miles per hour. The Nieuports here at Plessis are of the same type. I have also been flying a good deal here in the 140 H. P. Spad which makes a little better than 115 miles per hour. The new 200 H. P. Spad of which there are not as yet a great many at the front, makes about 125 miles per hour, which is moving along pretty lively.

I am enclosing you a letter which Chadwick wrote me when he was at Pau and I was still at Avord. It will tell you something of the work there. The monitor whose death he mentions killed himself doing a quick turn close to the ground. He slipped off on a wing and struck before he could right himself. The great danger to the experts is that they get to thinking there is nothing they cannot do. I make a practice of never doing anything out of the ordinary until I am at least 400 metres up and hope to be able to force myself to keep this rule. Then if anything goes wrong you can fall a couple of hundred metres without getting into trouble. We have young pilots here who try to show off by doing queer things just as they are rising. They remind me of the "expert" shot who flourishes a gun about his head and looks down the muzzle. The two types are about the same and are riding for a fall sooner or later.

After finishing the spiral work at Pau we did five hours of *vol de groupe* and then went to the class of acrobacy. When you arrive at the acrobacy hangars, the head mechanic greets you with a board on which is a long list of fines to be paid by the pilots for the benefit of the mechanics. For instance—bad landing 50 *centimes*; landing the

---
9. Solitary machine.

machine on its back, 3 *francs*; completely wrecking a machine 5 *francs*; putting your lunch in the machine, 1 *franc*; and many others. I caused loud shouts of glee by inadvertently (?) sitting in the monitor's special rocking chair from which he watches the acrobacy. This was chalked up at 1 *franc*, but was all they got against me I am glad to say. We only got about one hour of acrobacy at Pau, three flights of about 20 minutes each. The monitor first puts you in a machine on the ground, tells you what to do in order to perform the various evolutions, makes you go through the motions, and then sends you up to perform while everybody else stands around on the ground and watches.

The machines in this class are in the finest possible condition so as to avoid as much as possible the danger of breaking from undue strains put upon them by green pilots learning to do the stunts. The wing surface is only 13 sq. metres and they are I think the smallest biplane in existence. The Nieuports at the front have 15 sq. metres and the Spad more still. The 13 metre handles very quickly and having such small wings is less subject to strain and breaking.

The first thing we had to do was the much talked of "*vrille.*" The English call it a nose spin and the Americans a tail spin. You shut off the motor, put the machine into a loss of speed, throw all the controls to one side and it starts falling head first at the same time spinning very rapidly. The nose of the plane turns almost as though on a pivot while the tail describes circles. The machine falls vertically but does not spin vertically on its nose, on the contrary, as it turns, its directional axis makes an angle of about seventy degrees with the normal line of flight of the plane when flying level. To straighten out you simply put your controls in the centre, the machine stops spinning and dives straight for the ground and it is then very easy to pull it up straight and put on the motor. The *vrille* is very spectacular but in reality is extremely simple. The pilot does a few simple things which are hard to do wrong, and the machine does the rest.

Simple as the manoeuvre is, it has been the cause of a great many deaths, but there is no excuse for so many men being killed in doing their first *vrille*. The reason seems to be that they hear other green pilots talking about it until it gets on their nerves and then when they have started to do the *vrille*, they get excited and forget what to do in order to come out. If you do not put your controls in the centre the machine will keep on *vrilling* until it hits the ground. I have personally seen several machines fall this way and the men were always killed.

The *vrille* got its bad name in the early days of flying, for the old-type machines, once in one, would not as a rule come out no matter what the pilot did. As a matter of fact there is nothing hard or dangerous about it in a strong modern machine. If you have the motor running open you can only do a *vrille* for a very short time for you will soon get spinning so fast that the wings will tear off. This frequently happens when a pilot is killed in a fight. With the motor off or slowed down all the way, a good machine will *vrille* indefinitely without breaking. All young pilots should I think be taught how to go into and come out of a *vrille* before attempting any other forms of acrobacy, for in attempting to do some other stunt they will often get mixed up and unintentionally fall into a *vrille*. If however they already know how to do a *vrille* they will realise it the instant their machine starts into one and will be able to straighten out without difficulty.

The afternoon I arrived at Pau a French lieutenant evidently lost his head with the result that he started his *vrille* at 1500 metres and only ended it when he hit the ground, losing his life also. A machine in a *vrille* looks very much like a leaf falling off a tree. When you come out headed for the ground you are of course going very fast, much faster than the machine would fly on the level. The second time I tried it I thought I would try and count how many turns I made, and therefore got my eye on a big clump of woods under me. I counted the first time all right, but after that she went around so fast that the woods began to look like the blades of an electric fan, *i. e.*, all woods, so I gave up that count as a bad job. Have done a number of others since and it is really very good fun. In the Spad you fall just as fast but do not twist so quickly, so that the sensation is pleasanter. A new pilot doing his first *vrille* is told to start it at 1500 metres, keep his eye on his altimeter, and come out after he has fallen 200 metres. This gives him lots of time to try again if he does not get his controls in the centre the first time.

The other things we had to do were vertical "*virages*,"[10] which look easy but are in reality much the hardest of all to do properly; "*renversements*,"[11] and "*tournants*." [12]

To execute a *renversement* you pull your machine up a little into a climbing angle, put all your controls hard to the side on which you wish to turn and at the same time shut down the motor. This causes the machine to turn sharply over sideways and brings it out on its nose

---
10. Turns.
11. Immelmann turns.
12. Barrel rolls.

but facing in the opposite direction. You then open up the motor and level the machine out again by pulling in on your elevating controls. The result is the quickest possible way in which to make a 180 degree turn. If you begin by pulling the plane up at an angle of 45 degrees from the horizontal you will be slightly on your back just after the turn, the turn being made both on the lateral and the directional axis of the machine, that is to say sideways and not over backwards as in the loop. The same manoeuvre may be carried out without first pulling the plane into a climbing angle but will in this case result in the loss of about fifty metres of height. By climbing a little first or "zooming," as it is called in aviation slang, a *renversement* may be executed with the loss of little or no altitude.

To do a *tournant* the controls are handled in much the same way as for the *renversement* but the movement of them is accentuated and instead of straightening out after turning 180 degrees, you allow the machine to make a complete turn, rolling over on its back and then continuing right side up in its original direction. Both the *tournant* and the *renversement* may be done without slowing down the motor all the way and when done with the motor on are quicker and prettier to look at but they are also harder to control so exactly and subject the machine to a good deal of strain which seems unnecessary.

As they would only give us about an hour of acrobacy in all at Pau, we had no time to do more than try each manoeuvre out a few times and see how it should be done. Since then I have had another hour and a half of acrobacy here in the Spad and have learned to execute some of the stunts properly but am still in need of a great deal of practice. The machines here however are old ones which have been sent back to be used up, being no longer fit for service at the front. It is therefore not safe to do anything but ordinary flying in them as the wings will not stand it. You can see the ends of the wings wobbling with the vibrations of the motor in some of them. When we get to the front and have our own machine, a new one in fine condition, there will then be a chance to do a lot more practising.

There is only one Spad here on which we are allowed to do acrobacy and as there are a good many pilots, one does not often get a chance to use it. Personally I shall be glad to get to the front where I shall always have my own machine and become thoroughly familiar with it. There is always of course a certain amount of danger from school machines which are being continually abused by green pilots. By the time you get this letter, however, my schooling will all be behind me and I shall have been several weeks at the front. There is where the real schooling begins. You can fly to your heart's content and do all the practising you want and I hope to get in a great deal before taking on any Boches.

    I told you that they refused to let me go to the machine-gun school at Cazau. After Chadwick was there, an order came down from the colonel in command of the schools, directing that no more pilots were to go to Cazau. His reason was that the school is intended for the training of aeroplane *mitrailleurs*[13] who shoot from the two-seater machines with movable guns, and is only amusing, but not beneficial, for pilots who are to use a fixed gun on a one-seater. I don't agree with him on this and neither do the U. S. aviation officers with whom I have talked, but "orders is orders." It is just as important to know where to shoot with a fixed gun in order to hit a moving mark, as it is with a movable gun. Also it seems to me of the greatest importance to know in what position is it most difficult for the other fellow to shoot you. A great deal of our work will consist in attacking two-seater machines and the harder the shot you can give your opponent, the better.

    We got a little machine-gun work at Pau on the ground, and here I have so far had four flights of about fifteen minutes each, shooting at a round spot of sand on the ground, with a machine-gun from a Nieuport. The small fast *chasse* machines, one of which I shall have at the front, are all one-seaters in the French Army and your machine-gun is fixed. I think the French make a great mistake in giving so little shooting practice to their pilots and that it is very poor economy to hurry up a man's training by cutting down on such an important part of it. Once we reach our *escadrille* at the front, however, I think we will be given a good deal of additional training.

    This is about everything there is to tell you with regard to the training both here and at Pau. Chadwick and I are now merely awaiting our orders and getting in as much work as we can in the meantime. They are evidently holding us until they can put us together in the same *escadrille* as we asked. I now speak enough French to carry on an ordinary conversation and expect to have little difficulty with it after one month where I shall speak practically nothing else.

    Do not worry about me just because I am at the front instead of still in the schools. As I told you in my last letter, two-thirds of the deaths in the French aviation at Plessis and the front, *i.e.*, in the war

---

13. Machine-gunners.

zone, during the month of May, were from accident. You would not wonder at this if you could see the extraordinary things some of the French pilots do. Two poor fellows fell in a Farman and were burned to a crisp the day I reached here, just because the pilot did something in utter defiance of all the rules of flying. He pulled his machine up until it lost its speed and naturally he fell; although he righted her again about thirty metres from the ground, he then proceeded to make the same mistake over again and when the machine struck the ground she immediately went up in flames. Even after he saw he was going to smash, if he had had presence of mind enough to cut off his motor, there would probably have been no fire. Over and over again I have seen machines smashed to bits, but as the pilot cut off his-motor first, no fire resulted.

When a man does in aviation what the Farman pilot I mentioned above did, he might just as well take an automobile and run it head first into a wall or off a bridge and expect not to be hurt. I should say at a guess that the deaths in the French schools at least equal those at the front and more pilots kill themselves needlessly than the Germans ever shoot. No Americans have been killed in the schools since I came over and the Frenchmen who come to untimely ends by accident, are usually officers who are either too old or otherwise unadapted to aviation. There seem to be a good many students of this kind who are given a chance at aviation, as a reward of merit, but who are totally incapable of being made into good pilots.

I mentioned above the Frenchman who fell in a *vrille* the day I reached Pau. Two days later we all got "*repos*"[14] in the afternoon in order to attend his funeral. All the pilots in the school and a large number of mechanicians marched behind the hearse through the streets of Pau, in the regulation French military funeral. This man happened to be a Protestant and after the service in the church, we all marched on again to the cemetery. In the church two soldiers in full uniform, steel helmets and fixed bayonets, stood guard on each side of the casket during the reading of the service. At the grave, after the minister had finished, the captain of the school made quite a long speech and was in turn followed by some old duffer who represented some Order of which I could not discover the name. This seemed to me pretty trying on the deceased's two sisters and brother, the only members of his family present, but the rest of the proceeding was even worse.

These two poor women, who seemed completely broken up and

---

14. Leave.

were sobbing continuously, first had a long walk through the streets after their brother's body and then, after he had been laid in the vault, they stood side by side under a nearby shed while about sixty pilots and instructors lined up and filing past, shook each by the hand. It may seem a strange comparison, but the hand shaking reminded me of a crowd of wedding guests filing past the bride and groom. It must be an ordeal for the family at such a time and it is hard to see what comfort such a formality can be to anyone in trouble.

There was one other acrobatic stunt we learned at Pau which I did not tell you about and that is what is known as a wing slip. You put the machine sideways in a vertical position with the motor running at about two-thirds of its normal speed in order to prevent the plane from turning on its nose and diving. With the aid of the motor and by manipulating the controls, you can then make the machine fall sideways and it at the same time goes forward due to the pull of the motor. I generally start this manoeuvre by bracing one shoulder under the edge of the body alongside of my seat. Otherwise when you turn her to 90°, you fall up against the side and your belt is the only thing that holds you.

Also sometimes she slips over a little on her back and you get an unpleasant sensation of commencing to fall out although of course the belt would only let you leave the seat a few inches. The greatest possible speed can be attained in this way as the wings offer practically no resistance to the air and the only thing holding you back is the wind resistance against the side of the body of the machine. It is in this wing slip that you get a real impression of speed and you certainly do travel. The wind whistles through the wires and you fall a thousand feet in an incredibly short time. A conservative estimate of the speed would be I think 200 miles an hour, at least as fast as a man would fall through the air and infinitely faster than any machine will fly on the level. To come out of a wing slip you simply dive in the same direction that you are falling and then pull up straight. The stunt may of course be varied by slipping at a more gradual angle instead of coming down vertically and in this modified form is sometimes used as a means of losing height preparatory to landing.

I don't think it will take me long to settle down to the law again when the war is over. This sort of thing makes you appreciate the blessings of home and I shall be so glad to get back, that it will take quite some war to get me away again.

Plessis-Belleville. July 24, 1917.

We have just received our orders for which we have been waiting and Oliver and I leave tomorrow for the front. We have both been ready to go for the past ten days, but they have been holding us up for some reason or other. We asked to be sent out together and our request was granted and I am also glad to say that we are being sent to the crack group of the French army, the one in which Guynemer[15] and many other famous French aces are. It looks also as though we were going to get Spads, the best *chasse* machine that the French have. It is of course a single-seater combat machine. I do not know whether we shall be in the same *escadrille* with Guynemer or not, but do not believe so, as his is supposed to be the best *escadrille* in the service and I should hardly think that they would take in a couple of green-horns. A "*groupe de combat*" comprises four *escadrilles*. We are in the same group with the cracks, but I do not know what *escadrille* we shall be assigned to.

Our location will be along the north coast near Dunkirk. Unless all the omens fail there is going to be quite a bit of excitement in that region very shortly and we are very lucky to have an opportunity to get in it.

---

15. *Guynemer: Chevalier of the Air* by Henry Bordeaux & Mary R. Parkman, *Georges Guynemer, Knight of the Air* by Henry Bordeaux and *The Chevalier of Flight: Captain Guynemer* by Mary R. Parkman also published by Leonaur.

Insignia of Escadrille N. 73

Chapter 2
Escadrille N. 73

Bergues. July 28, 1917.

Just arrived at the front today and am in Escadrille N. 73, *Groupe de Combat* 12. The group is otherwise known as "*Le Groupe Brocard*" after its famous commander Brocard, who is one of the great French airmen. One of the *escadrilles* of the group is N. 3, more generally known as "*Les Cigognes*" or "The Storks" when translated into English. The name comes from their insignia, a stork painted on the sides of the fuselage[1] of each machine, and this squadron is easily the best known in the French aviation. The whole group carries the stork as its insignia, the bird being placed in different positions to distinguish the several escadrilles, and consequently the entire group is often referred to as "*Les Cigognes*." The original "*Cigognes*," however, which has gained such a wide reputation, is Escadrille N. 3.

This group is the most famous fighting one in the army and admittedly the best, so you can see that Chadwick and I were very lucky to get in it. It contains more famous fighting pilots than any of the other French flying units, one in particular Guynemer, who has to date brought down about 48 Boches officially and many more unofficially. To count on a man's record, a victory has to be seen and reported by two French observers *on the ground* or some such rule as this, so that a Boche shot down far behind the lines where no one but his comrades see him fall, does not help a pilot's total. Last evening Guynemer got one 25 kilometres in the German territory and as I sit here on the aerodrome he has just gotten into his machine and started off for the lines in search of another victim.

Chadwick and I and two other Americans who came with us, are

---

1. Body.

the first Americans to be sent to this group. An *escadrille* or squadron in the French service numbers about fifteen pilots and machines. We are indeed fortunate to get in this crack group, but as it has suffered rather heavily lately, they had to fill up, and so we got our chance. This morning the captain of one of the *escadrilles*[2] was killed and our own chief[3] was shot down with three bullets in his back but will pull through all right. He was shot down last night also, but only his machine was damaged. He went up again this morning and while attacking one Boche, another got him from behind. He has 17 Boches to his credit officially, so I guess he is entitled to the rest that his wounds will give him. The captain who was killed had gotten seven German machines officially, so we are sort of out of luck today, losing two such good men. It seems to come in bunches that way for some reason or other.

It looks as though I shall see lots of service and have a chance to learn a great deal before the time comes to transfer to the U. S. Army, if it does come. We hope to be able to stay where we are for a considerable length of time and that we shall not be forced to leave this French unit before we have learned a lot more about military aviation and have been able to make some return for all the training that we have received. This group is usually, like the Foreign Legion, moved about to the particular locality in which there is going to be an attack, so we shall see plenty of action. It was for instance at the battles of Verdun and the Somme and it seems that it is usually in the thick of it. For this reason it is obvious that I shall not be able to tell you where I am and must be very careful what I write. Since beginning this letter I have been talking to one of the officers about the censorship and have, as you will notice, been doing some censoring on my own account. No details that could possibly be of any military importance, so you will have to be content with much briefer and more general letters than I have been writing heretofore.

You will be glad to know that I got a S.P.A.D.[4] machine, the kind I hoped to get. Also I shall have a chance to do a good deal more practising before starting in in earnest. The officers are as usual very nice and willing to help in any way they can. We get a great deal of advice and information here which I have been anxious to get from the beginning. When the time comes to make our first trip in search of a real

---

2. Captain Auger of Escadrille N. 3.
3. Captain (then Lieutenant) Deullin, originally of Escadrille N. 3, but at this time commanding Escadrille N. 73.
4. *Société Pour l'Aviation et ses Deriv*es.

CAPTAIN GEORGES GUYNEMER

Taken at St. Pol-sur-Mer near Dunkirk, France, in September, 1917, shortly before his death. Captain Guynemer, who was at this time the French ace of aces, is standing in one of the hangars of his squadron with his machine "Vieux Charles" showing in the background. The machine is dismantled for repairs.

live Boche, we ought to feel able to give him some sort of a run for his money. Here's hoping that my first adversary is a young pilot like myself. Should hate to bump into a German ace for a starter.

Bergues, July 29, 1917.

Guynemer came back from his sortie last night having sent one more Boche to his happy hunting grounds in flames. This wonderful French pilot seems absolutely untiring and his skill must be something uncanny. Approximately 50 Boche officially means about 75 machines brought down altogether, and as most of his victims have been two-seaters, this represents I suppose something like 125 German pilots and machine-gunners, observers, etc., disposed of by one Frenchman. You can imagine how much nerve, skill and endurance it takes to accomplish this feat and live to tell the tale. I was much surprised when I saw him for the first time. He is small and very slight, more like cousin T—— than anyone else I can think of whom we know, indeed he looks something like him. He is 22 years old and without question the greatest individual fighter this war has produced. There are many things about him which I should like to tell you but which I am at present forbidden to talk about and which will therefore have to wait until later on when they are still interesting but no longer of military importance.

It is quite a sight to see a bunch of the "Storks" starting off at crack of dawn for a flight over the lines, or to see them coming home to roost at dusk. One sees here probably the finest flying in the world and it will be a great advantage to us young ones, who as yet are not real pilots by a long shot, to be able to watch these men work who really know the game. One is naturally anxious to get started, but I shall take your advice and go easy until I feel able to take care of myself. As you say, rashness only results in throwing yourself away to no purpose and foolhardiness is certainly no essential of bravery. As far as one can discover, the most successful men have been those who have known when not to sail in and take too great chances.

Bergues, July 30, 1917.

Our machines have not yet arrived and we shall probably have to wait some little time longer, so Chadwick and I have as yet done no flying since reaching the front. There is however plenty to do in the way of studying so the time does not hang heavily on our hands. There are maps of the locality to learn, types of Boche machines to familiarize oneself with and all kinds of things like this to keep one fully occupied. It is however irritating to be so near the scene of action and yet so far. When I was in the schools I used to think that I would wish I was back home again when the time came to go out over the lines. Maybe I still shall feel that way and my present enthusiasm is merely due to my excessive greenness. Just now, however, with the big guns roaring all day and all night in the distance and all of our companions in the fray except a few of us new ones who have no machines as yet, it makes you wish you could go out and get in it.

The guns sound like distant thunder. We are too far away to hear any but the big ones, but the explosions remind me more than anything else of the noise made by the paddle wheels of a steamer on the river on a quiet evening. You know how they sound in the distance as each blade hits the water. The noise of the guns has of course no such regular time as the sound of the paddle wheels, but the shots are I should say, considerably closer together than the blows of the paddles on the water. Remember that this represents only the big guns and that we are too far away to hear the 75's at all, and you will get some idea of how much fun the Boches are having at the other end where the projectiles are falling on their blessed heads.

We are very comfortably housed here in a big tent and *"everything in the garden is lovely"* except the mosquitoes, which are quite numerous and at least three times the size of Jersey's best. They are the first I have struck so far in France, but they are making up for lost time. They are honestly half as big as what we call a mosquito hawk and have a beak like a great blue heron. The first one I saw I mistook for one. One bit me on the right eye-lid the first night and I could hardly get my eye open in the morning. Then another one, who evidently saw me and had his eye for symmetry shocked by the sight, bit me on the other eye-lid the next night, so that yesterday my eyes about matched. Last night I fooled them by sleeping with my head under the covers and to-day my visage does not quite so nearly resemble the morning after a prize-fight.

A funny thing happened here a couple of days ago while some of the men were practising bomb dropping at a target on the flying field. The Spad can be fitted to carry a couple of small twenty-pound bombs which are dropped from a low altitude on troops and convoys on the roads behind the enemy lines. The bombs in question were filled simply with a small bursting charge and some stuff that would make a smoke, so that the aviator could see where they fell. One fellow let one go from about 3500 feet, but he had waited too long and it landed on a road within six feet of an English "Tommy" who was taking a quiet stroll. If it had ever hit him it would have pushed him out of sight. Everybody thought it a huge joke except the "Tommy," who was bored to death (or almost) and could not see anything funny about it. It is amusing to note the difference in the popular attitude towards such an episode, here and at home. With us the result would probably have been a law suit and a long argument on the legal theory of injury resulting from fright alone without physical contact.

You will be glad to hear that my commander, Commandant Brocard, seems from what little I have seen of him, to be the finest French officer I have yet met. He is a real man himself and takes that personal interest in the welfare and ability of his men, which means so much. It is quite evident that he means his men to know their business thoroughly before he sends them out.

I think Aunt K—— might like this place. My tent is in a field next to some farm buildings and the pasture is full of horses, cows, and three or four big fat sows. The latter are very inquisitive and every now and then try to come in and pay us a visit, but a heavy army shoe, well placed in the spare ribs, generally results in indignant grunts and a hasty withdrawal. We came in one day to find them all asleep in our tent. One old lady had her head in my suitcase where I keep my clean linen. She had first pushed open the lid and eaten a supply of chocolate I had secreted there. My laundry bill the following week amounted to twelve *francs*. We also have a large supply of dogs who travel with us. Five fat puppies run about the kitchen-dining-room tent and lick the plates and pots and pans. One is called "Spad" and another "Contact," the latter being the French expression meaning "throw on the switch of a motor." The other names I have not yet mastered.

At each advance in my training the food has improved until here it is first rate. As for my health, it has never been better, and my spirits are excellent. The work is interesting and I try to make it a rule to do little thinking about what I might be doing if it were not for this damn war. Do not worry if my letters are irregular as the censorship is now severe and will, I fear, subject the mails to long delays.

Bergues, August 10, 1917.

Have at last had a couple of flights over the lines and will try to tell you something about it, but in such general terms that the censor will not object. After almost incessant rain, fog, and very low clouds for ten days, it has finally cleared up enough in the last two days to allow the machines to go out for at least a part of each day. Yesterday morning I had my first trip out over the Boche lines and as the patrol of which I was a part, was quite a low one, I could see the whole show and you never saw such a mess in your life. At times we were as low as 800 metres and on our way home went down to 600 metres over the artillery where we could plainly see and hear the guns blazing away. Higher up, one can see the gun flashes, but the noise of one's motor drowns the sound of the shots.

I do not think there is much use in trying to describe what the battlefields look like. They beggar description, and you can get a clearer idea from the pictures in the *Illustrated London News*. The ground about the trenches and in fact the country for several miles on each side of the lines, reminds me more of some of those swamps which had been burnt over by a forest fire, which we saw on the way in to the Rangeley Lakes in Maine, than anything else I can think of. I know nothing else which gives an idea of the utter waste and destruction. The ground itself looks much like one of those hard lumps you sometimes find on the river shore which resemble a petrified sponge, or perhaps a piece of slag from an iron foundry, or again a photograph of the craters on the moon. For miles the shell holes are so close that they merge, and the earth is chewed up until the surface also somewhat resembles the top of a bowl of stiff oatmeal. Every little village and farm house is a wreck, the roofs, where any are left, are full of shell holes; but a few fragments of walls represent what is left of most of them. Some of the larger towns are just a dark smudge with a gutted ruin sticking up here and there.

This morning I went out on a patrol at daylight, a couple of thousand metres up this time, and the sight which greeted us as we approached the lines I shall never forget. It was much more remarkable than yesterday from a spectacular point of view. The sun was not yet up and the flashes from the guns, which you can see even in broad daylight, were very brilliant in the early dawn. There was quite a lively bombardment going on and the guns made me think of the fireflies on the lawn at home of a hot summer night, and I might say that I have never seen the fireflies thicker. This from our guns behind our own lines and the Boche fireflies at work further on but not so numerous. Over it all the drifting smoke of the battle and above, all the way from 1000 to 5000 metres, flocks of planes circling about.

Scattered about the planes the little puffs of smoke from the shells of the anti-aircraft guns of each side shooting at the other fellows' birds. Some kilometres behind the lines on each side a row of sausages, as the observation balloons are called, floating lazily at the ends of their long tethers. Add to this the sun rising on one side and the moon and a couple of big stars fading out on the other, and you may get some kind of a picture of what we see here every day.

It is a funny sensation to sail around up in the air and watch the shells bursting around you. If they are anywhere near, which they generally are if they are meant for you, the noise of the explosion is very clear and there is always the puff of smoke to show you what kind of a shot the man on the ground is. Bang, bang, they go, sometimes over, sometimes under where you hear them but they are hard to see, at the sides, behind or any old place. Don't get the idea that we are surrounded by a swarm of shells however. As you pass near a battery they may let go two or three, the next time perhaps a dozen and so on from time to time. We flew about over a given sector of Boche territory for pretty nearly two hours yesterday and something over an hour today, acting as guards for the bigger machines which take the pictures, regulate the artillery fire, etc. Expect to go out again later on today if the weather permits, which I doubt.

The Boche gunners are pretty good when you consider the terrific speed of the machines and that they were shooting at a range of two miles. The closest that any came to me that I saw was about 150 yards, but that is close enough to suit yours truly. Had to laugh at Chadwick when we came in yesterday. He said that when he saw the first shell that he knew was meant for him, he felt quite flattered to think that the Boche should have at last taken that much notice that he was in the war and "agin" them. As for me, when we are dodging around up there in the sky to throw the guns off their range, I feel like a blooming duck on the first day of the open season, and there are many other forms of flattery which I should prefer. Chadwick hates a Boche even more than I do and I think that is going pretty strong. The more one sees of them and of their work the more convinced one becomes that they are not simply a nation misled, but a very race of devils.

Bergues, August 12, 1917.

On my first trip out over the lines, some Boche machine-gunner or rifleman on the ground amused himself by plugging a bullet through one of my wings. Considering that we were never under 800 metres on this sortie, that Fritzie must be a regular Robin Hood. Probably it was just a lucky shot but I'll bet that fellow used to shoot ducks before the war. A bullet hole through the cloth of a wing practically does no harm at all, and the mechanics just glue a little patch over it when you come home. You can find these patches on the majority of the machines.

Since writing the first part of this letter I have had four or five more hours over the lines. This morning I was down as low as five hundred metres over our own trenches and got a wonderful view of everything. It is a beautiful clear day and one could see the individual soldiers in their places. Every little while a shell would land on a particular spot at which you were looking and you could see the mud, water, and smoke go up in a veritable fountain. A little further back were cannons and artillery trains moving about on the roads. It is remarkable to see the fields cultivated right up to the blasted area and many of them with a good sprinkling of shell holes. There is one town,[5] the name of which I had often seen in the *communiqués* before I left home, which lies in the centre of the area over which we patrol. It was I suppose half the size of Andalusia village, but like all little French towns the houses were set quite close together as in a city.

This place appeared on my map and although I thought I had the spot exactly located and searched carefully from only five hundred metres above it, I could find no trace of it. I asked a Frenchman and he explained the mystery by saying that it had been entirely blown off the map. There is absolutely no trace of it left that can be distinguished from the surrounding country. Even several macadamized roads which ran through it, are blown out of existence. Since the recent heavy rains it is often difficult to tell a trench line from a brook, and every shell hole is full of water. The ground reminds me also of the mud flat next to the wharf at Andalusia after we boys had been throwing a lot of rocks in it. The poor devils in the trenches must have a nice comfortable time of it.

Julian Biddle arrived yesterday and has been assigned to this *escadrille*. He had been sent to another group in a different locality, but asked to be sent here so as to be with me and they granted his request. I am glad he got here. He should make a good pilot.

You speak about the time when I shall write you an account of my first fight. That will probably not be for some time to come. We are at first given work which is least likely to get us into a real hot aerial battle and are instructed to keep out of them as much as possible for the time being until we become more proficient and accustomed to

---

5. Bixschoote.

A BAD SMASH.
The pilot escaped with a few cuts and minus a few teeth. Wreck of an English Sopwith Camel scout-machine at St. Pol-sur-Mer, August, 1917.

SPAD PLANES OF ESCADRILLE N. 73.
Lined up for review by the King and Queen of Belgium. Bergues, France, August 13, 1917.

the work. Of course if a comrade was attacked and having trouble one could not well stand around and watch him get shot up. Young pilots do not however go on excursions far into the Boche territory looking for trouble the way some of the old hands do. Practice is everything in this game as in all others and one is learning something every minute spent over the lines.

Bergues, August 13, 1917.

Was out again last night after writing and again this morning. Nothing much out of the ordinary except that the Boche anti-aircraft guns were pretty active this morning. I watched the shells bursting all around a machine about half a mile from us and the pilot doing all kinds of gyrations to throw them off. Just about that time a couple went off pretty close to me and as I noticed they had my altitude exactly, I quit watching the other fellow and started doing a few things on my own account. Last evening when we went out about six o'clock, one of those black summer thunder showers was drifting around. There was a lively bombardment going on and part of the battlefield was shrouded in semi-darkness. The flashes of the guns stood out very vividly and the smoke, mist and drifting rain squalls were about all that was needed to complete my idea of what the private domains of Old Nick probably look like.

August 14, 1917.

The King and Queen of Belgium received us here yesterday. I was introduced to them both and said a few words to the King. Will write you all about it soon but not now. My friend Oliver Chadwick has evidently just been killed. We are not absolutely sure yet but there is practically no hope. He was the best of them all and we have been together all the time for months. I had come to know him better than I have ever known any other man and he was as fine and fearless a Christian gentleman as ever lived. He was apparently shot down from 2000 metres in a combat and fell inside the German lines over the little destroyed town I have described. I am glad he died with his boots on as he wanted to, but my heart is sick and I cannot write you about it till later.

St. Pol-sur-Mer.[6] August 21, 1917.

Just a line to tell you that I am well, but I have so many letters to write that you will have to wait until next week before I shall be able to write you fully. My friend, Oliver Chadwick, was killed by the

---

6. One mile west of Dunkirk.

Boche on Tuesday. He sailed in to help out another machine that was being attacked and was in turn attacked from the rear by two other machines. At least this is what happened as far as we can learn. We are not even sure that the machine that was brought down in this manner was Oliver's, and as it fell in the Boche lines there is no way of verifying it, but the evidence is very bad and I am afraid there is little hope. There is the barest chance that he may be a prisoner, but it is very slim.

Then on the 18th Julian was killed; so it was a very bad week for the Americans here. I am terribly sorry about Julian and I naturally feel his loss very keenly for we were always very good friends and had had a lot of fun together since coming to France. He was an excellent pilot in the schools and extremely conscientious and hard working. He got his military license in a remarkably short time and sailed through all the tests without the slightest mishap. Once he had had time to gain a little experience here at the front I feel sure that he would have done very well. Julian and Oliver and I might have had some great Boche hunting expeditions together if luck had not broken so against them. I am glad to say that M—— arrived here the day after Oliver was lost, so I am not left the only American in the *escadrille*.

St. Pol-sub-Mer. August 24, 1917.

Got a rainy day today and as I have pretty well caught up on the writing I told you I had to do, I can now drop you a line about what has been going on recently. On August 13th we were inspected by the King and Queen of Belgium. We all got dressed up in our best and stood at attention while the king conferred some Belgian decorations on some of the men for bravery and the work they had done. I have some pictures of Oliver, Julian and myself standing in the line of pilots with the king and queen in front and shall send the photos along as soon as I have an opportunity. The commandant stopped in front of us and introduced us all three to the king and queen. You see we are the first American pilots in the *escadrille* and therefore somewhat of a curiosity so we sometimes receive attention which our rank would not ordinarily entitle us to. Shook hands with them and called them "Sire" and "*Madame*" as per the commandant's previous instructions. Had a few words with King Albert, who said he is hoping for great things when America gets her forces over here. Glad to say he spoke English as I was scared to death lest I might have to talk French to them. Kings and telephones get my goat when it comes to talking

French. I guess little Willie is some pumpkins hobnobbing with royalty and such, eh what!! The king is a very fine looking man and the queen is most attractive.

The next morning, the 14th, Oliver and I were not scheduled to fly until the afternoon, but as we were both anxious to get all the practice possible, we went to the field in the morning in the hope that they might need an extra man. A patrol was just going out and being short one man they asked Oliver to fill up. I saw him off and was a little disappointed that he had gotten the job instead of myself, as he already had an hour or two more over the fines than I had. He went out with three Frenchmen and never came back. They reported that at about 9.45, shortly after they had reached the fines, they lost track of Oliver while manoeuvring near some clouds. Shortly after lunch we received a telephone message that the infantry had seen a machine of the type Oliver was flying shot down in the course of a combat from about 2000 metres and fall about 1200 metres north of Bixschoote on a place known as the "*Ferme Carnot.*" According to the report, the French machine went to the assistance of an English one that was being attacked by a Boche, and at the same time was itself attacked from the rear, by two other Boches. The French machine was "*nettement descendu*" [7] as they say, and took a sheer fall of over 6000 feet until it crashed into the ground.

I had hoped against hope that there might be some mistake, that the machine was merely forced to land or perhaps that it was not Oliver's machine at all and that he might be only a prisoner. I have been doing everything I could think of to get all the detailed information possible as it will mean so much to his family to know just what happened and whether or not he is really dead. The commander has been very kind in trying to help me to collect this information, but it has seemed almost impossible to trace what clues we have. Where so many thousands are being killed, and have been for the past three years, a dead man, no longer able to help in the fight, is nothing, and men busy with the great business of war have no time to spend in trying to find one.

Oliver fell between the lines but very close to the German. The recent French advance has however put the spot just within our own lines and I wanted to go up myself and have a look but it seems impossible. I thought perhaps I might be able to find his body or the machine or something. Even though I could not do this, however, my

---

7. Clearly brought down.

KING ALBERT OF BELGIUM DECORATING AVIATORS.
In the group are, besides the King, Lieutenant Nungesser (30 Huns), Lieutenant de La Tour (9 Huns), Captain Heurtaux (21 Huns), Major Borcard (commanding "*Groupe de Combat 12*," French aviation), Bergues, France, August 13, 1917. The records of enemy planes brought down are as of the date of the picture.

QUEEN ELIZABETH OF BELGIUM GETTING OUT OF FRENCH PLANE.
After a flight at Bergues, France, August 13, 1917. In the group are Major Brocard, Queen Elizabeth, and Lieutenant (then Adjutant) René Fonck, who later became the ace of all the aces.

efforts seem to be bearing fruit and there seems to be no longer any doubt that the machine was Oliver's.

Today I received a photograph of the machine taken by a priest attached to the infantry, and also some details of what happened when the machine fell. It seems that both the Boche and French soldiers rushed out of their trenches to try and get the machine, and a fight followed in which both were forced to retire. The picture was taken after the advance a day or so later and shows a tangled mass of wreckage and beside it the dead body of a Boche. No trace could be found of Oliver's body, but this is easily explained by the fact that pilots often have papers on them of military importance and his body would therefore have been taken and searched. This would have been easy for the Germans to do at night as the machine was so close to their front line trench. I am now trying to get the number of the fallen machine and to find someone who actually saw it fall. I think then we shall have everything. What chance has a man who falls like that from such a height? I have seen the result of a fall of one tenth the distance or less, too often not to know. I have a large scale map showing the spot where he fell; it will of course always be impossible to find out where he is buried.

I wish you could have known Oliver Chadwick as I am sure he would have appealed to you as he did to me. He was the kind of man that it takes generations to make and then you only get them once in a thousand times. A man with a great deal of brains, he was also a very hard worker and had learned more about aviation and made himself into the best pilot I have ever seen for one of his experience. He was one of the very few that I have met over here who came over long before America entered the war, simply because he felt it was his duty to fight for what he knew was right. That was why he was fighting and what he was fully prepared to die for. His ideals were of the highest and he was morally I think the cleanest man I have ever known. Physically he had always been a splendid athlete and was a particularly fine specimen. Absolutely fearless and using his brains every minute, if he had only had a chance to really get started and to gain a little more experience, he should have developed into the best of them all. The Boche that got him certainly did a good job from their point of view, for if he had lived long enough to become really proficient, they would have known it to their sorrow and I doubt if they would ever have gotten him.

We were in the Law School together but I never saw much of him there, as we lived far apart and had a different set of friends. Since I came over here however and went to the aviation schools, we had been almost constantly together. We had lived together, eaten together, flown together and planned all our work together. Always a gentleman and thinking of the other fellow, he was the most congenial man to me that I had ever known. I had come to regard him as my best friend and it is astonishing how well you can get to know one with whom you work in this business, whom you often rely on for your life and who you know relies on you in the same way.

There is nothing I would not have done for Oliver Chadwick and I know he would have done the same for me. He was the finest man of his age that it has ever been my good fortune to meet and was my idea of what a gentleman should be. I am very glad to have known him and I think it did me a great deal of good. When a man of this rare stamp goes down almost unnoticed, it seems, it makes one appreciate what this war means. To me personally, his death naturally leaves a pretty big hole, but I am glad that if he had to die he died fighting as he wanted to. I know he himself never expected to survive the war, but his only fear was that he might be killed in some miserable accident.

He was a great favourite with all the instructors both because of his amiability and because they could not help but admire his skill and fearlessness. The commander here regarded him as one of the most courageous men he had ever had, which is saying a great deal in this organisation. One of the officers tried to tell me that Oliver should not have left his patrol and gone to help out the other machine. I think he did exactly what he should have done, he could not well stand by when he saw a comrade in trouble and leave him to shift for himself. What one admires in a man more than anything else is the doing of his duty regardless of the consequences to himself and this was Oliver all over. As soon as I heard what had happened I felt sure it was he. My great regret is that I could not have been on the same patrol as we usually stuck pretty close together and might have been able to help one another out.

Had an interesting experience one day when a French barrage fire was in full swing in preparation for an attack. I was out on a patrol which happened to be a low one, and my leader, a lieutenant, flew entirely too low for one's comfort. He got down in the territory of the French shells and in a barrage fire they are pretty thick. Every few minutes you would run into the eddy caused by a shell and your machine would rock from side to side and sometimes turn up on edge.

Once or twice they came close enough to hear them screech above the roar of the motor and the machine felt as though a giant had taken it and given it a mild shaking by the collar, so to speak. As a matter of fact we could have done better work flying above the trajectory and we served no particular purpose being where we were. We were still too high to fear any fire from the ground, but in any event I am against taking chances where there is nothing to be gained. Seems to me it is just playing into the other fellow's hands and I have no desire to start unnecessarily an argument with one of our own shells in midair. On any ordinary day shells in the air, other than antiaircraft, are not thick enough to bother about.

Another time, a few days ago, I was again up at about 16,000 feet, when an oil pipe broke and let all the oil run out. As there was no way of telling this, it was only a few minutes until my motor "grilled." That is to say, the bearings burnt out and she stopped as suddenly and completely as though I had thrown off the switch. As I was on the Boche side of the lines at the time, I thought I had better start hiking for my own side of the fence "*toot sweet.*" Every day as I had been flying back and forth from the lines, I had amused myself in looking for allied aviation fields so that in case of trouble I would know where to go, if I could not get back to my own field.

A small fast *chasse* machine is a hard thing to land without upsetting unless you have a good place to do it on, and this is especially true when the country is wet and full of shell holes. I therefore bethought me of a field near a certain town[8] which I knew was the nearest to the lines, although I had never been there. It was a long way off and I did not think I should be able to reach it, but it could do no harm to try, as from very high up one cannot make out a suitable place to land anyhow. There were too many clouds beneath me to make out the town very well, but I knew the general direction and started planing that way. When I got through the clouds at about 6000 feet up I could see the town and soon the aviation field. Having plenty of height it was easy to go there with room to spare and I landed without further trouble.

A motor in the condition of mine means changing it and putting in another so there was nothing for it but to go back to my base by motor, a distance of some thirty miles. What was my surprise to find that some of our Philadelphia doctors were serving at a field hospital near where I landed. After telephoning to my squadron, I went over to

---

8. Poperinghe, five miles northwest of Ypres, Belgium.

see them and found Drs. P——, M——, D——, and V——. I dined with them and spent the night and we discussed the affairs of the nations generally. Tomorrow I expect to go back and fly the machine home as the mechanics now have it in shape.

Dr. P—— told me that the Boche had bombed the hospital two out of the last three evenings. At first they thought it was a mistake, but when they kept it up it became apparent that there was no mistake. This is a big field hospital in white tents and lots of red crosses plainly visible. I have myself seen it from the air and you can see it more distinctly than anything else in the neighbourhood. A couple of days before, a bomb had landed on a cook shack about twenty yards from Dr. P——'s tent. The cook's leg came through the roof of the tent next door and the guy-ropes of Dr. P——'s tent were decorated with his entrails. Nice party don't you think? Another bomb landed right alongside of the tent occupied by D—— and V——. Luckily they had just answered a special call to operate that night and were not in their tent. A piece of bomb went through one of their pillows where one or the other, I have forgotten which, had just been sleeping. Their clothes were blown all over the lot and D—— exhibited numerous holes in the seat of his pants. Luckily he had not been in them at the time.

We stood around after supper at the time when brother Boche usually came along and waited for him to put in an appearance. We had not long to wait. Pretty soon we could hear his motors humming up in the sky and dozens of searchlights began to look for him. They picked up one of the raiders and the show beat any Fourth of July celebration you ever saw. The machine showed clear and white in the glare of the searchlights. It was a dark night but very clear, with millions of stars. On every side were the muzzle flashes of the anti-aircraft guns, the sky was filled with the flashes of the bursting shells, and the two seemingly joined by streams of tracer bullets from machine-guns. These latter look much like Roman candles except that they go much faster and keep on going up for thousands of feet instead of stopping short like the ball from a candle. Add to this the roar of the guns and bursting shells and you can imagine what a quiet evening in a field hospital back of the front is like.

The one Boche that we could see was driven off, but pretty soon we could hear others coming and this time so high up that the searchlights could not find them. As we stood there listening the sound of the motors seemed to have almost passed over us, when suddenly *siz-bang-bang*, and five or six bombs landed plumb in the camp. We threw ourselves flat for a moment and then went to see what had happened. You could hear cries coming from the direction where the bombs had fallen and the air was filled with dust and smoke. One bomb which fell within about seventy-five yards of us killed three men and wounded about six. Another lit right in a ward,—imagine the effect when it was full of wounded soldiers. The casualties in all amounted to about 34 killed and 125 wounded. The camp consists of four field hospitals joined together. Fifty *per cent* of the staff of one of the hospitals was knocked out. I enclose you two clippings describing similar atrocities. The one described in the clipping headed "The New Frightfulness" happened not far from here and I know it is true. Don't let anyone tell you that these things are mistakes. You can't bomb a hospital three times in four days and then put in an alibi about a mistake.

The clipping entitled "Do we hate enough?" seems to me to just about hit the nail on the head except for the mention of a possibility of ever again being friends with the Boches. They are beyond the pale of a decent man's friendship and should be considered as a race with which no Christian should have anything to do. I am frank to say that I am looking forward to the day when I shall, I hope, kill some of them, for I hate them as I would a snake and would kill them with as little compunction. They have not even the excuse of the ordinary murderer *i. e.* that he was not decently brought up and did not know any better. It goes without saying that in speaking of the Huns I am always speaking of the German people who, individually and as a nation, are responsible for this war and whom we are fighting, and not at all of loyal Allied or American citizens of German birth or descent.

I forgot to add that one of the nurses lost an eye, and you have of course seen in the papers the case of the *Belgian Prince*, where a submarine commander deliberately took the life belts away from 38 English seamen and then drowned them in cold blood. Shooting is too good for people of this sort. I have no particular malice against the Boches because they killed Chadwick as that was in a fair fight, as fights go out here. Except for the rotten explosive bullets that they use so much, they seem to play the game fairly well in the air when it comes to a combat. What they do when it comes to hospitals I have already told you.

St. Pol-sur-Mer. September 4th, 1917.

Have been trying to write for the past three evenings but it has been necessary to put the lights out and spend the time in or close to a dugout. There is a gorgeous moon now, just right for night bombardment work and the Huns have been making the most of it. Every night regularly they bomb a nearby town,[9] generally setting it on fire in several places. Since I began this letter I have been out in the dugout and there is a big fire raging at this moment. The Boches have dropped about fifteen bombs so far tonight and it is quite a remarkable sight to watch them hit. The incendiary ones light up the whole sky and the high explosives throw a huge fountain of sparks in all directions.

When they are bombing the town we stand outside and watch the show, but when they come our way we duck down our hole like a lot of rabbits. No one but a fool or a greenhorn will stand around and get blown up just for the sake of seeing the sights. When you add the searchlights, anti-aircraft guns, bursting shells, and machine-guns, to the fires and terrific explosions of the bombs, you have about all your eyes and ears can take in at one time. I shall never again I think, so much as take the trouble to walk around the corner to watch a fireworks display on the 4th of July.

St. Pol-sur-Mer, Sept. 8, 1917.

I told you in my last letter to Mother, which I had to cut short, that I had my first fight last Sunday morning. It did not amount to much, but it was a satisfaction to be able at last to let one's gun off at a Boche. On the morning in question, I was to go on a high patrol but my motor would not start at first so I did not get off until fifteen minutes after the others and had to go out to the lines by myself. When I got there I was still quite low, between 2000 and 2500 metres and ran into a low patrol of three machines from our *escadrille*. I thought they might possibly be my own crowd and joined them for a moment to find out. Just as I did so I saw five machines coming our way which I took for another Allied patrol starting on its way home.

The men with whom I was were all pretty green (like myself) and evidently did not see the other machines at all. They worked around toward our rear and although I still thought they were friends I did not like the way they acted and kept watching them over my shoulder. When they got quite close, say 150 metres, I suddenly saw the leader let drive at one of our men who was below me to my left. You can plainly see the flash of a machine-gun and the explosive bullets leave long streams of wavy smoke behind them in the air. In a big scrap where there is a lot of shooting the long hairs of smoke left by the

---

9. Dunkirk.

bullets sometimes make the planes look as though they were in the middle of an enormous cobweb.

The man who was shot at turned suddenly and dove to get out of the way; he got three bullets through the tail of his machine. As he turned, the five machines veered and I saw plainly that they were five Boche single-seater fighting planes. The particular type very much resembles one of ours and the *cocardes* are hard to see until one is quite close. Our other two machines kept going for our own lines, the pilots evidently being taken by surprise and a bit mixed up. One could not very well go off and leave the one man who had been shot at with five Boches after him, so I turned around short and flew towards them. They had already veered when our man whom they shot at turned toward them. Three of them went down and two went up. The three that went down wanted to go after our machine that had gone down, but I think they were afraid to do so when they saw me above them. Our man made a safe get-away anyhow.

I had a lovely chance to dive on the Boche below me, but every time I started I looked at the two above and they would begin to do the same thing to me. It is pure foolhardiness to attack, when you do not have to, with other enemy machines close above your head. That was the way Oliver was killed, but he had to go in. The five Boches kept retreating into their own territory and it was impossible to get close enough to really do much with one's shooting. The three below kept circling about close together, evidently in the hope that I would attack and give the two above their chance. I got a few shots at one of them but he was three hundred yards off and you can't do anything more than worry a machine at such a range except by sheer good luck. I then tried to get near the two upper ones, but they kept hiking for home, and although I got a few more long shots, I had to turn back as I was by myself and getting too far into the Boche territory, perhaps three or four miles or so.

On my way back the Boche "Archies" (anti-aircraft guns) tried to have some fun with me, but did not come close enough to amount to anything. The whole thing did not amount to more than a useful experience as most of the shooting was too far off to have any effect.

Was out on Wednesday morning on a high patrol and had a couple of other little set-tos from which I think I also got some experience, but that was about all. We were up as high as I have been so far, about 18,000 feet, and it is as cold as Christmas up there. Dressed warmly however you do not feel it much, except on your face, and I have now got something to cover most of that up. There were five of us this time and at about 16,000 feet we ran across three or four Boche fighting planes who were a little below us. We manoeuvred for position and attacked. I picked out one fellow and went for him, but after about six shots and just when I was getting close enough to do some business, my machine-gun quit owing to a cartridge missing fire. I tried to fix it at once, but she would not fix. Everyone had gotten pretty well separated during the fight and as there was one Boche above me in a fine position to attack and I could see no sign of my comrades, I started hiking for our side of the fence as fast as I could go. On the way I passed a Boche within a hundred yards going in the opposite direction liked a scared rabbit. I had to laugh to see him humping his machine up and down so as to make it hard to hit. He looked for all the world like a hopping rabbit and I guess he thought I was going to take a crack at him, but if he had only known it I was beating it for home just as hard as he was.

As soon as I got in quieter water I fixed my machine-gun and began looking for my patrol. I had not been going five minutes when I ran bang on a Boche two-seater all by itself. I was afraid to start shooting when I first wanted to as there are so many different allied machines that it is very hard for a greenhorn to tell them all from the German. I thought it was a Boche, but did not like to begin shooting until I was absolutely sure, so waited until he passed under my wing close enough to see his old Maltese crosses on his planes. I then turned around and went for him from above, which by the way, is a fool method to attack a two-seater, as it gives the machine-gunner, who sits behind the pilot, a beautiful shot at you. Usually the best way to do it is to get under his tail where he often does not see you and can't shoot without hitting his own tail. I guess I was a bit too anxious however and spoiled my own chance.

I could see the machine-gunner blazing away and could not get to close quarters without giving him a much better chance at me than I had at him. I aimed ahead of him about the distance that I thought was right and gave him a rip from my machine-gun. I could see the tracer bullets and they looked to me as though I hit him, but I could not be sure. At all events he started for home without a second's hesitation, full motor and diving slightly, which gives almost the greatest speed. I manoeuvred a little and gave it to him again and I hope I touched him up for the machine-gunner seemed to me to stop shooting. I went after him a third time, this time from behind his tail and we were both streaking it through the air at a scandalous pace.

I had my machine nosed down a bit and going full out, was overhauling him and had just begun to shoot again when my machine-gun jammed, this time from a broken cartridge and so that it was impossible to fix it in the air. We had been going for the Hun territory all the time, so that we were by this time several miles behind the German lines. With my machine-gun out of commission there was of course nothing to do but go home. Since that time we have been having poor weather again and I have not been over the lines.

I certainly hope I can become skilful enough before long to drop one of these fellows good and proper as the saying is. My chance at the two-seater was badly handled, as I had to do my shooting at about 200 yards, and this is entirely too far. The great majority of successful fights, practically all of them in fact, are fought from 100 to 10 yards. You must remember the terrific speeds of the machines, the fact that we have to point our whole machine, and the great distances covered in a few seconds, in order to understand why patrol formations get broken up in a fight and why there is so much shooting without result.

Also, when it is one machine against another, if one fellow sees the other coming a good way off and wants to get away, he can usually do it. It takes so little time to cover several miles, and a skilfully manoeuvred machine is very hard to hit anyhow. The majority of successful combats are cases of surprise, where you sneak up close behind another machine without his seeing you or where he is busy attacking still another machine, and you can drop on his rear unawares. There are exceptions, of course, but most fights seem to be like this. Of course if a number of machines attack one of the enemy, they can often on account of their numbers get him whether he sees them or not and no matter how hard he tries to get away. I think I could do a lot better with that two-seater another time, but a little experience like this is I guess the only way to learn.

It would be utterly impossible for the one man in a *chasse* machine to use a movable gun fired from the shoulder. There is no place where you could carry such a gun and you would not have room to use it if you could carry it. In our small planes, of which the greatest assets are speed and manageability, there is just room for the pilot and no more. He is entirely encased with nothing but his head sticking out and in addition is tightly strapped in his seat with straps coming up between his legs and over his shoulders. This precaution is both necessary and important for in the rush of a close encounter one will do things that would otherwise throw the pilot around inside the machine and possibly out of it.

There is not much news to tell you about this week as my work has been very quiet, due largely to the flying having been considerably interfered with by more bad weather. We have however had some clear nights and the Boches have been doing their best to make things lively by dropping a few bombs around. I have already told you what a night bombardment looks like and also of the wonderful sight presented by the defence against it. It is all very well to watch three or four times, but when they keep it up night after night so that you have to put the lights out and stay near a dugout just when you want to do some writing or go to bed, it becomes nothing but a nuisance and a bore.

Most of the bombs dropped near here have been aimed at the town, but now and then the Boches seem to take a shot at us. At all events, one night in the early part of this week, they dropped one about ten or fifteen feet from the side of our barracks and they sure did muss it up good and proper. We had gotten our room all nicely fixed up, but that bomb wrecked the whole works. M—— and I had bought ourselves a set of tea things, cups, saucers and plates, etc., so that we could make ourselves tea in the afternoon and have oatmeal, eggs, etc., in the morning. Everything went in one grand smash, including the tar paper walls and ceiling to our room. You never saw a prettier mess or a more complete wreck than our room appeared to be when we came groping in in the dark after the Boches had gone. We were, however, lucky that our room was on the opposite side of the building from that on which the bomb fell.

Some of the men opposite us were much worse off as the explosion pushed in their side of the building and tore parts of the roof off over their heads. The hole the bomb made in the ground was about four feet deep by about twelve across. Right close by stood our cook shack, but after the smoke had cleared away it was hard to recognise. I have taken some pictures and will send them along when they are developed and I think they will show you what happened much better than I can describe it. M—— and I had gone to a shelter some little distance away where we could be pretty safe and at the same time see what was going on.

When this particular bomb landed I said I thought it looked very close to our barracks and that we would have the laugh on the Boches if we went back and found that they had blown our room up when we were not there. We went to look after everything was comparatively quiet and sure enough our room had been blown up, but I am not so sure that the joke was all on the Boches. However, the bomb was not close enough to hurt any of our things except the plates, and after a couple of days' hard work we are now much better and more comfortably installed than we were before.

They did seem to have it in for us that night though, as another bomb dropped in a village at least a mile away, right on the house of the good woman to whom we send our laundry, incidentally blowing the week's wash literally to shreds. Pieces of the bomb which dropped "*chez nous*" went right through the barracks from one side to the other, in places fairly riddling it. Luckily everyone was in the shelters and not a soul was so much as scratched. Come to think of it the total casualties were one dog. He was asleep in his kennel in a tent and a piece of bomb came through the side of the tent, through the side of the wooden kennel, through the poor hound, out through the other side of the kennel, and where it went after that is hard to say.

I enclose you a snapshot of myself in flying togs standing in front of my machine and have cut it down until I do not think the censor can possibly object. Pretty good of me don't you think but so far as I have been able to discover I am certain that I am of no "military importance."

St. Pol-sur-Mer, Sept. 16th, 1917.

You will have seen in the papers long before you get this letter, that Capt. Guynemer, the greatest of them all, is gone. He and another officer went out on Tuesday morning to hunt the Hun. They were flying fairly high, somewhere around 16,000 feet I think, and Guynemer went down a little way to attack a two-seater while the lieutenant who was with him stayed up to protect his rear. About that time eight Boche single-seater machines put in an appearance and the lieutenant was kept busy trying to worry them and keep them from going down on the captain. He succeeded and none of the Boches dove down, but in the general mix-up he lost track of Guynemer and he has not been heard from since. He must have fallen in the Boche lines and I am afraid he was killed without much question.

The place where the fight occurred was over the Boche territory, but close enough to our lines to have allowed Guynemer to have reached them if he had been merely wounded. Also, if the Huns had taken him prisoner, we would certainly have heard of it before now.

They would be proud to get him and I am surprised that they have as yet made no announcement of his having been found.

The loss of this man is very great, as he was by all odds the greatest aviator and individual fighter the war has produced. I am awfully sorry, for if ever a man had won his spurs and deserved to live it was Capt. Guynemer. He had 53 Hun machines to his credit officially and I hoped that he had become so skilful that he would never be killed. As I have already written you, he was small and of a frail appearance. I believe his health was very far from good and the high altitudes sometimes made him so sick he had to come down. He would fly for a week and then go away for a rest, as he was not strong enough to stand any more. In the course of several hundred fights he had been shot down seven times and twice wounded. To keep at it under such circumstances and after all he had gone through, a man's heart has to be in the right place and no mistake. He certainly deserved to live the rest of his days in peace and one hates to see a man like that get it.

The evening before he disappeared, I was standing on the field when he landed with a dead motor caused by a bullet in it. There were three others through his wings. He had attacked another two-seater, something went wrong with his motor at the crucial moment and this gave the Boche a good shot at him and spoiled his own chance of bringing down his opponent. A little episode like this, however, rolled off his back like water off a duck, perhaps a little too easily I fear. Long immunity breeds a contempt of danger which is probably the greatest danger of all. Guynemer's loss naturally throws more or less of a gloom over everyone.

It is clear again this evening so I am going to close this letter before I have to start for a dugout. We were out in quest of the elusive Boche this afternoon and got up as high as I have yet been, between nineteen and twenty thousand feet, but had no luck. Saw a couple of them but they were above us and by the time we had gotten up to where they were they had run for home while we were still too far away to catch them. Reminds me of the old days when I used to chase what you were wont to call the "invisible duck."

St. Pol-sur-Mer, Sept. 22, 1917.

Father in his last letter said he thought having a Hun sneak up under your tail would be a great danger and he is quite right. Surprise is the thing to try to spring on the Boches and is the most important thing to avoid having them spring on you. I think my long training

CAPTAIN GUYNEMER ABOUT TO START ON THE LAST FLIGHT FROM WHICH HE EVER RETURNED.

He came back with his machine badly shot up. On his next flight, he was killed and fell near Poelkapelle, Belgium, September 11, 1917.

in looking for the festive duck has helped me considerably, as spotting a machine a long way off in the air comes to much the same thing. I have not been caught napping yet or even come close to it and hope I shall not be. The closest I have been was one day this week when we were flying just beneath some clouds. Five Huns used the clouds to sneak up in our rear and above us, and I know I did not see them until they were within about three hundred yards. There were four of us on the patrol and one of our men lagged a little too far behind. He did not see the Boches until just as a couple of them opened fire on him. He then did some quick manoeuvring to escape while the rest of us tried to get above them to help him out.

They had us at a great disadvantage being several hundred feet above. In the meantime our companion was in a difficult position with several Huns around him shooting at him and I was afraid they were going to get him, but he did some pretty good manoeuvring, making himself very hard to hit and they never even touched his machine. There was a heavy gale blowing that morning toward the German lines and I never realised before how far one could travel in a short time under such conditions. The rest of us had turned and chased those Huns into their own lines for only about a minute I think, before we turned back. There was a solid bank of clouds above us at about 12,000 feet and a lot more about 5000 feet lower down. I lost my companions in a cloud and not being able to see the ground had to fly back to our lines by compass.

It is a funny feeling flying along in clear air with clouds both above and below you and we do not often do it except in such a case as this, for one quickly loses one's bearings and there is generally no purpose to be accomplished. This time, however, I did not want to come down below the lower clouds for I knew I was well over the Boche territory. Once or twice when I passed over a hole so that I could see and be seen from the ground, the Huns would let go an anti-aircraft shell or two but they could not see me well enough to put them close enough to worry about. I flew by the compass for about ten minutes and when I dropped down within sight of the ground was only just over our own lines.

One has to be careful of a heavy wind like this and we have had a great deal of it, always toward the Hun lines. It is a great handicap, for in a combat one cannot manoeuvre without being quickly carried into the enemy territory where one is likely to be soon much outnumbered. The day after the above episode, I was trying to bag a Boche and got mixed up with a couple of them. Four of us were out on patrol and attacked a formation of six Albatross scouts. There was again a very heavy wind blowing into the German lines and in chasing a Boche I was carried well into his territory before I realised it. Just as I was getting close enough to shoot at him another Hun came up and then suddenly I saw five more coming behind him. We were all on the same level and I did not like the look of things at all, so turned back for our own lines. The two nearest Boches got on my tail, one at about sixty yards range and the other at perhaps a hundred, and when each opened up with his two machine-guns I never saw so many explosive bullets in my life, they seemed to me to be going by in regular flocks.

The thing to have done under ordinary circumstances would have been to have turned and fought it out with the two Huns who were shooting at me or at least to have manoeuvred with them until a better opportunity of getting away presented itself. In this case however, to have turned would have landed me in the middle of all seven of them and with the wind carrying us into Hunland I would have been out of luck. The only thing to do therefore was to keep flying for home at the same time throwing my machine around so as to present as difficult a target as possible. I did things I never knew I could do before and think I invented some new forms of acrobacy, for those Huns scared me out of about five years' growth.

Luckily for me one of the Frenchmen saw that I was in trouble and being above us all he was able to fly in over the Huns and scared them off. When we got back to our field after the flight I examined my machine expecting to find about a dozen holes in it. Was rather disappointed not to find any so I guess those Boches must have been very poor shots or more probably I am just very green and thought that I was in more trouble than I really was.

I have explained to you that it is quite a job to get any of these Huns here, but with a little luck and perseverance perhaps we may have one of them fly into some of the bullets that we strew about. Here's hoping so anyhow!

There is another moon now and we have been expecting more bombs, but thanks to cloudy nights we have been left in peace. By day we swear at clouds and by night we bless them. Sometimes they are handy in daytime also as for instance the other day when I was in the Hun territory by myself. I felt quite safe, for with clouds above and below, if I had run into too many enemy machines, a cloud affords a convenient refuge where you can easily lose them.

Bergues. Oct. 3, 1917.

The sector of the front where we do practically all our flying runs from Dixmude to Ypres. The Belgians are on our left and the English on our right here. As you are seeing by the papers, the British have been giving the Huns what for around Ypres and I hope we can keep it up and make substantial progress before the bad weather sets in. It has been much improved lately. When we fly really high Ostend is plainly visible and I often think of the days that you and Mother and I spent there, swimming, going to the races, etc. Times sure have changed! Not long ago several of us were protecting an artillery regulating machine when our big guns were trying to blow up the huge Hun gun that bombards Dunkirk.

This work was nearer the sea than usual, and at 16,000 feet Ostend looked almost as though you could drop a stone on it. It is interesting when this big Boche gun bombards at night. When she goes off our men signal it in from near the lines, they blow a whistle in Dunkirk and all the people take cover. Between one and two minutes later I should think, the shell arrives and there is an explosion which, with one exception, beats any other I have ever heard. After that you can hear the crash of falling bricks and broken houses.

The one exception I mentioned, was when our camp was bombed again about ten days ago. For the second time in ten days our cook shack was wiped out and my room wrecked along with the others. It took a lot of time to fix things up again, not to mention being a great nuisance. This time, I was in a trench with the other pilots just in front of the barracks. The trench had been prepared for such occasions and it certainly came in handy. Three bombs fell close to us, of which one was about thirty yards away and the other fifteen feet from the corner of the trench, where M—— and I were. It bulged in the side of the trench, blew our hats off and threw dirt all over us. The hole in the ground was about four feet deep by about ten or twelve across and needless to say this was the fellow that broke all my records for noise. I was not quite sure for a few seconds whether I was all there or not. As we were below the ground, however, it never troubled us though I thought it had about caved in one of my ear drums for a while, but that is all right now.

A night bombardment is a fine sight to watch from a safe distance but when you are yourself the target it is the most unpleasant thing

I have yet struck, especially when the novelty has worn off and you know what to expect. You always know when the Huns are coming by the anti-aircraft guns and the peculiar sound of their motors humming up among the stars. When these motors tell you they are almost overhead it is time to lay low in a trench. The bombs are usually dropped quite close together in groups of from four to eight perhaps. They of course fall in the line along which the course of the machine carries them.

Suppose the first one falls say three or four hundred yards from you and the next a hundred yards closer. It is not hard to judge whether you are approximately on that line or not. As a matter of fact the interval between bombs is generally fifty yards or less. When they come within a couple of hundred yards you can hear them whistle for several seconds before they strike, and they all sound uncomfortably close. You just squat there in a trench, knowing that they have got your line, listening to the oncoming hiss and wondering whether the next one is going to only fall in the trench with you or square in the middle of your back. If it comes good and close there is a blinding flash, a deafening explosion, dirt flies all over you and the ground rocks under your feet.

The nasty part about it is sitting there in the dark wondering whether the next one is going to blow you into kingdom come, and being perfectly helpless to prevent it. It gives you an idea of what the men in the trenches have to face constantly. I would rather take my chances in the air with a Hun any day, for there you can see your danger and what happens depends mostly on your own skill. The danger in the latter case is much greater comparatively speaking, but is not half so unpleasant. When you are down in a narrow trench the chances of a bomb falling in it or close enough to it to get you are very slight. Some of the shelters are covered and protect you against falling shrapnel and fragments of your own shells, but I rather prefer the open trench. If a big bomb fell on the roof of the ordinary shelter it would I think bury those it did not kill.

The next day we moved our camp, as things were getting too hot for comfort. Now we can lie in bed in the evening and watch them bomb Dunkirk and be glad we are not there, for the Huns do not know where our camp is and I don't think they will be able to spot it.

Bergues, Oct. 15, 1917.

You speak about the value of constant care and in this you certainly hit the nail on the head. I think the motto of every flyer should be to never take an unnecessary chance or one that will not produce some real gain if successful. Of the many accidents I feel sure that at least ninety-five *per cent* are caused by the carelessness, ignorance, or rashness of the pilot or by his failing to use his head. I have personally seen a painful number of accidents but I have yet to see one that was not directly due to one of these causes. As in anything else, as you become familiar with aviation and your machine, there is a natural tendency to relax and let your attention wander. To be able to relax is important or a pilot would never be much good and would soon wear out, but pipe-dreaming and carelessness when near the ground or over the lines is bound to be fatal sooner or later.

If you are where there are no Huns and have a couple of thousand feet under you, you can go to sleep if you like, for when the machine begins to fall you will wake up soon enough and in the modern fighting plane, flopping over sideways or any way in fact, is the least of the pilot's troubles. He does it every day on purpose to accustom himself to his machine and learn what it will do under all conditions. The cause of most accidents is carelessness in landing, and of most defeats in combat, the failure to watch the rear. This last is easier said than done for when a man is; trying to kill a Hun in front of him, if he pays too much attention to his own rear, his attention will be so distracted that he will never succeed in getting the man he is after.

One of our cracks got square the other day with the man who is reported to have killed Guynemer. This German was a captain and an observer in a two-seater. The Boche machine had flown far behind our lines to take pictures, but was very high, over twenty thousand feet, relying largely on his height for protection, for an ordinary fighting plane will not go that high. Our man,[10] who is very expert and has been a pilot for a long time, was in a particularly powerful machine and was the only one who saw the Boche who could get up to him. He climbed up under and behind his tail. Every time the Boche pilot would try to turn in order to give his gunner a shot, the Frenchman would slide around also, always keeping the Hun's own tail between himself and the machine-gunner, so that the latter could not shoot without shooting away his own controls.

In this manner he got right on top of the Boche, and at the first salvo put his machine-gun out of business and probably hit the gun-

---

10. Captain (then Adjutant) René Fonck, the ace of all the aces. At this time he had about fifteen German machines to his credit. At the end of the war he had increased his official record to seventy-five.

ner, *i. e.* the captain who is credited by the Huns with having shot Guynemer. After that there was nothing to it, the second dose the Frenchman gave him cut away the supports of the wings on one side so that they came out of position. The Hun flopped over on his back and Guynemer's supposed slayer fell out of the machine, taking a nice little tumble of twenty thousand feet. The machine and pilot tumbled end over end and as they went by, a number of other French machines waiting below who had not been able to get up, like a pack of wolves waiting for the leader to bring down the game, amused themselves taking pot shots at them. There is no secret about a small fighting plane often not being able to get up quite as high as a two-seater, which although slower has a larger wing surface and can consequently mount better where the air is thin and gives poor support.

Bergues, Oct. 16, 1917.

Today I was not listed to go out on patrol until the afternoon and as it was a nice morning, persuaded a Frenchman to go out with me on a "voluntary patrol" and see if we could not find some Huns. Am very glad we did for it is raining this afternoon so that we could not work, and also we sure did find the Huns this morning. I am ashamed of myself for not having brought one down but this is how it came about. We were flying along at about 16,000 feet and in front of us a rather heavy mist, something like that which one sees hanging low over the fields on an autumn evening. I was the leader and suddenly saw a two-seater machine come out of the mist toward me and perhaps two hundred yards below. At first I thought it was an Englishman until as he started to pass under me I saw his black Maltese crosses and the peculiar shape of his wings. I thought this was a great chance and it was if I had not made a mess of it. I did a short turn and dove down full speed to get under his tail, and the manoeuvre worked out very nicely for it landed me behind and under his tail where he could neither see nor shoot at me, the machine-gunner being blinded by his own tail planes.

I thought at the time that he could not have helped but see me when I dove down behind him and just as I was trying to lay my sights on him, the machine turned a little as though the pilot were trying to get into a position where his gunner could shoot. I was only about seventy-five yards away and I thought to myself that if there was to be some shooting I should be the one to start it. I accordingly blazed away without taking careful enough aim and although I hit him, for I could see the luminous bullets plainly, I did not get him in a vital spot. We were just about over the lines when I shot and the Hun started for home for all he was worth with little Willie after him and shooting when he could, but a wildly zigzagging machine is an awfully hard thing to hit. Not perhaps so hard to shoot holes through the wings, but the vital spots are very small. I chased that son of a gun about four miles into his own country until I saw four single-seater fighting planes coming up to his assistance and I had to give it up.

My companion had stayed up to protect my rear from four other Huns who appeared about the same time that I had attacked the fifth, and as in chasing the two-seater I had come down some three thousand feet, I lost track of him. In thinking this fight over I believe that Boche never knew I was there until I started to shoot. He certainly did act surprised then. If he did not know that I was there, I should have gotten much closer and aimed carefully before shooting at all. The tactics of practically all successful aerial fighters are to get quickly to very close quarters, fifty yards and often less, where they can fairly riddle the other fellow. Also, in attacking a two-seater, the closer one gets the safer it is, for it is easy to see that he will have to make a much greater movement in order to get an enemy out from under his tail if that enemy is only ten yards away, than if he is a hundred yards away. As you may imagine, the difficulties of aerial shooting are very great and if you can get right up against a Hun where you can give it to him point-blank with practically no correction to make for his speed, your task is much simplified.

Be that as it may, about ten minutes after I got back to my own lines and started to search for my companion, I looked up and there right over my head about six hundred yards was another Boche two-seater. I don't think he had seen me at that time and I started climbing up under him as fast as I could. Unfortunately I had a new motor which had just been installed and some of the wires, as I learned on coming down, were loose. My engine consequently did not give me anything like the power it should have and I was very slow in climbing at the high altitude, about thirteen or fourteen thousand feet. I gained height on the Hun but very slowly and pretty soon he took a turn and saw me, whereupon he also started for home. He had flown inside our lines while I was following him and I was under his tail perhaps five minutes in all, trying to get up to him, but after following him several miles into his own country the closest I could get to him was about 400 yards. It would have been very foolish to go as far into the enemy territory as would have been necessary in order to catch him. I took deliberate aim and gave him a good salvo, but he was much too far off to hit, save by the greatest good luck and I never touched him.

I had scarcely gotten back over the lines again when I spotted still another Boche two-seater several hundred yards below me and coming in my direction. I did a quick turn and dove to get behind his tail and as I did so saw that there were two and that from the way they manoeuvred they both saw me. I think the most difficult attack of all to make is upon a two-seater that sees you, for with a fixed gun ahead for the pilot and the machine-gunner in the rear with a movable gun they possess an enormous field of fire, and can shoot you almost anywhere except under their tails. The fire from the pilot's gun of a two-seater is, however, comparatively easy to avoid so that one can attack head on from in front, but this gives the attacker only the most difficult kind of a shot and requires great skill and experience. The way most attacks are made, is to get under the tail with all the speed possible so as to give the machine-gunner the hardest shot and little time to make it. I therefore dove for all I was worth and with your motor and gravity both taking you down you can get going so fast it is hard to breathe.

After the second encounter, as there was a good deal of mist, I had closed a little trap that I have over my sights so as to keep the glass from becoming foggy. My manoeuvre with these Huns came out all right and brought me within 40 yards of one of them behind and below. Every time he would start to turn I slid around with him and he did not fire a single shot. I certainly thought I had this fellow, but when I went to squint through the sights the trap was closed, and I could not see. I tried to open it and just as I was doing so the Boche pilot gave his machine a twist so that his tail no longer protected me and I saw the machine-gunner drawing a bead on me. "This is no place for me," says I and I ducked under his tail again, at the same time standing my machine vertically on her nose so as to get away while still protected by the tail. The machine-gunner fired not more than half a dozen shots I think but he luckily did not have time to do much aiming and never touched me. I started to go back at him again but we were getting very far into his own country and I had to give it up.

Was not that trick of closing the sights the worst dub trick you ever heard of? It carries me back to my early days of duck shooting on the river. How well I remember my feelings when I would work hard for a shot and then just when I thought I had him, have missed because in my haste I had forgotten to cock my gun or put off the safety. I had just the same feeling to-day only worse for I had set my heart on that Boche. I as a matter of fact have another set of open sights which I might have used, or I could have shot by simply watching my tracer bullets. Or again I could have stuck it out long enough to open up my regular sights and use them but I was so surprised that I guess I got a bit rattled and just did not think quickly enough. When I woke up it was too late. You may wonder what the other Boche was doing in the meantime. He was in the front of the one I was attacking and was where I could see him, so it was practically the same as only having one to deal with. You may also wonder why I should have missed the first fellow I shot at.

As I have said before, the whole business reminds me of the beginnings of duck shooting—there is just that same tendency to become over-anxious which one must conquer, and then too it makes a great difference when you have to keep ducking around under a Boche's tail to keep him from plugging you. Quickness is essential, but there is a certain quick deliberation which I think must be acquired by practice. Just the difference again between the quick unaimed snap shot of the beginner in wing shooting and the equally quick aimed shot of the old hand. And when the bird shoots back it does make an awful difference for when you see a machine-gun aimed at you with fire spurting out of it, there is, to me at least, a strong tendency to duck my head like a blooming ostrich rooting in the sand. Today was my first experience in attacking a two-seater from below and I think next time I shall be able to do much better. The only thing I accomplished today was driving those four Huns home off the lines and if they all go home another tune I shall deserve a good kick.

Don't get the idea that we have fights every time we fly. Until today I had not had so much as a shot at a Hun for three weeks although I had in that time done considerable flying. It seems to come in bunches for all three encounters today were within twenty-five minutes.

The clipping which I enclose about German "*Junkers*" is, I happen to know, substantially true. Have not seen any of this new type of machine as yet. They are I believe only for low work and are so heavily armoured that they cannot fly very high.

I think this is about all the news I have to tell you this time and here's hoping I shall soon be able to write of an encounter with a Hun that has a more successful ending.

It is very interesting to watch the changes that take place in a sector as the infantry under you attacks and advances. You can trace the advance by the slow changing of green fields and woods into a blasted wilderness which shows a mud brown colour from the air. Fields become a mass of shell holes filled with water and a wood turns from an expanse of green foliage into a few shattered and leafless trunks. For weeks I have watched in particular the destruction of a certain forest.[11] When I arrived at the front it was almost intact, here and there in the few open spaces one could see an occasional shell hole. Now one whole half of it which faces our fines is simply wiped out of existence and but for a few battered stumps, has melted until it looks almost like the surrounding quagmire of mud and shell holes. The other half has the appearance of a mangy dog.

Every now and then you notice that there is less green and more mud. This little forest is I suppose about four kilometres square and the change is necessarily gradual. One is naturally busy watching the air about him, but every week or so you will notice that the destruction of some landmark such as this forest has advanced another step. It is the same way with the little Belgian towns. By degrees they are obliterated until their sites are only distinguishable by a smudge a trifle darker in colour than the brown of the torn fields which once surrounded them.

Bergues, Oct. 17th.

Went out again this morning with the same Frenchman, looking for Huns. Got two more cracks at them. The first was too far to accomplish anything although I could see some of my bullets going between his wings and he and his comrade went home, as the boys say "Hell bent for Election." There were two of them just as there were yesterday but I could not get up close. The second fight was with another two-seater. I saw him coming toward me and let him pass about thirty yards over my head, then jerked my machine around quickly so as to put myself under his tail, but when I came around he was squarely in the sun and I lost him for a minute. He soon showed me where he was however for the machine-gunner opened up and fired a long burst. He did not shoot far enough ahead of me though, for I saw the stream of explosive bullets passing a couple of feet above my head.

Perhaps it was my imagination but it seemed to me that I could

---

11. Forest of Houthulst, northeast of Ypres.

feel the wind from the bullets as they passed. They certainly gave me a thrill and I lost no time in getting under his tail again. I had however tried to turn too quickly at the high altitude (16,000 feet) and my machine took me down about three hundred feet under him before I could stop it. This made the shooting position very poor for accurate work and although I hit him and could see the bullets passing on both sides of the body of his machine, they did no serious damage and only warmed him up and sent him home. No one who has not tried it realises what a difficult thing it is to get real accuracy in this sort of work, I know I never realised it before myself. Once more I have to say "wait until next time."

Paris, Oct. 20, 1917.

Arrived in Paris yesterday to fly a new machine back to the front. Had expected to get off today but am afraid it will be too foggy and may have to wait till the morning. This new machine is not for me I think, but you will be glad to know that it will probably only be a couple of weeks before I have the latest type, one which will out-fly and out-climb anything the Huns have. My present one is very good but the new ones are better and also mount two guns instead of one.

Had two more arguments with the Boches on the 18th. One in the morning was a long range hit and run scrap with a bunch of single-seater fighting machines where the object was more to drive them off than anything else. In the afternoon I found a two-seater by itself and think the pilot was a greenhorn for when I dove under his tail he got scared and started to beat it for home in a perfectly straight line. My position was perfect and the machine-gunner could not even see me, let alone shoot. I could have run into him if I had wanted to and thought I had him sure. Two shots and the machine-gun broke. I was so mad and disappointed I could have cried but here's hoping such bad luck is over and things will break my way next time. I have gotten a lot of valuable experience this week if nothing else.

Bergues. Oct. 30th, 1917.

You referred in your last letter to my speaking of going out alone with one other man over the lines. My reason for doing this is not at all because we have not enough men to fly in groups, but simply because two is the best number if you want to try to bring down some Huns. Two men patrols are nearly always voluntary "*vols de chasse*" and on such an expedition you can get a shot at many Huns who would take to the woods in the face of larger numbers. As you say, however, there is in aviation too much striving for individual success and not enough team work. This sort of thing produces some fine men, but kills unnecessarily a great many more. Although the Hun flyers are not up to the English or French, man for man, I have seen them bag our men on several occasions simply by always using their heads and working on a system and get off scot-free, although the man they got was probably better than any single one of them.

As for the statistics you say you saw in Baltimore, about all our best flyers having been killed, and many of the Germans being still alive, I think that they are mistaken. Practically all the big German aces are gone. Our men and the English have bagged several here in this sector this fall. On the other hand, there are a number of Frenchmen who have many Boche machines to their credit.

We have one fellow named Fonck in this group who only started in on chasse work last Spring, although he had been a pilot for a long time. Already he has about twenty Huns. He is a wonder, and with a little luck, should I think equal Guynemer's record. He is the fellow I wrote you about, who got the Boche who was reported to have killed Guynemer. He flies a great deal, and the regularity with which he nails them is extraordinary. A couple of days ago, he went out in the morning and brought one Hun down in flames, and killed a machine-gunner in another, only failing to get it because his engine went back on him.

In the afternoon Fonck went out again, brought another two-seater down in flames, and probably got a single-seater as well. When a man gets a few Huns and becomes recognised as very good he of course gets greater opportunities, and has the advantage of being among the first to get the newest and finest type of machine before the other pilots. But no matter what advantage of this sort he has, Fonck has won it and his record is none the less remarkable.

I hope when we are transferred to the U. S. forces the fact that we have our Government back of us will enable us to be among the first to get the best machines. As an improvement is made, it of course takes time to supply everyone, but the men who get the new type first get the jump on the others, so to speak, and have the great advantage of going after the Huns with a machine that will perform better than the Boche believe it will. For instance, if your machine will fly faster or climb higher and more quickly than the ordinary type will and the Hun that you are after bases his calculation on the performance of the ordinary type, you can easily see that you have a much better chance of fooling him. This keeping ahead of the times is, I think, of the utmost importance, and I hope the U. S. Government realises this. Turning out machines in large quantities and standardization have of course their advantages, but it would be a great mistake to load up with a lot of machines of a certain type and then by the time we could get them on the front in the spring find that they were out of date. The science of aeroplane building is still advancing very fast.

One of my reasons for hoping that after I have had my fling at the front I may be able to win a higher position is, because I should much like to have an opportunity of trying to cut out some of the frightful inefficiency and waste of time and effort that one sees on every side. It is sometimes perfectly appalling, and I can now understand what I could not understand before I came over, and that is, why the Germans have been able to do so well. What we know of their methods is of course only hearsay, but from all accounts, "efficiency and united effort" are their middle names—as the slang expression has it. The results they have accomplished certainly bear out this reputation.

What do you all think at home of the recent Hun invasion of Italy? The outlook is pretty gloomy, is it not, but I hope it may serve to make people in America realise that this war is not won yet by a long sight, and that if it is going to be won they have got to get into it for all they are worth. We certainly should do our utmost without complaining when one considers what a soft time of it we have had so far. Yesterday a Frenchman came to me with a letter he had received from a friend of his, an English infantry officer. It was written in English and he asked me to translate it for him. The Englishman was speaking of one of the recent attacks and said among other things, that he was sorry to have to write that Major X—— and his son Captain X—— had both been killed within an hour of each other. I thought at the time that this bit of news was going to be pretty hard on Mrs. X—— when it reached England, but this is what England has been going through for over three years now. Practically all her best young blood is gone. When the same sort of news reaches America a hundred thousand times or so, I guess we will wake up and realise that we have a war on our hands, if we do not realise it already.

The Italian business is certainly too bad and seems to be the direct result of the Russian fizzle. If the Russians had only done half their duty it seems likely that the war might have been ended this year, but now it doesn't seem possible that the end can come before another year at least.

Bergues, November 12th.

I am in a particularly bad humour this morning, so do not be surprised if it is to a certain extent reflected in this letter. Today is the most beautiful one that could be desired—better than any we have had for two weeks, and just what I have been waiting for. Three-quarters of an hour ago I was all dressed sitting in my machine, about to start out, when a mechanic discovered a leak in a gasoline tank, which means that it must be changed and that the machine will not be ready until the morning, so there goes another day to pot.

A few days ago I started out on a patrol with two lieutenants and on our way to the lines we saw a number of miles to one side of us a great many of our own anti-aircraft shells bursting. We went over to investigate and what did we run into but ten Hun Gothas and a couple of *chasse* machines flying over them for protection. The lieutenant who was leading our patrol says he shot at a couple of them, but I could not see him do it, as I was a little behind. The cover of my radiator had cracked and the water, mixed with glycerine to keep it from freezing, had sprayed out, covering my telescope sights, the windshield and my glasses, so that I could not see well. I had gotten a little behind the others in trying to clean things up with my handkerchief. At all events, the lieutenant's machine-gun went back on him, and he started back with the other lieutenant after him; seeing them both go, I thought they must be after a Hun that I had not seen, so I started to follow them, but when I could see no signs of a Boche in that direction, I turned back.

A Gotha machine, you know, is the enormous Hun machine that they use for their night bombing in the raids on England. They are almost as big as the Caproni which they have been recently demonstrating in the U. S. They have two motors and as a rule carry three or four men. They are unusually well armed with movable machine-guns, fore and aft, and the usual zone of safety under the tail is removed by means of a tunnel in the fuselage, which enables them to shoot under their tails. It therefore behooves you to "mind your eye," when you attack and to make sure you either get him or put his rear gunners out of business at least, for although you may be able to approach without giving him much of a shot it is impossible not to give him a shot in getting away.

These Gothas were the first that I had ever had a real look at for they are rarely seen by day; once or twice I have seen them in the distance over the lines. At all events, when I turned back, I spotted one Gotha off a little to one side of the squadron and somewhat over my head. As they were only about 9000 feet up climbing was easy and I started after him. They saw what I was up to however and the Hun drew in alongside of his companion for protection. Under these circumstances, it is foolishness to attack by yourself, for you will have at least two or three machine-gunners shooting at you with their movable guns and no way of protecting yourself when you want to shoot, for then you have to hold your machine steady. You will just get riddled with practically no chance of success to compensate for it. I accordingly looked for better game and saw another Gotha behind the squadron all by himself and below me. I flew around over him for a minute to see if the coast was clear and then dove down behind his tail. When I started after him he left the others and put for home as fast as he could go. All these Huns were well within our lines, and this was just what I wanted.

About this time I looked around to see if any other Huns were coming on my tail and there were two *chasse* machines just behind me in the sun. This gave me a jolt for with my glasses all fogged up it took me several seconds to make sure that they were English and not Huns. All the time the "Archie" shells were bursting in every direction, for in this sector at least, they often do not stop shooting just because one of their own machines goes after a Hun. As they generally shoot behind they come closer to you than to the Huns, and it always makes me sore. They did the same trick the day before when I was trying to sneak up under a Hun's tail. That time our guns were shooting at him and their guns shooting at me, so that between the two there was quite a bit of a bombardment. It seems to me that this is bad policy for it is comparatively rare that they hit a machine with the "Archies" and why bother a man who really has a good chance of, accomplishing something.

To come back to the Gotha, I got within 150 yards of him just behind his tail, so that he never fired a shot, but when I tried to aim everything was so gummed up I could not see the sights and the Gotha was nothing but a blur. Now as I have explained, these machines are regular battle ships of the air, and to get them you have got to fairly riddle them for they frequently carry two pilots in case one is killed. I had to give this one up without firing a shot and I have been wondering ever since whether I did what I should have. My mistake was, in not going in quicker, and if I had then had time to get right up close to him before he got into his own lines, I could probably have seen well enough to shoot anyhow.

On the only other time that I have seen Gothas by day they have been escorted by a whole flock of fighting planes. Being by myself on this occasion and not able to see clearly I don't mind saying those Huns had me nervous. But it was such a glorious chance and would have been such a triumph if I could have bagged him, that it was worth taking much bigger risks than one would usually take. The only Frenchman I ever heard of who got one was Captain Guynemer. I shall probably not have such a chance in six months, but if I do I shall certainly try to make better use of it. I am sort of ashamed of myself for not sticking to that Hun and perhaps accomplishing something.

The day before my experience with the Gotha I went out in the morning with the chief of the *escadrille*, Captain Deullin. It was the first time I had been out alone with him on a Hun hunting expedition and I was very glad of the opportunity to watch him fighting, for he is an old hand at the game and there is probably no one in the French Army more skilful than he. I am glad to say that I think he will now take me with him as a protection for his rear in other expeditions of the kind, and this protection business often gives the protector some splendid opportunities, not to mention the lot that one can learn by watching. I was glad to see that the captain's methods of attack were the same as I had been trying, although of course much more skilfully executed. He has a faster machine than mine and left me a little behind several times when he was attacking a two-seater. I only got a few very long shots at one.

He had one fight with some single-seater fighting machines which turned out better. I was right behind the captain and started down with him when he dove down to attack the highest of several Boche single-seaters. In my capacity as rear guard I was necessarily several hundred yards behind, and about the time that I started to follow the captain I caught sight of another Hun coming in behind me and on the same level. He was a good way off, but started to shoot at me, so I had to turn and chase him. When I started after him he also turned and started to run but I had no more than begun to follow him when still another put in an appearance above me, and I had to get out. In the meantime the captain had gotten close to his man but had to stop shooting at him to defend himself against a couple of others and in doing so lost sight of the Hun he had attacked. As soon as we landed, he told me he could not understand why the fellow had not fallen, for he had seen at least ten of his tracer bullets fired at point blank range apparently go right into the pilot's seat. Sure enough, a few minutes later confirmation came in that a Hun had fallen at that time and place. This made nineteen for Captain Deullin.

The afternoon that Captain Deullin got his Hun he asked me to go with him in his motor to have a look at the Boche as the machine had fallen in our lines, and besides we were not entirely sure whether the one reported was the same as the one the captain had shot. We had some little difficulty in locating the spot, for the report had not been entirely accurate, and neither I nor the captain had been able to see the Hun fall, having been otherwise occupied for the moment. Also, the fight took place some 15,000 feet up, and at this height no matter how hard you try to watch a machine it is usually lost to view before it hits the ground.

The trip to the lines was just what I have been wanting to do ever since I have reached the front, and it goes without saying it was most interesting. I have seen the same places hundreds of times from the air, but you do not get the detail that way. As you approach the lines, you come first to a country of occasional old shell holes, and villages with here and there a smashed house. As you go on, the shell holes become more and more frequent and the villages more and more completely demolished. We passed on to little hamlets, now used principally for the quartering of troops, where the gaping holes in the walls and the splintered trees gave evidence of the shelling they had received in the days before the Hun was driven back.

Then we drove through what is probably the most famous city [12] of the war, once a good sized town, with many fine buildings, among them a beautiful cathedral. I looked carefully to see and without exaggeration there is not a building left with a roof, or that is more than a gutted shell. Few of them are even this—the walls also being blown in, and the cathedral is typical of practically every house in the city, a pile of rubbish and broken stones, with here and there the battered fragment of a wall still standing. We shall never be able to make the Huns really pay for the damage they have done, but one cannot but look forward to the day when we shall be in a position to give them a bit of their own medicine in their own country.

The desolation of this city was as complete as it is possible to be in a city, but not so complete I think as that of the country beyond, where the hardest fighting of the war has now been raging for almost the past three and a half years. This country defies all description, and as I

---

12. Ypres.

have told you before, the nearest approach to it I know of in America is a northern swamp where a district once destroyed by a forest fire has been flooded. Every tree is a splintered, leafless wreck, killed as though by lightning, where indeed there is more than a stump left. The ground is a mass of merging holes, filled with water. It is easy to understand why the men are always in mud when one passes through this region, for as you drive along the road you are as if on a dike with the surrounding land below you.

There are little ridges of course but in many places the country lies below the road as do the marshes when you are approaching the Jersey coast. The ground is strewn with the wreckage of the war, especially near the road, broken wagons and junk of all kinds; once we came upon a number of used up tanks; now and then you pass a cemetery with its thousands of little wooden crosses, some bearing the name and rank and the legend "Killed in action June 27, 1916" for instance; others simply mark the grave of an unknown soldier fallen there. One cannot but think of how much lies behind each one of those little wooden crosses besides the bones which rest beneath it.

We went in the motor as far as the road would allow us, perhaps 1000 yards from the first line, and then got out and walked over about 200 yards to an artillery officer's dugout, to inquire for our Hun. The walking reminded me a little of wading for reedbirds in one of those very soft marshes on the river at home where you sink in up to your knees. We found that we were within 800 yards of where the Boche had fallen that morning, but it was practically dark by this time so we could not go up to have a look at him; this was disappointing as the machine was a new German type which we wished to see.[13]

The artillery officer had seen him fall and said that he had lost his wings on his way down, and all he saw coming was the body of the machine. The place we got to was up with the light artillery and of course considerably ahead of the heavy. By the time we started back, it was dark, blowing hard, with rain, and a more dismal sight you never beheld. Every second or so the desolate country would be fit up by the flash of one of our big guns, immediately followed by the crash of the explosion and the shriek of the shell as it passed out over our heads to the Boche lines.

Added to this, the whine and crash of the shells coming the other way, and in the distance on the front lines themselves, the *rat-tat-tat* of the machine-guns and the star shells going up and hanging in the sky

---

13. Pfalz.

THE LAST FLIGHT

Wreck of a French Spad brought down in the Ypres sector, August 1917. At the left of the picture is the body of the machine as it was broken off in teh crash, in the centre one wing and a wheel, in the lower right-hand corner a dead Hun soldier killed in the fight for possession of the wreck.

for a few seconds, with the brilliancy of an arc light. When moving in this country at night one can of course carry no light, but the flashes of the guns light up the road like very vivid heat lightning on a summer night. It is easy enough to distinguish the different sounds made by a "*depart*" and an "*arrive*," especially after one has had a little practice listening to both ends of the anti-aircraft gun firing, but I believe soldiers in the trenches can also distinguish between the whine of their own shells going out and the enemy's shells coming in. Of course if you happen to be able to spot the individual report of a gun and then hear the shell afterwards, you know that it is one of your own, but when this is not possible it is hard for a beginner to know which is which. They sound very much like a falling bomb.

I do not envy those infantrymen and artillerymen their jobs, but generally they would not swap with us for anything, so we are both satisfied with our branches of the service, and I guess it is just as well that it is that way. It is little wonder though that men get shell shock, sitting in one of those shell-holes—up to your middle in cold water and listening to the whine of the shells and wondering when one is coming to share your hole with you—must get frightfully on a man's nerves. As we retraced our steps across that bleak wind-swept morass in the face of the cold rain, groping around the shell craters by the light of the guns, I was mighty glad I had a warm bed to go to where I could only just hear those guns rumbling in the distance.

Bergues, November 13

Yesterday afternoon we had a little ceremony in honour of Captain Guynemer at which his last citation before the army was read and some of the other men received decorations. Just before it started, a most unfortunate accident occurred, about which I shall tell you, as it throws a little light on the death of Oliver. We were all standing on the field and a patrol from the *escadrille* was just going out. I could not go along, for as I told you my gasoline tank had to be changed. One of our men who went up was a captain, a new pilot, who had only been here about a week, and was starting on his first patrol over the lines. He had gotten up about 600 metres and as I watched him he executed a "*tournant*" and did it pretty well for a new man. My attention had been attracted however by the rough manner in which he handled his machine, the smooth grace of an old hand was lacking.

When he turned right side up after the "*tournant*," instead of going on he dove vertically on his nose at the same time doing a half turn in a *vrille* very slowly; then he dove straight again and then another slow turn; every minute I thought he would pull up, until he got within a couple of hundred metres of the ground, when I saw that something was wrong; he kept right on diving on his nose until he disappeared behind some trees half a mile away, then came a dull thud, and we knew that that was the end of the little captain. Such things are not pleasant to see; no one says much, for there is nothing to say, and you just stand there helpless and wait for the end.

What happened to make him fall no one knows, and you can only guess that upon doing the "*tournant*" he must have gotten rattled, and lost his head. So far as one could see, nothing broke about the machine, and I flew the same one a few weeks ago when mine was out of order, did barrel rolls and other forms of acrobacy and everything seemed perfectly strong. I was very sorry, for the captain seemed like a nice little fellow; he was a captain in the infantry who had been transferred to the aviation. Later in the afternoon I walked over to where the machine had fallen to have a look at it for I thought at the time that that was probably just the sort of a fall that Oliver had taken and I wanted to see if the wreck of this machine looked anything like the picture I sent you. What I found was almost a replica of that picture, which merely goes to confirm the report we received of the manner of Oliver's fall. In his case however it is of course possible that the machine was further demolished by shell fire.

Had some excitement today but I cannot write you about it now if this letter is to catch the next boat, so you will have to wait until next time.

Plessis-Belleville. November 18, 1917.

Here I am again at Plessis-Belleville and it seems a long time since Oliver and I left here together for the front in July. I flew an old machine down this morning and now have a little while before my train leaves for Paris. You see when a plane is considered no longer fit for service at the front, it is sent here to be used up for instruction purposes. The fact that a machine can no longer be used at the front does not necessarily mean that it is not strong, but simply that it has lost some of its efficiency and cannot climb as well or fly as fast as it once could. I had to come to Paris anyhow to get my own new machine and fly it back and as we had at the *escadrille* an old machine to be taken to the rear the captain told me to fly it down instead of going by train. As you may guess I vastly prefer the former method, for the trip is an interesting one and the time required to go by air is about one hour and a half as compared with fourteen or fifteen by train.

It was quite misty this morning so that I flew all the way at about six or eight hundred metres. Not being able to fly high and the visibility being very poor I came by way of the sea, keeping it always in sight until I struck the mouth of the Somme, then followed the river to Amiens and from there on down the railroad. The country is still new to me and I did not wish to get myself lost in the mist. Going back, if the weather permits I shall take the direct route behind the front, for I am anxious to get to know this section of the country. It may be very useful when we are in the U. S. Army. The return trip should also be very interesting, as it will take me over the country evacuated by the Germans last spring, the famous battlefield of the Somme and also that of Arras.

All this explains why I am now at Plessis-Belleville writing to you in the little Cafe de la Place, where I lived while I was here in training, and of which I think I have sent you a picture. Tomorrow morning I shall go to the great distributing station for aeroplanes near Paris, see that my machine is all right, take it up and try it out, and then next day (weather permitting) fly it back to the front.

Being here again, reminds me very much of Oliver, for it was here that I really came to know, and I hope appreciate him, and we did have lots of fun, flying together, and in off times taking long walks through a beautiful country and talking in frightful French to the people we met by the way. He knew more words than I did, but I think I could beat him sometimes on accent—New England and French inflections are a trifle different.

I have been thinking a good deal about Oliver lately, and I am sorry that I shall have to be again the sender of bad tidings to his father, for last Thursday I found his grave. I told you in one of my letters not long ago about a couple of the Frenchmen in our *escadrille* having been brought down, one was named Jolivet and the other Dron; you have pictures of them both, and I remember I sent you one of Dron, with a cigarette in his mouth and a little puppy in his arms. Captain Deullin went up to the lines some time ago to see if he could find where they had fallen, and when he came back reported that he had found the graves of both. He had not told me that he was going, for I should certainly have asked to go with him; he reported, to my surprise, that he had found the grave of Jolivet in almost exactly the same spot where I thought Oliver had fallen.

Thursday the whole *escadrille* went up behind the lines to arrange the graves of the two Frenchmen. I was glad to go and also glad of the opportunity to at last look personally for some trace of Oliver. When we arrived at what the captain thought was the grave of Jolivet, lying scattered about it were the fragments of a shattered plane. I at once searched for a number, and soon found what I was looking for, 1429, almost obliterated by the rains of the past three months. That was the number of Oliver's machine, and in the midst of the wreckage was a rough grave; at its head a wooden cross that someone had made by nailing two pieces of board together, and on the cross written with an indelible pencil "*Ici repose un aviateur inconnu.*"[14]

All around the grave a mass of shell holes filled with water, and the other decorations of a modern battlefield. I tried to describe to you before what it is like, and this was but a repetition of the rest, that is, at least in this sector. A flat low country torn almost beyond recognition by the shells, here and there the dead shattered trees sticking up from the mud and water, occasionally a dead horse and everywhere quantities of tangled barbed wire and cast-off material. Just beyond the grave was the German first line before the attack on August 16th. It is marked by a row of half-wrecked concrete shelters, pill boxes the English call them. Just beyond this a village,[15] but I stood on what had been the main street and did not know that there had been a village there until the captain showed it to me on the map. This little town has been so completely blown to pieces and churned into the mud that there is literally nothing left to distinguish it from the surrounding country. Not even a foundation stone left standing.

The grave is only about 1500 yards from our first lines and not far in front of the heavy artillery. I have marked it exactly on a map, and there can be no doubt whatever that this is where Oliver is buried. Although scattered and still further broken by the weather, the wreck of the machine is recognisable as the same as that shown in the picture taken by the priest, the same broken roof of a house in the foreground, and in the distance the same sticks and splintered trees.

I am having a plate engraved by one of our mechanics who was an engraver before the war; on it will be "Oliver Moulton Chadwick, of Lowell, Massachusetts, U. S., a Pilot in the French Aviation, born September 23rd, 1888; enlisted January 22nd, 1917; Killed in action August 14th, 1917." This will show that he was an American pilot in

---

14. Here lies an unknown aviator.
15. Langewaede.

the French service, enlisted as a volunteer before America entered the war. I think the simpler such things are, the better. Around the grave now is a little black wooden railing, which we put there, and a neat oaken cross, on the cross a bronze palm, with the inscription "*Mort pour la patrie.*" The captain and I are going back soon to put the plate on the cross and I have bought a little French flag and an American one, for I think he would like this. Also I thought I would try and get a few flowers. The spot should be a peaceful one after the war, for it will take years to make anything out of that country again. Just at present there is a great deal of artillery close behind; the roar of the guns was almost incessant when we were there and a stream of shells went whining overhead on the way to the Hun lines.

Paris. November 23rd.

In my last letter to father I mentioned at the end that I had had some excitement, which I would write to him about. That was ten days ago now, but I have really not had time since to write. What I referred to, was this. That afternoon I had gotten another American in one of the *escadrilles* in our group to go out with me and protect my tail while we tried to see if we could not find some Huns. For a while we did not see much, and then below us we spotted five single-seater fighting machines, who had evidently made a little excursion into our lines, and were just going back into their own. We attacked them together. My companion pulled up a little too soon to have allowed him a reasonable chance of accomplishing anything I think, but I, on the other hand, got in a little too far. You may think it sounds foolish or as if one was blowing a bit to talk about attacking five when we were only two, but an attack does not necessarily mean that you charge into the middle of them and mix it up.

On the contrary you can by diving at high speed from above get in some shots and then by using your great speed climb up above them again out of reach before they can get in a shot. If you remember to leave your motor on as you are diving and in this way to come down as fast as possible, without at the same time going so fast as to interfere with your shooting, the great speed gained in this way will enable you to make a short steep climb and thus regain a position perhaps two hundred metres above the heads of the Huns where they cannot effectively shoot at you. I am now of course speaking only of an attack on a group of single-seater machines. If the engagement ends here the chances of bringing one down are not great, but you can sometimes by such methods and by, for instance, hitting some part of one of the machines, so worry the Huns that one will in the general confusion get separated from his comrades so that you can get a fair crack at him.

This was about the first time I had had a chance to try it, however, and I made a botch of it. I saw I was getting in too close, but did, I think, hit one of the Huns, though not seriously. In my haste to get out, I made a false manoeuvre, and fell on my nose instead of climbing up, as I should have done. The result was, that the Hun I had been shooting at and who had turned, got behind me on my tail in a most unpleasant position, where he could shoot and I could not. Naturally I did not let him stay there long, but had to dodge and beat a retreat. He did manage to hit my machine a couple of times, one bullet through a wing and another through the body of the machine about six inches behind me, but never touched me and did my plane no harm whatever. It did not take much thinking to see that my little manoeuvre had been very badly executed.

My companion and I started off again to see what else we could find, and 15 minutes later I spotted six more Huns in almost the same place. This time four two-seaters with two single-seaters above and behind them acting as protection. The two-seaters were far enough below not to have to bother about, so I tried the same plan again and came down on the rear of one of the single-seaters. I blazed away at him and he made the same manoeuvre as the first one, but this time I kept shooting until very close, then sailed up over his head, did a quick turn, and dropped on his tail again. Before following him, I looked to see what the other single-seater was up to, and saw him bravely making tracks for home, leaving his friend to shift for himself. I therefore kept after the first, and poured in all about 200 shots into him, many of which I am sure hit the machine, for I could see the tracer bullets apparently go almost into the pilot. I think my first burst of bullets put his engine out of business for he did not seem able to dive very fast and I could catch him with ease.

Several times when he would do a *renversement* he would turn up and slide off on one wing, as though he were going to fall and I thought I had him sure. Three times I was so close, only about 30 feet, that I had to pull up to avoid running into him. I could see the Hun sitting there, staring up at me through his goggles, the colour of his bonnet and all the details of the show. This kept up from 4000 to 1800 metres, and he never got in a shot, I am glad to say. Why he did not fall, I do not know. There is however always a very good reason why they get away, I think, and that is because you do not hold quite close enough. I know the experience taught me a lesson about being too hasty in my shooting. I finally had to let him go because I caught sight of nine of his brethren coming to his rescue and when they started after me and began to shoot I thought discretion the better part of valor and got out. At this time the Boche was flopping about in the air and letting out a considerable quantity of smoke.

Being busy in the getting out, I could no longer watch my would-be victim, but the American who was with me and who had stayed above as a sort of rear guard was able to watch him and said that the last he saw of the Hun he was still going down in a spiral with black smoke coming out of his tail. The latter means a fire on board and if this was the case I think that Hun's flying days are over unless he gets a pair of wings in some Hun heaven—maybe they will have such a place full of beer and sausages—certainly Christians could not be expected to associate with them.

Be that as it may, I am sorry to say I could not get any confirmation by someone on the ground of the Boche having been seen to fall, so he does not count officially for me; if he fell, as I think he did, he came down considerably in his own lines. I wish I could have gotten him at the start for he then would have fallen in our lines, and the machine was one of the new type. *Mais si le Boche est mort, c'est la première chose.*[16] As the Frenchmen say when they bag one "*Un moins qui mange la soupe ce soir.*"[17] If that Boche ever did get down alive I am sure in my own mind that he is at least at present sojourning in the hospital. My manoeuvring worked out all right this time and if I can catch another like that and do not get him beyond question, I shall promptly admit that I am a punk aviator.

The next day I was out on another expedition with one of the lieutenants. We ran into a regular fleet of Hun machines, there were five of the huge Gotha bombers which carry three or four men each and about eighteen single-seaters protecting them. The lieutenant has been in the aviation since the beginning of the war and said he had never seen so many Huns at once. He tried to get a shot at the Gothas and in so doing flew directly under five Albatross single-seaters whom he entirely failed to see. I was some eight hundred yards behind him at the time for he was flying one of the new 220 H. P. Spads such as

---

16. But if the Boche is dead, that is the main thing.
17. One less who eats supper this evening.

the one I am about to get and when he had put on full speed in order to attack the Gothas, he left my old bus far behind.

I saw the Huns coming down on my companion and followed him as fast as I could but they attacked him before I could even get within long range of them. Luckily for him however they began shooting too far away, put a couple of bullets through his wings and warned him. He promptly stood on his nose and dove vertically for six thousand feet with his motor at extreme high speed. I never saw a machine go down so fast before and it is a wonder he did not pull his wings off. I think he would have in anything but a Spad. As it was, he stretched all the bracing wires between his wings out of tension and bent the wings themselves back an inch or two so that the whole plane had to be taken apart and re-regulated before he could fly it again. When I saw that the lieutenant had escaped I pulled out myself, for the five Huns who had jumped on him had not followed him down, and being still above me, there was not much that I could do. Looked around for some Hun who did not have so many friends with him but seeing nothing better than another group of five below me thought I would have a try at them.

Being by myself I had to keep above them and could not get a close shot but took a crack at the rear man anyhow and at least succeeded in making him sore. When I started to shoot the Boches turned and then as I pulled up above and to one side of them, the Hun at whom I had been shooting, sat his machine back on her tail and took a shot at me. I was at least one hundred and fifty yards from him and flying at right angles to him, a most difficult shot, but at that he managed to put a bullet through the side of my plane which missed my foot by two inches and brought up in the bed of the motor with a thud. It did not break anything however and I dug it out with my knife when I got home.

Since then I have not flown over the lines, due partly to bad weather and also to my trip to Paris. The little delay here is certainly worth it to get such a good machine. I shall be much safer in it for it will fly faster than anything the Huns have, will climb higher, and much more quickly than my old one, and mounts two machine-guns of an improved type, thereby greatly reducing the chance of gun jams. With it and any kind of weather I certainly hope that I shall soon be able to write you of a Boche that goes down and stays down officially.

Bergues. Nov. 27th, 1917.

My trip back from Paris was most interesting, but rather too eventful for comfort, considering it was an ordinary cross-country flight, with no Huns to complicate matters. I came, as I told you I would, by way of the front, going from Paris to Compiegne, and then over the territory evacuated last spring. The battlefield of the Somme looks much like our own sector here, villages, fields, trees, everything blown to atoms, except the Somme is more extensive, and one flies for miles and miles over this sort of country. I do not think, however, from the look I had at it that the Somme wreck is quite as complete, except in spots, as that here, for the fighting there, terrific as it was, was not as long drawn out as it has been here, and the country is not nearly so low and wet.

A marsh is a dreary sort of a place at best, unless it happens to be full of ducks. I passed the scene of the recent English advance before Cambrai, and could see the guns blazing away, although I did not go very close. Not having as yet any guns on my machine, I was naturally not anxious to fall in with some Boches. That advance by the British was certainly a great stroke and will I hope tend to relieve the tension on the Italian front. It does beat the devil how every time the Huns are beginning to feel the pinch they succeed in pulling off a coup of some sort to cheer their people up. Servia, Roumania, Russia and now the Italian success—each one must certainly add months at least to the duration of the war.

Everything went all right until I struck Arras, when I was met by a very strong north-west wind which very much reduced my speed. I had arrived at the field near Paris, ready to start in plenty of time, but my motor had not run properly at first so that I was delayed in getting off until I had only just sufficient time to make the trip before dark. When I left Paris the wind had been a little in my favour and not particularly strong. The trip down by the long route had only taken me an hour and three-quarters, so that as I was returning by the direct road, and left Paris at 20 minutes before three, I thought I would certainly get here by half past four when it begins to get dark in this country. The wind however shifted and became very strong and to add to my troubles my motor began to run badly, missing and throwing fire out of the exhaust, so that I had to keep constantly watching to see that the side of the machine did not get dangerously hot. Then I ran into a storm, which seems to have been bad all over the country; clouds, rain and mist forced me to fly under 200 metres, and darkness fell very suddenly.

All this makes it hard to find your way in a country you have never been over before, and in trying to figure out just what my motor was going to do, I got off the little strip of map I had and lost my bearings. I had a compass of course and knew approximately where I was, but as my gasoline was almost gone, and it was getting very dark, the only sensible thing was to land for the night. I accordingly searched for an aviation field, for in a hilly wooded country such as I was over, where good landing places are scarce, one is very likely to break one's machine in trying to land in an ordinary field, when one cannot see much and there is a heavy wind. I searched for 20 minutes, and although aviation fields are generally numerous behind the front, I could not find one for the life of me. I have had some rough rides before this, but this one beat them all.

Our machines are strong and stable, but the gale threw mine around like a canoe in a high sea. Under such conditions you will often strike a pocket in the air and the machine will drop so quickly that you shoot up out of your seat until pulled down by the safety belt. With a little room to spare under you, it makes no difference, but it is most unpleasant when very close to the ground. I much dreaded breaking my new machine in landing, for it is an excellent one of a sort which is scarce and hard to get and for which the captain had kindly given me a special order. Finally it got so dark that it was no use looking further for an aviation field and it was absolutely necessary to land without delay. I saw a field facing into the wind and in the lee of a woods, so that the force of the wind would be less, also some sort of an encampment next to the field where I thought they would probably take me in. I accordingly dropped into it with all the care I could muster and certainly breathed a sigh of relief when safely on the ground with everything intact.

I would not have broken that machine for anything for it would have seriously delayed my work out here before I could have gotten another. You can yourself generally get through a smash in landing with nothing worse than a few bruises, but a ditch or a hole in the ground is all it takes to turn a machine on its back and ruin it. I noticed a weather report saying the wind had blown 60 miles an hour that night on the coast and observations taken the next morning at a field near where I landed, showed 40 miles an hour, and this after the wind had somewhat gone down. It must have been blowing about 50 miles that evening, all of which goes to show how the war has advanced aviation, when one thinks of how a few years ago the machines were such that an ordinary good breeze made flyers hesitate about going up.

As soon as I landed, a number of Tommies came running up and then an officer, the latter evidently surprised to find my machine right side up, for he had thought that I was going to land in a ploughed field near by. As a matter of fact, I fell into great good luck, for the field where I landed was as smooth and firm as a prepared aerodrome.

With the help of the Tommies, we pushed my machine up under the lee of the woods, tethered it, covered up the engine and had a guard put over it for the night by the major of an English infantry regiment that was resting in the neighbourhood. Then the officer who had first appeared, a captain, took me in tow, and insisted that I come to his quarters for the night. I found that he was in command of a company of Chinese *coolies*, who had originally been stationed near us,[18] but had been forced to move because of the bombing they got from the Huns. One of these labour companies is much larger than the ordinary infantry company. This one was acting as foresters, working in the woods, getting out the timber which is so necessary for the construction of the quickly made roads across the battlefield over which the artillery and supplies are brought up.

The company is now enjoying perfect quiet and they deserve it after the way they caught it at their former camp. That camp was only about half a mile from where we used to be, and almost every clear night the Huns would bomb it. No matter what else they bombed, they always seemed to save a few for this camp. We used to watch the bombs fall, and wonder how many poor Chinks went up in smoke with each one. As a matter of fact, their casualties were heavy and the ignorant Chinamen were convinced that the Boches had it in for them particularly. You could see them any clear evening hiking across the fields with their blankets on their backs to sleep in the country, rather than stay in their camp. They became terrified, and it was very difficult to keep them in hand; the officers sometimes finding missing men many miles from home.

The officer told me of one instance where a bomb fell right through the roof of a little wooden hut, where four *coolies* were sleeping, but fortunately went deep into the soft soil before it exploded. The hut went straight up in the air and the coolies in every direction, but by some miracle none of them were hurt, except one who had his back burnt, but has since recovered. He is now in the hospital again, as the result of a friendly stab from one of his comrades. Naturally all this

---
18. At St. Pol-sur-Mer.

bombing did not nourish a very friendly feeling between the *coolies* and their tormentors the Huns. The *coolie* does not care a rap whether Germany is at war with China or England or anyone else, and I doubt whether many of them even know it; but these particular *coolies* do hold a most vivid and personal grudge against the Hun for having showered them with bombs and slaughtered their pals. The officer told me that they know the difference between the black cross of the German machine and the round *cocarde* of an Allied. He mentioned that it was a good thing for my health that I was not a Hun who had been forced to land in their midst, for the *coolies* would undoubtedly have torn me limb from limb and the officers could not possibly have stopped them.

In a little bit of a hut that served as a mess room I found three other English officers, and they took me in and were most kind and cordial, as indeed are all the Englishmen whom I have met over here. These fellows appreciate that we are all fighting for the same thing, and are most anxious to help out in any way they can. I have been forced to ask their assistance on several occasions, and there is nothing they will not do to make you feel at home and lend a helping hand. I found the same thing the next morning when the captain and I walked about four miles to a field of the Royal Flying Corps, which I had missed in the dark the night before, to ask for some gasoline, and tools to fix my engine. Immediately the major in command gave me a motor-lorry, all the gasoline I wanted, tools and two mechanics to fix the motor. He also wanted me to stay for lunch and invited me to come back for the night if I could not get off.

On another occasion, of which I long ago wrote to you, when I had another breakdown, the officer in command offered all the above things and besides sent me home 30 miles in one of his motors. It is this spirit and the way they fight that makes one admire them very much. I enclose you another list of citations for the V. C. as an example of the way these Englishmen go after the Huns. In reading these, remember that they are the official citations which, if anything, understate the facts and are not the flowery exaggerations of some newspaper reporter.

To return to the hut and the English officers of the labour company—I spent a most pleasant evening with them, sitting about their little stove, and swapping yarns. One of them had an extra bed in his tent, where he put me up for the night, each one insisting on giving up one of his blankets for me. I was mighty glad of them, as it was cold, and I thought the tent would take to aeroplaning itself at any minute, the way the gale howled outside. I also got three good meals, as I could not get my machine ready to leave before the following afternoon.

It is remarkable what a collection of men one will run into over here, especially in the English Army; of my four hosts last night, one had been a Methodist Episcopal Missionary in the Malay Peninsula, and spoke Chinese, another came from Siam, another from England, and the captain from Winnipeg, Canada, with a wife from Lansdale, near Doylestown, Pa., where he told me she now is. The fellow from Siam could not speak a word of Chinese, and it was most amusing to hear him cussing out his *coolie* boy servant in English, the boy not understanding a word of what was being said to him; one notices this trait in both the English and French, when they can't make someone of another tongue understand them they often pour out a perfect stream of talk to him which he could not possibly understand without a very thorough knowledge of the speaker's language.

Bergues, November 28th, 1917.

I forgot to tell you one or two rather amusing stories about the *coolies* that I heard from the English officer. One day some *coolies* were loading coal into a wagon and the sergeant of the gang had borrowed three Hun prisoners to help with the job; the Huns were filling sacks with coal and were casting them up to the *coolies*, when one of the latter, a great big strapping *coolie*, the largest of the lot, resting from his labour, stepped up to a Hun, and pointing his finger in his face, said "You bloody German, you no good. Dunkirk *Ziz-z-zBoom!!*" to which the Hun getting his meaning at once, replied: "Yes Dunkirk *Ziz-z-z Boom!* Ha-Ha-Ha!;" plainly indicating by the way he said it, that he was glad they had been bombed. He no sooner had the words out of his mouth when the big *coolie* jumped on him, grabbed him by the throat and the officers only got him off in time to keep him from killing that Hun; he mussed him up in great style as it was.

Another time, a yellow, dirty looking Chink met one of the other native soldiers, a coal black Kaffir boy; the Kaffir looked the Chink over and evidently decided he needed a bath, for he pointed at him and said "You washee, washee, good!!" The Chink looked nonplussed for a minute or so, and at a loss for a fitting retort, then he grinned at the black Kaffir, and replied "You Washee, washee, *no* good!!" Pretty good come back for the Chink, don't you think? If one could only draw like Bairnsfather, one could make a funny picture out of the incident.... I hope you can make sense out of this letter; I have been reading it over, and it seems to be chiefly a lot of corrections. Do you ever get sometimes so that you find the greatest difficulty in expressing what you wish to say, and then the next time, for no apparent reason, have no difficulty at all? I seem to be in the former condition today, so will call a halt.

Bergues, December 8th, 1917.

You already know that from one cause or another, I have not been able to get out on the lines for some time, and when I finally did get out last Wednesday, it was exactly three weeks since I had last seen them; the same old lines, except a little more blown up, for there had been a great deal of artillery activity in part of the sector. On Wednesday I started out at nine in the morning on a patrol, with two Frenchmen, a lieutenant being the leader. We were on the lines for some time without seeing any Huns except well within their own lines, although once or twice I think I saw where some came on the lines, but the others evidently did not agree with me, and the Boches, if there were any, were too far off to justify my leaving the patrol and going to investigate.

After a while however I noticed a two-seater of a type known as an Albatross which was flying up and down in his own lines. He was a long way off, but from the way he acted I thought he was just waiting for a clear path to slip across the lines, take his pictures or make some observations, and slip back again. I have had several encounters with two-seaters in the same locality at about the same time of day, and at about the same altitude, and accordingly kept my eye on this fellow, to see what he would do. Sometimes he would go way back into his own territory until he was just a speck in the sky, and then again would come just above the lines, evidently see us, and turn back again.

Now a patrol has the duty of protecting a certain sector and cannot go off and leave it, which is one reason why it does not usually offer the same chance to get a shot at the Huns that a voluntary chasse expedition does. If for instance I had been there with another man just looking for Boches and with no sector to protect, the thing to have done would obviously have been to fly deep into our own lines as if we were leaving, then climb up over that Hun's head and hang around with the sun at our backs, in the hope that he would not notice us, and wait for him to come into our territory. If he would not do this, you could go to him, but it is always better to get them in your own lines if possible, for you can then get a better shot without having to spend half the time watching your own rear, and ending up by being forced to retreat by the Boche's comrades coming up in force. Once I left the patrol and started after this Hun, but he evidently saw me at once and dove back into his own lines; I saw that I could not get any kind of a shot at him, so decided to wait a little longer. I rejoined the patrol, and we made a tour of perhaps ten minutes.

When we got back to the same place again, the lieutenant had gone down somewhat so that the Hun who was again just coming to the lines, evidently saw us some 400 metres below him instead of on the same level as before, thought he was safe, and came on into our lines. My companions apparently did not see him, so I turned to one side, flew directly under the Boche, going in the opposite direction, and then put myself below and behind him by doing a *renversement*. He saw me all the time, but I guess he thought he could do what he wanted, and get out before I could climb up and catch him. I must have followed him at least five minutes, first into our lines, then back above the lines again and then back once more.

All the time he was manoeuvring to keep me from getting behind his tail, where he could not see me, and doing it well, for in order to try to stay behind him and to manoeuvre so as to give him only a long, hard, right-angle shot, I had to fly further than he did, and accordingly could not catch him quickly. I did get up to his level though (4,700 metres) and when he finally started back for his own lines, I got directly behind his tail and put after him as fast as my bus would travel. When I got within 100 yards I tried to lay my sights on him, but being directly behind him the back draught from his propeller made my machine unsteady so that accurate shooting would have been impossible. I dove down 10 metres so as to get out of this and tried again.

After my sad experience with the single-seater, which I wrote you about, and which I think went down, but was not confirmed, I tried my best to shoot most carefully this time. All the time the Boche had not fired a shot, and from the way he acted I think he must have lost track of me behind his tail. Anyhow, I turned both my machine-guns loose and thought I saw my bullets going about right. My left hand gun only fired about a dozen shots and then broke, the Boche at the same time, giving a twist to the right to get me out from under his tail. I kept on plugging away with my other gun, shooting for the place where the pilot sits, and again I thought I saw the bullets going into the right spot.

After possibly thirty shots however my right gun also broke, and left me with nothing, and at the same time the Hun started to join in the shooting, firing perhaps twenty shots. By this time we were I suppose about 50 or 60 metres apart and I got under his tail quickly to get out of the way, so that I could not see just where the Boche was shooting, but am sure he came nowhere near me. There never was a truer saying than that there is nothing which upsets a man's accuracy so much as having the other fellow putting them very close to him. That is I think one of the principal reasons why accurate quick shooting is so important, not only for the damage it does but because to come very close is one of the best means of defence, even if you actually do not hit. At all events, with two broken guns, close proximity to a Hun is not a healthy locality, so I turned on my nose and dove out behind my friend, at the same time watching him over my shoulder to try to keep myself protected by his tail.

As I watched him he started diving until he was going down vertically and I could see the silver colour of his bottom and of the under sides of his wings, with the black Maltese crosses on them. It was a good sized machine, and very pretty, with the shining silver paint underneath to make it less visible against the sky and the sides just by the tail a brilliant red, this last being probably the individual mark of his *escadrille*, for I have seen the same kind of a machine before, painted in this way. When he got in a vertical nose dive, instead of going on straight down, he kept on turning until from flying toward his own lines right side up he was flying back into ours, upside down, and diving slowly in this position. This is of course a sign that all is not well on board and usually means that the pilot has fallen forward over his control stick, thus forcing the machine into a nose dive and then onto its back. You will read in the flying magazines about flying upside down but it is not what it is cracked up to be.

One often gets on one's back in certain manoeuvres, but only for an instant, and with always sufficient centrifugal force to keep one securely in place. In learning to loop the loop however I have gotten upside down for longer than I intended because the loop was not done properly, and it is not pleasant. You start to fall out and even though your belt holds you pretty tight in your seat, there is a tendency to grab the side of the machine; then whatever dirt is in the bottom of the machine falls over you, the oil, etc., fizzles out of the top of its tank and the motor starts to splutter and wants to stop due to the gasoline not feeding properly. All this and everything being upside down, gives you a queer feeling in your middle, and although in some specially constructed machines I believe it is possible to fly upside down, it is not at all my idea of a good time.

Hence when I saw my friend the Hun flying into our lines with his wheels in the air I thought he must be pretty sick, but after my previous experience, was expecting every minute to see him come to and fly home, while I watched him helpless, with two guns that would not work. I accordingly dove after him, holding my controls, first with one hand, and then the other, and working with first the right and then the left gun, and trying each in the hope of getting one of them going, and taking a few more shots. At the same time, it is necessary to watch your own rear to see that no one is after you, so that between this and trying to keep close to the Boche I had little time to spare. Pretty soon some English machines came over my head, which relieved my mind very much as to the rear, and allowed me to concentrate on the Boche and my guns. I worked away and incidentally said some things I never learned in Sunday-school, but it is exasperating when you could get a good shot and your gun wont work and you have visions of what should be an easy victim escaping you. There was nothing to do though in this case, for upon returning to the field, I found both my guns not simply jammed but actually broken, one so that it had to be taken off the machine and replaced.

While trying to fix the guns in the air I kept glancing down at the Boche; sometimes he was on his back, sometimes on his nose, and again diving almost normally, which was what made me think he might come to life. The machine was however evidently completely uncontrolled; I chased him down almost 4000 metres, faster than I have ever come down before, so fast that when we reached 1000 metres he was not more than perhaps 400 metres ahead of me. A quick, great change of altitude like this is most unpleasant, as your ears get all stopped up and it gives you a headache, but in a fight you do not at the time notice it, and this time I was very anxious to see just where the Boche fell so as to get him confirmed if he did go down. At a thousand metres however I had to pull up and use my hand pump, for all the pressure had run out of my gas tank, due to the unusually long dive with the motor shut down.

I lost sight of the Boche and did not see him hit the ground but after my motor was running nicely again I flew on down to 200 metres over the battlefield and searched for him, for he had fallen several kilometres within our lines, so that it was possible to go down low and have a look. Pretty soon I spotted him lying on his back in the mud, his top plane was mashed into the soft ground, but the rest of the machine was apparently remarkably intact when you consider the height from which he had fallen. Probably the machine flopped over flat on its back, or right side up, just before striking, and in this way the force of the fall was broken.

Shortly after I got back to our field, the official confirmation came in from the lines. The pilot and observer were of course both dead. The pilot was I think killed by one of my shots, or at least completely knocked out, for there was nothing serious the matter with his machine, and it fell only because it was uncontrolled. The machine-gunner was however alive after I had stopped shooting for I heard him shoot after I had finished. If he had been any kind of a decent man, or in fact anyone but a Hun, one could not but have felt sorry for him in such a situation. Not much fun falling 4,700 metres, especially going down comparatively slowly, knowing all the while what is coming at the end, and with some little time to think it over. Particularly bad I should think with a good machine, which only needs someone to set the controls straight in order to right it. Much better to catch on fire, or have the machine break, and get it over with right away.

Also after having had experience with the same thing oneself, one cannot help thinking of the comrades of these men, standing around the aerodrome, and wondering why they don't come back, and again of the people at home, who after they get the report "*Disparu*," keep wondering and hoping for months whether perhaps they might not only have been taken prisoner. It is a brutal business at best, but when you stop to think for a moment of what these Huns have done, of the horrors they have committed, of the suffering they have brought on innocent people, and of the millions of men dead before their time, all because of them, you don't feel much sympathy for the individual but rather look forward to the time when you can perhaps bag another.

We had a most unpleasant accident here on Thanksgiving Day. There is a French Squadron of Voisin night bombers stationed on our flying field, and although they only cross the lines at night, they do considerable practice flying during the day time. On Thanksgiving Day afternoon one of their machines was going up for a practice flight at the same time that a patrol from this group was leaving the ground for a flight over the lines. There was not much wind at the time, but what there was of it was coming from the West, so that all machines leaving the field should have done so facing in that direction. To do this, however, the Voisin would have had to roll on the ground all the way across the field, and to save himself this trouble the pilot started from just in front of his hangar flying South. A Spad was leaving the ground at the same time, going West. I was standing in front of our hangars and noticed the two machines approaching each other at right angles. Even before they got very close to one another, it was apparent that they must pass with very little room to spare, so I stopped and watched them.

The two planes were only about thirty yards high, and just before they came together, the Spad pilot saw the Voisin and pulled his machine into a sharp turn in a desperate attempt to avoid a collision, one of his guns going off in the air as he did so. It was too late however, and the right wing of the Spad hooked into the left wing of the Voisin; this swung the Spad around and it charged head first into the front of the Voisin, and then pitched headlong to the ground. There was a terrific crash as the two planes came together, and the air was filled with flying splinters. The force of the collision turned the Voisin upside down and it burst into flames even before it touched the ground. M—— and I were nearest to the accident, only about a hundred yards away, and were so horrified that we just stood there for a second with our mouths open, too startled to move.

Then we dashed across the field to the wreck, and M—— got his shoulder under the body of the Voisin and raised it up, while some of the Frenchmen and I dragged the men out of the blazing machine. There had been three men in it, two of whom were still in the body of the plane and as the wind was blowing the flames towards the rear, it was possible to get at the place where these men were. We dragged the pilot out, but his head was crushed, and he was obviously beyond helping. Then we dragged the observer out, and he was burning from head to foot, a bursting gasoline tank having evidently thrown its contents over him. The flames were shooting up two feet in the air from the man's clothing. I jerked off a heavy sweater which I was wearing, and dropping on my knees beside him managed to put most of the fire out, by rubbing him over with the sweater, using it as a sort of a sponge. The poor fellow's face and hands were burned black, and as we tore his clothes off, some very bad burns appeared over his ribs and on other parts of his body.

While we were working on the observer, I happened to glance up and caught sight of the third occupant of the Voisin, a mechanic. He had been thrown out of the body of the machine and as it lay on its

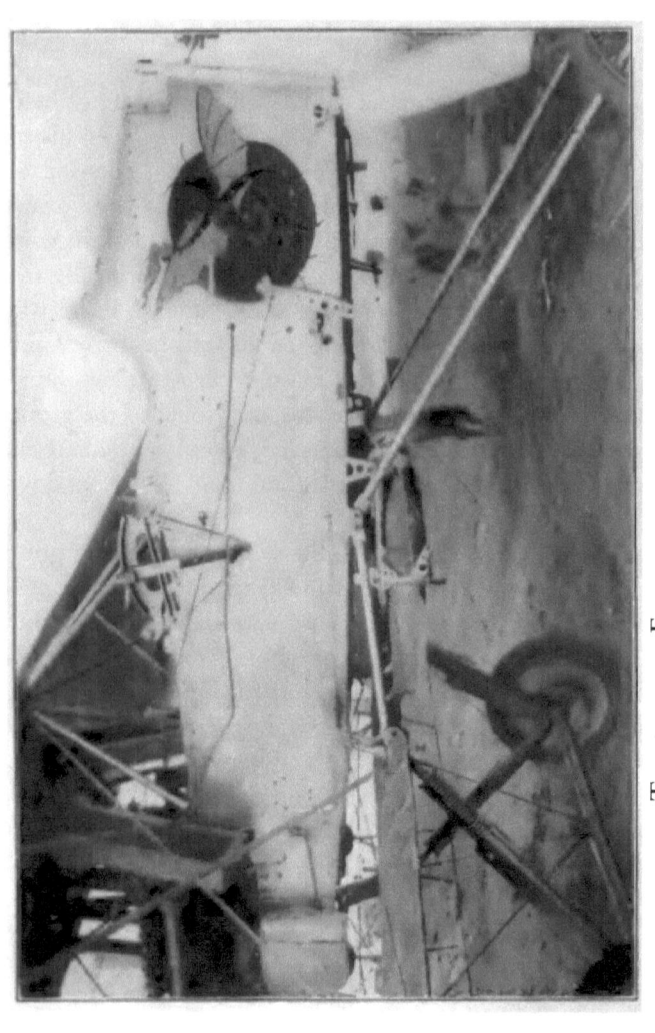

THE CAR OF A FRENCH NIGHT BOMBER, VOISIN TYPE

Note the squadron insignia painted on the side and the arrangement of the bombs in the rack below the car.

back, his feet were caught under the top wing, and his ankles apparently broken off. His arms had fallen over some of the wires and this held him erect as though he were standing up. The propeller of the Spad had evidently struck him in the face and had cut off the lower part of his jaw. His head was supported by some part of the machine and thus held in a natural position, and he stood there with his eyes wide open, staring at us, just as though he were alive. The place where he was caught was just behind the wings of the plane and right in the middle of the fire. The whole machine was a blazing furnace, and it was impossible to reach him. He was quite obviously dead anyhow, so it would have done no good, and we had to watch him burn up for all the world like a living man being burned at the stake, and a more gruesome sight I hope never to see.

The wreck of the Spad was lying a little off to one side, and had not caught fire, but as we dragged the pilot out, a man whom I know very well, he certainly looked as though his days were ended, for his face was ghostly pale and smeared all over with blood. It turned out afterwards, however, that he was hardly hurt at all, just shaken up and a couple of holes punched in his cheeks. In a week he was out of the Hospital and back with his squadron, as well as ever. The last I heard of the observer whom we dragged out of the burning Voisin, he was very sick, but was expected to recover.

A sight such as the above and the sickening smell of roasting human flesh that goes with it, goes a long way to impress upon one the absolute necessity of constant watchfulness when leaving or landing upon an aerodrome, and the importance of the strict enforcement of the rules of the flying field.

Bergues, December 9th, 1917.

You said in your last letter that you do not wonder that the French and English are tired of the war, and that they are entitled to rest after all they have been through. Of course they are sick of it and they have had a very hard time, but that hardly seems a sufficient reason for our not going after the Boche and trying to finish the war. I suppose you refer to my criticism of the attitude one sometimes sees which is typified by the question, "When is the war going to be over?" As though there was nothing to be done about it, a sort of a "When is it going to stop raining?" attitude instead of asking "How soon can we finish it?" The French have done much and done well, England has done and suffered much, and so will we before we are through, but how about the Hun? He is fighting a lot of nations and has suffered in his home life much more than any of the great Allies, but he is still going strong. The answer is forty years of training and preparation, combined with splendid system and conservation of energy, but even so it seems to me that he has more cause to be tired than we have.

Dunkirk. Dec. 24, 1917.

The group moved away from here two weeks ago and I should have gone with it but have been held over by a succession of troubles with my machine, coupled with some very bad weather.

Our new sector of the front will be in the famous "*Chemin des Dames*" region on the Aisne, where the French made their last advance a month or so ago. It will be a relief to get away from this flat, uninteresting region where we have been so long, and to miss some of the fog and dampness that come in from the sea. The weather where the group now is[19] should be much more favourable for our work, and according to all accounts the sector presents much better chances to get a shot at the Boche. I went there by train a few days ago while waiting for my machine to be repaired and the day I was there a Hun machine similar to the one I brought down came over our mess and that is 20 kilometres behind the lines.

He was of course very high, but was all alone and would have offered a splendid chance had one been up there. If you can catch a Boche like this you have all the time you want to manoeuvre, can attack without fear of interference by other machines, and if you miss him the first time can go after him again. Such opportunities were very rare in our old sector, but in the new, from what I hear, they are much more frequent, and even on the lines single Huns or small groups are much oftener met with. These photographic and daylight bombing machines which penetrate far behind the lines, rely largely on their great height for protection. The one we saw the other day had two French machines after him, and we watched them try to get him, but he was evidently too far above them and escaped without their doing more than worry him a little.

Such Huns are usually between 16,000 and 20,000 feet, generally nearer the latter figure. Down low, a thousand feet is for a good machine only a matter of perhaps a minute, but very high where the air is thin it is an entirely different proposition, and the time that it takes you to climb a thousand feet or two is often just the time the

---

19. At Chaudun, about six miles south of Soissons.

Hun needs in order to escape. Obviously the thing to do is to be there when they come along, and if possible be over them.

As I have told you before, *aviation de chasse* resembles in many respects other kinds of hunting; for instance, the pursuit of the festive duck. I have noticed that successful Hun hunters often owe their success to the same qualities which go to make a successful duck hunter, that is, patience and knowing where the birds use, so to speak. I know that many of the best chances I have had I have gotten at the same time of day, the same altitude and approximately the same locality; chances at machines which I had noticed tried to do a certain kind of work, such as taking pictures when the light was most favourable. I went and laid for them, and wish I could have the same chances over again, for I think I could bring down some of them which in my first attempt I hit, but let get away from me.

Reminds me again of my beginnings of shooting on the river, and how well I remember the fine shots I used to make a bungle of. When I get to our new sector I shall try to find out something of the habits of these birds and go up and lay for them when the weather is favourable. The country to which we have moved is very pretty, with woods, and streams, and rolling hills, and a seeming possibility of many interesting things to be discovered on walks through the country when the weather is unfavourable for flying. When I arrived, it was all very picturesque in a mantle of snow, with every tree and bush a beautiful bit of lace-work, each separate twig outlined by the soft snow and frost with which it was covered.

Father in his letter wonders if it is very cold high in the air at this time of year. It is bitter, and you notice the difference between now and summer time, although it is not nearly so pronounced as on the ground. Any water jumping out of your radiator, for instance, freezes at once, although it will also do this in summer very high up. I have never suffered from cold, however, as my rig is very good and entirely covers my face. The Spad, which I have always flown on the front, is probably as warm as any machine, particularly the new model, which is so arranged as to give you the benefit of much of the heat from the motor.

Paris. Jan. 7th, 1918.

As you know from my letters, the work that I have been able to do in the past six weeks has amounted to almost nothing, which makes me particularly sick when I think that I might in that time have gone home and been back again. I am now in Paris, having come down to see about the transfer to the American Army, and when I went to Headquarters I found that my release from the French service had gone through, and my commission in the American was ready and all I need do to become a U. S. officer is to take the oath.

The colonel who will be my chief was, he said, just on the point of sending for me, and wanted me to leave my *escadrille* at once, but I succeeded in persuading them not to make me do this, as I shall explain. After a man has been at the front for three or four months I think he gets in a position where he can in perhaps a month's time, granting the same opportunities to fly, learn as much as he did in all his previous work. The reason for this is that his work at first is so much limited by his inexperience. He should not begin too fast, and although the opportunities are there just the same, they are not there for him. That is to say, his lack of skill prevents his taking full advantage of the opportunities in the way he can after he has passed his preliminary stage at the front. Personally I feel confident that if I could only have the fights over again that I have already had I should certainly, with the advantage of my new machine and greater experience be able to bag at least two or three Huns instead of only one. And it was these chances that I had been hoping to get in the past six weeks, so it is mighty disappointing to have had them go by with so little accomplished. I am, therefore, very glad to have been able to arrange to return to my French squadron and stay there until there is actually something definite for me to do in the American service.

I got five hundred *francs* prize money today from the Franco-American Flying Corps for my first Hun. It seems rather poor sport getting money for killing people—too much like shooting for the market. It is, however, just a special sort of pay when you come down to it.

Paris, January 16, 1918.

You will probably be surprised when you receive my letter of last week on top of the cable which I sent you a few days later. I tried to do as I wrote in that letter to Father I intended doing, but things rather broke against me. The next day I flew back to my *escadrille* at the front only to find that during my absence Captain Deullin had received an order from headquarters that I was to be sent with several others to the Lafayette Escadrille. This because of my release from the French service and impending signing up with the U. S. As I told you in my last letter, however, this order had been changed, and instead of going to the Lafayette I am to do instruction work for several months. When the captain received the order he thought I could not fly with the *escadrille* any longer, so being short of machines he promptly assigned my new one to another pilot, who took it out and broke it in landing. When I arrived and found out about this, to say that I was sore would be putting it mildly. It had taken me over a month to get that machine all regulated to suit myself and the end of it all made the loss of time seem more discouraging than ever.

The captain was, however, not to blame, and as it turned out was reasonable in supposing as he did. He was very nice and offered to give me back my machine as soon as repaired (it was not badly broken) or to get me a new one at once. The commander of the group, however, called up headquarters and they said they had no provision for allowing Americans who had been released from the French service to remain in the group, but that they must either stay for the duration of the war or go to the American Escadrille as ordered. This, of course, settled it, and I returned to Paris the next day with all my things and have been here ever since.

Last Thursday I took the oath to support the Constitution, etc., etc., and since then have been awaiting my orders to report for duty. They should come any day now and in the meantime I have been doing some shopping, laying in new uniforms, etc. Am again staying at the Continental, have a nice comfortable room and have been putting in my time translating some notes written by Captain Deullin on "*Aviation de Chasse*." He gave me permission to do this and to add something of my own, and I am going to show the result to the U.S. officers in charge of the training of American pilots. I think something of the sort might be useful for the men learning to fly; I know from my own experience what a vague idea we used to have of the actual conditions at the front which we were endeavouring to prepare ourselves to meet, and I think a student can learn more in his period of training, and go about it more intelligently, if he knows as nearly as possible what he is getting ready for.

I am in many ways very sorry to leave the French service. In December I was promoted to the rank of sergeant and held that rank at the time of transferring to the U. S. Army in which I have been made a captain, but rank is not of great importance, and one naturally does not like to leave an organisation in which one has been well treated, when it has still so much work ahead of it for which every man is needed. Undoubtedly the immediate opportunities for flying on the front would have been greater, had I remained with the French, but I think it is the feeling of most Americans who have seen service on the front, that they should transfer to the American Air Service, which is of course badly in need of men with experience in flying under war conditions.

I have enjoyed my work with the French very much and I admire them immensely as must anyone who knows them. The more one sees of this war the more impressed one becomes with what France has done and how much the rest of the world owes to her. From the French I have always received the greatest kindness and consideration, and after nine months in their army my great regret is that I did not wake up a year or two sooner, as I should have, and enlist long before I did.

I have been very fortunate in my squadron commander. Captain Deullin, a thorough gentleman and a splendid fighter, to whom I owe a great deal of what I have learned about air fighting.

Paris, January 31, 1918.

I am still in Paris (almost a month now) waiting for final orders. It seems a great waste of time, and when it comes to delays the French Army certainly has nothing on the American. I am hoping to be definitely settled within a week, however, and when I am, will write you fully about it. The work which I was originally called in to do seems to have been so split up that it practically no longer exists as one job. Am doing everything I can to hurry things up as I am very sick of Paris and anxious to get started again. Are you so sure of what you say about how much America has done by way of preparation for the coming fight? A letter from Uncle J—— would seem to indicate the contrary and what I have seen over here is to the same effect. The preparation in aviation in which we are expected to do so much is certainly disappointing.

The difficulties encountered were of course to be expected, having in view the fact that America has never herself produced a single machine of any type which could be used on the front. It has, I think, been a great mistake to feed up to the public all the wild tales one sees in the papers about what the U. S. will do in the air this spring. Most of this rot is written by reporters who get their information second-hand and don't know what they are talking about. I fear the reality is going to be a great disappointment to the public and will cause a bit of a howl. Even the statements from men in the aviation at home who should know better, show in many cases the most profound ignorance of conditions and fundamentals.

The short article from the N.Y. *Times* which you enclosed in your last letter and which is entitled "Aviation has lost its romance" is just such another exhibition of ignorance. The writer has taken certain facts which he has seen in the papers and from them has proceeded to draw entirely erroneous conclusions, *i, e.,* because he hears that planes are now flying more in groups rather than singly as in the early days, he concludes that air fighting has lost its individuality and become like fighting on the ground. As you say, our work, does not sound much like what the article describes. It is true that there is more team work, so to speak, than formerly, but when the final fight comes it will never cease to be very much of an individual matter. The great speed of machines prohibits anything else.

 Insignia of Escadrille Lafayette (103rd Aero Squadron, A. E. F.)

Chapter 3
Escadrille Lafayette
(103rd aero squadron, A. E. F.)

Escadrille Lafayette,
La Noblette,[1] Feb. 18, 1918.

Have already written you all about the various complications in Paris which finally ended in my coming out here to the Escadrille Lafayette, so shall say no more about them. We have been having the most remarkable weather for this time of year, gorgeously clear days with an almost cloudless sky. Until the last three or four days it has been quite warm, but now it is clear and cold. When I think of all the rain and fog we had during October and November in Flanders it seems a shame things could not have been more seasonably arranged.

I have not got a machine of my own as yet, but yesterday I borrowed one from another pilot and flew around and got a good look at the country,[2] It is a great relief after the dreary wastes of Flanders, for it is rolling, with forests and patches of woods scattered about among very large fields, much like the sector we were in before I left the front in January. In fact, we are only a few miles from that other sector, and the country is even better for aviation, for should anything go wrong with your motor you can find a place to land almost anywhere. Yesterday M—— and I took a walk through the woods, mostly of pine, and I am going to do considerable more exploring before long. Flanders looks well enough from the air for all countries look flat when you are above them, but when it comes to living there, the sameness and lack of hills or woods of any size become very tiresome.

As for the Boches hereabouts, from what little I have seen they

---

1. About eight miles north of Châlons-sur-Marne.
2. The Champagne sector, between Reims and the Argonne Forest.

seem here also to have a habit of coming far into our lines to take pictures on clear days, so I am hoping that if I can get a good machine that will go really high, a little patient waiting may give me a crack at some of them. Those high boys well in your own lines and all by themselves offer a great chance once you can get up to them, but there lies the difficulty. Also it is not much fun waiting around at 20,000 feet this time of year. Yesterday I flew along behind the lines just in front of the sausage balloons, and as the day was clear got a very good look at things. Tomorrow I think I shall try to borrow a machine again and have another quiet look, for I am a great believer in knowing your country well before you start much scrapping. It is a great help to be always able to tell at a glance just where you are.

La Noblette, Feb. 19th, 1918.

Borrowed a machine again today and went out with H—— and another fellow for a look at the lines. It was another gorgeous winter day and one could see for miles behind the German lines. The lines themselves are very clearly marked by a broad belt of brown, pock-marked earth, from which the shells have blown everything, backed on both sides by the second and third-line trenches which show up very white and distinct in the light-coloured soil. Quite different from Flanders, where the marshy ground and dark soil make the trenches practically invisible unless you are very low and where the first lines are conspicuous by a complete absence of any trenches at all. In that quagmire, trenches are out of the question in a heavily shelled region, and the men just man the shell holes, most of which are half full of water. Here the condition of the ground is better, and I think I got a fairly-good idea of the country today. Major T——, who now commands the Lafayette squadron, has given me his machine for the time being, so I hope to get out soon again.

I am sorry to say that yesterday morning the Huns got a friend of mine named L—— who was in a French squadron which is stationed on this field. I used to know L—— at Avord and had seen quite a little of him recently as we had taken several walks together. Same old story of getting off by himself and not watching the rear carefully enough. He was on the other side of the lines and three Boches surprised him from the rear and evidently badly wounded him. He managed to keep his machine under control, however, and got several kilometres within our lines, but when he was still 500 metres from the ground it was evidently too much for him and he plunged head first the rest of the way. We buried him this afternoon in a little French military cemetery near here. The whole Lafayette squadron went, and there was a guard of honour of both American and French soldiers. L—— was a plain fellow but a good one just the same, who worked hard and fearlessly did his level best, and I am very sorry he had to go. I think I shall get a couple of flags for his grave, as I did for Oliver, if they are not already there.

Later on this afternoon I took a long walk by myself, and it certainly is a relief to get some air and exercise in the country again, after the weeks in Paris. Shall write you more of the country and the people when I have had time to explore further. Must stop now, as M—— wants to go to sleep. Certainly hope I shall hear from you before long.

Hospital at Mailly, March 12, 1918.

I have been laid up in this hospital for the past two weeks but regret that I cannot write you any hero (?) story about the cause of my being here. It was not a Boche bullet that laid me low, no such luck, nothing but a good old-fashioned case of the mumps. Rather thought that I had passed the age of such childish diseases, but it seems not, for I have had as pretty a case as you ever laid eyes on and a face shaped like a full moon. It is nearly over now, though, and I should be back at the squadron within a week.

You refer in one of your recent letters to what I said about the English being so decent. I suppose you have heard tales of how they force the brunt of the fighting on their Colonial Troops and that they have not taken over as much of the line as they should have. Such stories are lies, pure and simple, and generally, I think, of German manufacture, to stir up trouble. No troops fight harder than the English home troops, and if there was any comparison to be made, it would be that they do rather more than their share. As for England's effort in the war in general, all one need do is to consider the magnitude of her operations in Egypt, and Mesopotamia, Palestine, and S. Africa—all in addition to her enormous part on the western front and to the work of her navy. We may sometimes not admire her methods, because we think they are not always the best calculated to produce results, but no one can question that she has and is doing her best, and the nerve and spirit of the English fighting man is above criticism.

Do not pin too much faith on the reports you see of internal troubles in Germany. To me they seem to mean little or nothing, and

I should not be at all surprised if they were purposely put out by the German Government. The Allies are entirely too fond of taking comfort from such reports and thinking that all they have to do is to hang on and wait for the end. This is just what Germany wants them to do—that is, take it easy while she makes use of the time to get ready and hit another blow. When one considers how completely the government controls the German Press, it seems foolish to believe that anything emanates from Germany which is not meant to. With the Russian muddle I think the end never looked further away.

P. S.—Have been reading this epistle over and what I said about the English reminds me that we can hardly criticize them on matters of management after what I have seen of our own forces over here, and after all the talk we heard about how strong the Americans would be on this score! Have seen some interesting and also some disheartening things, since I entered the U. S. A., but being an officer I suppose I should say nothing.

La Noblette, March 19, 1918.

Here I am back at the squadron again and very glad to be here and out of the hospital, as I had no fun there at all, and was very much fed up with the place.

R—— had a narrow escape here the other day. I have written to you before about him and he is in my estimation the best man in this outfit, the kind of an American of whom we may be proud. There is none braver than he, and as I recounted to you in one of my letters last summer, his bravery very nearly cost him his life when he first went to the front as a flyer. I think he went a bit too strong at first but has been taking better care of himself lately, that is, until a few days ago, when he must have had a brainstorm. That he is here today to tell the tale is only due to his own skill and more particularly to the Goddess of Good Fortune. R—— was on for a patrol, and when he started noticed that for some reason he could not get his machine off the ground within the usual distance. He had to shut off his motor and stop in order to avoid running into the woods at the end of the field.

Instead of at once coming back to the hangar and examining his machine to see what was wrong, what does he do but turn around on the ground and roll to the extreme end of the field where he could get the longest possible run. He then started off again and this time managed to get up and went on out to the lines with the patrol. After they had been out for a while the leader saw a clear sky and an opportunity of making a dash some four miles into the German lines and attacking a captive observation balloon. This he did and R—— attacked in his turn, diving almost vertically on the balloon and shooting as he came. When he tried to pull up, however, he found that his elevating controls would not work and his machine consequently kept on diving for the ground a thousand meters or so below. He tried again to flatten out, putting on his motor and jerking on his controls as he did so. This time he managed to get the nose of his machine up, flew back to our lines and came in with the patrol after a full flight of some two hours. When he went to level off in landing, his controls again would not function properly, and he almost smashed up on the field, but just managed to get on the ground without breaking anything.

During the entire flight he flew with his controls out of their usual position in order to keep his plane in flying position. Upon examination of the machine to find out what was wrong, it turned out that the rivets which fasten the elevating planes to the controls had sheared off so that the only thing that was holding them was that the joint was a little stiff and gummed with paint. As it was, the joint slipped about and threw the controls out of position. It would be hardly possible to have a closer shave than this and to go up in the first place when one knows that the controls are not functioning properly is pure madness. I told R—— so, for if anyone has to be killed, R—— would be about the last man that I would want to see go. They did not get the balloon and when I asked R—— if he was tired of life he laughed and said "No, but I made the Boches pull their old balloon down anyhow." We have now corrected and reinforced the construction of the tails of the machines, so that the same thing cannot occur again.

You asked in one of your letters about Stewart Walcott, who was killed in December. I knew him at Avord and he was an extremely nice fellow, one of the best of the Americans in the Franco-American Flying Corps. Unfortunately, it is among this class that the great majority of the losses have occurred. The answer is simple—they do their best and fight.

Speaking of close calls, such as that of R——'s, I think many pilots do not take them enough to heart. It is all very well not to brood over such things and let them get on your nerves but at the same time there is no reason why one should not learn and profit by them. Many men when they have a narrow escape of one kind or another seem to quickly forget it just because they "got away with it" without coming to grief. It seems to me that it is a good idea to let such an experience sink in and try to always thereafter take every possible precaution against its happening again. One cannot keep too close an eye on machines no matter how good they are supposed to be or how much confidence one may have in the skill and care of one's mechanics. I know I have always tried to personally examine any machine I have flown, to the extent of sometimes almost making the mechanics in charge feel that I did not trust them. If they are any good, however, they understand when you explain your reasons to them and tell them that you would always do the same thing, for your own personal satisfaction, even if you knew that a dozen of the best mechanics in the land had just examined every bolt in the machine.

People talk of the progress that has been made in aviation and that will be made, and say that the day is coming when it will be as safe as automobiling. They don't know what they are talking about and the two cannot be compared. In an automobile if a wheel comes off or the steering gear breaks you perhaps roll in the ditch and that is all, provided you were not racing. In the air, if you lose a wing or your controls break, you are finished, at least until someone invents a sky hook or a means of getting out on a cloud and making repairs. In the case of broken controls, a skilful pilot can often save his neck, provided he has some of them left, but this depends largely on the inherent stability of the type of plane which he happens to be flying.

La Noblette, March 27th, 1918.

Have had several flights on the lines since last writing, but every time I go out things seem to be very quiet and I have not had a shot at a Boche yet. I led a patrol this morning and saw one two-seater fooling around low down far within his own lines. We went back into our lines and got in the sun in the hope that he would not see us and would come out where we could get a crack at him. Had no luck, however, for every time we got anywhere near him he would beat it back into his Hues so far that it was impossible to follow him with any chance of success.

Yesterday morning R———, another fellow and myself were out, and this time R——— was leading the show. We fooled around for an hour or so a little inside the German lines at about 3000 metres where the Boche "Archies" gave us quite a lively time. Then some clouds came along at about 1500 metres and R——— started into Germany flying above a line of clouds. The third man's motor was not going properly so that he was afraid to risk it and went back. All the time the "Archies" kept plugging away as there were not enough clouds to prevent their seeing us. When we got about fifteen kilometres into the German territory R—— dove down through a hole in the clouds and I followed close behind him. I flattened out at about 1000 metres to look for him and saw him 300 or 400 metres behind me. Turned to go back and join him but got mixed up in a low cloud which I had not noticed and when I came out could see no sign of him. Under me was a Boche hospital with a lot of red crosses on it. Their "Archies" and anti-aircraft machine-guns opened up in great shape and I don't mind saying that I felt mighty lonesome all by my little self with the front lines so far away I could not even see them at that height.

I thought R—— must have gone above the clouds again so I put on my power and climbed up but could see no sign of him. As my gasoline was getting low I came home without more delay and R—— came in a few minutes later. He reported that he had shot at a town and a small railway train, but I did not see him, as I was pretty busy watching the air for Hun machines. There seemed to be none out, however, for which I was rather glad, as should five or six of them get after you when in that position, they could give you a mighty poor time before you could get back to your own lines.

When we got back I told R—— I thought he used very poor judgment, for I cannot see the use of taking chances when there is nothing to be gained by it. What is the use of patrolling just inside the German lines where their "Archies" continually shoot you up and the black shell bursts give away your position and destroy practically all chance of springing a surprise. It seems to me much better to stay a little in your own lines or make short excursions into Hunland and out again, so that you are not much shot at and can at the same time see any German machines which it would be possible to attack. My theory is that you should allow a Boche to come as far as possible into your own lines before attacking, for then you have twice the chance of success. If he won't come, that is a different matter and you can go after him, but give him a chance to come.

Also at the time of an offensive, it is often necessary to adopt different tactics and to push the air fighting to far within the enemy lines, both for the better protection of our own two-seater machines, which at such a time are themselves penetrating further than usual into Hunland, as well as for the moral effect on our own forces and those of the Huns. Again, I can see no use in going miles into German territory in a quiet sector (so far as activity on the ground is concerned) just to shoot at ground targets from a height of 1500 metres where you have not one chance in a thousand of killing anything and a good chance of being brought down yourself. You don't prove anything and it does not seem to me to be the best way to win the war. At the time of an attack, when the roads behind the lines are full of troops, etc., which offer a good target, then is the time to go in and shoot them up, provided you do it at 100 or 200 metres height where you can really hit something.

The "Archies" do not often bring a plane down when one considers the number of machines fired at every day and the enormous expenditure of ammunition, but there is no use in letting them shoot at you just for the fun of it, particularly in this sector, where the German batteries are more accurate than any I have yet seen. They come too dam close for comfort. A few days ago R—— got a piece of a shell through a wing and another man got one in his tail. Yesterday, someone on the ground put a bullet through my tail, but that is, of course, much too far from me to be dangerous. Another thing about low flying in enemy territory is that all one needs is to have the motor stop or get a bullet in it and the best one can expect is to land and be taken prisoner. The English used to do a lot of this sort of thing and lost a great many men without accomplishing enough to make it worth while. They sent and still send their men out on a great many "strafing" expeditions. "Strafing" is aviation slang for flying low and attacking enemy troops with bombs and machine-gun fire.

At the time of an attack when the roads are full of troops and supply trains which offer good targets, strafing has a great effect and is undoubtedly of the highest importance. Its greatest effect is upon the morale of the troops attacked, for nothing gets on an infantryman's nerves like being shot up from the air before he even reaches the advanced positions. He feels that he has little or no protection against this sort of thing and that the only thing he can do about it is to hide. He is often afraid to shoot at a plane, for fear of giving away his own position, and thinks that if he makes a move the airman will spot him.

As a matter of fact the man in the air in his swiftly moving plane cannot see nearly as much as the man on the ground thinks he can. Things flash by so quickly that small details often pass unobserved. The infantryman's greatest protection against the low-flying machine lies in his rifle and machine-guns and he does not use them nearly as much as he should.

When he does shoot he is discouraged because his fire seldom seems to have much effect, forgetting that the vital parts of the machine which he must hit, in order to bring it down at once, are very small. To do this he must knock the pilot out, set the plane on fire or damage the motor so seriously as to cause it to stop. He may kill the observer, wound the pilot, or hit the motor or the plane, so as to ruin it for further service, but still the pilot may be able to get back to his own lines, and the man who shot him will think that he missed entirely.

In addition to this, fire from the ground gets on a pilot's nerves just as much as his shooting upsets the man on the ground. Losses to the Air Service when engaged in ground strafing are very heavy and almost all pilots will agree that they would rather do any other kind of work. A pilot's skill and experience are no protection to him against fire from the ground, and he feels about as helpless as do the troops he is strafing. He must also be constantly on his guard against attack from the air, and no matter how carefully he may watch, he will get into many difficult situations because his work takes him far into the enemy lines and low to the ground, so that Hun machines which may be above him can easily overtake him and come down on his back, even though he may have noticed them as soon as they came in sight. It is for these reasons that it has always seemed to me that strafing should be confined, as it is in the French service, to the period of an offensive, for in a quiet sector the dangers to the aeroplane are just as great, while ground targets being few and far between, there is little that the aviator can accomplish either by actual material destruction or by affecting the morale of troops.

If I ever get a squadron of my own, I know that there are some things they will not do. I prefer to take my chances flirting with a Hun where I have as good a chance as he has. Am glad to say that I am in command of one of the "flights" of this *escadrille* so that I generally lead the patrols that I am on and can take them where I please. Since I started on the present instalment of this letter, R—— has come in from a voluntary patrol with Major T—— and another fellow. They attacked a bunch of five Hun single-seaters and three two-seaters. R—— shot down two of the single-seaters and they are both already officially confirmed. He thinks he hit another one pretty hard but there is as yet no news of this third Boche. Pretty good work at that. I personally get more discouraged every day. Have just been out for the second time today and did not see a feather.

Worse than anything else, I can see from the way my motor is acting that it is not going to last more than about one more flight if I can manage to nurse it through that. And it is a brand-new motor and machine with only about five hours of flight. It seems to me that every time I get a machine something like this goes wrong and it is very disheartening after you have worked several days to get the guns and everything else properly regulated. When I have gotten out on the lines there has not been a sign of a Hun, and then the very next patrol runs into a bunch of them. R—— seems to attract the Huns, for he has had any number of fights except when I have been with him, and then we have not seen a thing.

Their fight this morning lasted almost half an hour in all, with intervals. They attacked the same bunch of Boches three or four times until their ammunition was all gone or guns jammed. R—— got one and then speared the other seven minutes later. Such a fight is, of course, not continuous, the machines attacking, then flying off, manoeuvring for position and going at it again.

One of my chief troubles with my machines has been that I have been trying to use a new type which is much superior to the old when it runs, being faster and better in every way. It has not proved a success, however, being continually out of order or the motor breaking down. I am through with it now, however, and am going back to the old type of machine that I had when I first went to the front. Nearly all the men here have them and they go very well, although I can fly rings around them with my machine when it will go. Have decided, however, that I would rather fly with the old type than sit on the ground and curse at the new.

La Noblette, April 9, 1918.

My letter this week must be brief, as we are moving tomorrow and it is late, with much packing still to be done. Of course, I cannot tell you where we are going, but it looks as though we were going to get in the big fight after all. Naturally, we are delighted, for it seems that this greatest of all battles may very likely make or break the war and being so near, it would be a pity to have had no part in it. It has seemed a waste of energy and material to sail around in what is generally a Hunless sky when there is so much to be done elsewhere. If the big battles on the Somme and south of it to the Aisne turn out as we hope, I think there will still be a weary lot of war to follow, but it should nevertheless prove the turning point.

Fismes,[3] April 13, 1918.

Yesterday was another of the most beautiful days imaginable and I have never seen the visibility better. From 15,000 feet you could see almost to the ends of the earth it seemed, and a large part of the great battlefield on which the present terrific struggle is going on, was spread out before us. I can tell you this without saying anything I should not, for this greatest of all battles extends over such a stretch of country that the mere fact that one is in it does not give any definite indication of where one really is. Yesterday we had not as yet had any definite duties assigned to us, so we got up a voluntary expedition in the morning and went out to see what there was to be seen. I was leading the show and we had not gotten to the lines when the white puffs of smoke from the French "Archies" showed me a Hun two-seater coming into our lines. He was very high and although we tried our best to climb up to him he saw us and got back to his lines before we could catch him.

Just as we got to the lines I spotted another two-seater trying the same trick and again tried to get up to him with no better results, although we got a good deal closer to this fellow, not, however, within even long range. As I have explained to you before, climbing around 15,000 feet where the air is thin is an entirely different part of speech from climbing when near the ground. It takes considerable time and if the Hun has a couple of thousand feet advantage of you, he must be a long way in your lines if you are going to catch him before he gets home. Yesterday we were out of luck, as we were just getting our height at the time and were still thousands of feet below the Huns.

After reaching the lines we flew about for more than an hour without seeing any Boche machines. In the beautiful clear air, however, we did get a most wonderful view of the country. Not far away, one of the largest and most beautiful cities of France[4] was under bombardment and was burning in a dozen places. There are no civilians left in this town now, I am glad to say, but the waste and destruction is sickening.

Finally I caught sight of two German machines flying far within their own lines and perhaps a thousand metres below us. They were too far in to offer any sort of a chance, so we went back a little into our own lines and flew about so that the Huns had the sun in their eyes. For at least ten minutes we waited and finally were rewarded by

---

3. In the *Chemin des Dames* sector, between Reims and Soissons.
4. Reims.

The remains of two Spad planes of the Escadrille Lafayette
After a successful German night bombing raid

seeing them start out for the lines, evidently thinking they had a clear coast. There had been four of us to begin with, but one man had lost the formation in some clouds and another had had to go in on account of motor trouble. As we started after the Boches, it was impossible to always keep in the sun, and they caught sight of us and started back into their lines. In turning, the two Huns drew up close beside each other in perfect defensive position, so that it was impossible to attack either without giving the observer of the other an excellent shot. Seeing this I manoeuvred around them for a second in the hope of getting them in a more favourable position. They did exactly what I wanted them to and one fell in behind the other so that it was possible to attack him as though his comrade were not there.

All this time I had thought that they were two-seater machines as in fact they were, but as I dove down to get under the tail of the rear Hun I noticed that he only had one set of struts between the wings on each side of the fuselage. Now I had never seen or heard of a Hun two-seater which did not have at least two sets of struts, while most single-seaters only have one. I therefore jumped to the conclusion that these machines were single-seaters after all, even though they were larger than the ordinary, for there is a new German single-seater which I have never seen, but which is considerably bigger than the older type usually met with. The machine also seemed a bit small for a two-seater. Hence I went after this fellow as I would a single-seater, diving on his back instead of going under his tail.

Have not had a fight for so long until this one (not a shot since December 5th, when I got my first) that I am afraid I started shooting too soon. However, I think I must have had the great good luck to hit the pilot with one of my first shots, for the Hun just kept flying along in a perfectly straight line without manoeuvring at all, giving one of the easiest targets imaginable. I could see my bullets hitting the machine and going all around the pilot's seat, and no man in his senses would fly straight ahead with this going on. Finally, got directly behind him, so that my shots raked the machine from end to end, and let him have at least a hundred of them. When within about forty yards, I suddenly saw the machine-gunner let go of his gun, throw up his arms and flop down out of sight in the body of the machine, and so realised that it was a two-seater after all.

About that time a lot of white smoke started to come out of the Hun's motor, evidently caused by the bullets hitting it, for the machine did not catch fire. Then he began to climb until he was at such a steep angle that the motor could not pull the machine up any further and it seemed to hang almost stationary for a few seconds. You have seen a duck when it is mortally shot climb straight up for a little, flutter a second or so and then fold its wings and fall. This Boche reminded me for all the world of such a bird. He finally slipped sideways on one wing and then plunged vertically on his nose, leaving a long trail of white smoke behind him. I circled above and watched him fall and have never seen a machine go down so fast before. He seemed to cover the nine thousand feet to the ground in almost no time at all. I watched him until he went head first into the ground and could distinctly see the machine all the time it was falling, but when it struck it just seemed to melt out of sight and I could see no trace of it on the ground. When a plane falls in this way the motor generally goes out of sight in the ground and the body is of course smashed to atoms, so I suppose the wreckage was too small to see from my height.

All the time the second Boche had been hiking for home as fast as he could go and had I been quick I should have had a good shot at him also, for he was only a couple of hundred yards away and directly in front of me. When the first one turned out to be a two-seater, however, it took me so much by surprise and he was so long about making up his mind to fall that by the time I woke up the other fellow was gone. Also, not knowing the sector, I thought we were a considerable distance in the German lines, when as a matter of fact we were just over them, and the Boche fell in No Man's Land. There was no trouble at all about the official confirmation, for almost as soon as we had landed on our own field, confirmation came in from several sausage balloons, the infantry, artillery, and from a couple of observers in aeroplanes who had seen the Boche fall.

A report also came in that a lot of Huns ran out of their trenches and gathered around the wreck of their machine on the ground, whereupon the French 75's amused themselves by dumping some shells in their midst. Rather rubbing it in, don't you think? I think I had a good deal of luck with this fellow. My machine-gun ran like a charm and never even hesitated.

Then, too, this was a rube way to go after a two-seater, for although it gives you a splendid shot, the machine-gunner has an even better one. As soon as you run into one who is a good shot you are going to have trouble, and the man who uses such tactics against two-seaters will not generally last long. In this case I think the machine-gunner must have been hit by one of my first shots, because he did not fire at all so far as I could see. I don't think I shall make this mistake again, however. The machine was evidently a new type of two-seater[5] which I had not heard of. It is rather small, the pilot and the machine-gunner sit very close together, and the plane is intended as a sort of combination pursuit and observation machine.

One of the other men in the squadron reported that he shot down a single-seater in flames half an hour after I got the two-seater, but we have as yet been able to get no confirmation. If he gets this one it will make four for him in a month, three of them in flames. Was rather surprised that mine did not catch fire, for I don't think I shall ever hit a machine harder than this one, due to the very easy shot he gave me. I saw not just a few bullets go into him but a regular stream of them, and I don't see how I could have missed his gas tank. There is a great advantage in setting a machine on fire, for there is then no possible doubt, and it can be seen to fall for miles, which makes confirmation much easier.

Went out on another voluntary patrol in the afternoon and tried to get a shot at another two-seater, but in attempting to surprise him made rather a mess of it, so that I never even got a shot. Then a little while later we spotted three single-seaters flying far within their lines, and I tried the same tactics of waiting in the sun for them to come out. Waited ten minutes and they would not come so went in after them. I got on one fellow's tail and one of the other men jumped on another, but both our guns jammed after only half a dozen shots or so. We were far in the German lines on the other side of their sausage balloons, so there was nothing for it but to clear out.

In the morning when we were after the two-seaters, my companion stayed over my head and protected the rear. He tried to get a whack at the second machine, but was unsuccessful. In making an attack it is a great comfort to know that your rear is protected and the man who does this protection work to my mind deserves a great deal more credit than he usually gets. On coming out of the German lines after the machine fell, their "Archies" opened up, but they didn't seem to be as good as they were in our last sector. There they were wonderful.

Was looking over the official reports the other day and saw an account of a most remarkable coincidence, and incidentally one of the hardest bits of luck imaginable. A German machine attacked a French sausage balloon so that the two observers were forced to jump in their

---

5. A Halberstadt.

parachutes. They were coming down all right when the German machine above them was hit by an "Archie" and blown to pieces. A piece fell on one of the parachutes, breaking it, and the Frenchman fell and was killed. That fellow certainly had no luck at all.

Fismes, 29 April, 1918.

Rien de neuf ici. Toujour la brume et le mauvais temps.[6] Now my French has about run out so we will continue in the mother tongue. But "*sans blag,*" [7] since last writing there has been practically nothing but fog, mist, and rain, with the exception of one day when it cleared up for a few hours. Got in a flight then, but outside of that have not had my machine off the ground. Hobey Baker and another fellow and myself went out and had hardly reached the lines before we bumped into three Hun *chasse* machines, Albatross. I was leading our patrol so attacked at once, as we had the advantage of height. Got on one Hun's tail and should have had a very good shot, but after a few shots my gun stopped again. Was able to fix it in a second but then the chance was gone and I never got as good a shot again.

I was square on the Boche's tail and saw several bullets miss him by inches but am afraid I shot when too far away. He turned under me and as I had fixed my gun by that time I dove and took another crack at him. He turned vertically on his nose, so much so he almost got on his back, and dove like a bullet. It was impossible to follow or watch him as that would have taken me below the other two Huns. This one is carried on the official reports as "probably" destroyed by me, but not confirmed. I do not think, however, that he fell or was seriously hit, for if he had gone down he would surely have been seen as we were just on the lines.

We were flying above a sea of white clouds with just enough holes in them to allow one to see sufficient of the country below to keep one's bearings. The fight began at about 11,000 feet and just as I attacked the first Hun I looked behind and above to see Baker and the other man going after the other two. They had no luck, however, as Baker's gun jammed after about twenty shots and the other fellow was having trouble with the pressure in his gas tank, so that he was able to do very little. When I looked again one of the three Boches was trying to get at me, so I left the one that had dived and took a try at this second one. I got on his back but that was about all the good it did me

---

6. Nothing new here. Always fog and bad weather.
7. No fooling.

for that fellow certainly could handle his machine.

He started diving toward our lines and I hoped that I could drive him down low to the ground, even if I could not hit him, and once close to the ground he would have to stop his stunts and either land or fly in something like a line, which would give me a decent shot at him. He went into a spiral with little Willie doing the same just behind and above him. We went down several thousand feet in this way, twisting and turning. I got some shots at him at close range but only the most difficult ones. Once when he did a *renversement* in front of me I had to pull up to keep from running into him. He tried to get above me, but as the advantage of height had been with me from the first, this was of course easy to prevent.

As we went down I glanced behind me to make sure of not being surprised from the rear and could see nothing of my companions, but two Huns were circling some 500 metres over our heads. They were so directly above that I doubt if they saw us, and at any rate I knew I could dive into the clouds if I got into a tight hole. The two above never came down, but having them there always worries you and distracts your attention by requiring too much watching of the rear. My Hun dove for a hole in the clouds, but in watching the others I had gotten several hundred yards behind him, and although I came through the same hole a couple of seconds later and went down under the clouds to 3,000 feet there was not a sign of him. Suppose he must have stayed in those clouds until he was well within his own lines.

The fact that there were two Boches above us when I was after this last one, making three in all, the original number, is what makes me think, among other things, that the first one did not go down, although of course a fourth might have come along. My personal opinion, however, is that that first Hun is now passing these rainy days drinking beer and calling the American the Boche equivalent of "*sale cochon*,"[8] because the American gave him a thrill and perhaps necessitated the changing of the wings on said Hun's "*joli* Cuckoo" by shooting a few holes in them. I am sorry to have gotten so little result out of these last few encounters but have at least learned a great deal, I think, and hope to be able to do better next time.

My experience in fighting with single-seater *chasse* machines has been very limited. It is the most exciting of all encounters but offers the most difficult chance for a decisive victory and consequently requires more skill in shooting to bring one of them down. These

7. Dirty pig.

Boche machines were very pretty, being clean and new looking, with the mark of one of the squadrons of Baron Von Richtofen's[8] famous group on the tail planes. The tails were painted in broad black and white diagonal bands, and one had a diamond-shaped mark on the side of his fuselage with some sort of an *"ensigne"* inside, which I could not make out. All my last three fights have been with this outfit and I should like very much to get one of them, for they are excellent pilots, supposed to be the best the Germans have. However, we shall not see them any more for a while at least, for we are moving again immediately. I would like to tell you where, but of course cannot.

You want to know what we have to eat and when I tell you, you will see that war is not so bad after all, when it comes to eating. For breakfast we have oatmeal, eggs to order with bacon, hot cakes about every other day, and coffee or tea. For lunch, one or two *hors d'oeuvres*, such as bully beef or canned salmon with mayonnaise, or perhaps canned asparagus. Then some sort of meat, veal or steak or mutton, for instance, with potatoes, and some other vegetable, a salad, and generally some dessert, such as canned fruit or a pudding. With this goes pretty good bread and butter. Finally we have a *demi-tasse* and always plenty of granulated sugar. We get stuff through the French when we want it and also through the American quartermaster; anything else we buy outside.

Our mess costs us 150 to 175 *francs* a month. For dinner we get soup, some meat again, a couple of vegetables, salad, sometimes nuts and sometimes a dessert, finishing up with coffee. So you see we are not to be pitied and you will now understand why I say that one of my greatest dangers is over-eating, especially when the weather is bad, not forgetting, of course, the ever-present danger of breaking one's neck by falling out of bed.

The *Challenge of the Present Crisis* arrived last week and I read it through at one sitting, as you suggested. I think it is excellent and certainly contains much food for thought. I cannot, however, at all agree with the author in his prayer to God to bless Germany (see p. 54-55). You remember the picture I sent you, *"Ne leur pardonnez pas, mon père, car ils savent ce qu'ils font."*[9] The same thing applies to the methods of the Huns in general and not simply to their bombing of women and

---

8. *Richthofen & Böelcke in Their Own Words* by Manfred Freiherr von Richthofen & Oswald Böelcke, *The Red Battle Flyer* by Manfred Freiherr von Richthofen & *An Aviator's Field Book* by Oswald Böelcke is also published by Leonaur.
9. *"Father, do not forgive them, for they know what they do."*

children. During this war I shall kill personally and help to kill as many Huns as possible, after it I shall never speak to or have anything to do with one except perhaps to tell him what I think of him and the rest of his tribe, and if I ever catch one in my house or my office, I promise you that he will go out faster than he came in, if it is in my power to make him. Fosdick in his book quotes Walt Whitman as having said "God damn the Turk." I think the same prayer would be even more suitable in the case of the Hun. You will say that I am bitter. I am and I should be ashamed of myself if I were not. I hate the Huns but I do not think my feeling is such as to interfere at all with such ability as I may have to help defeat them.

Leffrinckoucke,[10] May 7, 1918.

Our moving is completed for the time being at least, so now I have a chance to drop you a line. The bad weather continues almost incessantly so that we have been doing very little flying, but when it does clear up there should be plenty of action, for we are again in that sector where Oliver and I first arrived at the front last July. I have had a couple of flights over the lines, but the mist was so heavy that there was not a great deal going on in the air. On the first excursion I did have one short flirtation with a Hun two-seater, short because I again had trouble with my confounded gun. The Boche plane was a new type,[11] in appearance very much like some of the English machines and so marked as to carry out the deception. I started to let him pass under me and then noticing the peculiar markings, started down after him to make sure. Immediately he dove back into his own lines so we waited around for him to come out again. This time I got dead behind and under his tail at about fifty yards, but my gun quit after about eight shots, the Hun twisted sideways and the machine-gunner started shooting, so I ducked under his tail, stood on my nose and left him, with the least possible delay.

You have no idea how hard it is to follow the shooting instructions laid down in the notes I sent you, that is, to hold your fire until you are at close range and then to shoot with sufficient deliberation to be really accurate. There is the constant tendency to get "jumpy" and shoot too hurriedly, which one is continually striving to repress. As for my gun, such troubles are most discouraging and I have had my fill of them, so after this last fiasco I took it off the machine and put on a new one, first examining every part with the greatest care.

---

10. Three miles east of Dunkirk.
11. Hannoveranner.

Yesterday I tried it out on a target and it worked to perfection, firing a large number of shots without the slightest hitch. I hope, therefore, that things will go better from now on.

My other trip on the lines was a daylight patrol at the time of a particularly heavy artillery bombardment. For as far as one could see the guns on both sides were twinkling like the lights of a city in the distance, while in between the black and white puffs of the exploding shells and the little geysers of flying mud and debris were practically continuous, as thick as the large raindrops at the beginning of a summer shower. Above the fines many planes, all of them ours at this time, with hundreds of the little black clouds around them made by the Hun "Archies." The fines look, of course, much the same as they did when I first saw them and wrote to you describing what a sight they are, only the devastated area has spread enormously.

A green forest which I wrote you in the fall had taken on a very mangy appearance, has now almost entirely disappeared, until at present it is hard to distinguish from the fields, or rather what were once fields, which surrounded it. It is remarkable in how short a time a region may be transformed when it becomes the centre of heavy fighting. For instance, a village[12] which I visited last fall and which has been the scene of fighting for only the past two or three weeks, is now nothing but a heap of bricks and plaster with scarcely a wall standing. Last fall there was not a shell mark in the town. On this particular morning a certain much disputed hill [13] was receiving a large share of attention from the artillery and it looked like what I suppose a volcano in eruption does. The whole top of the hill seemed to be exploding every second, and certainly nothing could have lived upon it. In such a ease I believe only the approaches commanding the hill are held.

Not so long ago I had a chance to visit Reims and jumped at it. I had seen it often from the air, having flown over it day after day, but had never seen it from the ground. There are portions of the city which are not very badly battered in spite of the rain of shells to which it has been subjected almost since the war began. Until recently I think 1,835 was the record number for 24 hours, but I saw that one day a few weeks ago the Huns fired something over 3000 shells into the city. That was at the time when you may have noticed in the papers that the city was burning in a number of places more or less continuously for a week. For blocks around the cathedral, however,

---
12. Locre, southwest of Ypres.
13. Kemmel Hill, east of Locre and south of Ypres.

the buildings are completely wrecked and he a mass of broken bricks and plaster with jagged walls standing up from the debris. Fire has completed the destruction of what the shells had left. The cathedral itself is, I fear, beyond repair, although it is not in bad shape as compared with the buildings which surrounded it. The roof is gone and of course all the beautiful stained glass has been smashed to atoms. There are a number of direct hits visible on the walls and buttresses and the whole has been considerably scorched by fire.

A good deal of the intricate carving and pieces of statuary have been broken, but there is a great deal more which has not. The famous carved arches at the entrance (the cathedral faces away from the lines) with their thousands of little stone figures, have been protected by sand bags and seem to be almost intact. In fact, it was not as bad as I had feared and may still remain as a wonderful monument, although it can hardly again be used as a church. The afternoon we were there was very quiet with only a few shells falling in the distance. I took some pictures of the cathedral and the town about it which I shall send when I get a chance to have them developed. Thought of Mother and Uncle J—— and how they would have enjoyed being there, painful as it is to see the wreckage of such beautiful places.

Think we shall probably see another big effort by the Huns before long and this time we shall really be in it. The guns have been pounding away incessantly for the last two or three days and their steady rumble is plainly audible as I write. Every now and then the barracks shakes and the windows rattle when a particularly big one goes off. Our sleeping quarters here are, by the way, the most comfortable we have ever had. We are lodged in little huts made of corrugated sheet iron and shaped like a cylinder cut lengthwise in half, with the flat side on the ground. M—— , Hobe Baker, L——, and I have one together and are very nicely installed, each with a washstand in the corner by his bed, electric lights, and in the centre a table larger than any we have at home, with books, magazines, etc., and an oil lamp. Men in the aviation certainly have a cinch while they are not flying.

Leffrinckovcke, 13 May 1918.

Due to our moving I had not until today had a letter from home for two weeks, but at last they have come and I have been having a fine time reading them for the past two hours. It is blustering and raining outside as usual and M—— and Hobe Baker have gone off with an Englishman to see the front-line trenches. They met the Englishman recently and when he came for them today he asked me if I would not like to go up some other time. Naturally I said yes, but this afternoon I was just as glad to be left to myself so that I could drop you a line and read my letters. Also, as you know, I have already had several trips up to the front in this section when I was here with the French *escadrille*.

You will see by the papers that a great friend of Oliver's and mine is missing, poor old Jimmie Hall. He left this squadron about six weeks ago and went to one of the new American squadrons, and I had not seen him since he left. He was one of the very best men in this outfit and I am deeply sorry that he is gone. We know no more about what happened to him than what we have seen in the papers, but although he is evidently gone so far as this war is concerned, I hope that we may see him again some day. Jim has been in the war since 1914, first as a machine-gunner with the English, then in the French aviation and finally the American. He was a long time in the trenches with the British and you have read his book.

He has had several hair-breadth escapes so we hope that his good fairy has not altogether deserted him and that he may have pulled through this last and be only a prisoner. I certainly hope so, for there was a real man. He had been doing very well, and was a most valuable man, not only for his ability as a pilot, but also as an officer and a leader for our own men. I had gotten to know Jim quite well. He was a true friend and certainly no braver man ever lived. According to the newspaper reports he was shot down by a new type of German machine which has unusual climbing ability and can shoot at another machine above it much better than the ordinary single-seater with fixed guns. The report was that Jim was diving on one when it suddenly pulled up under him and got him from below, but of course this is only a newspaper report on which little reliance can be placed.

This new German machine is a tri-plane. It also has fixed guns like all other single-seater fighting machines, but is very light, so that it climbs with extraordinary speed and can stand very much on its tail to shoot. The last fight I had was with one of them just a couple of days ago when the weather cleared up long enough to let us get in one flight. I was leading a patrol of three other men when I saw this single triplane detach himself from a group and start into his own lines. I found afterwards that he had made an unsuccessful attack on some of our two-seaters and in doing so had evidently gotten separated from the rest of his patrol.

At all events the four of us jumped on him at about 5000 metres and everybody had a few cracks at him, but before we got to close range he started doing all kinds of stunts so that he made the hardest sort of a target. The other men seemed to think we had him and did not follow him down, but I have seen this sort of thing too often to take anything for granted and felt sure the Hun was just throwing his machine around in order to get away and that it was not out of control. Hence I kept after him, shooting whenever I could get my gun about on him. It worked to perfection this time and I must have fired about a hundred and fifty shots, some of them at as close as 40 yards range, or even less. But all the time he was doing spins, *renversements*, etc., and all the tricks of the trade. I know perfectly well I hit his machine a number of times, but did not have the luck or rather, was not accurate enough to set it on fire or get the pilot.

Once when I was diving seventy yards behind and above him, at high speed and plugging away, he suddenly pulled up into one of those steep climbs for which these machines are remarkable. I pulled up as quickly as I could without risk of breaking something, but the Hun ended up 75 yards above me, and rather had the advantage if he had used it properly. I put on my motor wide open, and by pulling my machine into a climb, was able to get my gun in line just as he started to turn. Gave him a blast and came pretty close; in fact, this was one of several times when I thought I might have gotten him.

Anyhow, it seemed to give him such a thrill, that he fell on his nose and passed below me again, where it was a simple matter to dive after him once more. I chased him down to 2,500 metres and then being alone and not knowing where I was, on account of many clouds below, except that I was a considerable distance on the German side of the fence, I had to give it up as a bad job. He got away all right for I saw him pull up and fly off home in a perfectly normal way. This new Hun machine can outclimb our Spads but is not as fast nor as strong and on account of its light weight you can catch them easily in a dive. If, therefore, one remembers their one strong point and watches out for it, they should not prove as difficult to handle as some of the other German types.

Have had three other fights since last writing, two of them with these same Fokker tri-planes. My gun has been working much better and twice the Huns went down but only, I think, as a means of escape. At the time of the second fight I was flying with one of our men whose name is F—— and who has been doing remarkably good work, having gotten seven Huns officially, in the past two months, two of them in one day, since we arrived in this sector. He has great nerve and audacity but takes a great many chances which would bring a less skilful man to grief. His great assets seem to be quickness of decision, getting to very close range, and then shooting with great accuracy.

On the occasion I speak of he was leading, and I wanted to watch him and see just what his methods were. We saw a number of Huns fooling around far in their own lines, and waited for some minutes for them to come out, but as they showed no inclination to come, we went in to see if we could not get a shot at them. There were about fourteen chasse machines in all, tri-plane Fokkers, Albatross, and Pfalz, three types of Hun single-seaters. F—— had a scrap with a couple of them and shot up one Fokker, which he saw go down in a spin almost to the ground. I did not get in it at first as I had to stay up to keep the rest of the army from going down on F——, but pretty soon I got a chance at a Pfalz, which got a bit off to one side of the others.

Fired about 15 shots when my gun stuck, but as it was I could not have fired any more shots to advantage anyhow, for the Hun went immediately onto his nose and then into a spin. Saw him go down this way for 1000 metres, but could not watch him further on account of the others which started after us in force. We asked confirmation on these Huns, but could get none, so I guess they did not crash, although if they did they may have been too far in their own lines to have been seen by our observers on the ground. We of course could not sail into the middle of an outfit like this, but you can often pick one off on the edge of a group and get away before the others can come to his assistance.

My other scrap was with a big Rumpler two-seater. I fired a hundred and fifty shots, and he about a hundred, I suppose. I hit him and had him about where I wanted him when some others came up and forced me to call it off. He went off smoking into his own lines, but did not go down. This makes nine fights now since I got my last official Hun. The machine-gun trouble has hindered me three or four times and knocked out a couple of the best chances, but one should be able to do better than this. My shooting has not been what it should be and I do not get close enough before beginning to fire.

May 25, 1918, Hopital de l'Ocean,
La Panne, Belgium.

I am really beginning to feel more like myself today, so am going to start on that promised letter. Not that I have been feeling very badly for I really have not, but the pain and inflammation in my knee has kept me rather tired and listless, so that it has seemed impossible to get up sufficient energy to do much writing.

I am very glad I sent you those cables at once for the only thing that I have seen in the papers about myself was incorrect and misleading. There was a notice in the Paris N.Y. *Herald* which said that my machine was seen to finally crash and that later I had been picked up in No Man's Land by a French patrol with a bullet through my leg. This would naturally give the impression that I was too seriously hurt to be able to help myself, so here is hoping you got one of my several cables in good time. I sent several through different channels on the chance that one might be delayed. I shall tell you from start to finish what happened, although you probably know most of it already.

On the morning of May 15th at about 9.30, Baker, Lieut. F—— and myself sallied forth, in response to a telephone call saying that there were a great many Huns on the lines and more of our machines were needed. We three were on the "alert" patrol for the morning and it is the duty of such a patrol to send out machines in response to special calls, etc. I was leading the party and when we got to the lines the Huns had evidently gone in, for there were none in sight except very far within their own lines. We cruised about for a while quite high up and F—— had to go in owing to motor trouble, leaving Baker and myself. I noticed a lone Boche two-seater sailing about in his own lines, but he was very low down and not in a good position to attack and I did not want to go down and lose all that altitude until we were sure the activity up above had quieted down. I mean the activity which had brought the telephone call, for we had certainly seen none ourselves to speak of. To go down from 4500 to 1000 metres and then have the Huns come along at the altitude you have just left, means that it will take you about fifteen minutes to get up to them again; and then, nine times out of ten, it is too late.

Accordingly, we took another turn about, and seeing nothing I went back to see if the lone two-seater was still there, and saw him still sailing around in wide circles, evidently regulating artillery fire. Also noticed a large white cloud just over the lines opposite and above the Hun, so I thought we might try to spring a little surprise on him. We dove down on our side of the cloud where he could not see us, flew along just above it until the Hun made a tura near the lines, when I ducked down through a hole and went for him. Unfortunately, he saw us coming, and when I was within 150 yards of him, up went his tail and he started diving full motor into his own country. I dove after him as fast as my bus would go and overhauled him a little but could not get to good close range; started shooting at about 100 yards range and the Boche commenced zigzagging as he dove. I got in about seventy-five shots, I suppose, and suddenly saw the machine-gunner apparently almost fall overboard, then throw up his arms and disappear in the fuselage.

Evidently he had gotten it even though the pilot had not. Just at this moment when I think with a few more shots I might have finished the whole outfit, my gun stuck, due to a defective cartridge and I had to give it up. I thought for a few minutes that the Hun might crash anyhow, but he pulled up just over some houses and very low down, for I could see his shadow on the ground close beside him as he dashed off out of sight into his own back areas. The scrap ended three or four miles in Hunland, and we got rather heavily "archied" coming out, but nothing close enough to be dangerous.

When we got back to our lines a few minutes' work sufficed to get my gun running again and we started up the lines in the direction of home, as our gasoline was getting low. Ten minutes after the first fight we were flying along inside our own lines, when I noticed a peculiar two-seater circling very low down between the trenches, he could not have been more than 600 metres up. I took him for an English infantry liaison machine, which he very much resembled, but then noticed that he seemed to circle into the Boche lines with remarkable impunity considering his very low altitude, so decided to investigate. Sure enough there were the old black crosses on him showing plainly as he swung almost under me in making a turn over our fines.

I said that this Hun was flying between the trenches as he was, but in this most terrible of all the battlefields that I have seen, you cannot distinguish the trenches from above, and in many places they consist simply of shell-holes joined together. The particular spot where we encountered this Hun is less than two miles from Oliver Chadwick's grave, so that from the pictures and descriptions I have already sent you, you know pretty much what the country is like. Very low and flat and the ground nothing but a conglomerate mass of shell-holes filled with water, and barbed wire. Here and there a wrecked concrete shelter or "pill box," and the shattered stumps of trees.

The only way that I knew that my friend was really a Hun was by his crosses, for it was the first Boche machine of the kind that I had ever seen, and indeed I have never heard of anyone that I know, running into one like it. He had a rounded body like some French machines, the tail was square and the lower wing much shorter than the upper, like many of the English two-seater observation planes. All the Hun two-seaters that I have ever seen or heard of before, have both the upper and lower wings approximately the same length. In addition to this it was the slowest bus you ever saw and I think I could go two miles to his one. All this leads me to believe that it was a new type of German armoured plane which they call "Junkers" and which I have read about in the aviation reports. They are built especially for this low infantry liaison work and are heavily armoured about the fuselage to protect them from fire from the ground. In consequence of their great weight they cannot go very high and are extremely slow.

This fellow must have been a squadron leader or something, for he had four big streamers attached to his wings, one on the top and another on the lower plane on each side. Perhaps, however, these may have merely been means of identification for the benefit of his own infantry, although it is very common for patrol leaders to carry such streamers so that their pilots may easily distinguish them from the other machines in the patrol. Personally I have a big blue band around the fuselage of my machine and also a blue nose, which serves the same purpose. Whether or not this fellow was what I think he was, I hope that when I am flying again I may see him or at least another like him and have another go at him. He certainly got the best of me, and I don't feel at all vindictive about it, as it was a perfectly fair fight, but just the same it would give me more satisfaction to bring that boy down than any five others. It would also be interesting to see whether his hide is thick enough to stand a good dose of armour-piercing bullets at short range. An incendiary bullet in his gas tank might also make his old boiler factory a warm place to fly in.

As soon as I was sure that the machine was really a Hun I dove down after him and made up my mind this time to get at good close range. I did, and ended up fifty yards directly behind his tail and slightly below, but I made one bad mistake, a real beginner's trick which was the cause of all my troubles. I evidently was not quite far enough below him and I had not fired more than one or two shots when I got caught in the back draught from his propeller, which joggled my machine about so that anything approaching accurate shooting became an impossibility. I saw one bullet go three feet to one side of him and another several feet on the other side, so stopped shooting for a second to get in better position.

Anyone with a little experience should know better than to get himself caught like this, especially myself, for I had the same thing happen with the first Hun I ever brought down. That time I dove down a little before shooting at all, and then fired from a good position a little lower down. Hence, when I found myself in the same trouble this time, I tried to remedy the situation in the same way, but in doing so I entirely failed, for the instant, to appreciate the very slow speed of the Hun. I was already close to him, and when I dove down and then pulled up to shoot, I found to my astonishment that I had overshot the mark and was almost directly under him, so much so that it was impossible to get my gun on him.

He started swerving from side to side to get me out from under him so that the machine-gunner could shoot, and I tried to stay under him, swerving as he did and at the same time slowing down my motor to the limit so as to try to let him get ahead of me enough to allow me to start shooting again. The Boche and I were at this time about twenty yards apart and if he had only had a trap-door in his bottom he might have brought me down by dropping a brick on my head. However, he did not need it. The Hun gave a twist which took me for an instant beyond the protection of his fuselage. It was only for a second or two, but that was sufficient for the observer, who proceeded to do the quickest and most accurate bit of shooting that I have yet run up against. As a rule in such a situation, you see the observer look over the side of his machine at you, and then swing his gun around on its pivot and point it in your direction. While he is doing this you have time to duck.

In this case, however, I saw a black-helmeted head appear over the edge of the Hun machine and almost at the same instant he fired, as quickly as you could snap-shoot with a pistol, or with a shot gun at a quail in the brush, for instance. In trying to slow down as much as possible I had gotten into almost a loss of speed, so that my machine did not perhaps answer to the controls as quickly as it otherwise would have. This, however, made no difference, for although I tried my best to swerve back under the Boche's body to get out of his line of fire, and in spite of the great quickness with which he shot, he was as accurate as he was quick and his very first shot came smashing through the front of my machine above the motor and caught me just on top of the left knee. It felt more like a crack on the leg from a fast-pitched baseball than anything else I know of except that there is also a sort of penetrating feeling one gets from a bullet.

How many more bullets hit the machine I don't know and never had a chance to find out, but my motor went dead at once, so that knocked out all chance of any further shots at the Boche. I dove under him out of his line of fire and then twisted sharply around and planed back for our own lines, trying to make the most of the little height I had. A glance at my gauges showed no pressure in the gas tank, and that together with the way in which the motor stopped made it quite obvious that the trouble was a severed pressure or main gasoline pipe. Now we carry a special little emergency tank which is operated by gravity and is for just such occasions. It will run ten or fifteen minutes, plenty of time to find a good landing place. I tried to turn it on but the little stop-cock would not budge, so I dropped my controls and letting the machine take care of itself for an instant, tried with both hands to move it. Still no effect; it had evidently also been put out of business by a bullet, probably the same which cut the main connections. It only took a few seconds to cover the distance to the ground, which could not have been more than three hundred yards after I had gotten turned in the right direction.

Kept working away until the last minute, trying to get the motor going, for everyone who knows this country also knows that it is utterly impossible to land any machine in it without crashing, let alone a Spad which requires at least as great speed for landing as any other type. All my efforts were useless, however, and I saw that there was nothing for it but to smash up as gracefully as possible. The thing that bothered me most, however, was not the smash, for that would probably only result in a little shaking up, but I thought I was further in the Hun lines than I was and had most unpleasant visions of spending the rest of the war in Germany, which is not at all my idea of a good time. If, however, it was No Man's Land where I was going down, I thought the Huns would probably turn their guns loose on my plane as soon as it crashed and that the best thing to do would be to get out and away from it as quickly as possible.

I held my machine off the ground as long as I could, with the double purpose of getting as far towards our own lines as possible and also so as to reduce my speed to a minimum before I touched the ground and the crash came. Braced myself inside my cockpit and tucked in my head like a blooming turtle in his shell. Just at the last moment I veered the plane a little to one side to avoid landing in the middle of a barbed wire entanglement and then the instant my wheels touched the ground, over my machine went in the middle of its back with a loud crash. As soon as it was over I unbuckled my belt and scrambling out lost no time in rolling into a nearby shell-hole.

I looked around, rather expecting to see a bunch of Huns running up to grab me but there was not a living soul in sight and the place seemed remarkably quiet. Twenty yards to one side was an old artillery observation post made of sand bags which looked as though it might make a fairly secure hiding place, so I decided to get there while the going was good, for I felt sure that it could not be long before things started to happen. I crawled towards this shelter as fast as I could go, trying always to keep out of sight in the shell-holes, rolling over the edges of the craters and half swimming, half wading through the water and muck with which they are filled.

On the way I passed a dilapidated lot of barbed wire. I suppose I reached the shelter in less than a minute after hitting the ground and just as I got there machine-guns seemed to open up all around. The Hun whom I had so unsuccessfully tried to bring down was flying overhead and I think shooting at the wreck of my machine, although I did not look to be sure. Then the Boche gunners in the trenches turned loose with a machine-gun or two on my plane and some of the English infantry began firing at the Hun plane to drive him off, while others, as I learned afterwards, fired at me, thinking that it was a Hun that had come down. The average infantryman, you know, does not know much about aviation, and sometimes finds it difficult to distinguish between his own planes and those of the enemy.

Altogether there was quite a rumpus, so I just lay low in my shelter, and as the bullets went singing by, was mighty glad I had a shelter to lie low in. The Boche plane was still flying around and I did not dare come out until he had gone for he would have seen me and potted me like a rat. While I waited I tore open my pants and had a look at my knee. It did not seem to amount to much—two or three holes as big as the end of your little finger and about a dozen little ones. It looked as though I had stopped a load of bird shot more than anything else. It bled very little, but I tied it up with my handkerchief anyhow to keep the mud and water out.

In less than five minutes after I had come down I heard the sound which I had been expecting and dreading, the whine of a Boche shell coming. The first one landed about a hundred yards over my plane but the line seemed to be perfect. I waited to see where the next one would go and the next five or six all landed in about the same place, perhaps seventy-five yards in front of me, but rather effectively cutting me off from the English trenches. They were all big ones (5.9 inch calibre) and came at perhaps 30-second intervals to start with, later they speeded up a bit and sent sometimes three or four over at the same time. They used high explosive, luckily for me, instead of shrapnel, but the H. E. makes a terrific commotion when it goes off and throws a column of mud and debris nearly a hundred yards in the air. Seems to have rather more bark than bite, however.

Pretty soon they began to come closer, and though I hated to leave my cosy shelter I decided to get moving again for if one of those boys had landed in my immediate vicinity, there is no doubt at all but that my shelter and I would have gone for a ride. It seemed just a question of time until this happened, so I took to crawling and swimming in shell-holes again. Stopped for a minute to rest in another little shelter, which was about the size of a chicken coop, and into which I could just fit myself by drawing my knees up under my chin. A couple of 5.9 shells went off just behind my little sand bag house, rocking it from side to side. This made crawling seem a very slow method of getting away, so decided to try running. Before my leg stiffened up it did not hurt much, but even so, with those big shells coming that close, I think I could give a pretty good imitation of running, without any legs at all.

While in the first shelter I had taken a good look at the sun and at the German and English lines of sausage balloons, so that I was fairly sure of my direction. Hence I waited until a shell had just burst and then got up and made a dash for it along the edge of a little old narrow gauge railway where the going was smoother. Had not gone far when a sniper's bullet cracked into a rail alongside of me and I heard the whiz of some more big shells coming. Down goes little Willie flat on his face in the ditch and *boom, boom, boom* went three of them just to one side. After their first long shots, the Hun artillery evidently got a couple of practically direct hits on my overturned machine, for they blew the wheels off, tore the wings from one side, and generally finished it, thereby making me exceedingly glad that I was no longer in it. After this they seemed to change their range again and began putting them back where the first ones had fallen and as I had by this time reached this spot they came much too close for. comfort. There was nothing for it but to get on as fast as possible, for crawling won't help you if one of these big fellows decides he wants to share your shell-hole.

I kept on running and crawling as opportunity offered and each

"IN FLANDERS FIELDS THE POPPIES BLOW."
Wreck of the machine shown, with the pilot's grave beside it.

A PORTION OF THE YPRES SECTOR.
Near the spot where the author was shot down on May 15, 1918. The ground shown is higher than that where the author came down, and the picture was taken after a dry spell. In the foreground are the remains of a trench after bombardment.

time I heard a shell coming dove head first into the nearest shell-hole. Am afraid my diving form was rather poor, for a Tommy told me later that they could see the splash I made all the way from their lines. But what is form among Allies? You can't imagine how the sound of a big one coming close makes you want to hug the mud in the bottom of any old hole that comes along. I guess I had the wind up all right (English for being scared) but then I am not used to this kind of war and I hope I shall never have to be. I struck two more lines of barbed wire entanglements which were in good condition and very thick.

I was afraid to stand up in full view of the Huns and try to climb over them, which would probably have only resulted in my getting completely tangled up, especially as I still had on my heavy fur-lined flying combination. Therefore in both cases I went under, rolling in each case into a big shell-hole, submerging up to my chin and swimming under, pushing the wire up with my hands as I went. Funny what one will think of in such a situation, but I had to laugh at myself as I remembered Bairnsfather's comic drawings, "The Better 'Ole" and "When do they feed the Sea Lion?" If you don't remember them, look them up in the collection of Bairnsfather drawings that I sent you by N—— and you will see what I mean. I don't think I ever really appreciated all there is in those drawings until then.

Finally I sat down in a shell-hole to take off my combination, for being soaking wet it weighed a ton and had me so all in I felt as though I could lug it no further. Just then I looked up and have never been so delighted in my life as when I saw half a dozen Tommies beckoning to me over a low parapet about fifty yards away. I was pretty well fed up with crawling and swimming by this time, so decided to cover that last fifty yards quickly, bullets or no bullets. Made a run for it and it is too bad someone did not have a stop-watch to take the time, for I think I was about two seconds flat. I fairly threw myself into that trench and then in an Irish brogue came the question, "Faith, and who are you?"

"I'm an American," says I, panting for breath, for I was a bit all in from running. This surprised them very much. Someone yelled over from another trench nearby to know if they had captured a Boche and one of the Tommies said, "Ay say Maitie, when you furst com down we was after thinkin' you was a bloody 'Un." They had been led astray by the different arrangement of the colours in the American cocarde, red, blue, and white reading from the outer circle in, instead of red, white, and blue, as in the French; and blue, white, and red, as in the English.

This trench where I ended up was an advanced post at the extreme end of a corner salient, so that my choice of direction was very lucky as it took me to the nearest possible friendly point. It was, however, completely isolated so that no one could go or come during the hours of daylight, and there was nothing for it but to wait until dark. I reached the trench about noon. The trench was manned by a platoon from an Irish regiment,[14] most of them from Ulster and, of course all volunteers, and a mighty good lot they were.

One of the stretcher bearers put some iodine and a bandage on my wound, and another fellow produced bread and butter with good hot Oxo soup, made on a little hard-alcohol stove. Cigarettes were plentiful and we settled down to an infantryman's day in the trenches for a change. The weather was beautiful, with a warm sun, and just a few fleecy clouds floating about. The Huns kept on for a while dropping 5.9's around the wreck of my poor machine, of which we could see a portion of a shattered wing from the trench, and then things subsided into what the men considered a rather quiet day.

There were no officers in the trench, the platoon being in charge of a couple of very intelligent and seemingly capable sergeants. We sat and chatted about the war and the affairs of the nations in general and every now and then someone would produce a cup of hot tea, cocoa, or coffee, with hard tack, bread, and butter and such knick-knacks. These men get their breakfast at 3.30 a. m., and then nothing comes near them again until 9.30 p. m., when it is dark enough to bring up supper, so naturally they take a lot of little odds and ends to spell them in between times. The trench was an open affair with no head protection except in one or two places where a piece of light sheet metal was thrown across, but this would of course stop nothing worse than a spent piece of shrapnel.

The Huns shelled our immediate vicinity very little except for four shells, the first of which fell a hundred yards away, the next fifty, and then two at about twenty-five yards on each side, straddling us. No one paid much attention to them; one or two of the men would look up, laugh and say, "Hey there, Jerry's wakin' up again." Several times we saw some Hun two-seaters in the distance and twice a patrol of single-seaters passed over, well up. Our "Archies" got after one patrol of four and split it all up so that I prayed that one of our own patrols might come along, for those four solitary Huns would have

---

14. Royal Irish Rifles.

made fine picking.

The English artillery was much more active and our own shells kept shrieking just above our heads all day long, for an hour or two in the afternoon becoming very lively indeed. We could watch the shells landing on the Hun trenches four or five hundred yards away, and throwing up great clouds of dirt and wreckage, and a most interesting and comforting sight it was.

Towards sundown the men began to get restless from the long hours of sitting in cramped positions, and commenced moving about in the trench, and showing their heads above the parapet in a way that seemed to be foolish. You may be sure that I did not show even the end of my nose, for having gotten that far I was taking no more chances than I had to. The sergeant cautioned them, but they did not pay much heed until suddenly "*crack*" and the dirt flew from the end of the parapet, where a sniper's bullet had landed. If it had been six inches higher a Tommy who was standing directly in line with it would have now been in Kingdom Come; but then this war is all "ifs" of that sort. This warning was luckily sufficient for pretty soon another bullet jostled a sand bag directly in front of where I was sitting.

After one more ineffectual try the sniper called it off, but the episode brought forth an anecdote from one of the men. He said that a year or so before he had been sitting in a trench when one of the men had carelessly shown his head. A sniper took a shot at him and missed by a couple of inches, to which the intended victim replied "Hey there, Jerry, missed me, didn't ye? 'ave another go at it" and stuck his head above the parapet again. Quick as a flash—*crack*—and a man next to him caught the foolhardy soldier as he fell with a ball squarely in the middle of his forehead. "Now," added the teller of this story, "that guy was just arsking for it and he got it. You guys there will get it too if you keeps on arskin, so help yourselves, but not me!" This was the wisdom of an old timer, and I think it was wisdom which many a soldier would do well to take to heart.

I had an interesting day with those fellows; they had seen a lot of service. Several of them had come over in 1914 and been at it ever since, many of them had been wounded, all the old timers seemed to have been. Finally as darkness began to fall an officer came on his rounds inquiring for "the missing airman," and I hobbled off across the duck boards after him, using an old pick handle as a cane, for my knee had grown very sore and stiff during the day. Our path was in plain view of the enemy trenches, but it was by this time too dusk for them to make us out so we were not disturbed.

A walk of four hundred yards brought us to company headquarters and there I had supper with three officers in their bomb-proof shelter. It reminded me more of a large dog kennel than anything else, and to negotiate the door it was necessary to crawl on all fours. The colonel had sent up word from battalion headquarters that he hoped that I would dine with him, but as the officers at company headquarters had also invited me I was glad to take the first meal available. The dugout where we ate served as a general dining-room for the officers and also as living quarters for two of them. It was perhaps three and a half feet high and certainly not more than eight by six feet in extent, but of course a vast improvement on what the men have. While on duty in the front lines they just flop down anywhere they can when it is not their turn on guard.

My day as an infantryman made me very glad to be in the aviation, but the peculiar part about it is that you will rarely if ever find a Tommy who envies us. I can't imagine anything much worse than the existence of these fellows with whom I spent the day in the front line trench. With nothing but an open trench to protect them, affording no place to rest or sleep, except by sitting on the bottom and leaning up against the side, and the trench necessarily so shallow from the nature of the ground that to stand upright meant exposing one's head and shoulders, they have to stick it there for stretches of a week at a time, and sometimes when there is an attack on and the reliefs are scarce, the sessions are much longer. The bottom of the trench is always full of water; the duck boards keep you out of it in dry weather, but when it is wet they are submerged. All day and night the shells fall around them, sometimes very thick, and again only at long intervals. If one lands in the trench or on the parapet, it of course means heavy casualties. The incautious showing of a head may bring a sniper's bullet or a burst of machine-gun fire at any minute.

The sergeant told me that he thought what made the men more "windy" than anything else in such an advanced post was the thought of being severely wounded and having to lie there all day before being able to get to a doctor. In a very serious case, where it meant life or death to get a man operated on at once, the stretcher bearers would of course chance it and take a patient in in full view of the Huns, but the sniping of stretcher bearers has become so common that this is only done when absolutely necessary. What a contrast to our cosy billets far in the rear, where we have nothing to fear when not flying other than an occasional bombing at night. Bad weather brings the hardest times of all to the infantry, while to the flying corps it means idleness in comfortable quarters. Nevertheless, the infantrymen will tell you every time that you earn your comforts and that you only fall once in an aeroplane, or words to like effect.

After supper with the company officers I crawled out of the dug-out and started on a walk of perhaps a half mile or more to the battalion headquarters, the nearest point to which an ambulance could come up. As we passed along the trench I noticed a couple of large fresh shell-holes that had blown in the edge of it, and my guide informed me that one of them had sent the company sergeant-major to Kingdom Come the night before.

By the time we were started across the duck-boards once more the last light had faded from the west and a brilliant moon in its first quarter lit up the whole scene. This country, as I have tried to describe it to you, is fantastic enough during the day, but by moonlight it becomes more so. Behind the trenches on both sides the sky is constantly lit up by the flashes of the guns, and their shells go whining overhead in weird fashion. It would not take much imagination to hear in them, the shrieks of the thousands of departed spirits, whose earthly carcasses are rotting in this same ground. The trenches themselves are lit every few seconds by star shells and there is a constant procession of signal lights and chains of luminous balls which look like those which come from the burst of a rocket. I do not know what they all mean except for certain kinds of chains of fiery balls which we call "flaming onions," and which I believe the Huns send up to guide their night-flying machines.

Every now and then there comes a burst of machinegun fire, from first one point and then another, as some gunner gets jumpy or thinks he sees something suspicious in the gloom of No Man's Land or the trenches beyond. The tracer bullets from the machine-guns make their contribution to the greatest display of fireworks imaginable. Above it all comes the throbbing of the motors of the night bombing planes of both sides as they cross the fines in search of their various objectives. Speaking of this, you may have noticed in the papers that the Huns have been again at their old tricks of bombing hospitals and been very successful at it, as they usually are at such work. As we trudged slowly along we passed reliefs coming up to take their turn in the trenches, stretchers loaded with hot suppers for the men, etc., etc., for those front lines in this flat country must be fed and supplied in the dark.

I could not help thinking of Andalusia with the same moon sparkling on the river, shining on the great white pillars of the house and throwing the shadows of the stately trees across the lawn on a peaceful spring evening. Quite a contrast to this wreck of Flanders.

Battalion headquarters reached at last. The doctor dressed my knee again and I went into the mess room, where I found the colonel. Headquarters proved to be a veritable mine, an intricate arrangement of corridors and rooms all sunk at least thirty feet below ground so as to be proof against the heaviest shells or bombs. Pumps were constantly working, drawing off the water, for otherwise such a place would be nothing but a well. The colonel produced a bottle of Scotch, for which I was very thankful, for I felt like a bracer. While I waited for the ambulance I told him what had happened and he seemed to think I had done well and been mighty lucky to get out of it, for it so happened that he had been in the front hues at the time I came down and had seen the whole show. He was most agreeable and we had a long talk, as the ambulance was a couple of hours in getting there. He was sending up one of his engineer officers to save anything he could from my machine and blow up the rest.

I discouraged this plan, for I recalled the sad experience of a French patrol which tried to reach a Hun machine that I brought down last month between the lines on the *Chemin des Dames*. I had had some eighty hours of flight out of my machine already, so it was about done anyway and not much of a loss, and the Hun artillery had pretty thoroughly finished what was left of it after the crash. We take great care not to mark on our maps anything on our side of the lines, so there was nothing the Huns could learn even if they did reach the wreck. Perhaps a few instruments, such as the compass and altimeter or even the machine-gun might have been saved, but to my mind the mere chance of this is not worth risking lives for. Needless to say, I had stopped for nothing once I hit the ground, but only lost an extra flying helmet and a pair of goggles, so far as my personal effects went.

I would like to emphasise again the kindness and cordiality which I have always met with at the hands of the English. This is the third time that I have been thrown upon their hospitality, and always with the same result. It has not been merely the officers but all ranks that have shown this spirit of fellowship. There was nothing that the men in the front trenches did not try to do for me. They were continually producing hot drinks, and insisted on sharing with me all the little comforts they had, and would hear of no refusal on my part. I learned that several of the men and two of the officers had volunteered to go out and bring me in out of No Man's Land in broad daylight. When I came in they were preparing to start. This meant leaving the comparative safety of their trenches, and taking a long chance of being killed on the possibility of being able to reach me, and bring me in, and would have required a large amount of nerve and self-sacrifice. For me it was a case of being "*between the devil and the deep sea*" and running one danger to escape a worse; but for them there was no such alternative.

As I have already told you, by the time I got to company headquarters I had two invitations to dinner and there was nothing for my comfort and assistance that these fellows did not think of. At last the ambulance arrived and proved to be one of Henry Ford's vintage. I was never so glad to see a "tin Lizzie" in my life, for I had had enough walking for the time being. Just as I piled in a poor fellow who had been gassed came staggering along, supported by two comrades. They propped him up in a corner of the ambulance and as we drove along in the darkness, for of course no lights can be shown, he sat there gurgling and gasping for breath, evidently in the greatest pain. Every now and then a spasm would strike him and it seemed as though he must choke to death. In spite of the modern masks, every time there is a bombardment with gas shells there are always a few men who get caught by it. The rotten stuff seems to lie for days in shell-holes and such places, and men will suddenly be affected when no gas has been sent over for a day or so. This is one form of war which the infantry has to face that, thank heaven, we are not troubled with.

We finally reached the ambulance headquarters about 3.30 a. m., and after getting an anti-tetanus injection I turned in on a cot for the rest of the night, just as day was breaking, for there was no ambulance going to the hospital until morning. My knee hurt too much to permit of sleep and there was a big British gun concealed in a woods nearby which kept pegging away, shaking the whole place at each discharge. This together with a lively bombardment going on further away, but which nevertheless sounded pretty close, would have made sleep an uncertain quantity anyhow for one accustomed to only more distant bombardments. Among the officers at this place were four American medical lieutenants who seemed like a very nice lot. I breakfasted with them and the English officers, among the latter a colonel, and felt rather ashamed of my sorry appearance.

I certainly looked more like a second-class soldier than an officer.

Since I have been acting as armament officer of the squadron I have taken to wearing a pair of enlisted men's breeches cut down to fit, for my work requires a certain amount of tinkering with machine-guns that plays havoc with one's uniform. Then the American tunic with its high, tight collar is almost impossible to fly in if one is to do any looking to the rear. Hence I wore simply a sweater over my army shirt, and have also stuck to my French *poilu* boots, the most comfortable and serviceable footwear I know. On the morning before, we had gone out unexpectedly, so that I had not had a chance to shave, and altogether in my torn breeches held together with a couple of safety pins, and the whole outfit caked with mud, I was indeed a sorry spectacle of an officer.

After sending off a cable to you I got an ambulance about 9 a. m. and started for a British casualty clearing station. I was sitting in front with the driver, and when about halfway there what should I see coming but one of the squadron light cars with Maj. T——, Hobey and M—— in it. I leaned out as we passed and yelled "Hey! Where are you going?" and when they saw who it was they all looked as though they had seen a ghost and nearly fell out of the car. The day before Hobey Baker had been unable to do much in the fight, owing to his having been out a little longer than I had and his gasoline being nearly all gone. He had seen me start down when the Hun shot me, and then smash up in No Man's Land. That afternoon they had gotten a report from the English that I had been seen to get out of the wreck and jump into a shell-hole and that a patrol would be sent out that night to try and find me. I had sent them a wireless the night before but it had not reached them, and when I tried to telephone had been unable to get them.

Not hearing from the English any report as to the result of the promised patrol they had naturally concluded that I had been killed or was at best a prisoner, more probably the former, and the major had sent in a report to headquarters that I was missing. I most sincerely hope that my cable reached you before this rumour got out. When I met them they were on their way to the front to see what news they could get of me, and as you may imagine they were a bit surprised when I yelled at them. We had a grand reunion and I think the people of the small village where we happened to meet thought that the American officers had gone crazy.

It *was* a bit dramatic. M—— and Hobey did not say much but both looked as though they were going to cry, and if I do say so myself, I think they were all glad to see me. The major offered to send me to any hospital I wanted, to Paris even; but as I knew this one to be so excellent, and near at hand, I asked to come here. I therefore left the English ambulance and went back to the squadron in the light car with the others, and then came directly here. At the squadron they were no less surprised to see me than the major, M—— and Hobey had been.

My knee was very painful and swollen, so I thought it best to take no chances, even though the wound did not on the surface look as though it amounted to much. I am glad I did, for an x-ray disclosed three fragments of the bullet lodged against the bone. They operated at once, and I think made a very good job of it. I did not remember that ether made you feel so sick. It is too bad there is no way of telling when one is going to get shot, so as not to have to take ether on top of a full meal.

May 27.

I have been writing this letter in instalments each day as I have had the chance, but it seems to have run on a great deal already, so I guess I had better bring it to a close and get it off. I asked the doctor the day before yesterday morning how much longer I should probably be here, and he said two weeks. I hope you will not be worried at my being in the hospital longer than I said in my cables that I should be. The wound has not proved much more than I at first thought, but the fact that the poisonous fragments of the bullet were in my knee for somewhat over twenty-four hours before they could be removed, has made it rather slower in healing than I had expected. I still exercise it three or four times daily, which is a nuisance, but has at least resulted in my now being able to bend my knee almost as far as the other.

The men from the squadron have brought me both good news and bad during the past few days. Of the former I am delighted to hear that Jim Hall is not dead but a prisoner and only slightly wounded. He has gone through so much and his luck has so wonderfully pulled him out of the fire before, that I almost felt it in my bones that it would not desert him this time. He is a great fellow and the Huns had better keep their eye on him or they will wake up some fine morning to find him back in France. When I spoke above of having been so badly dressed when I was shot down I had in mind also this very chance of being taken prisoner. When I was brought down I certainly looked like a soldier and had nothing with me to prove that I was an officer.

In my haste to get off I had even forgotten my pocketbook. This is a great mistake, and I shall not fly on the lines again without money in my pocket and enough uniform to prove my rank. If the Huns had caught me they would probably have had me cracking rocks behind the lines or going in for some other form of outdoor sport of this kind. Their treatment of prisoners is generally atrocious, but officers are evidently treated much better than the men, especially officers in the Flying Corps. Being an officer, one might as well have the benefit of this and then one could probably do something to better the condition of the men.

Have you noticed in the papers how Lieut. Fonck has been going? Forty-five officially now and with any luck he will easily beat Guynemer's record. He is a wonderful pilot and a perfectly marvellous shot, and seems to me to be easily the most skilful pursuit pilot that the war has produced so far. In all this time he has only gotten one bullet in his machine, and that through a wing. He never seems to get himself in a tight corner. I read with interest the clipping you sent me about him, for I know him, as he was in *Groupe do Combat* 12 when I was there.

June 2, 1918.

About a week ago the Hun long-range guns fired a few shells into this town, four of which exploded, the first doing practically all the damage. All the shells landed within three hundred yards of the hospital and it is most unpleasant, for one feels so helpless. I was lying in bed writing in the morning and heard the gun go off, but thought nothing of it, as the guns firing on the lines are plainly audible from here. A second or so later a big shell went screaming past the corner of the building, followed almost immediately by a loud explosion as it landed. This first shell struck squarely in the middle of a military laundry where a lot of women and young girls were busy washing and ironing soldiers' clothes. The result was about twenty-five killed and eighty wounded, the great majority women. I suppose the Huns are justified in firing into this town when one considers that there are a large number of troops quartered here; but just the same, it is one of the worst aspects of the war.

For an hour or more they were carrying by under the window of our room, a lot of poor women and girls all cut and covered with blood, and their cries were pitiful to hear. Outside the reception room there soon collected a crowd of weeping mothers and relatives, and it made your heart sick to see them. It is bad enough when the wounded are soldiers, for that is war; but when it comes to women, it seems like something worse than war. Granting that the Huns are justified in shelling this town now, one cannot but remember that it was they who started this hell on earth for their own ends. Forgiving and forgetting, with regard to such as they, is to my mind, as I have said before, not a sign of a Christian spirit but of pure weakness. If Christianity requires us to forgive them I am afraid that I am no Christian. We have no right to forget, and the memory of the millions who have died to defeat the Huns forbids that we should do so. When this war is won, it will have failed in one of its greatest purposes, if in the years to come the Huns are not made to pay in full, the penalty for their crimes, so that they may perhaps some day come to realise that it does not pay to be a beast. Do you wonder that so many wounded men are anxious to get at them again as soon as possible?

June 11, 1918.
Hopital de l'ocean, Vinckem, Belgium.

At last it is definitely decided that I am to leave this hospital tomorrow—just four weeks since I came here. When I came in I expected, as you know, to be laid up for only a short time; but knees seem to be very slow and contrary things with regard to getting well. Have been taking walks each day of a couple of miles, so you see I am all put together again. Major T—— is coming for me tomorrow to take me back to the squadron, stopping on the way at a French review, where a general is to confer decorations. Among the recipients of the *Croix de Guerre* will be several men from the squadron, of whom your angel child gets a cross with palm. This for making a darn fool of himself and letting a Hun shoot him, when if he had done as he should have, he ought to have plugged the Hun. It seems rather funny when one stops to think of it to get more credit for being shot down than you would for shooting down the other fellow.

Soon after writing my last letter to father, the whole hospital was evacuated from where we were on the sea, and we were moved some fifteen miles down the line. We are still about the same distance from the front and our sausage balloons are very plainly visible. As I was taking the air outside the hospital after supper a few evenings ago, a lone Hun came across the lines and shot down two of our balloons in flames. The evening before another one tried the same thing, at the same time, but missed the balloon, although he forced the observers to jump in their parachutes. The Boches were heavily "archied," but

LIEUTENANT RENE FONCK, THE ACE OF ACES,
IN FRONT OF HIS SPAD.

Lieutenant Fonck holds a cross cut from the machine of the Hun who was credited by the Germans with having shot Captain Guynemer. Shot down by Lieutenant Fonck three weeks after Captain Guynemer's death, near Poperinghe, Belgium.

got away safely both times, and I met a Belgian pilot[15] the other day who has brought down seven Hun balloons in flames in the past three weeks. You see, therefore, that ballooning is not such sure death as father seemed to think; true, they are more dangerous than attacking enemy machines, but, on the other hand, they are a great deal easier to get.

Another evening, a few days ago, I was taking a walk and saw something happen which I think must have occurred but a very few times during the war. The Boches were intermittently shelling one of our balloons with a big gun. They were coming fairly close, but the balloon kept changing its altitude to throw them off their range, and it is not often that a balloon is brought down by shell fire. They are too far behind the hues and the range is too elusive to make it pay. Both sides have rather given up shelling them, although they still occasionally indulge in the pastime. The evening in question I saw a shell burst a considerable distance above the balloon, and then as I watched another burst several minutes later and perhaps a hundred yards directly below. The balloon swung around and started skyward, at the same time drifting towards us in the light breeze.

The shell had cut the cable, a most remarkable piece of luck for the Huns when you consider that the range must have been at least eight miles. She had not gone far when two black dots dropped from the basket and then slowed up as their parachutes opened up. The observers came sailing down as their balloon went sailing away, getting higher and higher each minute. These captive balloons are equipped like free balloons with a safety-valve, etc., so that they can be brought quietly down by the observers in case they break away. These fellows evidently got frightened, however, and jumped as quickly as they could, without even stopping to open the safety valve. Naturally we don't want to lose a balloon with all the equipment in the basket, if it can be helped. A *chasse* machine was sent up from a nearby field and shot enough non-incendiary bullets into the gas bag to let it quietly down in our lines.

Perhaps a minute after the observers jumped, and as they were coming down side by side in their parachutes, the Huns took another pot at them, and the shell seemed to burst just between them, and very close; but, apparently, did no damage. It must be pretty poor fun to

---

15. Lieut. Coppens, who later became the Belgian ace of aces and at the end of the war had brought down about 35 German observation balloons, by far the largest number of balloons ever destroyed by one pilot.

be shot at while one is hanging to the end of a parachute in mid-air. The observer in such a situation is so utterly helpless that it has always seemed to me poor sport to shoot at him, but it has long been apparent that the Huns are devoid of all sporting instincts. If the Boches like this sort of thing I suppose we might as well give them a dose of their own medicine, and I think that the next time I go ballooning I may be tempted to pot the observer on his parachute. However, there is no use in trying to cross that bridge till we come to it. For one thing I shall be glad to leave tomorrow and that is so as to get away from the night bombing. The Huns have not hit this hospital yet, but they dropped one bomb a few nights ago within a hundred yards of it, and broke some windows, which is quite close enough.

This section seems to be a sort of highroad for them on their way to bomb other places, so that they are continually passing over at night and our "Archies" blazing away at them. One feels that they may let one go at any minute, and this keeps wounded men in a very nervous state, for they feel so helpless and with their wounds still fresh in their minds, they have no desire to collect any more or be blown to pieces in their beds. I do not think there is any worse side of the war or any dirtier trick than this bombing of hospitals. To illustrate the terrific power of a big bomb, I will tell you what happened several months ago in our more southern sector.

One night a large bomb fell squarely in the centre of a main road, a road with a solid foundation and paved with sturdy French cobblestones. Shortly afterwards an ambulance came along in the dark and ran into the hole. This was not a Ford ambulance, but a big French ambulance, larger than an ordinary big limousine car. Standing a little way off up the road the ambulance was not visible at all, being completely below the level of the road in the bomb hole. This will give you some idea of its size. One of our cars came along a while later and helped rescue the wounded men from the ambulance and take them to a hospital.

The other day I met the colonel who is in charge of this hospital walking in one of the corridors with Queen Elizabeth. I saluted as I passed them and then the colonel called me back and introduced me. The queen had evidently been surprised to see an American there and wanted to know what was the matter. She is most attractive and was very kind and considerate.

Next day I was standing in front of the hospital with a couple of British officers I know, when who should come up but the Prince of

Teck, the brother of Queen Mary of England. He is a brig.-general in the English army. He stopped and chatted for about five minutes and wanted to know what had happened to me. Now, of course, I do not mean to boast by telling you all this; but I just want you to realise the kind of a fellow I am, and appreciate the society in which I move. When I come home I don't know whether I shall be able to bring myself to associate with you ordinary folks or not!!

But "*sans blag*" I did stop and talk with the queen for about five minutes, or rather she stopped and talked with me. She started right off in English, so I did not have a chance to air my French on her. For future reference I might say that it is technique or etiquette or whatever you call it, when one is passing the time of day with royalty, to allow them to start the conversation. I spoke of having seen her last summer when she came with the king to *Groupe* 12, to confer decorations; but I don't think she understood me very well, for she looked at me in a blank sort of way, as if she thought my wound had affected my brain. I did not see the king this time. Both he and the queen seem to keep very busy, and do a great deal of good; they tell me the latter sometimes assists as a nurse in the operating room, and I know she goes very frequently to the hospitals.

There are a couple of English officers here in the hospital, one of them an observer of a British two-seater, who was shot in the leg a week ago while flying over Zeebrugge, taking pictures of the blocking ships sunk there. He did not have the luck I did, for the explosive bullet caught him above the ankle and exploded, almost tearing his leg off. He said he looked down and saw his foot turned around backwards, and then doubled up his knee to try and stop some of the bleeding. Fortunately his pilot was not hit, so was able to bring him right back and landed on the beach in front of the hospital. They had his leg off in half an hour after he landed. This boy's spirit is something wonderful, and you would think he had lost a ten cent piece instead of his right leg about six inches below the knee. He seems about twenty years old, and is a very attractive fellow.

He is, I think, the most cheerful man in the ward, and to hear him talk he seems to be looking forward with great amusement to trying to learn to walk properly with an artificial leg. He is keen to get a Belgian leg, as he hears they are lighter and much better than any of the others, and with this he says he thinks he can do about everything, except that he has his doubts about being able to dance. Even this man with his leg just off and not sewed up yet, is made to exercise his knee and hip-joints six times a day, so as not to have his muscles stiffen up. It is wonderful what this exercising seems to do. As you may imagine, however, it is rather heroic treatment, not only during the actual exercising but afterwards, for the movement starts all the cut muscles to aching, and it takes them quite a while to quiet down, just about in time for the next exercise. This Englishman had received a release to go back to England and finish his course in medicine, the same day he was hurt, but refused it.

50 Rue Bassano, Paris, June 17, 1918.

I finally got out of the hospital on the 12th, and after getting decorated (some hero, eh what? Yah! Ha!!) went back to the squadron. That evening a patrol was going out so I borrowed a machine and went along to see if the lines were still there. There was not a great deal going on. I was not leading the patrol, but was bringing up the rear as an extra man, for I was feeling a bit seedy still and did not want to have to stay through the whole patrol if I did not feel like it. Saw one chance to jump three Hun single-seaters but waited for a minute to let the leader of our patrol start things; he evidently did not see them, and then it was too late. We make it a hard and fast rule that other members of a patrol shall let the leader start a fight in his own way; for if two or three try to start it, each according to his own ideas, everything gets balled up.

A little later I saw what I took to be a Hun two-seater and thought I might be able to take it out on him for what one of his pals did to me on May 15th. Was behind the patrol by myself at the time so did not have to bother about the leader. Started to dive down after him and got myself all "het up" over the prospect, only to discover when I got nearer that he was an Englishman.

I felt a little queer and out of practice on the lines. After laying off for a month I think it takes a couple of flights to get one's hand in again. In climbing into the machine I strained my knee a little, and when I came back it had swelled up considerably, so I thought I had better go easy for a while, as I have no desire to spend any more time in the hospital. I therefore packed up and came to Paris the next day, bringing all my things with me, as I am not going back to the Lafayette. I was to go out as C. O. of a new squadron, but upon arriving here found that they had not been able to wait until I was in shape for active duty, so had given it to another man. I believe I am down to take the next squadron formed, and had expected to go back to the

Lafayette again the end of this week and fly with them until further orders came. However, orders came this morning, relieving me from duty with the Lafayette and directing me to report to Headquarters in a few days. I shall therefore leave Paris the end of this week, and will let you know when I find out what I am to be given to do.

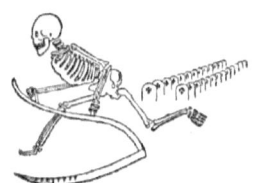

"Death the Great Reaper"
The Insignia of 13th Aero Squadron, A. E. F.[1]

Chapter 4

13th Aero Squadron, A. E. F.

Paris, June 22nd, 1918.

Just a line as I am in rather a rush and have not got a great deal of news for you anyhow, Paris being a much less fertile place for news than the front.

I have been made Commanding Officer of the 13th Aero Sqdn., a new *chasse* squadron being formed. Am lucky in being equipped with French Spads, the machine which I have always flown at the front, and which I prefer to all others. The machines are of the latest type, carrying two machine-guns, and should be very good if we have any luck with the motors and I can get some first-class mechanics. Have been rushing around here in Paris for the past few days finding out about my squadron equipment. Have most of the machines already and am going to a field near Paris this afternoon to try out a couple of them. The bodies of the machines are very strongly built and I have been to the factory, where I went over with the builders some weak points which had gradually developed at the front.

I was much encouraged to find that they knew of all these faults and had corrected them by reinforcing and changing the construction. I don't want to have any of my men losing his wings nor, in fact, would I care to lose my own. These planes are, I think, the strongest chasse machines made, and it is a great comfort to a pilot to feel that he has this extra strength in his machine in case he gets in a tight place and has to put his plane to unusual strains.

Tomorrow I go to headquarters near the American front to see about my personnel and pilots and shall then probably return to Paris

---

1. Copied from author's plane. Nicks in the blade of the scythe indicate individual pilots' victories; gravestones show combined victories of the squadron up to October 22, 1918, when the author left it.

Porte Super baby taxiing on the water

within a week to see further about equipment. I am very glad to get this squadron, as it will be fun getting it organised and then later on trying out at the front my ideas of the best chasse methods. There is much organisation work to be done, however, and I shall consider myself lucky if I can have the men flying on the lines a month from now. You see, therefore, that I shall be out of active flying for a month and by that time should be in perfect condition for anything. Indeed, I have been getting along so well that I am in good condition now. My knee is still a little weak if I should try to run, for instance, but beyond that I hardly notice it.

Paris, June 30, 1918.

Since last writing you I have been out to the American front[2], where we shall soon be flying, and am now in Paris again, making final arrangements about the machines, equipment, and pilots for my squadron. I flew down last Sunday and it is a long trip, as far as the old journey from Paris to Dunkirk. M—— has been assigned to my squadron and will be one of the flight commanders. I am getting two other men who have had some experience at the front, to act as the other two flight commanders. Three experienced men is the least number one can get along with in a squadron. This makes fifteen perfectly green men in the squadron; but we must do this, having so few experienced pilots. I intend to bend all my energies at first to keeping these fellows from going too strong and getting themselves killed before they know enough; to be able to protect themselves. I don't care if the squadron does not bring down many Huns for the first month or two, if the pilots can keep out of serious trouble and learn the game. If they can do this, I think they will in the end accomplish much more. Am glad to say that our sector is a fairly quiet one, and thus a very favourable place to train new men.

As to the question of my coming home, I am afraid that is impossible, for several reasons. I read carefully what you said about it, but you are wrong on some of your information. The French do not take their men away from the front after six months; and, in fact, a pilot's greatest efficiency is not reached until he has been there longer than that, for he really cannot learn the game in less than six months at the front. There have been one or two remarkable exceptions, perhaps; but I think it usually takes considerably more than six months. Take some of the great French pilots as an example of service at the front: Guyne-

---

2. Region of Toul.

mer was there two and a half years; Fonck has been at it for more than two years and so has Deullin, and I could mention many others.

Toul, July 26, 1918.

It is not long after daylight and I am sitting on the flying field in my combination waiting for a telephone call notifying us that some Fritzie has ventured across the lines, and needs attention. As a rule the C. O. escapes this rather tiresome business, which is taken care of by the other members of the squadron, but being short of experienced pilots, I am for the present myself acting as a flight commander until one of the other men has had sufficient experience to relieve me. Don't like the idea of a lot of green pilots flying on the lines without an old pilot to lead them.

We have not had much excitement as yet. The second day of active work on the lines one of my patrols ran onto a lone two-seater, got some shots at him, and he was officially confirmed as down before they got back to the field. Unfortunately for us, however, further reports came in a couple of days later that he had not gone down at all but had pulled up, after falling in a *vrille* to within a couple of hundred metres of the ground. His spin was just the old trick to escape, and after the patrol passed on he came back on the fines again, so that washed out that Boche.

The next day I was myself leading a patrol and spotted a single two-seater under us just over the lines. I attacked and one of the other men with me. Fired a hundred rounds at less than 100 yards range and the Hun went off smoking like a Christmas pudding from the place where his gas tank should be and I thought he was going to take fire. He did not, however, but pulled up close to the ground and then was seen to land in a field behind his own fines. This was the first fight I had had since being wounded, and found myself very rusty, after my two months' lay-off. The Hun manoeuvred well and I had considerable difficulty keeping myself covered by his tail, but should certainly have had him at that. I had not been able to get the necessary fittings for my own sight, so had nothing but an emergency sight to which I am not accustomed, and of which I had had to leave the regulation to the armourers, owing to many other things keeping me busy. I had trouble in lining these sights up and was much slower in shooting than I should have been.

Once when I thought I did have it on him noticed my tracer bullets going over the Hun's head. Upon returning to the field I tested my guns and sights on the target and found them to be six feet out. Moral—never let anyone else regulate your sights, a moral which I already fully appreciated and have always followed and shall certainly never stray from again. Have not had another shot since, as we have been having some bad, windy weather, but this cannot last and I am hoping soon to get even for my experience of May 15th.

The squadron is coming along pretty well, and I now have my full quota of pilots, and we are making regular patrols. In the fight the other day when I did not get that two-seater, two of the new men got separated from the patrol and lost themselves, finally landing far to the South. This in spite of all my talking about the importance of studying the map, and that before allowing any new pilot to go on the Hues, we have taken them around the whole sector a couple of times, well behind the lines, so that they could get their bearings. They finally got back all right without breaking anything, and I have now instituted a class in the geography of the sector for them and another man, who got lost and broke his machine in landing. Have told them that they don't fly until they can pass my examination—one of them flunked last night. Am doing the same thing for all new pilots coming to the squadron. This business of getting lost and having forced landings in consequence, is too expensive both in pilots and machines and is usually the result of pure carelessness or bone-headedness. The men are all anxious to fly, so I think they will soon learn their lesson in geography.

The new American pilots coming to the front are very encouraging, for they are as a whole a very nice lot of boys, keen, and anxious to get some Huns. There are, of course, some mediocre specimens, but they are the exception and the average is much better than among the French pilots with whom I trained, both in skill and morale. I do not mean this at all as a criticism of the French, for a comparison of our men when we are just entering the war, and still have all our best to draw upon, with the French material after four years of war, when the majority of their best young men have been killed, would be distinctly unfair. The trouble is to keep our men from going too strong at first and getting themselves into trouble before they have had sufficient experience to be able to protect themselves.

You will be glad to hear that we are insisting on team work and the patrols sticking together, and are discouraging the great tendency for one man to try to dash off by himself and be a hero at the expense of the whole. Any man who leaves a patrol for such a purpose will be put on the ground for a couple of weeks and confined to camp, and if he repeats the performance I shall send him to the rear. I think the sticking together plan will give better results in the long run and certainly less losses, and after all this is the combination that we are after.

I had a thrill a couple of weeks ago when I sent a new man up for his first ride in a Spad. In getting off the field, which is rather rough, he bumped a bit and bent an axle so that the wheel was at an angle of about 45 degrees, with the axle almost touching the ground. I knew that if he bounced at all when he landed the wheel would probably snap off or that the axle would at least catch in the ground and throw the machine over. As it was his first trip he would probably land fast so as to be sure not to lose his speed too soon, and I had visions of seeing him turn over at sixty miles an hour. I said goodbye to that new machine and only hoped that the pilot would not be killed or seriously injured.

There is almost nothing one can do to prevent such an accident once a machine gets up with a bad wheel, except stand on the side lines and hope for the best. While this man was flying around the field I sent a man out with a spare wheel to wave it at him in the hope that he would catch on to the fact that there was something wrong with his wheel and land as slowly as possible. Also sent for the doctor and the ambulance, got a stretcher ready and had men out on the field with fire extinguishers. A cold-blooded performance, perhaps, but I thought we might as well be ready for anything.

Luck was with us, however, and the pilot as he passed over the field saw the man waving the spare wheel and realised for the first time that something must be wrong. When flying your lower wings prevent you from seeing any part of the landing carriage. I held my breath when the plane came down to land but if the pilot had been flying for five years and had tried a thousand times he could not have made a softer landing. The bad axle held and the plane rolled along and stopped as though there was nothing at all the matter.

Toul, August 6th, 1918.

Here I have gone and let my letter-writing interval increase to ten days again, but without making too many excuses I do seem to have very little time to myself. What with trying to instruct these new men and also run the squadron, keep the planes in condition, etc., time does not hang at all heavily on my hands.

Have had a few scraps since last writing and, as I wrote you, I at first found myself rather rusty, but did better in the last one. One fight with a two-seater on July 31st resulted in some long-range shooting, but he was too far in his own lines, and saw me too soon, to allow me to get to close quarters, so nothing happened.

On the morning of the first I had two of my new men out, and we ran across four Fokker bi-planes. They are a new Hun single-seater chasse machine. We had the altitude and I put my patrol in the sun in the hope of being able to surprise them, but they saw us before we got within shooting distance. I tackled one and one of the new men another, while the third man of my patrol stayed up to protect the rear according to orders. I fired at rather long range and did not go in very close, for I caught sight of my companion chasing one Boche down below the others, forgetting entirely in his zeal that it is a good idea to watch one's tail. I accordingly laid off to try and watch him, but finally ended in losing sight of him in the heavy mist, and by that time it was too late to continue after the other Huns. I think they must have been a green bunch like ourselves, for they manoeuvred badly and one of them dove madly for home the instant he saw us, as though he was scared to death.

I did catch sight of one of them going down for a thousand metres in a vertical nose dive. The boy who followed the Hun down too low got some good close shots at him and was not bothered by the others, who were evidently afraid to follow him with the other man and myself still above them. The infantry reported the fight and said that two of the Huns were still going down vertically on their noses at 500 metres from the ground when they lost sight of them in the mist. As the fight took place at 4,000 metres I think those Huns must have at least been a bit scared, for a man does not dive 3,500 metres on his nose for the fun of the thing. It was impossible to see, however, whether or not they crashed, and on account of the mist and our being three or four miles in the Boche lines no confirmation could be obtained.

In the afternoon I was out again, this time with three of the new men. We were at 5,000 metres and had gone into the Hun lines to escort some of our bigger planes home from a long-distance day-bombing expedition. Nothing happened but a lot of "Archies," and we had just left the big machines after bringing them back into our lines, when I spotted three little black specks in the distance far within the Boche territory. They had evidently been following our bombers. I never thought we could catch them and they were too far in to pick a fight, which would be the first any of my patrol had ever had. I followed them anyhow to see where they would go and we chased along far behind them with the sun directly in our backs.

We must have been fifteen kilometres over the lines where the Huns were not expecting trouble and with the sun behind us they never noticed us at all. This business of flying far in the enemy territory would be dangerous for new men in a sector like Flanders and would not pay, but in this quiet sector if one has sufficient altitude it is safe enough. As you know, my motto is "*safety first*," particularly with the new men. After we had followed these Huns east for a couple of minutes they turned south towards the lines and I turned after them, trying always to keep the patrol directly between them and the sun. Diving slightly and with our motors almost wide open we overhauled them rapidly and by the time they reached their own lines we were only about 500 yards behind and above them.

Up to this time they evidently had not seen us, for they naturally expected trouble least of all from behind them in their own lines, and a machine behind you and above and in the sun is the hardest of all to see. Suddenly they saw us, each Hun did a *renversement*, and all three dove under us back into their own territory. I dove on one and gave him a burst as he passed under me, which apparently came very close, then did a *renversement* and dropped on the tail of another. Then my old machine-gun hoodoo started again. The first guns which I had on my new machine loaded with ordinary bullets had worked beautifully, but I had been hoping to get a balloon so had mounted an extra size balloon gun on one side and filled the other gun with nothing but incendiary ammunition, not so reliable a combination, but the only thing for balloons, as ordinary armour-piercing and tracer ammunition will not set them on fire.

These Boches were Albatross single-seater *chasse* planes and certainly were a good-looking lot with their greenish camouflaged wings and tails, and bodies made of bright yellow laminated wood. I fired a few more shots and then just as we had succeeded in separating one Hun from his companions and turning him to one side, I got the best chance that I have had since coming to the front. One of my patrol had also fired at a couple of the Huns and had had machine-gun trouble, and I saw him flying along beside a Boche not thirty metres from him, just as if they were doing a friendly patrol together. Each was making little nervous movements, as though he did not know exactly what to do, and I learned later that my man had been trying to fix his guns.

The Boche was evidently busy watching him and did not notice me as I slipped up behind him, and I made up my mind that this time I would take my time and make sure of him. Got within about forty yards and laid my sights very carefully in the middle of the pilot's back, pressed both triggers and not a single shot did I get out of either gun. One gun had stopped just as I stopped shooting the time before, so that I did not notice it, and I thought I had cleared the stoppage in the other. Don't think I have ever been much madder or more disappointed, and as on a former occasion, I guess I said some things Mother never taught me in Sunday-school. I was so close to that Hun that it seemed as if one might almost bring him down with a brick.

I started in to try to fix my guns for another shot and was behind the Boche and within easy range of him for at least a half minute while I worked with them. One gun was beyond repair as the band of cartridges had broken, but I managed to get the other one going again. It had not been working well, shooting only half a dozen shots and then stopping, so I tried to get very close and make my shots count. Twice I came down on his tail and gave it to him at forty or fifty yards, getting a few shots out of my gun each time, the Boche at the same time doing a *renversement*. Once I had to pull to one side to prevent running into him, and several times I saw my incendiary bullets go into his machine. It is a wonder he did not take fire. Each time I looked above and behind me I saw my Spads circling overhead, so I decided to try to stick to my friend until I got him. Once he fell several hundred yards apparently out of control and I thought I had him, but he went into a spiral again, as though he had regained control of his machine, so I kept after him and managed to clear the stoppage in my gun for, I think, the fourth time.

The Boche kept spiralling down and I after him, really too close, for I could not bring my gun to bear. We kept this up while we went down a thousand metres or more. Finally I let him get a little further away and was then able to drop on his tail again. Just as I was firing at him for the last time there came the "*clack, clack, clack*" of machine-guns close at hand and I felt several bullets hit my machine. Looking up I discovered another Hun who had come down behind my left wing to within forty metres without my ever seeing him. He had a hard right-angle shot but did pretty well at that, putting two bullets through one of my wings, one of which split an interplane strut and half severed a control, and two others through the body of my machine a little behind my seat.

They did no damage, however, beyond necessitating putting on a new wing before I could fly my plane again. I ducked so quickly that I fell into a *vrille*, but came out after making one turn, as I had no desire to get both Huns over my head. I dodged around for perhaps half a minute, all three of us within 100 metres, fixed my gun again and thought that if I could get a good shot at one of them and put him out of business or scare him off, I could then have an even thing of it with the other or get away if necessary. One's natural tendency to dive straight for home in such a situation is about the worst thing one could do, as it gives the other man just the chance he wants, that is, to dive directly behind and rake you in a straightaway shot.

I manoeuvred with these Huns to keep out of their line of fire and succeeded in doing so as the one I had been attacking was too sick to have much fight left in him. Then as I watched the Hun behind me, a third appeared diving down on my back, and I thought the only thing to do was to get out and run for home, as I do not fancy mixing it up with three of them low down and considerably in their own fines, when two out of the three have the jump on you. The Boche below and in front of me was in no position to shoot, so I did a *renversement* and dove under the two who were coming down from the rear, having first succeeded in getting a lucky burst into one of them, then as they passed over my head and lost me for an instant under their wings, did another *renversement* so as to head for home, and dove for our lines with my motor wide open.

By the time the Huns located me again I had a head start of three hundred yards and no Boche machine can catch one such as those we have when diving slightly with the motor wide open. One of them did some long-range shooting but came nowhere near me and I came home flying in zigzags with all the speed I could muster. That is the first time I have ever been caught by surprise and I hope the last. Don't imagine it happened because I am not in good condition or anything like that, as I was never more wide-awake. It was simply a case of being interested in the Boche in front of me and relying too much upon the rest of my patrol. They did their best and are very good men, but it is extremely difficult for a new man to follow a fast fight going on below him, especially if the planes are diving at high speed as I and that Boche were.

The show started at 5,000 metres and I ended up at 2,000; the rest of my patrol lost track of me during the fight and I never saw them again until we got back to our field. Then, again, the Hun who sur-

HUN-HUNTING WITH THE CAMERA

Photograph taken at 17,000 feet by a Belgian photographic machine. Note the Hun single-seater pursuit plane (Albatross type) at the left of the picture in the angle made by the cross-roads. It was flying about 3,000 feet below the Belgian machine when the picture was taken.

prised me came down just behind one of my wings, where I could not see him. It is fine to surprise the other fellow, but no fun at all when you are the one caught napping. At first I thought the two who attacked me when I was after the third Hun were the same that we had at first attacked, but from later developments it seems that they may have been two others. I was so busy getting away at the end of the fight that I had no time to see what happened to the Huns, and reported on coming back that I could not tell whether any of them went down or not. Next day in comes a report from an observation post that two of them crashed and both have been officially confirmed.

You asked me in your last letter how many I now have officially. This makes only four, as I have not had one confirmed since April 12, in spite of a number of fights and one machine-gunner of a two-seater that I shot the same day I was brought down. Was beginning to think I had forgotten how to shoot entirely, but getting these two makes me feel much better about being myself shot up by them, and also about May 15th. The other members of our patrol who took an active part in the fight will share in the confirmations, it being impossible to be sure who fired the shots which brought these Huns down. I was very glad, as you may imagine, to have had a hand in getting the squadron's first two official Huns.

Toul, August 7th, 1918.

I think the Boche aviation in this sector had a right lively day on August 1st. In the morning, just after my patrol had attacked the four Fokkers, the two that we did not shoot at ran into another patrol from one of the other squadrons in the group. This other patrol was led by a very good pilot named E—— with whom I used to be in the Lafayette. On this occasion he had two green men with him and he chased those two Huns almost to their own field, twenty-five kilometres behind the Boche lines. When he got back there he saw a Hun two-seater flying around at 600 metres near his own field, so dove down under his tail and gave it to him. E—— had too much speed as I did on May 15th and overshot the Boche, so he climbed up over him again and to his astonishment saw that there was no one in the machine-gunner's cockpit.

This was almost too good to be true, so E proceeded to sit on the Boche's tail at 30 yards' range and riddle him, the pilot being, of course, helpless so far as shooting was concerned. That poor Hun was evidently up simply trying out his motor in the security of his own back areas and had not bothered to take his gunner with him. E——finally shot him at only 150 metres' altitude and close to his own field where he crashed head first into the ground a complete wreck. In the meantime, however, one of the Fokkers had separated, and as the man was perfectly green and close to the ground miles behind the Boche lines, he was in a bad way. Luckily E—— saw his predicament, and although all his own ammunition was gone he dove down on the Fokker's back and scared him off so that the new man got away. Altogether a mighty fine piece of work on E——'s part.

Another patrol the same morning chased a Hun almost home and forced him to land in a wheatfield. They then proceeded to machine-gun some German hangars from a couple of hundred feet in broad daylight. Ticklish work, but it certainly does make the Huns nervous never to know when they are safe.

This is about all the news I have to give you. The weather has been poor, so that I have only been out once since August 1st. Went out at daylight then and flew over a *"coup de main"* being made by the American troops. The clouds were very low and kept us down between 200 and 300 metres, so that we had a wonderful view of the whole show; in fact I have never had a better look at a battlefield under heavy shell fire. The area covered was very small, but it was lively enough while it lasted. Behind us as we flew above the fines were the hundreds of brilliant flashes from our own artillery and beneath us and in front the shells breaking continuously on the German trenches and back areas.

Occasionally an ammunition dump would flare up and a small woods seemed to be veritably alive with bursting shells. At our low altitude the *"départs"*[3] and *"arrivés"*[4] were very loud and clear and we could at times hear the rattle of the machine-guns on the ground. Our observation balloons were hanging just below the heavy drifting clouds and the whole effect in the semi-darkness of the dawn was indeed picturesque. We saw no enemy planes at all, and the only excitement consisted in being shot at by our own infantry, which came about in this wise.

The sector which we had to cover was very short, only four or five miles long, so that we were continually passing backward and forward over the same ground. Each time we passed the point of a small woods, a burst of machine-gun fire on the ground was distinctly audible. No tracer bullets were used, so that it was not possible to see just what

---

3. Discharge of a camion.
4. Explosion of a shell.

they were shooting at, but it sounded very much to me as though we were the targets. A machine-gun fired up toward you makes a different sound from one fired along the ground at the enemy. We were so low, however, that one could hardly believe that the Infantry could fail to recognize us as their own planes.

As the machine-gun fire continued to break out each time we flew by the little woods I became convinced that they were firing at us and accordingly avoided this particular spot. Tried my best to locate the guns but they were too well concealed. I was mad enough to dive down and give them a dose of their own medicine, which might perhaps teach them to look before they shoot. Our green divisions in line for the first time are woefully ignorant of the Air Service and one continually hears of the "doughboys" complaining that they never see any planes with stars on their wings. I suppose they have seen the star insignia in the pictures in the magazines and on the war posters and do not know that this insignia has never been used on the front. We have always used the round *cocarde* like the French and English, except for the different arrangement of the colours. There is nothing more important than a proper understanding of the aviation on the part of the ground forces and *vice versa*, and a good liaison system between the two. The Huns seem to be way ahead of any of the Allies on this and it is about time we appreciated its importance.

Sure enough, when we returned to our field and examined our machines, three out of the four of us who had been on the patrol had from two to four bullet holes in his wings and tail. If the machine-gunners who fired at us had not been very poor shots they should have been able to bring us down, for we were flying back and forth only two hundred yards over their heads for about an hour. Later in the day a regular army lieutenant-colonel in the Air Service came to see me about it, saying that he had been in the front lines observing the attack and that the machine-guns which shot us up had been just to one side of him. He had sat there and watched them shoot because he also had thought that we were Huns.

Now our machines do not look anything like a Hun machine to one at all familiar with them, and one would think that by the tune an officer had risen to the rank of Lieutenant-Colonel in the Air Service it would have crossed his mind that it might be a good idea for him to study his own planes sufficiently to know what they look like. I have since been wondering what, believing us to be Huns, they thought our idea was in flying over their heads for an hour without ever attempting to fire a shot.

The Air Service is unfortunately burdened with a few regular officers who have done very little war flying on the front, but who fail to appreciate their lack of practical experience. I admit that they have not had much opportunity to gain experience, and a West Point training will not teach a man much about how an air patrol on the lines should be conducted. What one does object to, however, is the refusal of some of these officers to take advice from men who do know the game and to learn something about it in this way. There is one man of whom I am thinking who is a most glaring example of this smallminded type. He has under his command several men of long service on the front, men with fine records who have had more experience in air fighting than anyone in the American army, yet when these men attempt suggestions in a most friendly and loyal way to him as their commanding officer, he makes it very evident that their ideas are not wanted and that they are to understand that he and not they are running the organisation.

This attitude is entirely uncalled for, as the suggestions are made without the slightest intimation of any desire on the part of those making them to controvert his authority or to take credit to themselves for their ideas. This man also fails entirely to appreciate that an officer can make his subordinates realise that he means what he says without being unnecessarily disagreeable to them and thus making real co-operation impossible. The best officer and the one whose orders are never questioned is the one whose men love and admire him instead of fearing him. And the best soldiers do not really fear any officer, anyhow, and obey the bulldozing type only out of respect for his position as their commander and not from any respect or fear of the man. My friend might do pretty well as the commanding officer of some unit where unruly soldiers were sent for disciplinary purposes, but as the commander of an Air Service unit on the front he is mighty poor.

I do not mean this as a general criticism of the regular army officer in the Air Service, for there are some exceptionally good broadminded men among them who are just the opposite of the type I have attempted to describe.

Toul, August 15, 1918.

One of the patrols from the squadron which was out early this morning had a lively fight with four Fokkers and incidentally got one of them. The man who did most of the work is a new pilot named D—— who had as yet had very little experience and had never been in a real hot scrap before. In the fight this morning he first drove one Fokker off his flight commander's tail, thus extricating his companion from a very serious position. He then attacked another Hun at long range and finally still a third, this time at very close quarters. This last opponent seems to have been a very good pilot, for as they went at each other, head on, he put four bullets through one of D——s wings, one in his radiator and another half shot away a strut. Then the Hun swung around behind him and fired a bullet through his mirror. The mirror is designed to assist in seeing behind one and in a Spad is only about six inches from the pilot's face.

The next bullet cut the support of the mirror and blew it overboard, while still another creased his helmet. D—— said he was scared to death, but he certainly did not let that interfere with his determination to see the show through. With his plane riddled, water squirting over his feet from his punctured radiator and the motor heating up as a result, that youngster chased that Hun far into his own lines until he finally got him only 600 yards from the ground, and brought the Boche down in flames. One could not ask for a better exhibition of nerve and grit; you cannot realise how disconcerting it is to have bullets go smashing through your plane close beside you, especially to a new man. I know that when I first started in, I would have run for home under the same circumstances and would probably do so now. When D—— landed on the field after the fight he was naturally a bit excited. He came running over to me and said: "Gee, Captain! When that Hun broke my mirror and threw glass all over me, it for some reason made me so damn mad that I made up my mind I was going to get him." And he sure did. That boy deserves a lot of credit and I shall do my best to see that he gets it.[4]

Toul, Aug. 23, 1918.

I wish our mail came with something like regularity and I guess you are thinking the same thing about my letters if the service home is as poor as it is coming over. I get letters in a large batch about once every three weeks or a month and nothing at all in between. There is no comparison at all between our service and the French, but still I guess we have no cause to complain if we finally get our letters, for

---

4. D—— was awarded the American Distinguished Service Cross for the above exploit.

it must be a terrific job trying to get our men and supplies over. The news one gets in the papers these days is certainly good, and it really begins to look as though the Hun is pretty nearly finished as an offensive power. Is it not wonderful the way the entire aspect of the war has changed during the past couple of months? As I have so often said before, it is still a long way to the end, but it is a great thing to have it in sight.

There is nothing much new to tell you about this week aside from my experience with my fifth Hun, about the most interesting from my point of view that I have yet had. The squadron is going along about as usual and things seem to be turning out fairly well. I have some very good men whom I think will develop into first-class Boche getters. One of my men has had to quit due to heart trouble, as he fainted one day while playing baseball and I found out that he had fainted once before in the air but had said nothing about it. I got Col. N——, (an expert) to examine him and he said he should never fly on the front, so I am sending him off with a recommendation that he be used as an instructor on the ground. To allow him to fly would not be fair, in my opinion, either to the man himself or to the men who fly with him and must rely upon him. The man has had the same trouble for years and that he was ever passed for the Air Service is remarkable.

I will tell you something about that Rumpler two-seater I brought down last Friday morning, for it was in many ways very amusing. For about four days previous there had been a Hun coming over the camp high up every morning between 5.15 and 6 o'clock, evidently taking pictures and looking around to see what was going on behind our lines. He always got away safely as there was no one up there at that time and before anyone could leave the ground and climb up to him he would be home again. The "Archies" used to wake us up shooting at him. I thought I would go up early and lay for him, and accordingly got myself out of bed at 3.30 on Friday morning and took off at crack of dawn about 4.45.

For this sort of work I prefer to be alone, for one then has so much better chance of effecting a surprise attack and there is no chance of being caught unawares oneself by a bunch of Hun single-seaters. Climbed up to 5,600 metres and waited for Mr. Boche, remaining far within our lines so as to let him come in without scaring him off. I hung around for about an hour without seeing a thing and was beginning to cuss my luck for having picked the one morning when the Boche would not come over, when I saw far in the distance toward the lines the white puffs from our "Archie" shells. Then I made out the Hun among them, a tiny black speck on the horizon.

As soon as I saw him I turned around and flew off in the other direction, so as to get out of his way and let him come in, and also so as to put myself in the sun where he could not see me. I waited five or ten minutes while he kept sailing along into our lines, all the while gradually approaching him so that the sun was in his eyes. Finally he began to turn as though he thought he had gone far enough so I went after him, but his position was such that I could not keep my place in the sun while attacking him and he saw me before I got very close. He was only about 4,500 metres up, so by diving I overhauled him very quickly and went down under his tail with all the speed I could muster. The pilot manoeuvred very well and I had a hard time to keep myself covered, but managed to get in close and gave him a burst until I had to turn away to keep from running into him.

The pilot told me afterward that he heard the observer yell when I shot so I suppose I must have hit him. The machine appeared hard hit and for a minute I thought he was going down, so laid off and waited to see what would happen, as we were so far within our lines that I had ample time for another attack if necessary. We flew along for a minute or two, the observer firing a few scattered shots at long range, and then the pilot started for his own lines again. I went after him once more and coming up under his tail gave him a good burst at short range; when I stopped shooting I suppose we were ten or fifteen yards apart. This time I did better, for I got the observer in the stomach, shot the band of cartridges on his gun so it would not work, shot the synchronizing gear on the pilot's gun so that it was out of commission, and another bullet stopped the motor. I pulled away when I got too close and watched again to see what would happen, but even then the pilot tried to plane back to his own lines.

The observer had stopped shooting and I noticed his gun sticking straight up in the air, so thought he must be knocked out. There was lots of time and I climbed up over the Hun where I could look down in the observer's cockpit. There seemed to be no one there so I went down and gave him another dose, this time getting the pilot in the shoulder. By this time we were down to 2,000 metres and the pilot seeing that he could not possibly get back to his own lines, gave up and planed back into ours. I sat on his tail a couple of hundred yards away and watched him, for although it would have been an easy matter to have gone in and shot down the now defenceless Hun, it did not seem worth while when it was quite evident that he could not possibly escape. I thought at the time that it would be much nicer to get the machine intact if possible rather than simply a wreck.

We were right beside a river[5] which ran down a little valley with quite high hills on either side. By the river was a broad green field, smooth as a prepared golf course, and the Boche made for this. He just missed some telegraph wires and then made an absolutely perfect landing without so much as a bounce. I was afraid he would try to set his machine on fire or run away, so kept circling over his head, prepared to give it to him if he tried any tricks. For several minutes no one got out of the machine, and I thought both men must be knocked out, but pretty soon the pilot jumped down and I saw him standing by the tail of his machine. It seemed perfect ages before anyone came, and I fired my guns once or twice to attract attention.

Finally I saw some French soldiers running to the plane, and then a crowd quickly began to gather around it. I went down and landed a few hundred yards away and then turned and rolled back on the ground. Just before I got to the Boche plane there was a stone sticking up out of the ground about eight inches, grown over with grass, which I failed to notice, and I think it was almost the only stone in the whole field. Anyhow I hit it and caved in one of my wheels, which allowed a wing to touch the ground and snapped off several ribs. This was a bit disgusting, but I wanted to see that Boche, so stopped my motor and hopped out.

A great crowd of soldiers and civilians came dashing across the field and in the centre, between a couple of *gendarmes*, was the Boche pilot. He was a little short stocky fellow and had his coat off, with some blood soaking through his shirt. Surrounded as he was by a crowd of Frenchmen who looked none too friendly, but rather as though they would like to string him up, and rather pale from the scare he had just had, he was looking pretty miserable and downhearted. I could not help feeling sorry for him, so smiled and held out my hand. He just beamed all over and shook hands with a will. Tried both French and English on him, but it was no go, as he could not understand any better than I could his German. "*Nicht gobble-gobble,*" said he, or something that sounded like it, but the "*nicht*" was the only word I could make out. Then the *gendarmes* took him off to get his wound dressed and lock him up. The wound was a mere scratch and did not penetrate more than half an inch.

---

5. The Moselle.

By this time people had begun to come from everywhere and the place looked like the exit from a football game, the crowd was so large. I walked over to the German machine and they had just taken the observer out of his cockpit and laid him on the ground. Some of the Frenchmen told me he was dying, and he breathed his last just as I walked up. He was a fine big strapping fellow, twenty-one years old, and looked like a gentleman. It gave me a queer feeling to stand there and look at that dead boy whom I had never seen before, stretched out with two or three of my bullets through his stomach, his fast-glazing eyes staring wide open and that nasty yellow look just coming over his face. It is nice to get them down on our side of the lines where one can get the machine, but on the other hand, even though you know perfectly well that you have killed a man, it seems less personal if you do not see him. They are Huns and I will without hesitation kill as many as I can, for it has to be done, but, just the same, they are human beings, and one cannot help remembering that they have a mother somewhere who will be wondering what has happened to them.

I have got a little parachute to which I am attaching a note giving the names of the men and a short statement of what happened to them, and this I shall drop over the German lines the first clear day. Lieut. Putnam brought down another two-seater in our lines a couple of days ago, and we are going to combine on the note. His machine came down in flames, however, so that there was almost nothing left but the motor, but by giving them the motor number they will, of course, know who the men were. The Hun aviation in this sector is very good about doing the same thing and sending us information about any of our men who are lost, so the least we can do is to reciprocate.

As I was standing there a *gendarme* went through the dead observer's pockets but did not find much except a pair of eye-glasses and a half-empty flask of whiskey. The former he gave to me and I have them. Inside the case was the man's name, "Lt. Groschel." The pilot's name was Johann Eichner and I enclose his card. Please keep it as a souvenir. The long word under his name is not an address but is the German for "Air pilot."

The Hun machine was absolutely intact except for about thirty bullet holes in various parts of its anatomy, which did not at all spoil its appearance, but made it unfit for flying. He had quite a few holes in his wings, a sign of inaccurate shooting, but once when I was very close to him he turned and dove quickly and I got into the back wash from his propeller. This threw my machine about, and as I had both guns going at the time I sprayed bullets all over the sky. The pictures which I am enclosing will give you a much better idea of a Boche two-seater than anything I could write.

Toul, Sept. 1, 1918.

I am writing twice in succession to you, as this letter is more or less of a continuation of my last, so please explain to Mother and tell her not to get jealous.

To take up the thread of my letter of last week about where I left off, after looking the Boche plane over and getting the *gendarmes* to put a guard on both it and my own so that the crowd would not tear them to pieces for souvenirs, I walked up to a nearby village[6] to telephone to the squadron. Finally got them and told them to send over some mechanics with a truck and trailer, so as to repair my machine and also take the Boche machine apart and cart it back to camp. After telephoning I went with a friendly *gendarme* to the house of one of his friends, and they provided me with some very welcome coffee and cheese and crackers, for I was beginning to feel a bit empty after my early start. While I was getting this breakfast, a very pretty little daughter of the house, aged about six, came shyly in, holding to her mother's skirts, and presented me with a beautiful little bouquet of fresh roses which she had just picked for me. The roses were set off by sprigs of some other sort of a flower with which I am not familiar. I enclose a bit of it for Mother's benefit. So you see I still get along all right with the children, and also with the old folks, as will appear later on in this story.

After breakfasting I walked back with my *gendarme* friend to the field where the planes were, and you never saw such a crowd in your life. Pretty soon the major who commands the group arrived and then a number of pilots from the squadron, together with mechanics. Then a French general put in an appearance and made me stand up in front of the Boche plane with my flowers in my hand while he took my picture. I felt awfully foolish during this procedure with about three thousand people looking on, but you will see from the enclosed photo what a sweet and girlish smile I managed to assume. Don't you think it goes well with the flowers? I was going to put the flowers out of sight somewhere, but suddenly remembered that the little girl had come down to the field with her mother and was standing there in

---

6. Bouxières-aux-Dames, about five miles north of Nancy.

the crowd looking at me, so I was afraid it might hurt her feelings if I did not keep the flowers. I therefore stood there with my posies like some June bride, looking as self-conscious as I felt.

It was fortunate that the general was there, however, for the *gendarmes* had orders not to allow any picture-taking, but the general changed all that and one of my sergeants got a lot of good ones.

After my mechanics had put a new wheel on my machine and repaired the broken wing-tip, I flew back to our field, leaving them to take the Rumpler to pieces and load it on the trailer. This they did, and the whole caboodle reached camp that afternoon. I think the crew of my plane had the time of their lives that day. On the way back to camp they had to pass through a very large town[7] and the sergeant in charge of my crew sat up in the cockpit of the German machine and rode through the streets as though he were Napoleon himself. Then after we had removed some things from the plane here at camp, the colonel in command of the "Wing" ordered it set up on exhibition in the public square of a nearby town.[8] My crew again did the work and seemed to enjoy it immensely.

We got all kinds of souvenirs from that Boche, and one of the enclosed pictures shows my photographer-sergeant sitting among some of them. The camera was a beauty with large Zeiss lenses of the finest grade. I wanted very much to keep it for Uncle J———, as he could have gotten splendid pictures with it. These lenses are too expensive for most private individuals to buy. It so happens, however, that such lenses are needed in our own service, for the Germans can make better ones than any of the Allies. I therefore had to turn the camera over to our technical department, but hope some day to get it back.

At the extreme left of the same picture is the Hun observer's map, the dark line on it being some of his gore. The map I turned over to the intelligence department, but expect to get it back before long. All the other things in the picture I am keeping in addition to a couple of splendid undamaged machine-guns and a lot of Boche ammunition. A few days ago the enlisted men of the squadron presented me with a very handsome cane made from the laminated wood of the German propeller, and beautifully inlaid with pieces of the brass gasoline tank. Of all the souvenirs, however, I think the pictures are probably the best.

The next day Major D——— and I, together with a pilot from one

---

7. Nancy
8. Toul.

of the squadrons who spoke German, went to the headquarters of the French Army in this sector to see the German pilot. He seemed all right and had his coat on over his wounded arm, so that you would never have known he had been touched. Through an interpreter we had a long talk with him; he was very communicative and told us many things that we wanted to know. He seemed thankful to have escaped with his life and was anxious to answer my questions, for I think he realised that after I had knocked out his observer I could have killed him if I had wanted to.

He even went so far as to tell us the unit to which he belonged, the number of machines in his squadron, and to show us on the map the location of his aerodrome. He may, of course, have been lying about these, particularly the latter, for no man with any sand at all would give away the position of his field. In all the other answers he gave, however, I think he was sincere, for his responses were much too promptly and freely given to have been false, and he did not speak at all like a man who was lying. He was not an officer, but he was by no means stupid, quite the contrary, but even so I don't think he was cleverer enough to make up all the things he told us. One thing he wanted to know was whether pilots captured by the Allies were as well treated as our pilots who landed in Germany. He said that the officer pilots captured were sent to a camp near to and very like the camp to which they send their own pilots when they are in need of a rest. They are comfortably housed, have good meals with meat twice a day and are allowed to go and come as they please so long as they give their word not to attempt to escape and report back at night.

This again, of course, may have been an exaggeration[9] in order to try to get good treatment for himself, but even if it was true, I guess the joker in the pack was the *proviso* about not attempting to escape, for few men would care to give their word on this for more than a very limited period. The Boche also told us that the German pilots were very well fed but that the men in the trenches had a miserable time of it in this respect. We did not get around to asking him about the civilian population. With regard to our combat he said it would have been a different story had he had his old observer with him, that it was Lt. Groschel's first trip across the lines and he had not shot at me very much. It was small comfort to him, I think, when we told him that his observer's gun had been put out of commission at the beginning of the fight and that, therefore, he could hardly be blamed

---

9. From reports of prisoners since received, it was certainly a false statement.

for not shooting more than he did.

One interesting thing we found in the Hun plane was a small, innocent-looking iron box about the size and shape of an ordinary brick. It was screwed to the floor of the observer's cockpit. Printed on the top of the box in German were the words "Beware. Danger of death." One of the words was "*Vorsicht*," which I remembered as having been painted on the cases of caps which exploded in that Admiralty case we had in the office. At first we never noticed the thing, it was so small and inconspicuous, until a French major pointed it out. We then cautiously removed it and brought it back to camp. I gave orders that it be put away carefully in a safe place, for it should have been turned over to the Ordnance Department. Unfortunately the man to whom I gave the orders misunderstood me and thought I said I wanted it done away with.

In my absence, therefore, they took it out in a field and tied it to a tree, fastened a rope to the small handle on top of the box after unfastening the safety wire which held this down, then pulled the handle out and ran. Just five minutes later that little infernal machine went off with a report like an ordinary aerial bomb. It blew a hole in the ground a foot deep by three feet across and cut down the tree to which it was tied and another small one beside it. The trees were eight and four inches in diameter respectively and of solid live wood. The Boche pilot told us that all German machines except the single-seaters now carry these bombs so as to destroy the plane in case of a forced landing in enemy territory. He had not pulled the handle because he was not sure that his observer was dead and he could not get him out of the machine by himself. I had heard of these things before but had never seen one.

I remember hearing of one case where a Hun plane was forced to land in Belgium. The pilot and observer got out and walked off to one side surrounded by soldiers, but never said anything about having released the fuse of the bomb. A lot of Belgian soldiers gathered about the machine and the bomb went off, killing a large number of them. Whereupon the other soldiers promptly slaughtered the two Huns.

The Boche pilot went on to say that he did not like American pilots, for he had been shot down in flames by two of them about the middle of last May. Luckily for him he was able to land his machine and jump out before she burned up. Two weeks before, about the first of May, he got some bullets in his motor which put it out of business, but as he had lots of height he was able to glide well into his own lines and land safely. His last encounter when I brought him down on Aug. 16th was, therefore, his third experience at being brought down. He said he had been flying for five years and I believe him, for he certainly handled his machine well and had his observer not been knocked out at the beginning, he would have given him some good shots at me. Eichner said he had almost finished his term of service at the front, and in three weeks would have been sent to the rear as an instructor. Pretty rum luck to get knocked down just at the end like that.

This Boche was so communicative that we wished very much that we could have had more time to talk to him. The circumstances under which we questioned him were very unfavourable for getting the most out of him. He was in a small room with four American and three French officers, being continually plied with questions by them. If we could have taken him somewhere, given him a good dinner and a few drinks, and then gotten to swapping yarns in a friendly way about the war instead of firing a lot of direct questions at him, I think he would have told us everything he knew about Germany. He seemed more worried about not having anything to shave or brush his hair with than anything else.

Also he had, the night before he was brought down, given his observer a hundred *marks* to buy him a flask of whiskey, which had only cost four *marks*. He wanted to know if the change had been found on the observer's body, for he did not have much cash with him to see him through till the end of the war. I felt like giving him some, but thought the guard would probably take it from him, and then also a Hun is not entitled to many favours, so I gave him a package of cigarettes and called it square at that. He seemed pleased, said he thought the captain (being me) seemed like a pretty nice sort of a fellow, and wanted to know my name, so we exchanged cards and I have already sent you his. The one I gave him had "Andalusia, Pa.," on it so if he calls on you after the war do not be surprised. Unfortunately the pilot who acted as interpreter and who could read German script was drowned a few days ago while bathing in a creek near by. I enclose you the leaves from the note-book which you sent me for Xmas, on which Eichner wrote his name and address as well as that of his observer. The rest of it says that he was brought down in combat but only slightly wounded, while the observer was killed. He wrote this with the idea that I would drop his note over the lines, but I shall drop a copy.

Had a hot scrap with another Rumpler the other day and we only lost him by the hardest kind of luck. The flight was the most disappointing and at the same time the most extraordinary encounter I have ever been mixed up in. Have no time to write you about it now but will save it for my next. The gist of it was that I drove a Rumpler two-seater from 5,500 to 50 metres, four miles inside our lines, shot the observer's gun away from him, and then when I had him lashed to the mast had to let him get away because the belt in one gun broke and I had fired all the cartridges out of the other in driving him down. For ten minutes I manoeuvred around him without being able to fire a shot, but trying to run him into a tree or a house or hoping that someone on the ground would come along and bring him down with a brick.

P. S.—Forgot to tell you what I referred to above when I said I still got along with the old folks as well as the children. When I went back to the field where the German plane was, an effusive middle-aged French lady grabbed my hand and insisted on kissing it, before the whole crowd, much to my confusion. These poor people do not know the difference between a photographic and reconnaissance plane such as the Rumpler and the night bombing machines. The region where my Hun came down had been very heavily bombed, so the civilians look upon anyone who brings down a Hun as their deliverer from torment. I tell you all this to show you that I am still quite a man with the ladies, provided they are under the age of twelve or more than about forty-five. In between these ages I seem to be about as hopeless as ever.

Toul, September 20th, 1918.

Many happy returns of the day, even though it will be a month late when you get it. It really begins to look as though we shall be able to celebrate your next birthday together, for I think the old Boche is beginning to get a bit worried by the constant hammering the Allies are now giving him from one end of the front to the other. This is only a line to let you know that I am well and flourishing, for I have been and still am so busy that extensive letter-writing is well-nigh impossible. We have had a big week and the squadron has done some good work, although I am sorry to say that we have also had a hard knock and lost too many men. In three days—September 13th-15th—we shot down officially eight German machines, all single-seater fighting planes. In the same time, however, we ourselves lost six men, two of them being among my best pilots and one particularly as valuable a

Observer's cockpit and machine-gun of machine shown facing page 242. Note how the cartridge-belt has been broken by a bullet, thus putting the gun out of action.

pilot and as fine a man as there was in the squadron.

It makes me sick at heart to see these boys go, especially when I know that all but perhaps one or two of our losses were entirely unnecessary and should never have occurred. In the American aviation it is the same as in the infantry, the great trouble is that the new men will get carried away with themselves in a combat and go too strong. I have talked and preached and harped on the importance of care ever since the formation of the squadron, but it seems that the only thing which makes most men remember is bitter experience. When a man has seen his friends shot down around him or has been nearly killed himself a few times, he begins to realise what he may get himself in for and thinks twice before he takes wild chances which do not pay. These fellows we lost had plenty of nerve, but as I said before some of them went too strong and others evidently got separated from the formation in the course of a combat, and then instead of returning to our lines at once, fooled around by themselves in the German lines trying to pick up the rest of the patrol. There were plenty of Huns about and I suppose my men must have fallen in with superior numbers and been overwhelmed.

Of the six I myself saw one shot down in the course of a fight in which we brought down two Huns and in the same fight I saw another of my men following a Boche far into his own lines at only about 100 metres altitude. I was afraid he would get himself into trouble and tried to watch him, at the same time endeavouring to get the patrol together, for we had become very much scattered during the fight. It happened, however, that I was flying an extra plane without any distinguishing marks on it, while my own machine was being repaired. It was, therefore, difficult for the other men to recognize me, and being unable to collect them I went in by myself to watch the man who was still chasing a Hun just above the tree tops. He followed him fifteen kilometres into the German lines and then I saw him attacked by two Fokkers and manoeuvring very well to protect himself. I dove to help him and would have been in plenty of time had my motor not stopped, owing to some dirt in the gas line. This forced me to pull up for several seconds, but I got her going again and dove down over the fight as fast as I could go, but by the time I had come from 2,000 to 600 metres altitude the Huns had shot my man's motor and forced him to land.

There were lots of Boche about and as we were on the far side of one of their balloons and the machine-guns and "Archies" on the ground were making it pretty hot for me I had to pull out. I tried to get a shot at the two Huns, but before I could come up with them they flew back toward their own aerodrome, which was only a short distance from where the fight took place, and there was nothing more I could do then, but to my dying day I shall feel that I should have been able to save that boy. Perhaps not, but just the same I am afraid I hesitated an instant too long. I could not see him get out of his machine, so perhaps he was wounded. I only hope he was not killed.[10] He was certainly conscious when he landed, for he brought his machine down very well and although it went up on its nose as though a wheel had rolled into a hole, it was not even going fast enough to turn over.

Still another man was caught by surprise by a gang of Huns whom the two other men who were with him saw and were able to get away from. He was a flight commander and an excellent pilot and why he was surprised with all the warning he had, I cannot guess.

The other three men none of us saw even attacked, and what happened to them no one knows; they just did not come back.[11]

We have orders now to attack Hun observation balloons whenever possible and to burn them up, or at least force the Huns to pull them down. During a patrol the other day I noticed one balloon very clearly, and at the end of the patrol went down to take a shot at it. My guns were not equipped with incendiary ammunition at the time, but on each patrol we have some pilot whose guns are loaded for balloons. Before going out I had told the men that we would attack balloons if we saw any up, and accordingly dove down on this one to show the pilot who was loaded for balloons that I wanted him to attack it.

---

10. This pilot had a most remarkable escape. The motor, body, and wings of his plane were riddled with bullets and he himself got several through his clothes but was unwounded. He was made prisoner and returned after the signing of the armistice.
11. Of these three men one got lost in the course of a fight among some clouds and was forced to land in the German lines, while another had his motor fail him when he was attempting to save the man to whose assistance the author also tried to go, as described above. The result was that he too was forced to land in enemy territory and was taken prisoner. The third pilot mentioned earlier in these letters as D—— and as having brought down a Hun machine in flames after his own plane had been riddled, was shot down with one bullet through his leg and with his right arm practically torn off above the elbow by an explosive bullet. He fainted in the air, but recovered consciousness sufficiently to partly right his machine before it crashed to the ground. By great good fortune he was not killed, and after spending two months in a German hospital, where his arm was amputated, returned after the signing of the armistice.

As we dove down on the balloon I opened fire at three or four hundred yards range, much farther than I would have if I had hoped to be able to set it on fire myself. Having only armour-piercing and tracer ammunition, however, I knew that this was practically impossible, and shot more to point out the balloon to my companion than for anything else. The Huns did not pull the balloon down nearly as fast as usual when they saw us coming, and several anti-aircraft machine-guns opened up on us when we were still twelve hundred yards above them. As I was diving I noticed one in particular shooting at me, and the incendiary ammunition which they use makes the gun appear at long range something like a huge watering-pot spraying its contents up toward you.

When I first opened fire I aimed directly for the balloon without allowing for the fall of my bullets at long range, and noticed the stream of shots passing just under the edge of the gas-bag and about into the observer's basket. Two of us fired perhaps three hundred and fifty rounds into that sausage, but we only shot a lot of holes in it and nothing happened, for the man who had the balloon ammunition did not see it at all. Then we started back for our lines, about eight miles away, and I never before have run into such hot anti-aircraft fire. There must have been a dozen machine-guns firing at us from every possible angle, and it seemed as though the Huns had turned loose every "Archie" gun in the sector. We flew along for what seemed an age in a perfect cloud of shell-bursts, ducking and diving this way and that to throw the gunners off their range, but every way one turned it seemed as though a shell would go off in front and others on each side. Being only five or six hundred yards from the ground, the machine-guns could be plainly heard, and these, mingled with the explosions of the bursting shells, made quite a rumpus. It certainly is remarkable, though, how much shooting can be done without hitting anything, for none of our planes was so much as touched by either the machine-guns or the "Archies."

The most peculiar part of the whole thing, however, was that with two planes right on top of that balloon shooting it full of holes, the observers did not jump out in their parachutes. I do not believe that any observer in his sober senses would stick to his basket under such circumstances, and at first thought that my shots which I saw apparently going into the basket must have hit the observers. Upon thinking it over, however, I am inclined to believe that the whole thing was a trap. I have heard of decoy balloons about which are placed particularly strong anti-aircraft defences. In such cases the ranges and angles of fire are very carefully worked out ahead of time, the idea being to decoy enemy planes to attack the balloon, and thus get them down within good range of the guns. Such a decoy of course carries no observers. If this is what we ran into, the decoy worked first-rate, but I can't say so much for the men behind the guns.

Balloons seem to be my hoodoo and it does not look as if I should ever get one. Each chance I have had my guns have either jammed or I have had no incendiary ammunition. Then I load up with incendiaries, go out and run into some Hun planes. The incendiary bullets then jam or make so much smoke I can hardly see the Hun and this makes me mad, so that I get rid of the incendiaries again, and so it goes.

Captain Deullin, of N. 73, came around to the squadron and had dinner with me the other evening. I have also dined with him once or twice and he is now in command of *Groupe de Chasse* 19 of the French Aviation. We got talking over the old days when we were in Flanders a year ago, and he told me a most amusing sequel to a fight which I remember he had there.

He was out by himself one day, flying very high, a considerable distance inside the Boche lines, east of Ypres. He ran across a formation of half a dozen Albatross scouts, and being above them, tried to dive down and pick one of them off. There was one Hun in particular who had his machine very gaudily painted up in red and yellow and all the colours of the rainbow, whom Deullin tried to shoot. This Hun would deliberately fly up under him, offering an apparently good chance, but as soon as Deullin would start to dive down on him he would begin side-slipping and doing *renversements* down into the middle of his companions who kept circling in close formation just below him.

This was, of course, nothing but the old Hun trick of trying to decoy an enemy down into the middle of a group of their machines, so that they could all jump on him, but Deullin is too old a hand to fall for any stuff like that. He tried for fifteen minutes to get that brightly coloured Hun but could never get a decent shot at him and said that he was without exception the most skilful German pilot that he had ever run across. Finally he had to give it up, as his supply of gasoline was getting low, so he started back to his own lines, the Huns following along below and behind him. On the way he ran across a solitary Albatross, took him by surprise, and shot him down in flames.

Six months later, when Deullin was down on the Soissons sector, he heard that a well known German ace had been brought down slightly wounded, in the French lines. As Deullin speaks German, he thought it might be interesting to talk to the Hun, so he went over to see him. He asked him how long he had been flying in the Soissons sector, and the Hun said that he had only been there a little while, as his squadron had always been stationed in Flanders. Deullin told him that he also had been in Flanders, suggested that they might have met up there, and then told him the story about his fight. He mentioned the peculiar way in which the brightly coloured Albatross had been painted, and the time and place at which the fight took place. The Hun smiled and said: "Why, yes, that was I. I remember that very well." Deullin then said: "And did you see that Albatross of yours that I shot down in flames, just after our fight?" To which the Hun replied: "Yes, I saw him; didn't he burn nicely?"

P. S.—I was mixed up in one or two of the fights this week but do not think my shooting had anything to do with bringing down any of the Huns, so they do not count for me personally.

Belrain,[12] Sept. 29, 1918.

Once again I am sending you just a line after an interval of ten days, to let you know that I am well. We have been going through a period of the toughest fighting I have ever experienced since I have been on the front, but I think the old Boches have been having a still tougher time than we have. I am sorry to say that the squadron has had still further losses, although we have managed to keep our victories ahead of the losses. On the 26th[13] I lost two new men who had come out to replace some of those lost in the first offensive. You cannot guess how I hate to put these new boys into the hardest kind of fighting, while they are still so totally inexperienced that they do not know how to properly protect themselves. One knows perfectly well when one sends them out that some of them are going to be killed, whereas, if they could be given a little preliminary experience in a quiet sector, they would have a much better chance and would individually probably accomplish a great deal more.

There is no time for this now, however. The Huns are on the run and the thing to do is to throw in everything we have so as to get them running so fast they cannot stop. A green man is worth more *now*, green as he is, than he would be a couple of months hence if he were saved and given additional training. Hence with each squadron

---

12. About ten miles north of Bar-le-Duc.
13. The first day of the Argonne offensive.

doing as much work as it can possibly handle at full strength and after having had such heavy losses in this squadron, it is absolutely necessary to throw the green men in, and when they don't come back, one simply has to grin and bear it.

We sallied forth on the morning of the 26th shortly after daylight and had a dozen machines flying in two formations one above the other. I was leading the lower formation myself and we had not been long on the lines before I spotted seven biplane Fokker single-seater fighting machines coming in the distance. We had the altitude on them so I passed over them and then dropped on the rear man. Unfortunately he saw me just before I opened fire and turned sharply under me. I gave it to him at about fifty yards, but the shot was a very difficult one, and although my tracer bullets seemed to be going in about the right place I could not be sure that I got him. There was no time to watch him after my first burst.

Going down after this one put me on the same level with the rest of them, about 4,200 metres, and as they all turned back I saw that I was going to charge right through the middle of them. Jammed on my motor full speed and pulled up for all I was worth, passing just above the heads of all six. Then did a *renversement* and dropped on the tail of the last man, who had, I think, been the leader. Perhaps he did not see me for a moment because I got behind him at about fifty metres and had a dead shot at him. Gave him a good burst and he turned over and started to fall. I think he was pretty sick, for I saw my tracer bullets going into him, but again was unable to watch this Hun go down on account of the others. I attacked a third, but had to shoot at too long range to be effective.

By this time I thought the fight had progressed far enough into the German lines, considering that there were new men along and we had lost considerable altitude during the combat. I therefore pulled up and endeavoured to get my formation together, signalling the other planes to fall into their positions. Collected a couple of them and with the upper formation well together and above we started for our lines. Just then I caught sight of six or seven machines far in the German lines, so far away that it was impossible to tell which were Fokkers and which Spads. They were manoeuvring, however, as though in combat, and I knew that if any of my men were there they must be greatly outnumbered and much too far in the Boche lines.

I turned and dove full speed toward the fight and soon made out a Spad manoeuvring wildly, trying to shake off two Fokkers which were on his tail at point-blank range. He was in a bad way and I prayed that I should not this time be too late. Just then to my right I saw a second Spad making for our lines, closely pursued by two other Fokkers, so I dove down on them and drove them off and then turned to help out the first Spad. He was nowhere to be seen, although I caught a glimpse of his two pursuers making for home.

One of my men did not return from this fight, so I am afraid that they must have gotten him. Once more the same old story of a man forgetting that there is any danger other than that which may come from the machine which he is attacking. This is, of course, much the lesser danger. In this fight we had everything in our favour and there was no reason why anyone should have gotten in trouble if they would only not get carried away with themselves. It is splendid the way these boys will sail in and fight, but no amount of warning seems to teach them the necessary caution if they are to live long at the game. Only bitter experience teaches them, and that is dearly paid for. The man who was being pursued by the Fokkers which I drove off was a major temporarily attached to the squadron to get some practical experience. He got it all right. He is an extremely nice fellow and I am glad to say he got safely back to our lines. In the course of this fight we shot up four or five Huns, but only two were confirmed.[14]

Later in the day on the 26th we got orders for a strafing party on some roads well in the German lines. "Strafing," you will recall, is aviation slang for bombing and shooting up troops, etc., on the roads, from very low altitudes, two or three hundred metres. It is most unpleasant and dangerous work, for one gets shot up from the ground, against which there is no protection, and then any Huns who may come along in the air have you at a great disadvantage. I could not go out on this show as several of my flight commanders were laid up and I had to take out a high patrol shortly afterward. Seven Fokkers came down on the strafing party, and although my men shot down one Hun, one of ours did not return. It is a rotten situation to put a green man in, but I fail to see how it can be helped. Am glad to say, however, that I don't think we shall have much more of this work to do. The Boches we got on the 26th make fifteen for the squadron, but the losses have

---

14. The pilot who failed to return from this fight was shot down, wounded, in the German lines. He returned after the armistice with the information that a second group of Fokkers had come into the combat in addition to the original seven, and that instead of two, eight Huns were actually brought down, four of whom he himself saw dead on the ground.

been much in excess of what they should have been, eight in all.

Will have to stop now so as to get this letter off, but there is not much other news to give you anyhow. We have moved since I last wrote but have only gone a little way up the line, not so very far from where we were. The fight on the 26th took place just north of the most famous city of the war, so I shall leave you to guess the exact location.[15] My Hun had four large red and white squares on the centre section of his top plane, the marking of a rather famous German squadron which we call the checkerboards, for the squares look like part of a checkerboard.[16] I glanced over the side of my machine at the Hun as he spun down below me only twenty or thirty yards away and could plainly see his markings.

Belrain, Oct. 8, 1918.

Since we moved from our old station[17] our mail has been very much delayed, so that for several weeks we received none at all, but a few days ago came a very welcome letter from you and Mother. I was mighty glad to hear that everything is going along smoothly at home and that you are all well. Things are moving along about the same here, plenty of work and no little excitement, but the weather has been almost continuously bad and has made the flying hard and not productive of many Boches to our credit. We get out almost every day but are all the time flying in low clouds, squalls of rain, etc., which make it unpleasant. Under ordinary conditions we would not be flying at all, but during a push weather conditions make little difference. The squadron got a couple of Huns this week, but I was not in either of the fights, as I have been having bad luck with my machine and had to give up a patrol four or five times in succession due to motor trouble.

Forgot to tell you that I now have a new machine of a special type mounting a most murderous weapon of a gun. I cannot tell you just what this gun is, but if I ever hit a Boche with it he should come down in small pieces. The trouble is to hit them, for the gun only shoots once and then must be reloaded by hand. The machine was made specially by the French for poor Dave Putnam, the American "*As des As*," who was taken by surprise by eight Huns at the beginning of the St. Mihiel offensive and brought down. I was awfully sorry

---

15. Verdun.
16. Reported as one of the squadrons of the Von Richthofen group.
17. Toul. The squadron moved from Toul at the end of the St. Mihiel offensive, to a field south of the Argonne Forest, in preparation for the Argonne offensive.

about Putnam, as I knew him quite well, and he was a fine, fearless, unassuming fellow, who had done some wonderful work. We found him in our lines with two bullets through his heart.

The machine I mention is the only one of its kind in the American service, so I am very anxious to try it out. They gave it to me when Putnam was killed. Guynemer had one and Fonck and Deullin each have one and have used them with fair success. I do not mean by this statement to be trying to class myself with them, so don't start to kid me on that score. This special gun is difficult to use, but if a shot ever hits a Hun he might just as well say his prayers and give up, if he has time to think about anything at all. I have my regular machine in addition, and we have really been so busy that I have not had time to try out the new one. It handles differently from our ordinary machines and I wish to get considerable practice before I go monkeying around any Huns with it, for I should hate to be knocked by some Heinie just because I could not manoeuvre my new plane quickly.[18]

Give my regards to everyone in the office. How is Y—— these days? I have not heard from him for ages. Has he any offspring yet? I remember last fall I bet him I could get a Boche before he had any children.

Belrain, Oct. 14, 1918.

What do you all think of the news from all the fronts and the peace prospects from the Huns? It certainly is wonderful and it really begins to look at last as though they are getting a bit weak in the knees. My guess is that it will either be all over by the time you receive this letter or that we will have at least another year of it. I have heretofore thought the latter certain, but it now looks as if the former is the more probable, and I surely hope so. We must stick at it all the harder for the time being until the war is ended as it should be, but the end cannot come any too soon to please me. I spent all of yesterday searching the battlefield for one of my men who was killed about ten days ago, and a few hours spent on the ground near the front lines impresses the hor-

---

18. The gun mentioned was a 37 mm. cannon, which shot through the hub of the propeller. It fired two kinds of ammunition, one like a huge shotgun cartridge loaded with a lot of slugs, and the other a combination incendiary and high-explosive shell, which would explode upon contact with any part of an aeroplane. If, therefore, a hit was scored even on the wing of an enemy machine, the resulting explosion would blow the wing off. It would consequently not be necessary with this gun, as it is with a machine-gun, to hit that small area of a machine, which is ordinarily its only vital spot, in order to bring it down.

ror of it all upon one more than a month's flying over the same lines.

The man I speak of had a bit of the hardest luck that it is possible for a flyer to have. His name was Armstrong and he was one of my flight commanders and about the most valuable man I had. Besides being an extremely nice fellow and a very skilful pilot, he had a head on his shoulders which he used all the time which made him invaluable as a leader of the younger men. He had learned to appreciate the two principal points in this game, *i. e.,* that there is a great difference between foolhardiness and true courage, and that nine-tenths of the danger comes from another enemy than the one which you are attacking. The realisation of these points, coupled with nerve and perseverance, are, I think, the most important qualities of a successful pilot.

Armstrong took the lead of a patrol one cloudy day when I was forced to come back owing to motor trouble. Shortly after the patrol reached the lines they sighted half a dozen Fokkers and dove to attack them. Owing to the low clouds they were only about 600 metres up and our artillery was sending over a heavy barrage. Just as Armstrong opened up on a Fokker, one of his pilots who was fifty yards in rear of him suddenly saw his right wings and tail fly off while the rest of the machine fell in a cloud of black smoke, leaving the air filled with fragments of the plane. He had run squarely into one of our big shells on its way to Germany. There could be no other explanation, for the fight was just inside our lines and the patrol was not being fired on by anti-aircraft guns at the time.

This same thing has happened a number of times before, but it is comparatively rare, and coming as it did to one of our best men just when every experienced man in the squadron is so badly needed, was about as tough a bit of luck as one could imagine. An intimate friend of Armstrong and I searched high and low yesterday for some trace of him, but could find nothing. We expect to try again shortly; for after my experience with Oliver I know how much this would mean to Armstrong's family and to his young wife, whom he married just before sailing for France.

Armstrong had a very close friend who has now taken his place in the squadron as a flight commander, and there were two other men who were also about as close friends as I think it is possible for two men to be. Both these pairs were old friends and had been constantly together in their training and work at the front just as Oliver and I were. Now one is gone from each and the distress of the other two is indeed pitiful to see and I think I know how they feel. The loss of their dearest friend has shaken them as nothing else could and, although it will probably make better men of them in the end, the process is a very painful one. One of these men fought six Huns single-handed and at a low altitude ten miles in the German lines in his efforts to save his friend. He brought down one Hun and was almost killed himself, and I have recommended him for the D. S. C. for his courage.

The fighting on the ground in this sector has been terrific recently and the opposition stronger, I think, than at any other part of the front. The Huns seem to have massed a large part of their best troops opposite us, and in addition to this the country is hilly and naturally suitable for defence. Walking over the battlefield was a very interesting though gloomy sight, for the day was stormy, with a cold, drizzling rain. Everywhere one went were evidences of the recent advance, rifles and bayonets lying about in the grass, here and there various articles of cast-off clothing and equipment, and occasionally a knot of bloody bandages or a blood-soaked shirt where some poor devil had been trying to tie up his wounds. As you go forward you pass rows of holes scooped out by the advancing infantry, each one just big enough to hold one man.

In one of these, rather deeper than the others, I noticed where some fellow had evidently taken shelter until help came to him. In his pit were his mess-kit and some empty emergency ration tins, all lying in a pool of dark blood. While we were there our artillery was hard at it but the Boche shelling was only very intermittent. Every now and then you would hear the whine of a shell coming which reminded me very much of May 15th, although none of them came very close to us. Now that the Huns are squealing for peace I wish that I could take President Wilson, who is evidently going to have a good deal to say about the terms, and walk with him over some of these battlefields. Let him look at a battle in progress, and at all the wreckage behind it, at the fragments lying about of what were once men and horses and at a once beautiful country now reduced to a barren desert.

If he could see the ambulances with their gruesome loads, and the less severely wounded hobbling along toward the rear, many of them covered with blood and having wounds which would ordinarily call for an ambulance but having to walk none the less to make room for others worse off than they. If he could then pay a visit to a first-aid dressing-post and to the receiving and operating rooms of a field-hospital, the latter a veritable butcher shop, I am sure that he would feel as most of the men at the front feel, that there can be no decent peace until the Huns are utterly and completely defeated and made to pay the full price for all the misery that they have caused. I hope those higher up appreciate this as it is, but a little view of the real thing would bring it home to them as all the pictures and descriptions in the world never can.

Some of the men that I have lost from this squadron have been of the best and it makes one sick at heart to see these splendid young fellows, the finest that we can produce and men who cannot be replaced, dropping off singly and in bunches. Of their families I know nothing, but knowing the men themselves and the stuff that was in them, one knows that their people must be of the right sort and one can easily imagine the sorrow that must be caused by the loss of such men. If any but the right kind of a peace should come, one would always feel that all these fine fives had been sacrificed in vain.

We have been having a long stretch of bad weather, so that there has not been much flying, for which I have been rather thankful in a way, as the men needed the rest. I have personally only had one fight since last writing and that a very unsuccessful one. We were out one day protecting some of our "Liberty" day bombers and I caught a Fokker napping who had gotten off to one side of his patrol and was entirely taken up with trying to get a shot at the Liberties. I dropped down on him and sneaked up behind without his seeing me, but lost him by my same old trick of shooting too soon. I thought he was going to see me and duck, when I should have known that he probably would not see me. I opened fire at about a hundred yards range and gave him about forty shots, some of which I am sure hit his machine, but did not have the luck to get the pilot.

He pulled up in my face into a *renversement* and dove on his nose to escape, while I was prevented from following him by the rest of the Hun patrol, which was off to one side, and by my job of protecting the Liberties. Was so disgusted at missing him anyhow that I sort of felt that having missed such an easy chance I did not care much if the Boche did get away. If I had only waited as I should have until I was right on top of him I could not well have missed him. I certainly am an idiot not to have learned better judgment by this time. The fight I mentioned in one of my earlier letters, when I said that F—— was sitting on a nearby hill watching the whole show, occurred in this wise.

About a week after I got that Rumpler three of us were out looking for another one and found him at 5,500 metres, a considerable distance in our lines, I had a stronger motor than the others and climbed up under him first, and made him turn to protect himself. I drove him down a little, never getting very close, and then we all three pounced on him and shot the observer's gun away from him so that the Him was practically helpless and should have been easy meat. Then the Fates turned against us, for one of my men's motor failed him so that he had to land while both the other fellow's guns jammed. He pulled up for a minute to fix them and lost the fight, for just at that moment I and the Hun were playing hide-and-go-seek around the edges of some big white puffy clouds.

I kept after the Boche (another Rumpler with a big white number 8 on the side of his fuselage), but he manoeuvred very well and made it almost impossible to get a decent shot at him. I would give him a burst now and then to turn him and drive him down low in our lines where he would have to stop his tricks, relying all the time on having two men with me to help finish him off. Finally I drove him down to 50 metres, about a mile in front of F——'s balloon and some four miles in our lines. That day my own machine was out of commission and I was flying a plane especially equipped with large balloon guns shooting incendiary ammunition.

They do not carry as much ammunition and are not as reliable as our ordinary guns and I had fired a good many shots at long range to drive the Hun down rather than with any thought of getting him at such a distance. Then, to my consternation, when I had gotten the Boche just where I wanted him I found that my companions were nowhere to be seen and that I had fired all the ammunition out of one gun, while the band in the other was broken. While I had been shooting I had, of course, had to manoeuvre so as to protect myself, for even after we silenced the observer's gun it was some little time before I realised that he could not shoot and saw that his gun was pointing idly up in the air beside him. When I saw that Boche skimming the tree-tops and just before I discovered that my own guns were useless, I had visions of getting another Rumpler intact with two prisoners this time. Reckon I was a bit too cocky from my previous experience. Unfortunately the Boche had a good motor this time and would not land, but kept trying to get back to his lines.

When I found that I could not shoot I kept manoeuvring with him, and for ten minutes tried to run him into the trees or a house or to herd him over to the balloon where the machine-gunners on the ground could get him. Tried every bluff I could think of to make him land, diving down and coming up under his tail as though I was going to shoot him, and several times pulling up when the nose of my machine was only a few feet from him, in the hope that he would think that a wild American was trying to run him down and thus scare him into landing. All the time the observer was standing facing me in his cockpit, and as I would dive down on him he would lean over, tap the pilot on the shoulder and yell in his ear which way to turn, at the same time pointing first one direction and then another. I think I would almost recognise that fellow; he had a small brown moustache and a rather pasty face and was wearing one of those big round cork helmets that we used to have in the schools.

During these proceedings the Boche pilot's gun was all right, but it is not very hard to keep out of the way of that. Finally after ten minutes or so of this game the Huns caught on to the fact that I could not shoot and started for home, allowing me to do more or less as I pleased. Made one last effort to bluff them as we reached the hues, but it was no use and the observer even went so far as to wave at me as I turned off for the last time. Then what did they do but turn around and chase me home several miles into our lines, the pilot plugging away at me with his gun.

We had climbed up three or four hundred metres by this time and I have always wondered what our "doughboys" must have thought when they saw one of their Spads dashing full speed for home with a big old Rumpler on his tail. As you know, the Rumpler is a two-seater reconnaissance machine, which usually only fights to protect itself when attacked. I had no trouble in getting out of his way, but it was the most ignominious thing I ever had happen to me and I have not gotten over feeling sore about it to this day. It was just like having a Hun tied to a tree and then having to let him go, for all the hard part was over, and all that was needed to finish him was half a dozen more shots. I kept praying all the time that another one of our machines would come along or that someone walking down the road would bring the Boche down with a pistol or a brick or any old thing. Can you beat the whole thing for a crazy combat? When I saw that he was going to get away I almost cried with mortification.

Hobe Baker has certainly had a run of the hardest kind of luck. Both he and M—— were recommended by me to take squadrons of their own and each was given a squadron, but Hobe came ahead of M——, and was the first to go. As bad luck would have it. Baker's squadron was not yet ready, while the one which M—— was given a week later was all ready to go to the front. Now M——'s squadron has been operating on the front for six weeks while Hobe is still in the rear and has not even got his pilots and machines yet, and there seemed to be no immediate prospect of his getting them when I last heard from him. It is too bad, for Hobe is one of the very best, a very skilful pilot, and has all the nerve in the world and is a thorough gentleman. He is one of the fairest, most straightforward fellows I know and should make an excellent squadron commander, but he has struck rum luck from the start. I know how he frets in his present position and wishes he could be here at the front with us again.

Things have been going along about as usual here lately, almost continuous rain and bad weather. The constant damp has laid a good many of the men up with grippe, but I have personally been very well except for a slight cold, which is practically gone now. Had one clear day, day before yesterday, and in leading a high patrol I managed to get my nose and upper lip frostbitten; they are healing now and I am a pretty sight but quite well just the same. Had a little excitement on this flight, but no results, I fear. I spotted five Fokkers sailing along a short distance in their lines and slid around behind them to attack the high one. Before we got very close I saw a lone Fokker away from the others and flying straight into our lines. This looked like easy meat so I took after him, tagging along behind him for a mile to let him go as far as he would into our territory. When he got a mile or so in I put on my motor full speed and came diving down on top of him, all the time searching the sky for others, as I felt sure that the Huns were up to one of their old tricks.

The lone Boche had, I think, been watching us all the time, for when I got within a hundred yards of him and before I would have opened fire, he started to turn back under me, offering only the most difficult kind of a shot. I gave it to him and hit him, I think, and then pulled up to fix one of my guns which had jammed, and to look for the other Boches. Two of the men with me shot at the Boche and we followed him down a little, he continually working back into his own lines. Then I saw his little game, for here came his five friends, and he trying to lead us in under them. As soon as I caught sight of them I pulled up and started to climb, at the same time waving my wings as a signal for the patrol to stop chasing the single Hun and fall into position.

One man, however, a most excellent pilot and one of my flight commanders, did not see me pull up, and I saw him do just what I had feared all along. He dove down after the first Hun, entirely failing to see the others coming above, then as he pulled up after shooting he pulled directly into the faces of three Fokkers, all of whom had altitude on him. The only thing he could do was to run, but this is no easy matter with a couple of Huns close on your tail. I saw my pilot turn and start ducking back for our lines, with two Boches close after him. I was by that time above the whole gang, so, as our man came toward me with the two Boches behind him, I stood on my nose and dove for all I was worth, both guns wide open and aiming in front of the Huns.

There was no time to really aim, as I was afraid that a delay of a second might mean the end of our pilot, so I just sprayed the sky in front of the Huns with tracer and incendiary bullets, in the hope of being able to distract their attention sufficiently to let our fellow get away. I think the fuss I created did make them hesitate a little, and the Spad took advantage of this to dive like mad, and got safely away without a single bullet hole in him. I had myself gotten under the top Boches by this time, so pursued my usual policy, "*He who fights and runs away,*" etc., and lit out for home before they got close enough to bother me. Altogether a rather unsuccessful party, but one in which I think our men learned a few things.

But the nerve of that solitary Boche to let us jump him so that he could lead us into a trap, and the confidence he must have had, both in himself and his companions! If we did not get him we at least gave him the thrill of his life, and I think his mechanics will be busy for a day or two changing wings and patching holes. He was one of the most gaudily painted boys you ever laid eyes on, bright red wings and fuselage as far back as the pilot's seat, and the rest of the body pure white with black crosses. In the middle of his top plane a black and white checkerboard.[19]

I also recognised the markings of the others as one of the best-known Hun squadrons, broad black and white bands, the same as a gang that I had a fight with over Noyon last April. Some of the Huns with red wings have the rest of their machines a brilliant sky blue and are really beautiful to look at. There is a great deal of the best German chasse concentrated on our sector now and the pilots are certainly good, there is no use denying that fact. They have lots of fight in them and the way some of them can throw their machines around in the

---

19. A few days later it was reported by American observers on the ground that this German had crashed in his own lines. A good illustration of how impossible it often is for a pilot to be certain whether or not he has brought down his antagonist.

air shows clearly that they are old hands at the game. I wrote you a while ago that I plugged one of this checkerboard crew, but I would like to drop one of that red-winged outfit. We knocked a couple of them down in the last offensive but they got more of us than we did of them.

Gave myself quite a thrill the other day when we were out on a strafing expedition. A great deal of traffic was reported on a certain road[20] about five miles inside the Hun lines and we were ordered to attack it with machine-guns and bombs. I was leading a patrol of about seven machines, but when we got back near the road there seemed to be nothing on it at all. We therefore flew over and dropped our bombs on some cars standing in a railroad yard along a river,[21] and then came down along the road to make sure that there was nothing there. Seeing nothing, I fired a number of rounds into a village [22] where there seemed to be a few soldiers, and then caught sight of a big Hun wagon, which looked like an old-fashioned prairie-schooner, going slowly down the road, drawn by four horses. I dove down over the trees, and shot one of the rear horses, but did not have time to watch the result, for something went wrong with the timing mechanism of one of my guns and I shot three or four holes through my own propeller, knocking several big hunks out of it.

The effect of this is to throw the propeller out of balance, and my motor started to vibrate as though it were going to jump right out of the machine. The motor acted as if it might stop at any moment, and, being five miles inside the Hun lines and only two hundred yards high, I had most unpleasant visions of ignominiously ending the war by shooting myself down in Germany. Slowed my motor down as much as possible to have it still keep me going, and nursed it along, so that it brought me back to our lines, where I landed on an advance flying field until a new propeller could be sent up from the squadron. In flying back to our lines I found it rather hard to force oneself to fly along at extreme slow speed just over the heads of a lot of Heinies, who, of course, take delight in shooting at you. There were evidently no good bird shots among them, however, for they never touched me.

One of the other squadrons in this group had an amusing time with a Hun a few days ago. Eight of them caught a solitary two-seater

---

20. From Dun-sur-Meuse to Banthéville.
21 At Dun-sur-Meuse.
22. Aincreville.

in our lines and surrounded him, the Hun got scared and dove down to 600 metres, all the time following down the course of a river[23] which runs into our lines. Some of the pilots thought that perhaps they could make the Boche land and have some fun with his machine, and get some souvenirs, but the Hun observer kept taking pot-shots at them all the time. Finally one youngster went down right beside the Boche and motioned for him to land, but for reply the observer shot the stuffing out of him, blowing a hole in his wind shield right in front of his nose and starting a fire in his machine. This made the American pilot a bit sore, to say the least, so he sailed into the Hun, shot the pilot through the head and set the plane on fire. Just before he hit the ground the observer jumped out and then the Hun machine spread itself all over a field.

The American, having a small fire on board himself, had to get down as quickly as possible, which he did, but unfortunately picked out a barbed-wire entanglement. This wiped off his landing gear, while he and his machine turned a somersault over the wire and brought up upside down. He was never even scratched, so crawls out of his machine, grabs his pistol, and dashes over to where the Boches were for fear they might get away from him. As one of them had just fallen 300 feet and the other was burning up in the wreck of his machine, this was a rather unnecessary but amusing precaution. Some of these young pilots of ours do the craziest things you ever heard of, but the nerve of some of them and the way they will fight is simply great. They are constantly confronting the Huns with the unexpected and getting away with it by the very audacity of their methods.

One often hears tales of men who have landed behind the German lines and been able to get away again, but I never personally knew of a case until the other day. A new pilot from this group got separated from the rest of his formation during a fight which took place far the other side of the lines. Two Huns got on his tail and although he tried everything he could think of to get rid of them, he could not shake them off, and they ran him right down to the ground and forced him to land in their lines. His plane was badly shot up, but by great good fortune neither he nor his motor was hit. When he landed he left his motor turning over slowly and lay over in his cockpit as though he had been shot, the Huns all the time circling about just above his head. They evidently thought he was done for, for after looking him over they flew away, whereupon our pilot took off and came home. A

---

23. The Meuse.

A DIRECT HIT.
Spad plane of the author's squadron which had a forced landing three miles from the lines but within sight of the German observation-balloons. Until the Hun artillery obtained this hit there was nothing the matter with the machine but a broken gasoline line.

THE END OF A FAMOUS AMERICAN ACE.
Brought down near Limey, France, in the St. Mihiel sector, on the first day of the offensive, September, 1018.

mighty neat trick, but the next man who tries it is going to be out of luck, for the Huns probably will not be satisfied until they have shot him to pieces.

I would like to say a word about the enlisted men of the American Air Service units as I have seen them on the front. The men of my own squadron are, I know, an exceptional lot, and one could ask for no better, and although I do not believe the general average can come up to the standard of the men of the 13th Squadron, it is nevertheless very good. The men are intelligent, hard-working, and conscientious. They as a whole take pride in their machines and in their pilots, and you cannot imagine what a comfort it is to a pilot to feel that his mechanics are careful and have his safety at heart. When the enlisted personnel first came out, they had had very little experience with the type of motor which we use,[24] and although this lack of experience caused us some minor troubles, the men pitched in with a will and overcame this handicap in a remarkably short time.

The pride and affection which a good pilot can inspire in his mechanics and the grief of the men when their own particular aviator does not come back, is sometimes very touching.

When a pilot does not return from the last afternoon patrol before dark, we put out gasoline flares on the field to guide him home, in case he loses his way in the dusk. The Spad only carries sufficient gasoline to stay in the air for about two hours and twenty minutes, and yet I have seen a mechanic insist on keeping the flares burning until 9 o'clock at night for a man who had gone out at 4. Other men telling him that it was useless had no effect, for he said he knew that there was not any Hun good enough to kill his pilot, and that he just had to come back. I am glad to say that this fellow's faith was rewarded, for his pilot showed up the next day, having had a forced landing far from his home field. I have seen other mechanics sit down and cry like children when we would come back from a fight and tell them that their pilot had gone down, and, again, I have known them to walk around for half the night, unable to sleep, because their man was missing.

---

24. The Hispano-Suiza 220 H. P.

INSIGNIA OF U. S. MILITARY PILOT

CHAPTER 5
4th Pursuit Group, A. E. F.

Oct. 27, 1918, 4th Pursuit Group,
American E. F., Toul.

As you will see by the heading of this letter I am no longer with the 13th Aero Squadron. Two days ago I received orders relieving me of that command, and have been made C. O. of the 4th Pursuit Group, which comprises four chasse squadrons and one squadron for the overhaul of motors, headquarters work, etc. Have got three squadrons now and the other two arrive in a week's time. The group, however, is an entirely new one, as are several of the squadrons in it, and it is up to me to organise it and get it working as soon as possible. As I have as yet hardly any group headquarters staff or organisation to operate with and have somewhere between 1,000 and 1,100 officers and men to look after, you may imagine that time does not hang heavily on my hands.

I guess this new job pretty nearly finishes my days of active flying on the lines, although I did manage to bring with me my special machine which I must try out on a Boche the first chance I get. By the way, that Hun with the red wings I wrote you about last week was confirmed, so I guess he was not quite so smart as he thought he was. Expect to have so much organisation work to do in the next month that I doubt very much if I shall be able to fly at all during that time. The weather continues punk, though, so I guess I am not missing much. Have been figuring it out roughly and the property, planes, trucks, etc., which I have in the group comes to about ($2,000,000) two million dollars in money value. When one considers what a small item a single group is in the whole army one does not wonder that you are all having Liberty Loan drives at home.

P. S.—The boy with the red wings makes my seventh official Hun.

Toul, Nov. 12, 1918

It is hard to believe that the whole show is really over and that we shall probably never have to fight again. Yesterday morning they called me up from headquarters and said that no more patrols were to go out as the armistice went into effect at 11 a. m. I hung up the receiver with a sort of a "Well! What do we do now?" feeling. It is a wonderful relief to have it over, but it does leave you with a very much "let down" feeling, as though one had suddenly lost one's job. Having been at it so long it almost seems as though one had never done anything else and that one's reason for existing had suddenly ceased. I wish I could simply drop everything and come home, but I fear that time is still a long way off. With 125 officers and about 950 men on my hands I shall be mighty busy devising means to keep them well and amused and out of mischief.

Then again, this being only an armistice, the formation of the group, gathering of supplies, planes, etc., goes on as usual as though the war were to last forever, so that I shall be just as busy as if nothing had happened. Our days of air fighting are over, I guess, but the administration and organisation work goes on as usual and I am mighty sick of it. We shall be a sort of international police for a while, but here's hoping they hurry up with the peace confab so that we can all close up shop and come home. About our only chance for excitement will be strafing some Hun riot, which would be lots of fun. That is the way I like to fight, against someone who cannot y do much shooting back and turning one's machine-guns on a Boche revolution ought to furnish no end of amusement to us bloodthirsty fighting guys!! It will be immensely interesting, though, if we should be sent up to the Rhine and live among the Hun population for a while. One thing this young man intends to do in such a situation is to always carry a couple of automatics about with him, for having seen the War through this far he has no desire to have some swine of a Hun stab him in the back on a dark night.

What do you all think of the armistice terms? If they go through with them they do not leave the Hun much chalice to start the war again, do they? There does not seem one chance in a thousand that there will be any more fighting outside of what the Boches may do to each other if there is a revolution. When one thinks of the critical situation in which we were last June, it seems nothing less than a miracle that this wonderful change should have come about and the war be over in so short a time. I suppose Foch will be considered the world's greatest general and he certainly deserves it. No man ever had as difficult and stupendous a job handed over to him, and it is hard to see how he could have handled it better.

Had to interrupt this epistle this afternoon and have just now come in from a movie show which we set up for the men in an old barn. One of the squadron commanders bought a first-rate machine the other day and we get a new set of pictures each day through the Y. M. C. A. Tonight was the first show and the pictures were really splendid, as good as anything you ever saw in a first-class movie house at home. The show tonight was *The Three Things*—you remember that little story about the war by Mary Shipman Andrews. We must try to get a lot of comics of the Charley Chaplin variety; I think they appeal to the men more than anything; one gets a bit fed up on this war business. The movie machine cost 3,700 *francs*, but we charge a small admission fee, and if the attendance tonight continues it will not take long to pay for the apparatus. The girl who took the heroine's part tonight was the prettiest thing you ever saw. I would like to see her in real life, just to see how much of it was make-up; the original article would probably be an awful disappointment.

A peculiar thing happened here day before yesterday. It cleared up for a spell and a Rumpler came in over the field very high up, our attention being attracted by the "Archies" blazing away at him. For fifteen months I have watched "Archie" shoot at Hun planes and never saw him hit one yet, but on the last day of the War, as we watched this fellow, he suddenly went into a spin as a shell burst near him and spun down for about 2,000 metres. The observer fell overboard and then the pilot straightened his machine out and suddenly popped overboard with a parachute, leaving his machine to take care of itself. Down she came and dove head first into the ground with a crash that we could hear two miles away. It seemed to take the pilot forever to come down in his parachute, but he finally landed perfectly all right. He said the "Archie" did not get him but that he side-slipped into a spin by accident and his observer fell out.

Why he should have jumped from a perfectly good machine, even though his observer was gone, is hard to see, for there were none of our planes anywhere about. I think, the man must have been lying, although I must admit that the "Archies" did not appear to be coming very close to him. He said that they were all expecting the armistice to be signed, and that his C. O. had told the squadron that no one need fly, but that he and his observer had gone out anyhow for a bit of a joy-ride. They got it all right. The observer hit so hard he made a great big hole in the ground.

Speaking of guardian angels, as parachutes are dubbed in the air service, I remember one which worked very well, but perhaps not just as the Huns intended it to. During the fighting near Reims last spring a Hun two-seater was attacked by several French Spads. The Boche pilot put his machine into a spin and allowed it to fall a long distance in this way, this, of course, being merely a ruse to escape. He evidently put up a pretty good bluff, because his observer got scared, and thinking that his pilot had been hit, jumped overboard in his parachute. Just before the plane reached the ground, however, the pilot straightened her out and flew safely back to his own lines, while the observer with his parachute landed equally safely in our lines.

I wish I could get off for a few days and go to Paris, for there are a number of people there I should like to see, to say nothing of the tremendous celebration they must be having. I ran over to Nancy last night in my car, and if the spree in Paris was like the one there, it must have been a wild night on the *boulevards*. Am afraid, however, that I shall have to miss it all, for there seems to be little prospect of my getting away just now. Perhaps a little later I can arrange it. I hope so, for I feel pretty stale and think a few days' change would do me good. I will admit now that there have been days recently when I did not want to fly a bit, the losses in the squadron were so heavy that it was hard not to let it get on one's nerves. Twelve pilots in three weeks is pretty hard on the morale of the ten who are left. I am speaking of the original members, for a squadron is, of course, kept up to strength by replacements. Things went much better afterward, however, and for a month we had no losses at all and the squadron did some good work.

A couple of days after I left it seven of them jumped on seven Fokkers and shot down six without any of our men even getting their planes shot up. That is a clean-up which is hard to beat; in fact, the most successful fight I have ever heard of and I certainly hated to miss it. Now the open season for Huns is over and you can't half guess how glad I am. Tonight the moon is shining and we admire it instead of swearing at it and taking to the dugouts. It is almost too good to be true to think that before very long we shall be home again. There have naturally been a good many days when the chance of ever getting back again seemed a bit slim, and it is hard to realise that I shall some day be shooting ducks on the river once more. The losses in the 13th Squadron were pretty high, but recent reports received through the Red Cross make things look brighter.

Of the eleven men who went down inside the German lines up to the time of my leaving the squadron, six were not killed but are prisoners, some of them wounded, but just how badly we do not know. During offensives such as we have had in the last couple of months considerable losses are, of course, to be expected. I remember that in my old French squadron during the four months of the battle for the Passchendaele ridge, we lost nine out of the original fourteen, but of these nine two were killed in accidents.

Paris, Dec. 1, 1918.

Since arriving here I have seen my old friend H—— who has just come back from a German prison-camp. You will remember that I wrote to you last spring that he had been shot down for the second time, but had this time gone down behind the German lines. I got from him the story of what happened to him, and although we all thought he had already had about as narrow an escape as a man could have and live to tell the tale, he went it one better this time.

H was in a fight with some Albatross single-seaters, and was diving steeply down on the tail of one of them. Evidently one of his wings was defective, for a large part of the cloth suddenly tore loose and ripped off. This unbalanced his machine, and he started to go down in a slow spin, but by using his motor and putting all his controls to one side he was able to right his plane and started back for our lines. About this time the German "Archies" started to take a hand in the fight, and H—— received a direct hit from a 77 shell. He was flying a type of plane[1] which has a rotary motor, in which, as you know, the cylinders are set about the crank shaft in much the same way as the spokes of a wheel are set around the hub. The shell stuck between two cylinders but failed to explode. It must, of course, have been pretty nearly at the top of its trajectory, or it would have knocked the motor all to pieces anyhow.

As it was, the impact tossed H——'s plane about in the air and stopped the motor and he was then no longer able to control his crippled machine. He fell once more into a spin, going down in this way for many thousand feet until he finally crashed in Hunland. His motor had been so nearly carried away by the shell that when he struck the ground it fell off the machine and rolled away to one side, where it was later found with the unexploded shell still stuck between

---

1. Nieuport, type 28.

the cylinders.

H—— himself broke both his ankles in the crash, one of them very badly. He spent several months in a Hun hospital and was then sent to a prison-camp. When I saw him he walked with a slight limp, but aside from that was as well as ever. If anybody can beat his experiences for hairbreadth escapes I would like to hear about them. His guardian angel has certainly stuck to him through thick and thin.

Hobe Baker and some of the pilots in his squadron had a peculiar fight with a Hun two-seater a few days before the armistice. They met him very high up, about 20,000 feet. Hobe gave him a burst from behind and must have hit the pilot, for the Hun flopped over on his back and the observer fell out, coming down with a thud a considerable distance in our lines. The machine fell upside down for four or five thousand feet, when the pilot evidently came to, for he righted his plane and tried to get back to his own lines. Hobe and one of his men jumped on him again and fairly riddled him, and the Boche finally crashed about a mile in Hunland.

About a week after the signing of the armistice we crossed the lines and went up to the wreck of the plane. In it and scattered all about it we found a lot of propaganda leaflets, which the Huns had been engaged in dropping among our infantry when they ran into our patrol. The leaflets are printed in French on one side and English on the other and are headed: "The German People Offers Peace." I enclose you one of them. You will notice that even at this stage of the game they still maintain their right to attack passenger steamers carrying war material. I think the veiled threat contained in the paragraph "Who is to blame, if the hitherto undestroyed towns and villages of France and Belgium sink in ashes?" is rather significant.

The practice of dropping propaganda from aeroplanes is now, of course, an old one. I remember when we used to drop copies of some of President Wilson's speeches. You may recall that the Huns once sentenced two Englishmen to long terms of imprisonment who had been forced to come down in their lines after dropping propaganda. Is it not typical of the logic of the Hun mind that a man who drops bombs is merely committing an act of war, while he who drops bits of paper is considered a criminal?

I am glad to say that Lieut. Fonck pulled through the war all right, and ended up with a score of seventy-five or seventy-six official Huns, I am not sure which. This is top score for the Allies, and the highest authentic record of anyone pilot during the war. Fonck's actual score

The German People Offers Peace.

The new German democratic government has this programme:

"The will of the people is the highest law."

The German people wants quickly to end the slaughter.

The new German popular government therefore has offered an

Armistice

and has declared itself ready for

Peace

on the basis of justice and reconciliation of nations.

It is the will of the German people that it should live in **peace with all peoples**, honestly and loyally.

What has the new German popular government done so far to put into practice the will of the people and to prove its good and upright intentions?

a) The new German government has appealed to President Wilson to bring about peace.

   It has recognized and accepted all the principles which President Wilson proclaimed as a basis for a general lasting peace of justice among the nations.

b) The new German government has solemnly declared its readiness to evacuate Belgium and to restore it.

c) The new German government is ready to come to an honest understanding with France about

Alsace-Lorraine.

d) The new German government has restricted the **U-boat War.**

   No passengers steamers not carrying troops or war material will be attacked in future.

e) The new German government has declared that it will **withdraw all** German troops back over the German frontier.

f) — The new German government has asked the Allied Governments to name commissioners to agree upon the practical measures of the evacuation of Belgium and France.

These are the deeds of the new German popular government. Can these be called mere words, or bluff, or propaganda?

Who is to blame, if an armistice is not called now?

Who is to blame if daily thousands of brave soldiers needlessly have to shed their blood and die?

Who is to blame, if the hitherto undestroyed **towns and villages of France** and Belgium sink in ashes?

Who is to blame, if hundreds of thousands of unhappy **women and children** are driven from their homes to hunger and freeze?

The German people offers its hand for peace.

is much higher even than this, and it is safe to say without exaggeration that he brought down somewhere between one hundred and one hundred and twenty German machines. I remember very well how in Flanders in the Fall of 1917 he used to come back from a flight and ask for confirmations on sometimes two and sometimes three or four Huns whom he was practically certain he had gotten, and yet he could get only one of them confirmed.

Taking everything into consideration, Fonck is, to my mind, in a class by himself as a fighting pilot. There have been many other great pilots just as brave, such as Guynemer and Ball, but none of them have combined with it Fonck's marvellous skill. I know that up to the time that I left *Groupe* 12 of the French Aviation, Fonck had been hit only once, having then gotten one bullet through a wing. I saw Captain Deullin the other day and he told me that he had maintained this record to the end, throughout hundreds of fights. It is hard for one not familiar with air fighting to realise what this means. Luck has, of course, had something to do with it, but I think the principal reason lies in Fonck's almost uncanny shooting ability, and his faculty of almost being able to smell a Hun, and thus always get the jump on him.

I have been doing a good deal of thinking lately about the tactics of air fighting, and have come to the conclusion that I have often been overcautious. I know that if the war had gone on I would have materially changed my own methods, particularly in the matter of attacking two-seaters. I have always tried to take them from the rear and below, and to protect myself by keeping in the blind spot behind their tails. This is a first-rate method if the Hun does not see you, but the trouble is to get there, and he will almost always see you before you get in shooting position. In this way you lose the tremendous advantage of a surprise, and as the Hun is always manoeuvring to try to get you out from the vulnerable spot beneath his tail, you nearly always have an unsteady target and consequently one which is hard to hit. Particularly if one is above one's enemy when one catches sight of him, I think that an attack carried out with great speed from above would give better results.

One would then rely for protection upon the element of surprise, speed, and particularly upon accurate shooting. Reliable machine-guns would, of course, be of the greatest importance, as they always are. If you missed him, or anything went wrong, you would probably have to protect yourself by keeping right on going and passing down below him. The shooting would certainly be simplified, for the Hun two-seater pilot would not have the same reason to manoeuvre his plane. For a green man such a method of attack would be rather dangerous, but for an experienced pilot I think it would offer much greater chances of success, and I wish that I had come to this conclusion before it was too late to try it out.

Now that the war is over the question which naturally presents itself to one's mind is "Is it over too soon?" There is no question about it that it would have been a great satisfaction if we could have gone on and gotten into Germany and given them a taste of what they have been giving us for the last four years. Do you think the Huns are repentant for what they have done? As has been so often said, the Hun is fundamentally in his nature a bully, and like all bullies begins to whine for mercy when he finds that he is getting the worst of it. But put him back where he was in 1914 and 1915, when he thought he was going to win, and he would commit the same outrages, only worse, so as to get square for having been thwarted this time.

And do you suppose for one moment that the Hun thinks he is licked? Not a bit of it! And if we in future years forget what he has done and do not make him feel it, he never will realise it. The Allies are the ones who will dictate the terms of peace, and if we use our power and make those terms strong enough, the fact that he is beaten should be brought home to the Hun. If we do this, then, of course, the war ended none too soon, for satisfying as it would have been to have invaded Germany, the cost in the lives of our men would have been too great to have continued the fight a day after it became unnecessary.

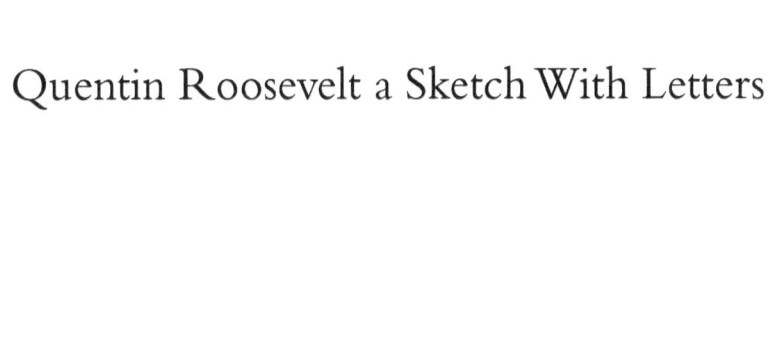
Quentin Roosevelt a Sketch With Letters

Quentin Roosevelt
Mineola, May 1917

Contents

Foreword	227
Before the War	229
The Way of the Eagle	243
The Last Patrol	305
Official Judgment	323
"The Judgment of His Peers"	329
Verses	354

Only those are fit to live who do not fear to die, and none are fit to die who have shrunk from the joy of life and the duty of life. Both life and death are parts of the same Great Adventure. Never yet was worthy adventure worthily carried through by the man who put his personal safety first.
     Theodore Roosevelt.

Foreword

Three years ago today, (as time of first publication), Quentin Roosevelt fell in France in an aerial combat over the German lines. He was buried by the enemy with military honours near the little town of Chamery.

Two weeks later when the Soissons salient was wiped out the Three Hundred and Third Engineers found his grave. The American burial service was read over the grave and the Engineers raised a new cross, and placed a shaft to mark where the airplane had fallen. Quentin Roosevelt was not yet twenty-one when he was shot down; still years count for but little in the record of a life; one man at twenty may have accomplished more and leave more behind to mourn his loss than another who saw a century out. Quentin Roosevelt to casual acquaintances typified the light-hearted *joie de vivre* (there is no English phrase that can quite convey the meaning) which freshened all who came in contact with it, but underneath it all there lay the stern purpose and high resolve of one who realises the essential seriousness of life.

K R.

July 14, 1921.

CHAPTER 1

Before the War

Quentin Roosevelt was born in Washington on November 19, 1897, six months before his father enlisted for the war to free Cuba. As a boy he attended the public schools in Washington. The last year of his father's second term as president he went to the Episcopal High School at Alexandria, Virginia.

The following summer—that of 1909—he spent in Europe. He had always been interested in mechanics, and in a letter to Ambler Blackford, a son of the principal of the school, he tells of his first sight of an airplane.

> We have had a wonderful time here and seen lots. We were at Rheims and saw all the aeroplanes flying, and saw Curtis who won the Gordon Bennett cup for swiftest flight. You don't know how pretty it was to see all the aeroplanes sailing at a time. At one time there were four in the air. It was the prettiest thing I ever saw. The prettiest one was a monoplane called the Antoinette, which looks like a great big bird in the air. It does not wiggle at all and goes very fast. It is awfully pretty turning.
> Isn't Notre Dame wonderful? I think anything could be religious in it. And the Louvre, I think it would take at least a year to see it. I have some of the pictures. I think the little Infanta Margarita by Velazquez is the cunningest thing I ever saw, and I think they are all very beautiful. We have been to Rouen and everywhere.
> Tell S. that I am sending him a model of an aeroplane that winds up with a rubber band. They work quite well. I have one which can fly a hundred yards, and goes higher than my head! Much love to all from
>
> Quentin.

That autumn on his return to this country he entered Groton School as a first former. His bent for mechanics, which was not inherited, and his love of reading, which was inherited, found expression in the school magazine. Quentin became an editor and also worked as typesetter and general overseer in the more practical part of publishing. It was in the printing-room that he enjoyed himself most when at Groton.

In January, 1915, with the World War launched upon It's first winter, he wrote the following story for *The Grotonian*:

One Man with a Dream

The train stopped with a jerk, the doors flew open, and the crowd surged out toward the street. I made my way slowly to the taxi stand and hailed a waiting machine. '4 West fifty-seventh street, and make it fast,' I said. The man glanced at me quickly, hesitated, and then said, 'Why that's John Amsden's house, isn't it?'

'Yes,' I said, 'make it in less than ten minutes and you get a fiver.'

The machine started to the street, dove around the corner into thirty-fourth, and then across. The traffic seemed strangely crowded:—we barely moved behind a stream of street cars and autos. Finally came Broadway and I saw the reason. Herald Square was packed with people,—a tense, silent crowd, all watching the bulletin boards. I strained to catch a glimpse and made out, under the flaring arc lights, '10.45—Drs. Waring and McEwen report John Amsden is doing as well as can be expected. He is partially conscious.'

I hammered on the window of the taxi stand, as the man turned, cried to him to hurry. The traffic was still blocked, however, and we were hemmed in. I looked at the board again. Another notice was being rolled up. '11—Condition slightly improved.' Strained faces in the crowd relaxed. I could see one man turning to another and clapping him on the back, a smile of relief on his face. So that was the reason. That was why I had received the telegram, 'John needs you. Come at once.'

The traffic began to move, and soon we were racing up Fifth Avenue, 42nd, 48th, St. Patrick's Cathedral,—at last 57th. Two policemen guarded the entrance of the street. I was evidently expected, for they let me through with a glance at my card.

The door was open, and I went into the familiar hallway with It's carved oak stairs. The contrast was startling. Outside the crowded streets;—inside, dead silence. I went upstairs. Low voices came from the back of the house. Someone inside was speaking:—'It must have been that speech in Union Square that did it. The doctors say it is pneumonia. His system is so overworked that he can't fight the disease.'
Another man spoke up, 'Something had to crack. No man can work at fever heat for weeks on end.'
I pushed open the door and entered. Three men were seated before the fire, all of them men whom I knew. My cousin Arthur, who was a reporter on the *Globe*, Charles Wright, the actor, and Pearson, the critic. Arthur sprang to his feet as I entered. 'I'm afraid It's too late. Cousin Fred,' he said, 'the doctors have given orders that no one is to see him.'
Hopeless, I sat down. Why had I gone away? I might have known something would happen to him.
'Tell me,' I said.
'There's not much to tell,' said Pearson. 'He would speak at that mass meeting in Union Square Friday. It was drizzling a little and he caught a chill. That and overwork brought on pneumonia. That's about all.'
We lapsed into silence, each thinking of the man above who was fighting for breath. The fire flickered, and then died out. Arthur spoke up:
'You were with him. Tell us about it.'
'It was like a dream,' I said, 'A dream come true.
'John Amsden and I roomed together at college. I think that was the beginning of our friendship. He never did much there, that is, in any serious way. He worked a little, went to every dance in or out of Boston, and that was about all. He had not the physique for an athlete, and though he had several things published in the *Advocate*, he gradually let it drop, and never tried for editor. He did not have to work for a living, for his father's millions were waiting for him so there was no incentive. People said that he had lost what little capacity he had ever had for work while in college.
'After college he led the life that all those lead who belong to the class reformers and Socialists call the idle rich. His winters were spent in Aiken or Palm Beach; his summers in Europe,

with interludes of Meadowbrook and Tuxedo. I doubt if he ever did anything more than this for twelve years. Even his friends, who always claimed that he would some day develop, gave up hope. He seemed to have arrived at the end of his development.

'Last summer we arranged to go abroad together for a bicycle trip through Holland and Belgium. That was in July. August found us in Belgium, travelling slowly from place to place. To make a long story short, we were caught in the whirlwind of the war. We saw the fall of Liege and we followed in the track of the invader as he tramped through Belgium. We saw towns levelled, cathedrals shelled, smelt the smell of the battlefield, saw the fleeing people, homes burned, husbands and fathers gone, the soldier dead, his rifle in his hand, the priest with his crucifix,—we saw it all.

'To John it was a revelation. He had never before felt the horror of death, never seen the human soul apart from It's polished covering. What death he had seen had been decorous, honoured, attended with peace and quiet. He had barely realised the fact that suffering existed,—that the horrors of war were any more than a novelist's term.

'Following in war's path had brought it all home to him with an appalling nearness. All the sorrows he had never known, all the emotions he had never felt,—he went through it all, saw the feelings of people, not mirrored in a book or veneered by etiquette, but sharp, bitter, unconquerable. In him it brought out all the character that had lain hid. All the crusader spirit of his ancestors came to the top. He was fired with it. In his reaction he thought of his former life almost with loathing. It seemed to him almost unbelievable that America could be callous to the suffering, to the horror of what he saw before his very eyes. He felt he was chosen, that it was his duty to tell of Belgium.

'He decided quite suddenly. "I'm going back, Fred," he said, "to tell the people at home about this. They must understand, they must help."

'We made our way to the coast, as best we could, and at last got a steamer for America. On our voyage we talked of the people at home often. It never occurred to him that people would not understand, that they would not see as he did. He could not conceive of anyone remaining unmoved in the face of suffering such as we had seen.

'We parted at the dock. The next day, as I sat at home, the telephone rang. It was John. "Fred," he said, "I must have a talk with you."

'We agreed, finally, that I was to come over and see him.

'He was sitting in this room before the fire, as we are now, when I came in. In all my life I have never seen a look of utter hopelessness such as there was on his face. "It's all wrong," he said, "they don't see. I can't understand it."

'He told me then, how he had been to his friends, had spoken to them, and the effect of his words. "They wouldn't even listen to me. They wouldn't even listen! I tried to tell about it all but they cut me short. Harry Wilding wanted to tell me about the baseball the Giants were playing. Schuyler had a scheme he wanted me to finance,—to charter a steamer and send over a cargo of silk socks to Belgium. Said it was a great opportunity now that the German market was closed." He laughed, dully, and, pulling aside the shade pointed out the window.

'"There," he said, "there it is. That is the explanation. That is the American spirit; America's countersign; her God."

'I looked. A huge sign showed in electric lights:

The New National Magazine
James Fried's article on What There is in the War for the U. S. A.

'"Yes," said John, bitterly, "that is the acid test of the 'Great American Nation's' feelings. What do we get out of it?"

'He gazed into the depths of the fire, and I watched the shadows come and go on his face. Suddenly his expression changed, and his eyes sparkled with the light of battle. "I have it," he cried, "I shall write the play of the war. I shall bring war home to the people as it has never been brought before. I shall challenge the nation."

'That was the beginning of his great play. He worked feverishly, at high pressure,—writing far into the night.

'In three weeks it was done. I remember the joy on his face as he came to the door. "It's done, Fred," he said.

"He would not let me read it, though I begged him to. The first night, so he said, was the test. He wanted me to see it then for the first time, and so I waited. As you know, Eisenstein agreed, after the first reading, to put it on as soon a company could be got together.

'Then, at last, came the first night. All New York seemed to be there. It had been wonderfully advertised. All over the city, great placards with the name, *War*, in red, and then John Amsden, underneath. I had to fight my way,—but you were there—you remember.'

Pearson nodded.

'You remember how it was received. Not a sound from the whole packed house. Not a clap, not a cheer, not even the shuffling that a crowd of people generally make. It was a tense, uplifted audience. A woman in front of me was crying as the curtain fell, and the crowd filed out silently. No one was discussing the play in the lobby when I came out. It was too great, beyond unthinking praise. Men went home and thought over it.

'By morning it was famous. In every paper it appeared on the front page. Critics called it a sermon of the stage.

'That was four weeks ago. Since then the presses have been running to capacity printing it, it has been played all over the country. People have telegraphed him by the thousand, asking him to speak. He has been hailed as another prophet who should preach of America's duty in this war.

'He was asked to speak at Union Square before I left. You know the rest—.'

I stopped, and we sat in silence for a while, each busied with his own thoughts. The clock in the Metropolitan tower began to chime. I looked out the window onto the quiet street. Across was Broadway, with It's lights, It's passing crowds. I could just see the top of the huge sign at Columbus Circle:—'*Charles Wright* in *War*'. I thought of the great crowd gathered at Herald Square. The clock struck the hour,-ten-eleven-twelve.

The deep boom died away. There was a noise of footsteps on the stairs. It was the doctor. We sprang to our feet. 'How is he; doctor?' said Arthur; his voice sounding cracked and strained.

The doctor looked at us, his face worn and white and lined, and shook his head slowly. He turned and went out without a word.

'Oh, it can't be true,' cried Arthur. 'There must be something wrong. Why should he die.'

'It can't be helped, boy' said Pearson, 'It was fate. God's plans seem mysterious to our cramped view.' He quoted softly:

One man with a dream, at pleasure
Shall go forth and conquer a crown.

Quentin had a remarkable gift for descriptive writing, and particularly delighted in short sketches, usually with the element of fantastic mysticism predominant. The two brief stories following were written while he was serving in France.

In Line of Duty

The service pistol is a merciless thing.

Up there above my desk it hangs, between Hilda's picture and the instrument board, always loaded, always ready. Yes; always ready, always loaded; that's the watchword of our service,—even now as we lie idly awash, charging our batteries. It's pleasanter this way, though, with the fresh air cleaning off the fumes of the last nights run. And then, when you're on the surface, there aren't so many noises, or at least I know them all. Sometimes when we are submerged I hear sounds,—ones that I cant account for, I swear they're only imagination, though. You can almost hear them now; the soft deadened whisper of stumpy fingers groping and pawing at the edges of our plates. It's all foolishness, all foolishness! Here I am, the senior commander of the imperial submarine service, with a record that even an admiral might envy, worrying like any child over noises that don't exist,—mere imagination.

Kuhlman is responsible. He was mad and I should have put him in irons. I remember when first he came aboard. The old admiral was there, and said to me, 'Take him and make a man of him.' So I gave him responsibility, put him in charge of the forward tubes. Off the coast of Ireland we were, and sure of work before long.

We got it, too,—a big boat, one of their crack liners. I was sorry we had to do it, for there were many women and children among her passengers, but what else could I do? She had been warned; and in war there is no pity.

I let young Kuhlman have the shot, and then, as there was no convoy and no guns, we rose to watch the effect. It is very sudden death, a torpedo. One moment you are but two days from port; the next the boats are manned and the band plays as she sinks. It was a bad night, and there were many of the boats that they could not launch. She sank very quickly, and we submerged again, for it was too rough for us,—and so we lay for two days while the storm went on above. Then it blew itself out, and luckily too, for two days below are hard on the nerves. Kuhlman felt it most, for he had never before seen death, and the sight of that ship sinking from the torpedo that he had fired, had been too much for him. So we came up, and were lying on the surface, just as we are now, while we officers smoked upon deck. After two days like that, the air seems very sweet, and it is good to live again, and cease to be a machine.

Only as we stood there something came drifting down upon us,—something white that glinted in the sunlight. It was quite close before I saw what it was,—too close. Somehow the current caught it and brought it alongside, and it seemed to stick to us in the little wash that lapped our sides. All the flesh was gone from the head,—the fish had been at it,—and the bare skull shone like polished ivory as it bobbed up and down and the water washed in and out of the empty eyes. It had been a common sailor off the ship we had sunk two days before, and across the chest of the suit you could see the letters 'Cunard Line.' It drifted on, but with it went all the life of the air, and I ordered the men below.

It must have been that that started Kuhlman. I had grown quite attached to him, for he seemed only a boy, for all of his moustaches. And yet, at first, even I did not notice any change. Then he took to coming in and sitting talking to me in my room, and I began to wonder. He said he liked the company. Only, as I found out, the real reason was that he was afraid to be alone. Later he told me about it. In the beginning it used only to bother him at night when the lights were out. Then, as he lay in bed, they would begin. He would hear them outside in the water, talking to one another, in dead voiceless words, the salt water in their mouths. And always their talk was of him. 'He fired the torpedo,' they seemed to say, and then he would hear the fumbling of soft, sodden fingers tearing at the rivets.

Later he began to see faces, dreadful, greenish, water logged ones, long strings of sea weed in their hair. And worst of all they were all faces he knew, friends and family at home, that stared at him with blind dead resentment. They became worse and more insistent, and he began to go round with his eyes fixed in front of him, for he said they watched him from the corners.

He slept with his lights turned on. I did my best to talk him out of it, but I knew that we would soon lay up for our month in port, and I thought that would cure him. Then we put in to take on oil for our last two weeks, and they gave me a bundle of papers. Kuhlman was in my room at the time, and I tossed them to him to read, for I thought it might cheer him. I was busy myself, looking over my new orders, and the reports from other commanders.

Over my shoulder I called to him some question about the news. There was no answer, and after a bit I turned around to look at him. He was sitting, the paper spread before him on the desk, and as I looked, he got up and fumbled for the door handle. His face was dead white, and on it the look of one who has seen something very terrible,—something more than one should see. I stood for a moment doing nothing, for the look on his face had driven all thoughts from my head and then, stupidly, I looked to the paper for the explanation. There was little enough in it,—politics, the war, a new invention, and at the top of the page the pictures of some people, a family I judged, with father, mother, and a sweet-faced girl of about twenty. I looked closer, and saw under the pictures, 'drowned in the *Caronia* disaster.' Even then I could not see the reason for that look in his face. Orders were orders, and he'd have to learn that in war people were killed, and not always the guilty,—and it was all part of the game. Suddenly there was the roar of a shot. I was in his room before the echoes died along the iron walls, but of course it was too late.

He lay bent over his desk, the pistol still clutched in his hands. Then, at last, I saw the reason. In a little gold frame before him was a girl's picture, the same that I had just seen in the paper, now blotched with his blood, he had written in his round, boyish hand,—'Ah, dearest; *mea magna culpa.*'

A bad, bad business it was. The bullet at that range, had torn his face terribly, and yet somehow I was relieved, glad almost. I am sure that his eyes would have been,—not nice.

That was a month ago and I am still at sea. I thought when I got back after that run I would ask for a rest,—I had begun myself to hear things that were not of the ship. But once in port, they told me I was chosen to take this, our newest, on her maiden run. What could I do? It was an honour they offered me. All the same, I wish the captain's quarters were not like those on my old ship. When I came in, and saw the bare iron walls just as before, with that grim pistol in its clips by the instrument board, I seemed to see him again. And now, three weeks out, it is growing worse. I dare not turn the lights out, for if I do, instead of the luminous dials of my instrument board I see only his poor shattered head, with great eyes that call me.

Perhaps he was right, after all. The service pistol is a merciful thing.

THE GREATEST GIFT

'What is the greatest blessing' I mused, as I sat at my window. And the warm breath of spring, sweet with the scent of flowers and green things growing whispered softly 'Life. Life is the greatest gift. To live and feel no fear lest the grim hand that stays not smite. What higher have the gods to give?'

In my heart youth cried assent, and full of the horror of that gray and merciless one who spares no man, I went forth into the crowded ways. Everywhere was life, and the beauty of things living. As pleasant music to my ears were the cries of children and all the many voices of the street. Death seemed but some foul vampire that lay in gloating cruelty waiting to take all from me.

I wandered whither my feet led me, careless of all save my thoughts until I came on a street to me unknown, a dark street heavy with the dust of centuries. Grey lichens clung about the houses' eaves, and in the shapeless wind-worn carvings. No children played upon the steps and on the cobbled pavement no traffic passed. The roar of the world without was lost, for sound itself seemed choked with age, and my footfall waked echoes long dead that fled wailing past the sombre houses and died among the wind worn tiles. One door alone stood open, mysterious, beckoning, and through it I passed as one who enters in a dream, a place familiar, yet of the dream. All within lay shrouded in gloom save for a little glow ahead, and toward It's soft crimson I went, my hands against the velvet arras.

And now I saw whence the light came. A ball of crystal in whose clouded heart the crimson light rose and fell with steady beat lay between the paws of an ebony sphinx, that crouched before a tall chair of ebony. In the light lay mystery, and the very air was heavy with the secret of old forgotten dreams.

The scent of spice and sandalwood, of incense and of myrrh. I stood in silence and past me went my thoughts, that drifted in a sea of memories dim and griefs long past. But in on them came a voice, deep and clear, yet a part of the silence, that said: 'What do you in the memories of the past, whose heart is with the present, to whom life and all that lies before alone are fair.'

With slow steps muffled in the crimson carpet I went into the circle of warm, glowing light and was aware of one who sat buried in the great chair. Face and hand alone were visible, for the velvet gown merged indefinitely into the ebony of the chair. One hand showed, yellow and shrivelled with age, while ridged tendons like twisted wires stretched to long fingers tipped with yellow and pointed nails.

On the face, too, lay the mark of ages, for over the skull the skin stretched wrinkled and creased like an ancient parchment. Deep sunk in their sockets glowed eyes that held me and searched my soul. There was in them age, to which to the end of time we were young; tragic age, the bitter sorrow of ten thousand years; sorrow such as had the dead eyes of Œdipus. As I looked in them all fear left me,—and only an awe and a pity too deep for words remained. Yet when I spoke it was as a child that answers, and yet is intent on the question it would ask before even it speaks. 'Why should not I dwell in memories past, to enjoy the more what life may hold?'

He spoke again, and his voice was as a hand held out to one that gropes in darkness: 'May not life then rise above itself—has it no higher to offer than its little span, and must death ever lie, a secret terror, black upon the mind? Is death a penalty that the Gods exact of a man whether evil or fair has been his lot? Through my crystal must all mortals pass when the fires of life are flickering low;—look now, in your ignorance, upon the face of Death.'

I looked at the crystal, and deep in its heart saw pictures that came and went as the light rose and fell. Each seemed to tell a tale familiar, though the time was short and the faces strange.

An old man lay dying, his children round him, on his face peace, and the happiness of one whose life is well spent, who after the long day's toil waits gladly for the end.

The crystal blurred and another scene was there. A woman lay dying, but none were there to watch save desolation and utter loneliness, for she had lived beyond her time, all that might have cared were dead, and on her face shone only a great relief.

Many pictures I saw, and where the dying were young, I saw the struggle against death. Yet Youth did not fear death,—rather they feared to lose life, It's cup still full. Where age lay dying was no struggle—only rest after the fever and fret of life. At length I turned to him who sat silent in the great chair, and asked humbly: 'What of you—will not you, too, pass in the crystal's crimson mist?'

'I,' he cried bitterly, and his voice swelled till its deep grief filled the velvet hung chamber with tragedy unspeakable, 'I have sinned too deeply, I may not die. Of the Gods I asked too much. I wished for all that was theirs to give,—for life eternal. They gave it me and now is their gift as gall and bitter wormwood to my soul. All that I ever loved or knew is dead for thrice a thousand years. Alone I go down the endless ages. Aye, the very gods have changed. Moloch and Ishtar, Zeus the Thunder, Jove to whom prayed the Romans, and Jehovah of the Hebrews—all are gone and forgotten of man. Their temples are ruins, their priests are dead, and still I live on; I who have lost all that for which men live. O, blind and more than blind, who would forever be free from death; death for whose kindly touch in years to come you pray. Of what value is immortality when all that makes our little lives is mortal.'

He ceased, but the memory of his words throbbed in dumb agony round the arras, nor did it die, as mortal speech is wont. Into the depths of me it sank, and I fled from his presence. Death, whom I had cursed, seemed now a kindly friend, who, when we tire of our toys, and all our little mortal playthings are faded and broken, comes soft-handed to heal all with his dreamless quiet.

And within me my soul cried out: 'Yes. Ah, yes! Death, death and oblivion are God's greatest gifts.'

In the fall of 1915 Quentin went to Harvard. He was unable to take part in athletics because of a fall he had had in a hunting trip in Arizona. His horse had slipped among the slide rock, and Quentin's back was wrenched and twisted so severely that in spite of constant treatment it never fully recovered. He suffered acute pain from it when he took any strenuous form of exercise.

Bubbling over with life, he entered into every other phase of college life. His taste for literature was almost as catholic as his father's, and his room was strewn with volumes of prose and poetry—histories, essays, novels, detective stories, and epic poems. At one time he was greatly interested in demonology and witchcraft, and combed the second-hand bookstores for grimy tomes on this subject.

Intent on following his line of mathematics and mechanics, he took many difficult courses, but his trials were leavened with a sense of humour that could not be downed.

27 Everett St.
Cambridge, Mass.
February 14, 1916

To " The Father of Quentin Roosevelt" Oyster Bay, N.Y.

Dear Sir:—The enclosed verses were written by your son Quentin at the end of his blue book in the midyear examination in my course, Mathematics A, a few days ago. They strike me as so capital that I want to pass them along.

On account of his illness the boy did not do very well in the first half year, but I think he knows what he is about, and have good hopes for a better showing at the end of the course.

Hoping that you will enjoy these verses as much as I do (he would probably regard sending them to you as a gross breach of confidence!) I am

Very sincerely yours
Edward V. Huntington
Associate Professor of Mathematics
in Harvard University.

Ode to a Math A. Exam.

If it be not fair to me,
What care I how fair it be?

1.

How can I work when my brain is whirling?
What can I do if I've got the grippe?
Why make a bluff at a knowledge that's lacking?
What is the use if I don't give a rip?

2

Cosine and tangent, cotangent, abscissa.
Dance like dry leaves through my sneeze-shattered

head. Square root of a^2 plus b^2 plus k^2
Gibber and grin in the questions I've read.

3

Self centred circles and polar coordinates.
Triangles twisted and octagons wild,
Loci whose weirdness defies all description,
Mountains of zeros all carefully piled.

4

Still I plod on in a dull desperation,
Head aching dismally, ready to sip
Goblets of strychnine or morphine or vitriol.
How can I work when I've got the grippe?

He made two trips, during the summer holidays, in the West—one with his father and his brother Archie, and one with some Western friends.

When at home his taste still ran to mechanics, and he would buy a broken-down motorcycle for sixteen dollars, or a ramshackle automobile for fifty, and doctor his purchase up until it could convey him from place to place, albeit with some uncertainty. His parents once suggested that he and Archie should be given a communal automobile, but the latter explained that it would be quite useless, for he would want the car to run and take him from place to place, whereas Quentin would spend all the time taking the motor down and putting it together again.

CHAPTER 2

The Way of the Eagle

PART 1—TRYING HIS WINGS

In spite of his crippled back Quentin went to one of the Plattsburg camps the summer before the United States entered the war. Through the employment of unlimited determination and grit and the understanding consideration of his superiors he managed to last through the course.

In his letters he spoke bitterly of the attitude of the administration:

February 1917.

I just got a very discouraged letter from my Hon. Pa. We are a pretty sordid lot, aren't we, to want to sit looking on while England and France fight our battles and pan gold into our pockets? I wondered, as I sat by my fire, whether there are any dreams in our land any more. How can there be, for it is lands like ours, and Germany, that kill the nation's dreams, and then the people drop into oblivion. Rome died only when the little dreams and fancies of its people gave way to their lust for ease and pleasure, power and gold. I wonder if we are trending the same way—

When war was declared all four sons turned to their father for advice and assistance in regard to the most rapid manner to get into active service. Quentin first planned to join the Canadian flying forces, but upon confirmation of the rumour that an American flying school was to be started immediately he decided that he would not materially speed up his entrance into active service by going to Canada, and accordingly altered his plans and enlisted for the Mineola camp.

April, 1917.

Excuse this scrawl, scribbled on the train,—there's a reason! Wild excitement! I have been put in the aviation school at Mineola instead of the one at Newport News. I discovered, after I had gotten down to the station, that there is a 1.35 train for Washington that I could have taken, and so stayed with you at the Mid. Frol. However, I settled down in the 12.30 and woke up the next a.m. at Washington with that evil tempered, sandpaper-clothed feeling of filth which is the trade mark of all midnight trains. A bath, and such, at Alice's was a successful remedy, and I trotted down to the War Department, to start in on a complicated little game of catch as catch can, with the Aviation authorities. Their policy is one of mystery. You ask for an application whereupon a little coloured "pusson" takes you in tow through some twenty miles of stairs to an equally little white man who gives you a blank. The rest of your day is spent in taking that little blank for visits to various dens in the building.

Next comes your physical exam., over which a hypochondriac with the darkest views of his fellowmen, presides. After two hours of a twentieth-century refinement of the inquisition you are pronounced fit, and travel on again for your mental test. The presiding deity there is a gentleman who feels like David,—or was it Isaiah—that all men are liars. And the questions: "What is the average age of the Dodo?" the correct answer should be 37. "What is the average sex." but to go on.

It really did take me two days to get by all the red tape, and apparently I was miraculously lucky at that.

First his instructors and later his pupils agreed that Quentin was gifted with that sixth sense that singles out the born aviator. Some men have an ability to call forth from machinery the best that is in it; it is a power analogous to that bestowed upon occasional horsemen, and is even more inexplicable. Quentin possessed this gift to a very marked degree, and when the first detachment of aviators was sent across to France he was among them, as was his boyhood friend, Hamilton Coolidge. The two boys had been at Groton and Harvard together, they were at the same aviators' schools in France, and went up to the line together, serving in neighbouring squadrons, Coolidge lived to become one of the most distinguished American aces, and when he was brought down on October 27, 1918, by a direct hit from an antiaircraft gun, his loss was bitterly felt by officer and enlisted man alike.

On July 23, 1917, they sailed from New York on the *Orduña*.

> 25 July, 1917.
> We are apparently to put into Halifax and there wait for a convoy, goodness knows how long! ... There is literally nobody on board except soldiers. Cousin Katy, and five or six extraneous nonentities that bob up and down on the smoking room horizon. It's by way of being very dull, for shuffle board, bridge, and reading become boring in time and even the springs of conversation can eventually be pumped dry. Our outfit are really mighty fine fellows, all of them. We've organised one of those interminable bridge-games, and as we play for a quarter of a cent a point there is not much chance of any great financial transactions either way..... a thoroughly satisfactory arrangement—*magnifique et pas cher*.
> Monday, after I left you I trotted down to the boat... I don't mind confessing I felt pretty down when I saw the Statue of Liberty and the New York sky line dropping below the horizon.
> Thanks, Mother dear, for the "Lute of Jade." It was just the sort of present that could cheer me up. When I opened it that first night I didn't know what it was, but it made the most tremendous difference, and of course I love it. It is sitting beside me as I write, looking friendly and very "family and home" like.

The next letter was from Halifax, where the transport was held waiting for the convoy.

> I found a paper bundle in my cabin when I returned, which mother had left. I opened it and found, neatly wrapped in a napkin,—a loaf of bread, lots of chocolate, and a knife, with a note saying it was from Margaret, the cook! I half expected to find my pyjamas full of messages from Mary, after that.
> The long stay here has been pretty hard on everybody, for you can't help feeling it would have been much pleasanter to put in a week more in New York! Otherwise I am fairly well settled in existence of a uniform and appalling dullness. We've been trying boxing for exercise but yesterday I succeeded in getting one on the nose which the doctor thinks may have broken it. It

doesn't look crushed, though, so I think he may be wrong.
The "little clock" is a great satisfaction and sits sociably by my bed, beside the bottle of Poland water. The bread and chocolate is just finished and was a howling success. Please thank Margaret. This letter is merely a goodbye one, for total atrophy of the brain has resulted from this long stay.

August 10th

As it looks as if we were really getting somewhere, for they promise we will be in by tomorrow,—so I shall telegraph you then. I was going to send this from London, but things are so uncertain that I cannot be sure we will ever get there at all, let alone be there long enough to get letters off. There is a chance we will go direct to Folkestone. At the moment I feel as if anywhere on shore would be better than this boat. She's comfortable, and the food is O. K., but three weeks—Columbus could have given us a good race at that rate. There's really astonishingly little going on, on Shipboard. All the regular ship games and such like have died from overwork, and our chief amusement is betting on when we arrive. . . . Otherwise our life is spent in anticipation, which, though a great solace, makes but poor reading in a letter.

Paris,—August 18th
39 Rue Villejust

Starting way back at Liverpool,—when I finished my last letter to you we were in sight of the lights at the mouth of the Mersey, and I had decided that we were just about to go in when our destroyer convoy began a lot of promiscuous signalling and round we faced and tore full speed down the channel. I had a horrid moment, for I began to feel that we were destined to take the place of the flying Dutchman. I could almost hear the "man in the smoking room" on board ship ten years hence, as he told over his whiskey and soda how he once had seen the lost *Orduña*—grey mist pouring from her rusted funnel, go tearing past—leaving no wake behind her—the sunlight showing through the rotted ribs of her boats,—and had heard the rattle of the skeleton soldiers that drilled on her mildewed decks to the wail of a ghastly band.

However, Sunday morning at five my dreams were rudely shattered by the thumping of the anchor chain and we were in

Liverpool. There we were met with bad news. Alas for all our pleasant schemes of London. We were packed into a filthy little troop-train with an engine of a type once used on the New York elevated, and shot off at once to Folkestone. There after an uneventful night we boarded the channel steamer. It was hard to realise that I had gone through England. Somehow, I don't feel as if I should ever really see it until we go abroad. I shall never have "permission" to go there, for if I get long enough to go there I shall wait over and get an extension to go home to you. England is lovely though. The hedge rows are green, and the little canals mirror the sky, and all about there is a kind of "lots of time" quiet, as the war were an idle speculation, and not hideous reality. The little thatched cottages and the funny old bridges seem all venerable apostles of peace.

In France, though, it is different. Even on the run up from Boulogne to Paris the signs of war were everywhere. Every little while there would come a concentrating camp of some sort,—a food depot, or a gang of Chinese, or German prisoners that worked along the railroad tracks. And then came Paris, so late at night that I, for one, was glad enough to sleepily turn into my room, and drop off, too tired to care about baggages or the frenzied protests of the hotel concierge.

Next morning about eleven I woke, and after a breakfast of war bread and eggs—no more *brioches et miel*—reported at headquarters. There was all sorts of news. None of our nine officers are to be used for flying, at least for the present. The trouble is that we are going into this war, of course, on a vast scale, and that means a vast organisation. A huge American school is to be built in the central part of France,—it has to be provided with an administration, and officers have to be trained to take charge of instruction in bombing, anti-aircraft, reconnaissance, and the various other highly specialised forms of work. The net result is that all of our nine are placed in one or another kind of ground job, and scattered to the four winds of heaven.

I report tomorrow at the American School—fairly near where Tommy is—to take the place of Seth, who has gone with our enlisted men to a French school. The work I know nothing of as yet.—I'll report as soon as I've begun. I don't fancy that I shall care very much for it, though. However, whatever it is, it's all in the days run and part of our business, which is to eliminate the Hun. I shall probably have no flying for at least two months,—and during all that time will not get into the *Zone des Armées*, if that pleases you. I confess I'm sorry, for I wanted to get started flying, and have it over with. I know my back wouldn't last very long. The thing that I realise more each day I am here, is how serious a proposition this war has become. Back in the states no one realises how important it is. I would give my boots to get hold of some of them who said to me that all this war needed was our wealth. Of course they need it,—but someone, Napoleon I think, said that you can't beat a nation by starving it or bankrupting it.

We have before us the task of driving the Bosche back, and overwhelming him, and no amount of talk, of airplane fleets that loom large only in the minds of the newspaper writers, can remove his presence from before us. Paris shows that, for it is not the Paris that we used to love, the Paris of five years past. The streets are there, but the crowds are different. There are no more young men in the crowds unless in uniform. Everywhere you see women in black, and there is no more cheerful shouting and laughing. Many, many of the women have a haunted look in their eyes, as if they had seen something too terrible for forgetfulness. They make one realise the weight that lies on all alike now. There is a sobering like no other feeling I know in the sight of a boy my age helped along the street by someone who takes pity on his poor blind eyes. It all makes me feel older.

> Issoudun—Aug. 20—1917
> Monday night.

I've only time for a very short note, as this is to go by a truck driver who is leaving for Paris. After all sorts of excitements, I'm settled down here definitely, with Cord for running partner. My job isn't half bad either. I'm supply officer for the camp, which consists principally in keeping a fleet of fifty-two motor trucks in running order and at the proper place. I also have to look after endless supplies of gasoline, and tools that are all jumbled into one vast pile, straight from the ship. In between times I act as the buffer between irate railroad officials full of jabbering complaints, and equally angry American construction officers who would like to consign the entire French railroad system to Hell, way billed collect farther on. Altogether, I've got a reasonably busy job! However it's very good fun—lots more responsibility than I've ever had,—in fact lots more than I'd think of attempting back home. Only being out here, with no one else to do it, we have to, that's all.

Its hard, though, to realise that it's war. We're stuck five miles out of a typical little French town,—the old tower and Hotel de Ville dating back to Richard Coeur de Lion's time,—with no appreciable improvements in sanitation during the last six hundred years. There isn't a bathtub within less than twenty-five miles! In fact on Sunday Cord and I became so desperate that we took to our motorcycles,—as supply and quartermaster officers we have them,—and went off twenty miles to the nearest river to swim. It seemed preposterously un-war like,—motorcycling off for a Sunday swim, and then lying on our backs and watching the sunset as we talked of the place that seems pleasantest to our minds now—Long Island. We both agreed that we hadn't realised how much we loved it until we were away. I think he's been a little homesick down here,—it is a forsaken hole. However mail gets here, and apparently it's equally quick whether by the Farmer's Loan and Trust or the Military mail.

I've had a letter from father and one from mother dated the thirtieth which came in less than three weeks *via* the Farmer's Loan and Trust.

I have no idea how long I shall be here. I'm afraid it will be months before I even get in a plane again. Both Cord and I feel that we would like our jobs a lot more if they came after we had been a couple of months at the front.

August 23rd.

I have been so very busy that this is the first chance I have had for a half an hour to write letters in. As I wrote Mother, I am now at the American Aviation School, or rather what will be the American School. Mother knows where it is and I am not allowed to mention the name. At the moment it looks as little like an Aviation School as anything I have seen. We have about two hundred men, and are busily employed getting all the vast equipment necessary to the school unloaded. With my usual evil luck I am stuck here as supply officer, a job for which I am as little gifted as possible. Judging by the way I have mishandled the ten thousand kinds of red tape which I have struck, my only destination after the war will be Atlanta State Prison.

I'm in the midst of a tremendous fight with the quartermaster up the line, as he refuses to allow me a motor-machine-shop, without which I can not possibly keep my trucks in commission. I also have been unable to get any sort of American reading material. Will you ask Mother to send me anything she has in the line of books, that will keep me up on what's going on outside—fact, fancy and fiction. You have no idea how thoroughly isolated we are out here in the A. E. F.

Eleanor treated me wonderfully in Paris. She has a really delightful house from the military viewpoint—good bed, piano, lots of room, bath tub, nice servants and even a garden, and, which is the best of all, "family" in the shape of herself.

Wednesday August 22nd.
Issoudun U. S. Aviation School
(or rather soon-to-be-school).

I can truly say now that I am a *blessé du guerre*, for in the last two days I have been in two motorcycle smashups. The first one was yesterday. I was on my way over to Nevers—eighty miles from here—to arrange about some supplies, and Cord, who is mess sergeant, had gone with me on his machine. We were passing a truck, with him in the lead when, for some unknown reason, he slowed up. I was coming on him, so I slammed on my brake, which jammed, and I started on down the road skidding side and every which way. Cord put on power and got out of the way, but as my brake was locked I could do nothing so I saw a bully spill coming my way, and tried my best to get clear of the truck. The next thing I remember is lying on the bank with Cord and the truck driver pouring water on me and trying to put first-aid compresses on my face. I was pretty well bunged up—a couple of deep cuts on my face, some loose teeth and two hands with not much palm left.

By luck we happened to be near the aviation school where Tommy is—we had intended to stop there—and I was bundled into the truck and sent over there to the hospital and bandaged up. Then, after about an hour, I went over to the barracks and saw Tommy, while I was waiting for one of our cars to come for me. He is in very good form, and is flying very well. In fact, an instructor told me that he thought that Tommy would be the first one of his class to make an "ace" which is pretty good, I think. I got back last night—bringing all sorts of messages to you from Tommy and thanks for your letter—and started out to write to you but found that my hands were too bad, and was sent off to bed by the doctor.

By the way, those two letters,—to Tim and Tommy—nearly got me into a row. They were spotted by a customs official, opened, and read, and I was nearly jailed for life for attempting to bring them in. That *en passant*. At all events this morning, stiff all over, and about an inch deep in bandage, I had to go in town to see about loading some cars. As there was no auto, I went *via* motorcycle side car, and on the way in the man who was driving ran into the wall of a house and shot me out on to my ear. That time I reopened both hands and laid out one hip with a bad cut and bone bruise,—so that at the moment, though in excellent form, I am somewhat dilapidated.

I'm beginning to rather like my job—except for smashups. It is quite interesting trying out the different men, and seeing how each turns out, how to get the best out of them, and how to size them up. I suppose it all makes up experience. There's some good news. We are having a hangar shipped down to us at once, so I suppose we shall soon have planes. At the moment they look pretty far off.

August 25, 1917.

Today I was at Bourges and had my lunch at a queer little tavern, black with age, that lies in the corner of an old castle wall. Over the doorway hangs a faded sign, "*Aux trois raisins noirs*" and up by the wall runs a little, crooked alley, half cobblestone, half steps, that is called *Rue Cassecou*. I know you would have loved it,—and *Madame* who stands at your table, red cheeked and with the white cap that the peasant women wear, while *Monsieur le proprietaire,* cooks the omelet. I took an hour off from my work, for there were places that cried for exploration,—narrow, winding streets that might lead anywhere, and finally did bring me to the cathedral. It has one square tower, but all around the walls are buttressed, like those in Notre Dame.

It is surrounded by a cluster of crooked little streets, whose houses seem as grey and ancient as the gargoyles on the tower. I went in, for there was no service. Once inside it seemed like another world. There was quiet so deep that I could hear the patter of the sacristan's feet as he came toward me, and the whispers of two old peasant women who knelt at a little shrine in the wall. It is like Chartres, for as you come in you see only the sombre gloom of the vaulted arches, and then as you pass on you look back on the glory of a great rose window. There was one window,—a virgin with a veil,—before whom candles were lit,—that was so lovely that I burnt before her a candle.

I shall be very glad to get any books that you can send me. At the moment my library consists of the collected works of Gaston Leblanc, father of Arsène Lupin, and the *Pageant of English Poetry*, and *The Wind in the Willows*.

I wonder if I ever told you my pet prayer,—almost the only one that I care for. It was written, I think, by Bishop Potter. "*Lord, protect us all the day long of our troublous life on earth, until the shadows lengthen and the evening comes, and the busy world is hushed, the fever of life is over, and our work is done. Then in Thy mercy grant us a safe lodging and peace at the last, through Jesus Christ, our Lord.*" I've always loved it, and now, when life is hard, and all that is dearest to me is far away, it is a comfort to think that sometime all this will be past, and that we will have peace.

August 28, 1917.

You know, there are periods when I curse the day that I ever learned French. I am one of the two officers in camp who can talk it, so that outside of my regular supply work I get sent off all over the country on wild goose chases after material with nothing but a rather limited French vocabulary to go on.

Last Saturday was one,—and typical of most of the others. I was sleeping like a log at about six in the morning—it's good and cold then, too—when someone grabbed my foot and shook it, to wake me. I turned over sleepily, and with one eye open, remarked that though I didn't know who the Hellespont it was, I extended the hospitality of any spot outside my tent. There was a sort of pause, and then the person went on in an apologetic way, "I'm Major Hyles." And it was! Of course that woke me up, so I slid out of my warm sleeping bag into clammy clothes, and found out what the matter was. He wanted apparently, a pump, a switch, and an extra locomotive,—for which I was to scour the country, and not return empty handed.

That being the case I hopped on my motorcycle—it was the first day the doctor let me ride since my accident—and disappeared, breakfastless, into the scenery. Twelve o'clock found me at a town about 30 miles away, tired and dusty with over a hundred miles to the bad, and no success. However things began to look better and after having seen several regiments of *M. le Chef de Sections*, and *Chef de Districts*, I got the engine and arranged to have five trucks over at eight the next morning for the switch. Of pump however, there was no sign, until I found one in the barn at the back of a manufacturing company's shops, and then I started back, reported in town to the captain, and came out here to my tent, about 9:30, all in, and with pleasant prospect of getting up at six in the morning and going over with the trucks for the switch.

September 5, 1917.

My hours have been getting progressively longer. I start in with six o'clock breakfast and work till five. Then I go over with Cord to the French camp to fly, which means that I don't get back to bed until between nine and ten. It's a mighty long day,—and the work's tiresome. We are arranging for the storing and unpacking of all the equipment,—and as it ranges from rock crushers to flash lights,—and has all to be listed, checked with an invoice from the states,—stored according to classification and then cross indexed in a filing system, I am as busy as several hivefuls of bees.

Then on top of that there's flying which I don't think I'd do if it weren't for Cord. He has been relieved from his quartermaster job, and so hasn't much to do. Consequently he has arranged that he and I go over to the French school and fly. We flew twice with instructors, and then went alone,—as (except for the controls) the machines aren't much different from the Curtis. They are as safe as an auto, as safe really as the old Curtis. All this doesn't interfere with the fact that a seventeen mile motorcycle ride, a flight, and then back by night aren't very resting. In fact my back just about quit on me, so I struck, and this afternoon called off work at five thirty, washed and *shaved* (though there's no particular reason to over here!).

September 6, 1917.

Last night, just after I had finished writing to you, a tremendous thunderstorm struck us. I was in bed,—dozing,—and luxuriating in the fact that it was half-past eight and I was all ready to go to sleep,—when a regular cloud burst hit the camp. Inside of five minutes my tent had become the housing for a very respectable water course,—a fact which I discovered when it started to wash off some of my clothes. I hastily moved everything above high water mark, and then turned over to a sleep, punctuated by leaks, and one visit from a water-soaked dog, that fled to my bed for refuge.

In the morning our camp had settled into a sea of gumbo mud. I got down to my office for work, and after a strenuous two hours succeeded in getting six of the trucks out onto the road. The others were buried axle deep in mud, and so we left them for dry weather. Consequently my day was peaceful—interrupted only by the arrival of a French general, described to me by my supply sergeant as "a French admiral, or something, all dolled up in gold lace, who's a jabbering after you out there."

P. S. Next morning 6:30 a.m.—And the winds blew and the rains fell and the centre of my tent has become a water course,—so now I am an *évacué*—alas and alackaday-de! It's rained all night

September 7.

There's been a temporary cessation of work due to flood conditions so I have a chance to write to you. I have never seen such a place for rain. It started in last night just about the time I got to bed, and poured, beginning with a thunderstorm. I settled in for a comfortable sleep, as my tent didn't leak, when I noticed the beginning of a water course across my tent floor. I had just time to put everything up on my trunk when it began to come through in dead earnest. I don't mind a river bed as a geological formation, but I can't say that I think much of it as a resting place.

This morning when I woke up there was about an inch of water everywhere, and I had the pleasant job of getting into damp clothes while perched precariously on the edge of my cot. When I got down to my office, and supply department, I found another flood. The roof leaks in about seventeen different places, and the supply staff were clustered around the few

Ararats afforded by desks and tool benches. Consequently there wasn't much work ahead, for the trucks are all mired down so deeply that it would be almost impossible to even get them out to the road, and even the most enthusiastic of motorcyclists wouldn't try the roads through all this. So, after about an hour of work on a filing system we are fixing up for our tools I had to give it up, as the rain spattered down onto the file cards, and I am calling it a day and writing to you instead.

We are really beginning to get settled in here in spite of the weather, and I think we shall overcome that, for I am going to start building cinder roads as soon as the weather clears enough, to get my trucks through to the railroad tracks. I hope they will really get the school itself started soon, and then maybe there will be barracks for us instead of tents. The trouble is that garages for trucks, and sheds for tools and equipment are much more important than sheds for mere men, and so they have to come first.

I have gotten in a certain amount of flying over at a French school, some seventeen miles from here. I go over there with Cord at five thirty when the work is over here and get in about a half an hour's flight. I can't do it very often though, for I am having a certain amount of trouble with my back, and I don't want to have it give out on me while I am still supply officer. About every third day I call my work done at five thirty, and settle down to a book and a pipe until eight thirty bed time, and so I make out pretty well. I don't know when I am going to be put regularly into flying service again. I am afraid that it won't be for some time, to judge by the way things are going. Still, I haven't got Ted's point of view, and I'm certain I'll get in in plenty of time. I'm not in the least afraid that the war will be done before I've had my whack at the Boche. I have to go up to Paris on business next week, and I hope I shall get a chance to see Arch and Ted then, for Eleanor thinks that they are going to try and get back en permission. I won't have much time for them, as I have to get vast quantities of parts for motorcycles and trucks, but I am going to stay with Eleanor.

I haven't heard a sound from the States for over a week now, so I suppose there must have been some mix up in the mails at the post office. I suppose they will get to me in the end, though, for I have gotten two letters from Eleanor that came by way of the military post office.

My fingers are getting so cold that typewriting is becoming an illegible attempt, so I shall even call it off for the rest of the day. Lots of love to all the family, and thanks for all your letters. Mother dearest, from,

Quentin.

39 Rue de Villejust,
September 13, 1917.

Just last Monday the order came through that Cord and I were assigned to the 1st Aero Squadron, and then to report there at once for flying. I could not leave, as there was no one to take my place as supply officer. However, I did start up to Paris at once, as there were all sorts of things that I needed for my supply department. It seems to be an interminable job getting things here in France, so I shall probably be up here with Eleanor for several days more. As a matter of fact I was very sorry to leave the supply department just at this moment. I had expected to leave it about three months later. As it is I leave just when I was beginning to get things running well, and when I had really become attached to the men that were under me.

When I told my supply sergeant he said nothing at all for a minute and then "Oh Hell, sir, can't you take me with you to that outfit." which I thought was pretty nice of him. However I had to do it. I rather think that if I had wanted to I could have stayed with the job,— but it wasn't worth it. If I had stuck this time it meant that I was running the risk of being stuck with it permanently, a sort of *embusqué* occupation. And so I am changed, and become the juniorest of junior lieutenants in an outfit composed mostly of regular army fliers. Still I get back to planes again—and it means that I'll probably see service fairly soon. I was beginning to feel rather like an *embusqué*,—but this changes it all. I rather think we'll first be down where Tommy is,—and so I'll be able to get hold of him. As soon as I get with the squadron I'll give you all the news of it.

One rather amusing thing happened—amusing because it was so typically American. The commandant where we were is a regular old French war dog, with a string of medals across his chest. The other day at dinner I heard him give a great roar of laughter, and so naturally I asked him what was amusing him so.

It appears that he had admired a dog belonging to one of our captains, whereupon the captain,—a long, scrawny individual with a strongly American sense of humour and delightful blue eyes with a concealed twinkle in them, explained to him in laborious French that the dog was all right, yes, but that its mother had *"plus de medailles que vous n'en avez, mon commandant."*
Paris is as delightful as ever, though I have been too busy to see very much of it,—at least of the parts that we'll see when we go here after the war. Most of my goings and comings have been in obscure garages and warehouses with addresses like 14 Rue Roger Bacon and 64 Quai de Billy.

29 Avenue du Bois de Boulogne
September 15th, 1917.

Eleanor originally had a bad cold, but she has succeeded in passing it on to me, now, and is as bright as a button. We went out for a spree last night,—dinner at Premiers and then a French play. It was a farce, and "I give you my word" it was the darndest. I was perfectly weak from laughing by the end of it, but scandalous is no name. I shan't even say anything about it—for you couldn't retail the plot to anyone. Then today, after a morning of business, I took an afternoon off and went shopping with Eleanor. We started out rather prosaically with heavy woollen underclothes, slippers and a pair of boots.

Then Eleanor decided that she wanted to give me a wrapper for a birthday present. I voted against a heavy, warm one, because I felt that everything I have over here was practical and suggested preparations for a long stay in uniform in the field. So we went to Liberty's and I got—or rather chose the material for—a silk one, rather like my pet blue one at home. It may be a bad plan to do "after the war" shopping, but I want on my birthday to have things that remind me of peace, and not of this war.

September 20, 1917.
Thursday.

I don't mind so much an out and out slacker, who says he is afraid, or unwilling to go, but I hate the one that gets a bulletproof job in the Red Cross or Y. M. C. A., and then proceeds to talk of "doing his bit."

★★★★★★

Monday afternoon I arrived back here again, all prepared to

leave at once for the First Squadron. The major met me at the station, and on the way out in the car began talking to me about Colonel Bolling's visit—he was down at camp. Suddenly he said,—"I gave you a darned good recommendation to him, but why are you changing to that other outfit? You don't gain much, for you're getting some flying over here, and the experience you've gained in the supply work you've done here, is worth twice what you can get out of the job of plain flying lieutenant"

Of course, it was a big surprise to me,—but the upshot was that I agreed to put it before the colonel,—Colonel Bolling is second in command of American Air Service in France. To my surprise, he agreed with the major. He said "the only reason I was transferring you was for the flying—if you are getting your flying here, stay by all means. You have apparently made a good job of this one,—and the reason I sent you down in the first place, was to give you experience. If I were you, I should stay, for it will count a good deal more in a man's favour if he has made a good job of something like this supply position of yours, than if he has merely flown as junior lieutenant in a squadron."

After that of course I stayed, especially as he promised to put me in a squadron at the front as soon as they got started sending them up there. I am glad in a way, for now I know for certain that I shall not be *embusquéd* here, and I had become quite attached to the men working for me. Five or six of them came round, when they heard that I was going to go, and told me that they were very sorry to hear it. My sergeant asked me to get him transferred into the outfit I was going to. It really made me feel quite—well, a lump in my throat, if you know the feeling. Last night,—or rather yesterday, I received orders to have trucks in to receive about two hundred men, coming from one of the ports. I got the trucks and went with them myself,—just to be on the safe side. I sat around the station till midnight, for the troops were being sent in a freight train, which was late of course. Then the train appeared, and when I went up to greet the officer, who should it be but Phil Carroll, with his outfit, just arrived. I nearly collapsed, out of combined surprise and satisfaction. Of course, after business was over, I made him tell me all the news of all Long Island.

September 30th, 1917.
Sunday.

Today, being Sunday, was inspection and so when it was over I went off to look around the country. It is glorious weather now,—the roads bright and dusty, with flurries of fallen leaves whirling across them, and that feeling in the air which says, despite the golden countryside, that autumn is passing fast into winter. I wandered where the roads lead me, past little farmhouses, nestling close to great stacks of hay, and pleasant fields where the little boys ran out from their sheep to watch me pass, and the sheep dogs barked disapproval,—past little towns, barely more than a cluster of houses, with their weather worn little church, and cobble stoned streets.

The afternoon was passing, and I was beginning to think of camp once more, when I came upon a somewhat larger town,—over whose roofs I saw an old tower rising. And so, as I came opposite I stopped to look a minute. It had been an old *château*,—gone partly to ruin,—and round it had grown the town,—where It's front must have been was a little inn, with the sign "*Au Lion Noir.*" The old arch was still there,—where the knights went out to battle in times past,—and I could see through it a courtyard, all bright in the afternoon sun, with little tables, and back of them the old wall with flowers in the windows,—and rusted iron gratings.

And as I looked, out came the innkeeper, a great blue apron round him, to know if I would not stop and have some beer,— "*car vous devez avoir soif sur la grande route.*" And so I came in and sat in the courtyard, watching the pigeons wheel and circle back to their nests in the holes where the tower roof had fallen. I was told all about the old tower,—how it was old, very old,—but now fallen into ruin,—save where it was used for the inn,— even the great stairway, whose rafters I could trace along the side of the walls, was half gone. But yet, so *Monsieur* said,—"*on y est bien, mon cher,*" for so he called me,—I was "*mon cher,*"—an American coming to fight for France. And then, at length, it was time to go, and I put my hand in my pocket to pay,—when *Monsieur* stopped me with "*non, non, non,—il ne faut pas faire ça.*" Arguments were useless,—and so finally we parted,—and just as I was going he brought out a little black brass snuff box, and offered me some, which I took, though I loathed it. And when I left he told me to return, with my friends, and visit him again.

October 8 and 10, 1917.

The flower I'm enclosing is mimosa. I don't know if it will keep It's perfume, but it's too lovely now. Yesterday the major and an English captain who has been *reformé* sailed over across the bay to a funny little bit of a fishing village. There's the most glorious grove of mimosa there—part of the grounds of the parish church. It's all in bloom now, golden yellow avenues of it with a heavy sweet scent that fills the air. It was a hot afternoon, with no clouds overhead, and down in the grove, with no noise of the outside world except the trickle of a brook and the clatter of an old peasant woman's *sabots* as she went up and down tending the trees, the war seemed very far away and unreal.

No one in the village seemed to be of this century even. The tiny winding street is made of oyster shells,—and bordering it were little, low, white washed houses with overhanging eaves. The wharf was deserted except for a few old men in the big, patched trousers they wear here, that look like bloomers,—and where the sunlight came through the open doors you could see the polished brass candlesticks on the mantelpiece, warm red bricks on the floor, and children playing in the sunlight.

It was more like a page from a sketch book than a real place,—and utterly apart from war, and flying, with all the hurry and noise of the camp. We stopped at the inn—it was a combination of inn, general store, social centre—and took oysters, for which the town is famous, while the old proprietress chattered around and to us like a nice, motherly old hen. She told us that the *Ancre d'Or*, that was the inn's name, had been in their family for over a hundred years,—the men fishing while the women-folk ran the inn. Then, after complimenting her on her oysters—at which she beamed all over—we left while she bobbed "*au revoir messieu*" in the doorway. "And so," as Samuel Pepys said, "*To bed.*"

The autumn is well here, often two weeks of dismal, chilly rain and mist, and the country side is bright with It's brave resistance to the frosty nights. All along the road the trees are showing brilliant yellows and crimsons,—with here and there a clump of sombre pines,—or a *château* on the cliffs, its towers in sharp silhouette against the sky. The fallen leaves swirl and dance among the eddies of white dust along the *"grand routes,"*—and everything and everyone seems to be living life to It's fullest before the dreary dark of the long winter nights set in. The Loire country is exquisite,—little *châteaux*, and funny, ancient villages, that round the ruins of some castle, or else bustling modern cities like Nantes,—that contrast strangely,—the street cars and broad asphalt streets, with the old castle, and It's net work of narrow winding alleys in their midst.

Aviation Camp
November 1, 1917.

During the last few weeks I have been chasing all over the lot and so haven't had any chance to write you and tell you the news of myself. Added to that my last letter, which I sent to you by a transport officer two weeks ago was unfortunately delayed. I found out today, just by accident, that he was in the hospital as the result of a too protracted spree, and that his ship had sailed without him, so I shall have to go back into the dim distant periods of the past over two weeks ago to tell you all that has happened.

In the first place, I was sent away from here with orders to go down to one of our ports of debarkation and take charge of a lot of Hudson touring cars which were to be taken overland to Paris. I got down there in great spirits, for of course it was a regular spree to get away from this camp for about a week wandering all over France in a brand new touring car. However, I found when I got down to the port that things weren't going to be quite as easy as I had thought. In the first place the cars weren't even unloaded from the boat, and there didn't seem to be much chance of my getting them off for weeks, as the stevedores were crowded up with work.

After one day I decided that particular place was no sort of location for me so I began to hunt around for some way to hurry things up. The captain of the ship proved to be the solution. She is a merchant ship, taken over by the government for the transport service, with the same old merchant captain. He and I got on excellently—he came from Arlington, Mass., which was an instant bond in common, and so I ended up by living on the boat, and using the ship's crew and winches to unload and my own men to get the cars out, so that they were out on the dock in three days. I had my own truck men down with me to take charge of them so we got them assembled in short time and in four days were out on the road again.

It was a delightful run up. All through Brittany and then up the valley of the Loire. I have got a little *"presink"* for you which I am going to send home by the first person. It is a very cunning little enamel cross that comes from Hervé Kiel's town,—do you remember? The valley of the Loire is really lovely. I hadn't realised before how lovely France was, for our region, though it is pretty, is very monotonous, with nothing except the perpetual run of farmhouses—which you soon become accustomed to. The Loire valley is all different, though, for it is never the same.

Part of the time you are driving high up on the crest of the hills, with the Loire like a silver thread down below you, and the country, "pleasant France," spread beneath you with no hint of the war that is raging in the North, or again you drop down into the valley where you can watch the little towns and *châteaux* silhouetted against the sky. I saw so many places that I wanted to stop and investigate and couldn't,—funny little towns where the street winds around between houses, and under the ruined walls of the *château* to which the houses cling, or little grimy inns, "*les Trois Raisins Noirs*" or "*le Cheval qui Boite*," all of which I am sure had all sorts of nice things in them to see. However, we could only stop very occasionally for meals, and so I didn't get a chance to do much more than see the country as I passed through.

I did however, on the second day get a chance to stop off at Chartres and burn a candle in the cathedral. I had no idea that the road went through there, when all of a sudden I saw off on the horizon the towers of a cathedral and thought that it must be that. So I called a halt, and while the men went off and got lunch I went in the cathedral. Do you remember the last time we were there,—when I was so busy trying to find out about the window, and we went out with Mr. Thoron? Goodness but that seems ages and ages ago. However, I finally got to Paris, and arrived in on Eleanor out of a clear sky, to find myself a very welcome guest as she had been feeling very lonely. The next morning I reported to headquarters and then went back to Eleanor's to get over the last of a slight attack of some sort of malaria that I had contracted in the run up.

When I reported to headquarters two days later I had the most horrid blow. I found that I was slated to take a detachment of fifty men to be taught the supply officer job in England. Of course I kicked. It seemed to be getting too far afield from flying and too far up in the supply work for me. However I had no success and went down to Issoudun again feeling rather low about it. Once down here however, I found that Jim Miller didn't want me to be taken away and after much telephoning to Paris I think it has been arranged that I am to stay here. I shall know tomorrow as I am going up to Paris again.

As a matter of fact I am going to have a bully job here. There is one of the squadrons here that is all disorganised. It got over here under an officer who was a poor bone head with no idea of how to get on with the men and the result is that there is no sort of morale to it at all. The men don't care whether they are out in the guard house or not, and they are in a frightful state. And yet they come from the same place as our crowd and are really exactly as good stuff. So they are going to put me in command of it here, to see what I can make of it. I am very much pleased, of course, for if I get away with it it means a very big step toward getting my own squadron to take out in the spring when we start sending our squadrons out to the front. It also is rather nice for they were very nice to me when they said that they would put me on, though they do refer to it as a dirty job. I don't care, for I think I can make it. I am going to get about five of my old crew transferred to it and then start in when I get back from Paris.

If everything works all right I am to stick here until they get the other fields working, for the plan is to have five fields working within a radius of ten miles, and am then to move over and take charge of one of the outlying fields. The idea is that they put one squadron in each field, and complete it's training and at the same time get it working in together before they send it out to the front. It sounds as though it were going to be a bully chance to get away from any taint of supply officer and to get back into the flying end in the right way. I am very cheerful.

December 8, 1917.

I am commanding officer of what is called the Headquarters

detachment. It includes about six hundred cadets and forty officers. I have to see that cadet affairs work properly,—that all the officers do their work,—and most of all, I am the one the colonel hops on if there's any complaint about the cadets. It is really no job for a flying lieutenant. In the first place—it takes all of my time,—or rather should take all of it, to the exclusion of flying. And then, too, it is pretty hard to command and discipline thirty nine other lieutenants when you are of the same rank and only a few months sooner. I have been working nights on the thing trying to get it organised,—then stealing a couple of hours off in the day to fly. The real trouble is that it doesn't get me anywhere. I suppose it can all be classed as experience,—but I feel a little as if it were just "one more dirty job."

My commanding officer now is my old Mineola one,—though, which helps, for he says he will let me get away as soon as they start sending any men out to the front. At the moment, though, it doesn't look as if any of us would get out for a couple of months. What I am hoping is to be sent up in a British squadron some time toward the end of January, but I am not sure how much chance there is for anything like that. What one wants so rarely happens in this army. At all events, I am now plugging along from day to day, doing my work, and enjoying my flying.

These little fast machines are delightful. You feel so at home in them, for there is just room in the cockpit for you and your controls, and not an inch more. And then they're so quick to act. It's not like piloting a great lumbering Curtis, for you could do two loops in a Nieuport during the time it takes a Curtis to do one. It's frightfully cold, now, though. Even in my teddy-bear,—that's what they call those aviator suits,—I freeze pretty generally, if I try any ceiling work. If it's freezing down below it is *some* cold up about fifteen thousand. Aviation has considerably altered my views on religion. I don't see how the angels stand it. Do you remember that delightful grey muffler you made me? It's very soft, either Angora or camel's hair I think,—and is now doing yeoman duty bridging the gap between the top of my suit and the bottom of my helmet. I think it is bringing me luck, too, for I am flying much better, now that I wear it every day. As a matter of fact I am wearing just about everything movable 'round my room now, and expect to for the next four months or so.

I had an exciting time two weeks ago with a plane. I was taking off, and had just got my wheels clear when a bit of mud got thrown against the propeller and broke it. One of the pieces went through the gasoline tank and before the wheels were really down on the ground again, or before I even had a chance to cut the switch, the whole thing was in flames. I made a wild snatch at my safety belt, got it undone, and slid out of the plane on the double-quick time. It cant have taken me more than thirty seconds, and yet when I got out, my boots and pant legs were on fire.

As a matter of fact, it's marvellous the amount you get away with in these planes. Two fellows in the last week have gone straight into the ground in *vrilles*, totally wrecking the plane,— and yet neither one is seriously hurt. The worst one of the two came down about three hundred feet, hit the ground so hard that he pushed the engine back where the rudder bar should be and the rudder bar under the seat,—and yet didn't break any bones. He will be out of the hospital in three weeks they think. All he got is a couple of bad cuts on his face from the wind shield and a stove-in chest. I've decided that nothing short of shooting a man or breaking a control is fatal!

December 16

Here goes for a very long letter, full of all sorts of news, for I've just met the man who was supposed to take my last long letter home. He was an officer on one of our ships, whom I happened to know, and is back in Paris now, for his ship—and my letter were sunk. As a matter of fact, this is the first chance I've had to write for I really have been busy. At the moment though I am confined to bed, the result of a mild attack of pneumonia. I had had a cough for a month, which suddenly developed into that. I'm sorry, for I've lots of work to do,—but It's a rather pleasant rest.

To begin 'way back—after I got back from my work of taking cars to Paris, I found that I had another job waiting for me. I was put in command of a squadron in quarantine for mumps. They had been under a bad C. O. and were pretty thoroughly disorganised. I had Ham Coolidge for my second in command

and two other very nice fellows from out West. I followed the Brushwood Boy's principle of sweating the fat off 'em and the beef on. First I put in two days making them clean out their barracks, and fix things up generally. Then I took them out and drilled and hiked until I know I was good and tired so I rather think they were. It worked like a charm, though, for after about two weeks they were all in fine shape. Really, the American of the mechanic class is a pretty fine specimen, I think. You see all the mechanics,—the skilled labour, has gone into the aviation service,—so you do get a good crowd. At all events, just about the time I had got them really going, another reorganisation hit us.

That has been the trouble all along in the Air Service. The first lot of regulars that they sent over here in the aviation weren't much. They were mostly men who had not made themselves useful enough in the States to keep them. They got over here, and found that the reserve officers who had been sent were a far more capable crowd. Then, instead of turning in and trying to work together as far as possible they tried to buck the reserves. You see, nearly all of them—the regulars I mean—came over here as captains, and as they are now either majors or colonels,—they've gone promotion wild. They have been hanging on, trying to prove that the reserve officers were useless. We had about three months of that, and then, thank heaven, Washington realised what was going on, and sent over a complete new organisation.

(The letter at that moment was interrupted by Major Goldthwaite, who came in and blew the roof off me for trying to write or do anything like that. This is continued two days later.)

I have just started to really convalesce, and am being allowed to read and write again. I was really quite sick for a while, a good deal sicker than I thought I was, and so, as soon as my temperature began to go down again I thought I was good for letter writing and reading. The medico sat on that scheme, though, so today is my first day of doing anything at all for ten days. I am to be kept in bed here until I am well enough to make the trip safely, and then am to be sent up for a two weeks' sick leave, when I shall see Eleanor in Paris, and get all fixed up again.

We have now got a real man-size organisation over here now,

and it has struck our school down here, for we now have my old Mineola K. O. He has made the most tremendous difference to the place. He was responsible for my last change in job, though. Just after he came here, when they made the new organisation, he made me commanding officer of what is known officially as the headquarters detachment. That consists of all the cadets and some fifty officers. You probably don't know what the cadets are, as no one back in the states, including the war department, seems to have any very definite idea about them. The original idea was that, as all fliers were to be officers, all flying students should be cadets. It's a good idea, too,—I wish they'd had it when I was at Mineola, for I'd have gotten a hundred dollars a month instead of forty. At all events the edict went forth that all students were cadets.

Then some lunatic got the idea that there was a crying need for pilots over here, that we were ready for six hundred students a month, and some other pipe dream, so they started shipping over untrained cadets by the hundred to France. Of course we have no earthly means of coping with them, and never wanted them in the first place. What with the troubles we have had in getting construction gangs and materials, I doubt if this school will be ready for six hundred pilots by next June, let alone six hundred a month now. What is more, and what they didn't seem to realise back in Washington, we are an advanced school, and have no facilities for training beginners. Consequently, we have now about six hundred non-flying cadets here with nothing in the world for them to do, and apparently no chance of their flying in the next couple of months.

The colonel, when he put me in command, told me I was to try and get things straightened out as far as possible, and then make a detailed report on the state of things. I started in and found I was up against a most tremendous job. The cadets had no organisation at all. They were being used for guard duty, and nothing else, and there is nothing more demoralising for a lot of men than doing guard under frightful conditions, and nothing else. I started in, and after two days, sent in a report as long as a presidential message, asking that more enlisted men be detailed to relieve the guard, that arrangements be made to ship off cadets to preliminary schools if possible, and that if there were any vacancies for non flying commissions in the air service, they be issued to cadets on a competitive examination.

Then I got together the officers, and picked out six assistants who I knew would work and were good fellows, and arranged that the seven of us be excused from regular flying formations. Thus we could work at the cadets and tuck in our flying whenever we had a spare moment. Then we divided them up into organisations of two hundred and fifty and started to lick them into some sort of military shape. Outside of the non-fliers, I now have one hundred and fifty fliers, and twenty navy fliers—known unofficially as the flying fish—and we have got them working out fairly well, though it's a pretty unsatisfactory situation at best. I know if I were a cadet I should feel justified in kicking, if, after being enlisted because I had a college education and was recommended by all sorts of people as good aviation material, I was used as a guard for an aviation camp with the prospect of flying in four or five months.

The doctor has come in and ordered me to lie down again, so I must stop. I have been a perfect pig about not writing more, and from now on you will see a vast change in the news from me, for I have loved your letters. The trouble is that writing home makes me get gloomy, for then you start looking at the war as a whole,—an impossible system. I have given it up entirely, and take it day by day. The only really satisfactory thing is that flying is wonderful fun on these new machines. I wish you could see them. We can do stunts that you would think were impossible after watching a Curtis wallow along through the air.

The doctor is in again.

Lots of love, and I'll write again as soon as I'm out of the hospital,

Quent.

December 18, 1917.

I am in the hospital, the result of a mild case of pneumonia. You see, I have been trailing around here through mud and cold, and draughty, unheated barracks for the last month with a tremendous cold and cough. About three weeks ago it got pretty bad, but as I had lots of work on hand and no one else that I wanted to do it, I kept on going. About a week and a half ago it really began to hit me, and I turned into bed one night with a fever of one hundred and four. There was no place in the hospital—our camp has still slightly elementary sides to it, and so I stayed here in the officers barracks in my room, under the charge of one of the doctors, being fed by the Red Cross, embodied by Miss Givenwilson. I was pretty sick for a couple of days, but now I'm well on the road to recovery. As soon as I am well enough I am to be sent off on a two weeks leave to recuperate, which I will start with Eleanor at Paris. I have written father a long letter just yesterday, so some of this may be repetition.

I am rather sorry to have to leave for so long just at this moment, as both my flying and my other job are very interesting. However, there's lots of war left to go round for all of us, I'm thinking. I wish you could see the flying we are doing over here, though, for it is a revelation to the Mineola educated eye. When I first got over here I wondered why every flier was not killed within the first three months of his flying. Now I have changed so far the other way that I feel as though a man could hardly drive one of these machines into an accident, short of completely losing his head.

We have had very good luck so far on this field, and though we have had a good many pretty nasty smashes, no one has been killed yet, or even permanently injured. And yet the French monitors make us do all the wild flying stunts that were considered tom fool tricks back home. Formation flying is the prettiest, though. They send about seven machines up at a time, to practice squadron and formation flying; *vol de groupe* they call it. It looks fairly easy, too, but when you get up in the air trying to keep a hundred and twenty horse power kite in It's position in a V formation with planes on either side of you, you begin to hold different ideas as to its easiness.

I am rather tireder than I thought I was, so I shall stop, and write to you soon again.

Quentin.

Friday, Dec. 28, 1917.
Obviously on the train.

I did not write till today, for even though I was with Eleanor, Christmas was ghastly. It was the first Christmas I had ever spent away from home in my life, and there was nothing to help it out.

At the moment, I am bounding south to get some warm

weather. The prospect is discouraging. I stayed in Paris as long as I could, with Eleanor, and was finally ordered out by the medico. At the last minute two of Eleanor's workers got sick, so she couldn't come, and I am now gloriously ensconced in one of those gilded horrors that the trustful Frenchman considers a *"wagon lit,"* trying to persuade myself that a temperature cold enough to make one see one's breath is a pleasant vacation. I suggested a little heat in the car, but the cold hearted lady who rules the car informed that *"c'est la guerre,"* a fact of which I was already dimly aware,—and then retired to her little stove at the back of car.

I think I have at last managed to pry myself away from that beastly camp. I had it all arranged that I was to go up with an R.N.A.S. squadron, and just at the last moment it was sat on by headquarters, on the grounds that it was not part of their scheme. Their scheme!

—Off the train and at Marseilles— The trouble with their scheme is that it bargains for a vast development, not to come to the height of It's power until next August at the earliest, and, unless I miss my bet, the Bosche is going to do his very best to finish the war, and incidentally, the Americans now in it, this spring. And spring, in the military sense, is fairly close. I've got a hunch that within six weeks or so things are going to be just about as hot up on the front as they have been since the Marne or Verdun. And, consequently, I rather hope I shall be in a French squadron within three weeks. I would have to have ten days machine gun work at Cazeau, but after that—Anyway, I'm dead sick of being in the L. of C, to all intents and purposes as much of an *embuscé* as ———, or ———. There's one thing—if I change camps at all, after Cazeau, it will be for the front. Once I have got there I shall feel a lot easier in my mind,—for it will be six months since I left you, pretty soon, and for all I have done to help the war I might have stayed at home.

I wish you'd tell the Hon. Pa, that if any of the big bugs happen to be talking of it,—its a darned shame if they cut out fliers extra pay. General Pershing cabled advising it, because the aviation Headquarters is in very wrong with him,—but all that it does is make us the goats because the man higher up made mistakes. Both British and French pay their fliers extra,—the British 68%,—while we only get 25%, which they want to take away. And it's not true that it's easier than the infantry,—look at the number of pilots, and the number of casualties.

January 7, 1918.

Next day we took an afternoon off, for I wanted to go to *Notre Dame des Victo*ires. I've always intended to, for it's the church to which all the *poilus* go just before they return to the front. It really is quite thrilling. You come in, and at first can't see very much, as there's semi-darkness inside. Then as your eyes get accustomed you can make out the people. There were no lights except at the altar,—which was ablaze with candles. Eleanor and I each lit our candle, and then went back to sit for a moment and watch. There was no service going on; it was the middle of the afternoon, and yet the church was full of people,—all come to pray for victory. We sat for a while and then, gradually, I began to distinguish things,—for the brightness of the altar only emphasized the gloom around. All around the walls, in cases, were rows upon rows of medals,—*legion d'honneur, croix de guerre*, and others I did not recognise,—in some there were crossed swords, and old flags,—all given in thanks for victory, and safe return from the wars.

January 15, 1918.

After all the excitement, and worrying, and discussing, I am on my way back to my same old camp. I don't know how long I shall stay there,—I don't know anything about what is going to be done with me, and nobody else does. I have finally given up, in despair, all attempt to squeeze any definite information out of the casual mob that constitutes our headquarters. The future is crammed with any number of possibilities, most of them highly discouraging. I shall know a little more by tonight, when I have seen Ham and Cord, so I'll either write you again or lengthen this.

Of course I hated leaving Eleanor's to come back to the same dingy old camp, where I'll be cold, wet, and muddy most of the time. And then, Eleanor has been so very nice. You don't know what a trump she is. During this last long stay I really got to know her quite well,—and we had a very particularly nice time playing around and doing all sorts of impossible things. Poor thing,—it's hard being so near and yet so far from Ted. And then, the time when he will begin his very dangerous work is coming very near.

Why, why don't the people at home realise what lies before them? I have been reading the papers from the states lately, and it is painful. Our policy seems to be one of verbal camouflage. The little tin-god civilians and army fossils that sit in Washington seem to do nothing but lie,—about German weakness,—which is easy, for they have never been in touch with the realness of German strength,—and about our own strength, which is inexcusable. They've all seen the reports of how things go over here,—and yet they choose to lie, deliberately and publicly, about them. I saw one official statement about the hundred squadrons we are forming to be on the front by June. That doesn't seem funny to us over here,—it seems criminal, for they will expect us to produce the result that one hundred squadrons would have. The one comforting thing is that all the rest of the services are as badly off.

There's one good thing about going to the front—I shall be so busy worrying about the safety of my own neck that I shan't have time to worry about the way the war is going.

I only hope I'll get up there soon—it seems such a solution for all sorts of difficulties. You get clear of all the little worries and jealousies that fill up life behind the lines, and you have only the big eventuality to face,—all the others arrange for themselves if you are fighting. And then, I feel I owe it to the family—to father, and especially to Arch and Ted who are out there already and facing the dangers of it, to get out myself.

January 17th, 1918.

Things have cheered up a lot since last I wrote you. I knew they would. This place is a squalid hole to come back to, and I knew that first day would be awful, and so it was. And so I wrote to you, because I was discouraged and writing you helps. By now, however, I have gotten settled into my work, and there is nothing so narrowing as one's own job. So I have religiously resolved to look at nothing but the immediate future. Of course I know how bad it all is,—but I'm trying to forget it for this little space.

My leave has shown it's effects in my flying. Just before I left I was really doing very badly. Now, however, I am flying really pretty well, and it has become fun again, not work. If I keep on as I am now I shall be ready for the front in three weeks, and then I hope I shall be able to get out. Of course it will be at least a month before I get to the front,—but still it's encouraging to think I'm getting appreciably nearer. The scheme now is to put us up for six months,—by us I mean Cord, Ham and all our crowd who have been working here at the school. Then, if we are still alive,—we will be taken back here to work behind the lines, for six months fighting will use us up pretty thoroughly and we will need the rest of work behind the lines. It's a good idea, and perfectly true,—so I have firmly decided not to get shot down during my first six months. I hope the war is over before I have a second!!

This letter is scrawly and scratchy because it is written on a little wooden bench while I wait for Cord. We are going to dinner tonight and have had about fifteen different delays, I rather expect to go out to one of the outlying fields pretty soon, and as Cord is in charge of one, I am arranging to move over to his. So I've been doing a good deal of tearing around.

Camp is a good deal the same as ever,—by that meaning muddy and dingy. A mid-winter thaw has contributed largely to the mud. However, it makes altitude flying a lot easier on us. I have to do a five thousand meter altitude test, so I speak feelingly.

Same Old Camp, January 22.

I have loved all your letters, and only wish there were something I could do about the ones I write. I know they are unutterably dull and uninteresting, but somehow, I don't seem to be able to write interesting ones, principally, I suppose, because the things I am doing are not very much different, except as far as the types of planes we are using, from what is being done at any of the camps at home.

I am very busy at the moment finishing up my flying. I at last succeeded in getting permission to do nothing but fly, as the doctor said that I would have to be on light duty if I went back to the camp at all. The result has been that for the last week I have flown practically all the time, and am now going to go over to Cord Meyer's field to finish up with my combat work and group flying on machines of a type that are still in use at

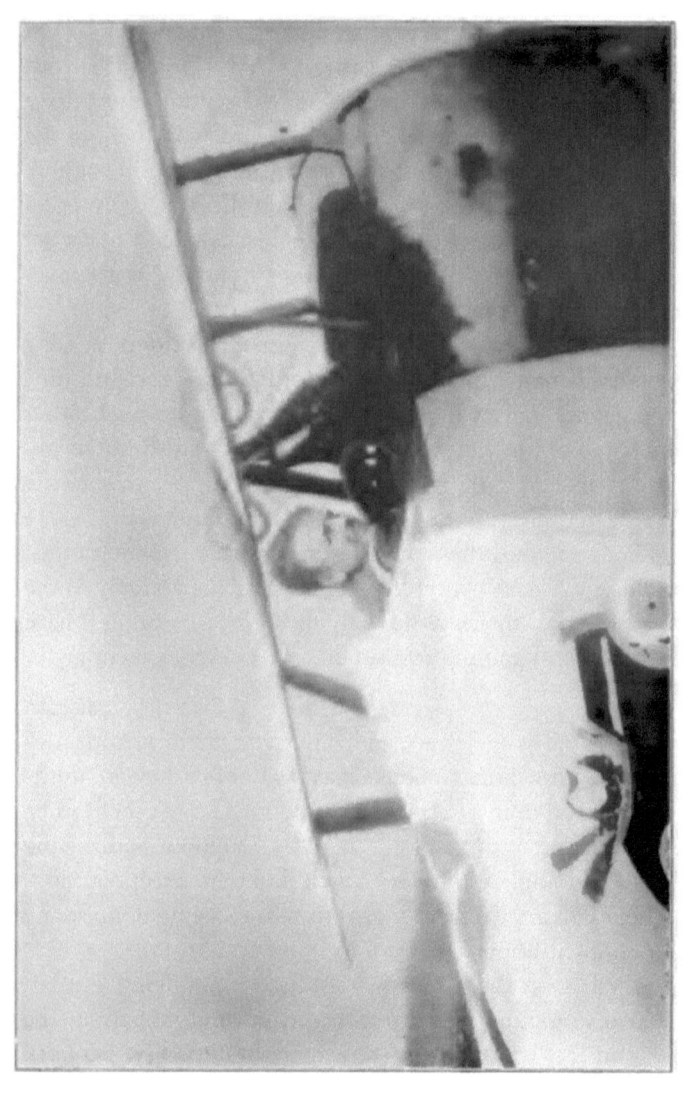

Lieutenant Quentin Roosevelt at field seven in his beloved "Dock Yack" plane

the front. I expect to have a bully time, and tho I rather hate to be doing nothing at all, yet there is a glorious sense of relief, when you aren't feeling very well, to know that you have no earthly responsibilities except keeping your neck intact when you are flying.

I had rather a hard time with my flying last week, thanks to having been sick, for I had to do my acrobatics, which is rather scary even when you are feeling thoroughly fit. As I wasn't I hated to have to get into a machine and go up and do my stunts, for the work they give us here in acrobacy is certainly wicked. They have one that they call a *glissade* that is the fastest thing I have ever run into in my life. You bank your machine up perpendicularly and then with your motor turning up at about three quarters speed, so as to keep the nose of the machine up, you slip perpendicularly down toward the ground. It's far faster than a straight nose dive, for you haven't got all the head resistance of the wings to hinder you. I got into it, and after coming down three hundred meters, in it, got over onto my back, and, as I was all mixed up as to my whereabouts, didn't have the slightest idea of where I was or anything. I got down to within about a hundred metres of the earth before I finally did get over onto my right side again.

I will be all right now though, for I know how to do the various stunts, and I won't feel that I have to do things I don't know anything about. I am going to get to work on them again next week, and get them perfected, for even though you don't use all of them on the front, they are enormously valuable, because they give you absolute confidence in your machine, and teach you how to get out of any kind of difficulty you happen to get into.

I suppose things are sliding along at home in their usual slip shod fashion, and that we are somehow getting our things ready to make some sort of effort toward becoming a factor in the war. It is a little discouraging to us over here, though, to pick up a New York paper and read a statement that the Production Board has put out saying that the work toward getting a fleet of two thousand and ten thousand fliers at the front is progressing very rapidly. Considering the fact that all our flying for the next spring and early summer will have to be done on French made machines supplied to us through the courtesy of the French government, I wish someone who knew the truth would get up and say what liars they are. I suppose that they consider it satisfactory if we have the two thousand planes by the fall of 1919. The French are beginning to see how much talk there was in a good deal of what we said. They grant us only one thing, good material. For the rest, they are turning back again and making plans to count on us at least six months later than they had expected from what we promised them.

In Camp, January 23, 1918.

Again a long gap between letters;—I'm afraid that I have lost my former faculty for writing letters. Somehow, when I have any time to myself, I always seem to either have some sort of official correspondence to write, like letters to the adjutant general's office, or else I am just plain tired out, and know the letter would be dull, uninteresting, and probably gloomy.

As you may gather from the heading, I am back in camp again. I left Eleanor's just a week ago. I could have stayed away on leave for two weeks longer,—Major Goldthwaite told me that I ought to,—but just at that moment Warrington came back with the news that Ted and Arch were going up very shortly, so I decided to take a chance and go back here as I was in order to get my training finished, and get out. So I trotted back, and arrived as usual, in a pouring rain storm.

This is really the muddiest country I have ever run across in my life. I don't see why the Frenchmen don't turn into frogs, by natural selection, after a thousand years of it. However, the camp is beginning to really get whipped into shape. The flying training has become more or less routine, and the construction is about half finished. When I got back, I was marked unfit for anything except light duty, so I was relieved of all duties other than flying, which was what I had been working for. Naturally, my flying improved about fifty *per cent*, for you can't fly and have your mind on something else at the same time. The result is that I am moving out to the *perfectionnement* school tomorrow, and in three weeks at the outside, will have finished my flying and be ready to go for my machine gun work, and then the front. The French machine gun course at Cazeau takes about ten days, so I think I can count on the front in a month, for they have promised to send me out as soon as I am ready.

I shall have a very good time for the next three weeks too, for the field I am going to is run by Cord Meyer. Consequently it is all arranged that I am to move in and room with him as soon as I get there, and generally have a good time. We have evolved a system for giving ourselves a good time when we are not working that goes like a charm. All the planes over at that field are the little monoplane fighters, and consequently very fast. So we have arranged when we have a day off,—and unless there has been bad weather during the week, there is no flying or work, other than the necessary inspections on Sunday,—we go off on voyages. He takes his plane, and I take mine, and we go off to someone of the French landing fields within a hundred or so miles of here. It is good fun, and also good flying practise, for the more time you get in the air, the better you are off, I have decided.

I have just finished up my acrobacy, doing it all in one day. It was rather strenuous, and I don't mind saying that I hope I don't get many more days like that. To begin with, the day before, I had taken an altitude test, going up to four thousand metres, and staying there for fifteen minutes. I did it all right, but thanks to having just gotten over being sick, it got to my lungs rather, and I picked up a bad cough and had rather a hard time breathing. The doctor says that I will probably be that way for a month more, but as it doesn't bother me under three thou, and I won't have to do any ceiling work now until I get to the front, I don't particularly care.

The doctor just happened along, and as I am not supposed to stay up after 9.30 at the moment, has packed me off to bed. I shall write again as soon as I get over to the other field. Best love to all the family, and *"un bon baiser"* to you, mother dear, from

Quentin.

Romorantin
January 27, 1918.

I am over at Cord's field now, and will,—with any luck—be ready for my machine gun work in two weeks. After that it's a question of getting myself grafted out of the school—which I think I can manage. The flying is wonderful, though, with these new machines I don't like it, from the point of view of personal comfort, for the motors are much harder to manage. You have the same plane,—practically, with one hundred and twenty horse instead of eighty,—and for some reason the one hundred and twenty motor is much harder to keep running. It's very easy to stall it when you're doing stunts and almost impossible to catch it again. Generally a stalled motor means a landing wherever you happen to be, with these birds.

The thing that makes up for it is the power you get. You can climb at the most astonishing rate,—and do perfectly wicked "*chandelles*" A *chandelle*,—in case I haven't told you about one, is a steep climb in a vertical turn. It's very hard to do well, wonderful fun when you can do it, and most important for fighting when you get out there. I am practising a lot on all of them, and getting in about three hours flying a day,—which is about all you can comfortably stand. As it is I'm always glad when I get into my ancient sleeping bag, and settle down for a night's rest.

In camp, on the 29th of January. Such a funny, and rather a pleasant thing has happened,—all at once today I got a whole lot of packages in a lump. I think they must have been missent, or else held at the post office through some mistake. At all events there were all sorts of things. (This, by the way, is being typewritten under difficulties, as I have the typewriter on my knees, and no light worth speaking of.) Then there were also three books from you, which I loved. They were detective stories, the last one being the *Black Eagle Myst*ery. I'm wondering now whether you have sent any others, and hope you have. They really made me quite homesick, for there was a sort of undefined presence to them, as of father in the train, and then the catchall. I am forwarding them on to Eleanor when I have finished them, for I know she will appreciate them quite as much as I do. We never get any of that sort of thing over here. The best we can do in the line of home reading is the Sat. *Eve. Post,*—and even that at times is rather inadequate. So nearly anything, no matter how common it is over home, is a novelty here. Do send me some more books, or magazines, or anything from a blue Ribbon Garage bill up, for I very much appreciate the ones I have got—not Garage bills.

At the moment I am doing what I have really wanted to do all along which is finish up my flying. I am at the last stage now, and should be finished in about ten days, or so. We are doing formation flying now, which is a revelation to you after what we did back home. They will detail two men to go on a reconnaissance, make a plan of a camp fifty miles from here, or something like that. Then they will detail another five men to go along in patrol formation acting as escort and protection against Boche patrols. In formation you fly rather the way geese do, in V shape, with the second men just higher than the leader and so on. At first it's rather scary, for you have to stick close together, but once you get over that it begins to be amusing, for you have to watch your plane and motor all the time without looking at them,—a rather Irish statement. What I mean is that you have to be able to watch the other men so as to keep your place in line, and at the same time manage your plane. We get the most tremendous amount of flying in in a day, for I did three hours and a half yesterday, and over four hours today.

I have been having a continual fight with the doctors, though, and incidentally with myself. The trouble is that I have been getting in so much flying lately that I am tired out most of the time. The net result was that I collected another cough, as my lung wasn't quite fixed up. I had been feeling rather poorly, but I was pretty anxious to get my flying done, so I was keeping on. Then to day, I dropped over to the main camp to see Ham, and there was caught by Major Goldthwait. The first thing he decided, after looking me over, was that I had measles, because I had a cold, and a temp, and there was a suspicious rash on me. I finally persuaded him out of that, and then he turned on the other tack, and said that my vitality was low, and that I was very likely to get something if I didn't look out, and ended with orders for me to go on light duty, and do no work for a week. I don't know what I am going to do about it, for I certainly can't quit flying for a week right now, when I am finishing up. In the first place, they are getting ready to send a couple of squadrons up within a reasonably short time, and I am going to have a hard enough time anyway trying to get myself a place in one of them. I think I shall wait and see how things turn out.

In the meantime I am going to bed at the noble hour of eight thirty, which means that there won't be very much more to this letter. I hope that by now you are getting my letters regularly again, after my lapse from virtue,—I have posted them to you in a variety of ways, by French mail, and military mail, so I hope they have started to arrive.

I am enclosing some snow drops that I found over at Romorantin. They reminded me so much of Oyster Bay, and hunting for the first one out in front of the *porte-cochere*. I suppose that they will be out by the time you get this, if my mail is any indication. At all events, they go to show that, even if I have been very bad about writing, there *are* places I would rather be, and persons I would rather see, than the A.E.F provides. Give my love to all the family; I am writing father tomorrow. Goodbye, and *un bon baiser*, from,

Quent.

February 3, 1918.

We all went over to the funeral of those two fellows that were killed. I was flying above it and so I couldn't tell so well. The coffins were escorted by a platoon of American soldiers, and one of French sent out from the French post. Then, flying just above, were two of the French pilots, in the larger machines. They are marvellous pilots, and it was really beautiful to watch them crossing and recrossing over the cortege in beautiful smooth right-angled S turns. Then, just as they were lowering the coffins, another Frenchman dropped down in a long swoop, his motor almost dead,—dropped a wreath on them, and then swung of?.

All the time we were up above, flying at about five hundred meters, in formation. We had a ten formation, two "Vs" of five, circling round and round till it was over. They say that from the ground it was very impressive,—for there, being buried, were two fellows we had all known and flown with a few days before,—and round them and over, the planes circling, paying a last tribute. It takes away some of the bare horror that the two little twisted heaps of wrecked planes and twisted motors leaves. You realise that perhaps, after all, we don't entirely, like the Boche, "put our trust in reeking tube or iron shard."

Soon after being detailed to Issodun Quentin met the Normants who were living at Romorantin, and instead of having one "*marraine*," he found himself with a whole family, grandparents, parents, and grandchildren to accept him. He always referred to the Normants as his "Family in France," and was devoted to one and all. What their friendship and unfailing hospitality meant to Quentin and Ham can never be estimated. Only those who have experienced the wholehearted generous kindliness with which French families greeted the Americans who went over to serve can begin to realise what it meant.

Romorantin Sunday, February 16, 1918.
Friday afternoon, we got orders over at our field to have eighteen men ready to go out in a squadron the next morning. Of course when I heard that, I thought "at last, we've got our first squadron going out." So I went hotfoot over to the main camp to see the colonel and get permission to go out with that squadron. He refused, absolutely,—and of course I put up a tremendous kick. After I'd got all through kicking he said:

> I'll tell you why I do that. That squadron that is going out is merely a political move,—sent so we can say we have a squadron at the front. They haven't even got machines for them yet,—or any sort of an organisation to allow for breakage and spare parts. What will happen to them is that they will move out into a camp that is not yet finished, up in the zone of the advance,—and then sit there for a month, until our organisation can take care of them, when they will probably form not the first squadron, but the finishing school staff of the zone of the advance. I am going to keep you back here for that reason, but I will do this. I'll send you out to the front as soon as Meyer gets back, and send you out in a real squadron, either English or French.

So you can imagine how cheerful I am. Cord ought to be back within two weeks, and then I get sent out in his place in a real squadron, with real machines, and men who know something about the game. I rather think it will be a French squadron, as I can talk French. At all events,—cheers!—in about two weeks I'll have stopped being *embusqué* Quentin.

Things are also rather amusing over at the field now, for besides the eighteen, twenty more were taken out, to be used as instructors, and to learn bombing. Consequently, I have only seven students now, so you can imagine how much flying I am arranging for them. It is the first time that I've really had enough planes to do what I wanted, so I am giving them all sorts of stunt flying and formation work the others didn't have. I'll bet they're better pilots than any of the others when I get through with them. And all the time, I am working on my flying, and watching the calendar till Cord comes back.

I took Ham over here with me this Sunday. We have been intending to do it for a long time, and now that he is plane tester over at my field, I can take him out, on expeditions, as I am in charge of all the planes over there. We had any amount of fun doing it—it's lots more amusement touring the country in a plane if you can look over your shoulder and see someone else sitting up in his machine just over your wing-tip. I knew Ham would love it over here,—and he is having a bully time. We have a great big room, with a bathroom to ourselves,—and altogether, it's civilization again. It's now 10:30 a. m. and we've just finished breakfast, so I hear Ham making a tremendous rumpus in his bath next door, and occasionally hurling some insult at me.

February 17, 1918.
Same Old Camp

It's been quite a long time since my last letter, and all sorts of water has flowed under the bridge since then, but I am up against the discouraging fact that I am not sure when my last letter was, so please excuse if I repeat. In the first place, I got your letter, together with ones from father and Ethel, and was particularly glad to get them, especially yours, for it hasn't been pleasant being under the ban, however well deserved it may have been. We haven't had exactly a mild winter ourselves over here, though it hasn't been as bad as it must have been on L. I. After one frightfully cold snap, when we had snow all the time, and flying was most unpleasant, we had nearly a month of delightful weather, almost like spring, but now the weather man seems to have had another relapse, and all the winter clothes and fur lined boots have come out again.

It's rather of a bore, because with the work I am doing now I have to get in a lot of flying of the most uninteresting sort, where I merely take out a patrol of men and try to lose them, or get them so mixed up that they can't show on the map where they have been when they come down again. It means about two hours of straight-away flying, with nothing in the world to relieve the monotony of it except twisting about, and trying to find some part of the country within a radius of seventy five or eighty miles that I have not already investigated.

It's not so bad when the weather is warm, for you sit back in your plane, and let the controls loose, and think of when the war will end, or what Long Island would look like now, or some other pleasing fiction. But now, there is always some part of you that gets cold. Either It's your forehead, or one finger tip, or your feet; but whatever it is, it serves to keep your mind off any more amusing thought. You try your hardest to project yourself out into the fields of speculation, and always after a few seconds you find yourself back up against the one disgusting truth that that particular finger or whatever it is is cold.

February 21, 1918.
Letter No. 1.

I'm at the moment indulging in the not over satisfactory feeling of knowing that I've done what I ought to have done, even though it wasn't what was pleasantest. I was given the chance of being permanently—that is for the next three months—stationed at Paris, to deliver planes to the various depots. You see, the heart of the aeroplane industry is Paris,—for all the big factories are there. Consequently, we have American testers, who receive the planes, test them, and then accept or reject them. If they are accepted they have to be flown to their various destinations. I was to be in charge of that particular branch, and to arrange for the deliveries. It would be wonderful fun, of course, for I'd be flying all over France—out to the front as well as to the various schools behind the lines. There would be a certain amount of good experience in it, too, but the trouble is, it's a job for a man back from the front for a rest,—or one who's had a bad crash and lost his nerve. It's no occupation for me who have never been to the front.

And so I turned it down, and I've been thinking, rather regretfully, of the good times I might have had in Paris. I would like to get a job testing, though, for I think that is valuable work. I don't think there's much chance of that. A tester is never an *embusqué*, for after all, you can't call a man a slacker whose job is testing planes to see if they're strong enough, and well built enough to stand service. Besides, a tester gets wonderful flying experience, for he flies all kinds of machines, and, in case he gets a machine, that is what the French call "*malreglé*," he has a slight sample of what flying at the front may be like with part of your controlling surfaces shot away.

So, I am still in my old work here, and having a rather amusing time, for I am not exactly sure what I am. I feel a little like the song, "Am I the Governor General, or a hobo,"—for no one, least of all headquarters, can make out just what my status is. I am hanging on like grim death, until I can get sent out to the front. Once I have had my three weeks or so with the French or English, I will have some sort of a foundation to base on, but till then, I'll probably remain an official mystery.

In the meantime, I am getting in all kinds of flying, and I think, accomplishing a certain amount in the line of training the new men at the same time. Yesterday I took a group of ten off for a reconnaisance. They all had their maps, and the object was to make them keep formation and at the same time make out from the map where they are going. It's good practice for them, but by way of being dull for me,—so I thought I'd liven it up by doing a couple of *virrages à la vertical*, and generally fooling round the sky. I did that for about five minutes,—always keeping the general direction I was going, but more or less wagging my tail en route, and then looked around for the formation, which should have been following above in two nice "Vs" of five. Instead, they were scattered all over the landscape like flies. I stopped doing everything at that, and flew in a straight line, so that gradually they formed up again. Then when I got back I asked what was the matter, and found that they had tried to follow my movements. Of course, it's absolutely impossible, in formation, to do anything like that,—and I told them so. I've also been polishing up my acrobacy a good bit lately, so that I can do it without thinking.

February 23, 1918.
No. 2.

Not much news this time, except one rather sad bit. Al Sturtevant has been shot down. I heard it from Bob Lovett. He was patrolling, doing seaplane work, when he had the bad luck to run into a squadron of Bosche planes, out on some sort of reconnaisance. Of course he didn't have a chance. They shot him down,—so thoroughly that even the plane was totally destroyed, and sank. Poor Al,—he's the first of that bunch whom we knew and played round with, that is gone. Still,—there's no better way,—if one has got to die. It solves things so easily, for you've nothing to worry about it, and even the people whom you leave have the great comfort of knowing how you died. It's really very fine, the way he went, fighting hopelessly, against enormous odds,—and then thirty seconds of horror and it's all over—for they say that on the average it's all over in that length of time, after a plane's been hit.

PART 2—TRAINING FOR COMBAT

March 7th.

I am down at Cazaux, it's where they teach the *chasse* pilots machine gun work, it is interesting and very valuable. From what I can gather about half the game in *"chasse"* is good machine gun work.

It has been really a kind of vacation to come down here, for although we work pretty hard, it's nice and warm and we are right on the ocean living in a big summer resort hotel. The colonel was awfully nice about it too, for he said I would still keep my status on the flying staff and be eligible to go out next in line with a French or British Squadron.

Our own affairs are going along about the same. They train pilots and send them up to depots at the front and then leave them there with no planes to fly. You will get all of that from General Wood. One thing that is making trouble is the fact that we seem to be a door mat for G. H. Q. and the line. The first they got us on was cutting flying pay—when every other army in the world pays their flyers extra. Then the new service stripe regulations came out, and we got it in the neck again. In the aviation section one has to be six months in actual combat at the front to get a stripe; that means that a mechanic working near the front and bombarded every night has nothing to distinguish him from the Washington *embusqué*. A pilot has to last six months and they hardly ever keep a *chasse* pilot up more than three. Also, someone like Ham Coolidge for instance, who is testing planes back at the school and doing dangerous work gets no credit and yet we kill on an average of one a week at the school. There, my wail is done!

March 7, 1918.
Letter No. 6

General Wood was out here yesterday,—and as he is leaving very shortly, is going to take these back with him. So, as this will get to you probably a good deal before my last few, I'm going to repeat myself. To begin with, I'm at Cazaux, at the French *École de Tir Aerien*. They teach you the machine gun side of *chasse* work. I was very strongly advised to do it by Colonel Kilner,— as he considers it very valuable training. He also promised to keep me on my training staff status, so that when I get back I can be sent out with either in British or French *escadrilles*. In the meantime I'm having a most interesting time back here. They start out with explanations of the mechanism and jams in the various types of machine guns.

Then after some work on the ground,—shooting at targets,— shooting from boat at targets, and shooting at little balloons, you start in on air work. First there are no guns on the planes and you have to go up a couple of thousand metres, drop over a paper parachute, and then chase it, manoeuvring round it. After that you start, beginning on fixed balloons and ending with a sleeve towed by another plane. In all that work they keep record of your shots, and count the hits afterward. It's a three weeks' course, and I do not get finished until the eighteenth, and then, after two days in Paris, I'll go back to Issoudun again. From there, if things work as I hope, I go out with the French or British very shortly. However, I've given up prophesying as to when I'll be anywhere. I went to Cazaux on ten hour's notice.

March, 1918.

The only unpleasant part is that the machines here are the most awful old crocks. They have been in service for ages, and have old motors and fuselages and wings that are all warped and bent out of shape. Consequently, the French warn you when you go up, to be very careful to do no sort of acrobacy at all, and not even try any steep dives with them to vertical *virages*. That's all very well, but they also expect you to follow the parachutes all the time, and make good scores when you are shooting at the machines.

You get up in the air, and get excited over trying to follow up the parachute, or whatever it is you are trying to shoot at, and you forget all about your machine except as a means of keeping your sights on the target. As a matter of fact one of our fellows was killed just last week, in a machine that was supposed to be perfectly all right. He was doing combat work at about fifteen hundred, when for some reason or other, just as he was straightening out of a dive, his wings folded up on him. Of course he didn't have a chance. He was a Cornell boy, named Hagedorn.

Quentin made an excellent record at Cazaux; his score card was afterward sent to his family, and the note on the bottom reads: "*Très bon pilote. Atterrissages très reguliers. Très bon tireur. Esprit très militaire, Beaucoup d'allant.*"

As we are all living at Arcachon,—incidentally, I've actually got a room and bath at a hotel,—I dine with four or five officers every night, and have a most delightful time. Last night we gave a little dinner, to a couple of French aces, back for a month's rest. One had nine, and the other eleven Boche,—so you can see they were pretty good. Things went well,—and they were most interesting, telling about various times they had had. One of them started as observer, was captured, kept in a reprisal camp for five weeks, and finally escaped, *via* the lines, and across No Man's Land to the French again. After that, he became a *chasse* pilot! Finally one of them got up, and proposed a toast to America,—with the best speech I've heard in a long time. He has a wonderful gift for the dramatic,—and he finished with, "and gentlemen, when we dine together again, and the war is over, may there be no empty places." That's only a bald attempt at conveying the sense, for it was beautifully done.

Cazaux, March 12th.

Down here things are very pleasant. We have been having the most glorious weather, warm and spring-like. The result is that they have increased our hours of work, so that we have to be upon the field from seven in the morning to seven in the evening, with only lunch time out. It makes a pretty long day of it and bed looks very pleasant by 9:30.

Sunday was a half holiday so we went off for an expedition, the Major, Lou Bredin, myself and an English captain named Ainsley. You would have loved it. We went away across the bay on a little nondescript sort of sloop, which her owner called a *canot*. The bay is closed up at the mouth with a sort of strait with high dunes on each side that go all the way along the ocean up into the pine forests. It's curious country—nothing but sand and pine trees, planted by Napoleon's orders (not the sand). I have flown for miles over it and except for occasional bare patches of sand it's deserted—no clearings, no houses—nothing. Only along the coast there are little fishing villages.

We went out to one of them on our sail and stopped to look at a grove of mimosa in bloom. You have seen it of course and know how lovely it is. The whole thing was like an artist's sketch book. The men wear blue and brown shirts and red baggy trousers, all toned and softened by salt water, so that there are no sharp edges to the colours. The women too, when they are working at the oyster farms wear the same red trousers. We explored it all—there were fully fifteen houses—and then sailed back and so, like Samuel Pepys, "*to bed*."

I leave in five days, although what I shall do, or where I shall go, heavens knows!

March 29

Its been quite a long time since I last wrote home, and all sorts of things have happened. In the first place; I have finished up my work at Cazaux, and am back again at the same old camp. I finished up there on the twenty-second and went up for a forty eight hour pass in Paris, hoping to be able to get out to see Arch. I found when I got up there that it was impossible, as he is still in an evacuation hospital in the zone of the advance, and I was not able to get passes to go out there. However I did see Eleanor, who was up in Paris, and having a horrid time, because she too had been unable to get out to see Arch. She had tried pulling every string she could, and the general opinion was that it would be impossible to do it, and that if she did do it this time, it would be the last chance she would have. She talked it over with Doctor Lambert, and also with several people who had just seen Archie, and they all agreed that his wounds were not serious enough to warrant that.

As she said, it is a good deal better, if she is only going to be able to do it once, to wait until a time when one of us is very seriously wounded and needs her more. Also, they are expecting to move Arch into Paris very shortly, and so she will see him and be able to look after him as soon as he gets up there.

She has gone down to Aix again, leaving word that as soon as it is definitely known when Arch is to be moved, she is to be telegraphed so that she can come up to him.

As a matter of fact I was rather glad to get away from Paris, for the offensive was starting, and it wasn't much of a time for playing around, or doing anything at all but getting back to one's job. There's no use talking about the offensive because it will be all past history by the time you get this, and also because we don't know anything about it down here. The one thing we do know is that our chasse planes are being held up now by a new shortage—machine guns. They have so far got only enough for the first squadron. The other squadron is doing decoy work—a most profitless occupation to my mind. They are sent out over the lines escorted by two French planes with machine guns. The object is to get the German to attack them. Then they leave for home in a hurry and let the Frenchmen look after the Boche. It seems foolish to have to work that way, but we can't choose. They've done one rather delightful thing though. As you know, each squadron on the front has some special insignia. Guynemer's, for instance, was the Stork, there are the Leopards, the Indians, and lots of others. The poor souls who have to go across without machine guns have adopted a decoy duck, with one leg stuck out stiffly in front as if it were doing a goose step. They have got it painted on all their planes.

I am at the moment in charge of training at the finishing field here, and expecting my orders any day. There is no vacancy at the present, as we have no planes, but I am to be sent up as soon as there is any. All schemes of going up in French squadrons and such have been disarranged by the offensive, and I rather doubt if they will start working smoothly again until the offensive is finished. In the meantime, Ham and I are sitting here, doing our work from day to day with an eye on the mail each morning, and a hope that it will have orders. In a way I'm not so sorry, for it has given me the chance to get out of a streak of bad flying that I had gotten into. I think it was the result of the landing field at Cazaux, complicated with not feeling awfully well.

When I got back to this part of the world again I started in with a very heavy cold, and had to turn in for a day or two, as the doctor thought I was going to get another attack of pneumonia. Then when I started to fly I found that, either as a result of that or as a result of a landing field at Cazaux that is as smooth as a billiard table, my landings had all gone to the bad. I smashed one plane up beautifully when I started out. It was really a very neat job, for I landed with a drift, touched one wing, and then, as there was a high wind, did three complete summersaults (spelling?) ending up on my back. I crawled out of it with nothing more than a couple of scratches. So now I'm flying most of the time, getting into practise. I've got to go now, as there is a plane out *en panne* that I have got to locate. Lots of love to all the family, from

Quent.

March 30, 1918.

I've flown a certain amount because, being in charge of training, I've had to decide whether it was fit for flying. It's quite amusing to fly in very windy weather. Yesterday when I cut my motor to come down, I found I was making almost no headway against the wind. So I came down turning over about a thousand, and feeling as if I were in a delivery cart on a cobble stone road. She slapped and thumped on the gusts of wind like a flat bottomed boat in a sea. Altogether, flying for me has been amusing. Yesterday before coming over here it rained until five in the afternoon. Ham and I had almost given up the idea, when we noticed the clouds beginning to separate. I said try it anyhow, and so we started. It was funny flying weather. We went through the first set of clouds at about three hundred metres. Then there was clear air for about a thousand metres, with only occasional banks, and finally a solid ceiling at about thirteen hundred.

So we took the middle flying fairly high and watching for the ground between clouds to see where we were. I had a most unpleasant time of it just at the end, for I was really scared, and It's the only time I have been, in the air. We were just about five miles from here, and I was getting ready to nose her down and come through the clouds to land when for some unknown reason I began to feel faint and dizzy. I'm free to confess that I was scared, good and scared. However there was nothing to do except trust to luck, so I nosed her down, and went for the landing. As luck would have it,—I happened to have just hit it rightly, and I came in on that glide with only a couple of S's to slow me up. I was mighty glad, though, when I got on to good, solid ground again.

Sunday, April 6, 1918.

Ham and I are planning a big party very shortly. We are both going to take the seven day leave which the army gives us every four months,—only we are going to take it by plane. We'll probably cruise all over the map,—drop in and see Eleanor at Aix les Bains, and generally have a marvellous time. Don't you think it sounds like good fun? The one draw back is that my plane looks like a Liberty Bond ad. The mechanics in the hangar said that they were going to arrange a little surprise for me during the four rainy days that we've had,—and they lived up to their word. They've got a huge American shield with white wings stretching across the top plane. Then running round the fuselage they have two spiral red and blue stripes ending in a little circle with the American insignia right back of the cockpit. Even the wheel covers are painted up. The net result is that wherever I land the plane collects a large crowd instantly. I'm getting some pictures taken of it, and if they're any good I'll send them to you. It's *v.* sporty.

April 15, 1918.

Please excuse this very spurious paper, for I have been too busy to get away from camp during the last week to get any more respectable variety.

Things are beginning to hum here at the school. For one thing, we hear that they are not going to send any more pilots over from the states for the present, which is about the first sensible decision that they have made as regards the Air Service. As it is they must have about two thousand pilots over here, and Heaven knows it will be ages before we have enough machines for even half that number. Not one of the bunch that were at Cazaux with me have got out to the front yet, and there doesn't seem to be much chance of their doing so in the immediate future.

It seems an awful pity, too, for with the way things are going on the front now, I can't help but think that all the pilots that can be handled ought to be sent up there in French and English squadrons if we can't provide the machines for them ourselves.

Still, the major says that he is certain that they will not let anyone go up with the French, as the last pilot that we sent up there only got as far as Paris and was then held up on account of the offensive.

I wonder if they are hearing all the news about the offensive back in the states, and if they realise how serious it is. I'm rather afraid of talking about it, first because I am a little leary of the censor, and next because, being in the rear as we are, I doubt if we know as much even as you do in the U. S. A. All we do know is that It's a mighty serious business, and that it's our business to get into it as soon as possible. In the meantime I am working my hardest trying to get the students that go through here as well trained as possible, and incidentally flying myself a lot.

I am getting my air work down pretty well now, for I don't think there's any sort of a stunt that I haven't tried. Ham who is here testing, goes up with me every day for combat work, which is most interesting. The other day he came over in a new type of plane, that they are just putting in on the front, and we had a bully time with it. I went up in mine, which is of course specially taken care of by the mechanics and we chased each other around for about a half an hour.

I just got a note from Arch to say that he was doing finely, and also hear from the papers that he has been moved to Mrs. Reid's hospital in Paris. I am going to fly up there next Saturday, if it's decent weather, and spend Sunday with him. It's about a hundred and fifty miles, and I can make it in about an hour and a quarter. Eleanor is already up there with him, as I just got her telegram asking when I could get up there to see him.

I have just gotten one piece of news that is very bad, if true. It is that Cord is reported missing. I have been over in the major's office all day trying to get official confirmation of the rumour, and as yet have succeeded in hearing nothing about it. I don't see how it can be possible, for he was as good a pilot as any I have seen here, which means as any in the U. S. A. S. So I'm still hoping.

Do you remember when you sent me this poem?[1] It was two years ago, in a clipping in one of your letters. I remember loving it then, and it's rather curious to run across it again, so I am sending it on to you, as I have a copy I made of the other.

---

1. *Christ in Flanders*.

This seems a rather short letter, but we are all so full of the offensive over here that it doesn't leave much room for anything else except "shop" in our heads. I'm so glad father is getting all right again. Lots of love to Ethel and Co. and to you especially, from your loving,

Quentin.

May 4, 1918.

Its been perfect ages since I last wrote to you, and I've got a variety of reasons for not having done so. The one real one is that I had one hand laid up in an accident and aside from that haven't been feeling decently for quite a while now. It started a little while after I got back from Cazaux. I had been feeling all overish for quite a while, and then one day when I was off on a voyage my motor blew up on me, and I had to come down for a forced landing. As luck would have it, some fool people got in my way, just as I was coming in to land, and as between hitting them or crashing, I took the latter, and hung myself up nicely in some trees. I reduced the plane to kindling wood, and got out of it myself whole but rather battered. Among other odds and ends, I had a bad wrist which reduced my epistolary efficiency. That in itself wasn't anything particular, but it was part of a vague general uncomfortableness. Ham and I talked things over, and found that we both were about in the same fix.

It boiled down to this, that we both were heartily sick of the work we were doing, and that we wanted to get out to the front, or anywhere away from this mud ridden hole. I had got to the point where even the sight of a flying student filled me with loathing. It is rather hard to teach men to fly, and send them on through the school, when you can see no future in sight for them. I knew that the men we were sending through would just be sent to a gunnery school, and then have to hang around goodness only knows how long until there were any planes for them to fly. And knowing that it was awfully hard to get up any enthusiasm for a job, which I hated anyway. The long and the short of it was that Ham and I both decided, independent of the other, that we were stale.

So I went to the major and asked him if he could not arrange to have Ham take a leave. He said that on account of the offensive, leaves were being discontinued, but that he would allow Ham to take a plane on a cross country to Paris. So he sent for Ham and told him this, whereupon Ham told him some long song and dance about me, resulting in our both being sent off with our planes for a six days' rest in Paris. Don't you think that was pretty nice of him? It made the most tremendous difference to me, for now I am back here again, and though I don't like the work, yet I do see how useless it is to kick about it and not do it, when there is no chance to go out to the front anyway. The major has promised us anyway that as soon as any bunch goes out to the front he will see that our names are on the list.

Eleanor is up in Paris now looking after Archie so I stayed with her and naturally had a bully time. She really has been a perfect trump about the way she has taken care of all of us. As a matter of fact, neither she nor I think Arch is very well. He is very thin, and is in the horrid position now of not knowing what is going to happen to him. It will be about five months, so the major at the hospital says, before he will be fit for active service again, and the question is what to do. Myself, I can't see why he wasn't sent back to the states as soon as they evacuated him from the Z of A. As it is, he is in the hospital, getting better slowly. I think he would have been much better off if he had been sent back to the states to convalesce.

May 4, 1918.

There are some nice things about aviation, really. It seems to be the one part of the war in which brother Boche has the instincts of a sportsman and a gentleman. Of course the service is as full of wild stories as a boarding school, and this one I'm not sure about,—though I think It's so. After Guynemer was brought down a Boche flew over his squadron's airdrome and dropped a letter saying that his funeral would be on a certain date and that four Frenchmen would be given safe conduct to land on the German field and attend it. They accepted it, and flew over, landed on the German field, were received by the Germans, attended the funeral and then went back. It's rather a fine thing if true, and I do know for certain that they know where Guynemer's grave is, so it may be true.

Then just shortly ago. Baron von Richthofen the German ace, was brought down by the English. They buried him with full military honours,—three French aces and three English aces for his pall bearers. It must have been most impressive, the French and English soldiers standing to attention as they lowered him into his grave while the English chaplain read the burial service over him. All those are the little things that will make up the traditions of the service after the war's over. And it is a nice thing to know that the things that you are to some extent a part of will be the traditions of the service. That and the certainty that there will be plenty of war left even when I get up there, helps to make Issoudun a little more bearable.

May 12, 1918.

Its been perfect ages since I wrote to you, and again I'm ashamed of myself, but I am also ashamed of my mail from the states, for I haven't gotten a single letter from there of more recent date than the third of April. I don't know what has been happening to them, for most of the other people here have gotten them as recently as the eighteenth. I hope they weren't sunk.

I've got uncommonly little news that's worth the repeating. To begin with, I am still back at the same old place, and with no more definite prospect of getting out. Thank goodness, from what we can get in the papers. General Wood seems to have tried to give the people some idea of just what their wonderful aircraft production board has accomplished for them with It's six hundred and twenty five millions and It's glorious prospectuses. I only hope that it isn't too late to get things rolling over there. This certainly does look as if we were in for a good long run of it, doesn't it? Arch and I were discussing it, in the cheerfully ignorant fashion in which everyone does who is over here, and we don't think there's a chance of their being beaten for a year and a half more. Or rather, we don't think it will last through more than one more winter.

But of course, I'd have said the same thing last fall. They can certainly put over an offensive when they make up their mind to, in spite of "insufficient man-power" and all the rest of that line. The one thing that we've heard that has pleased us in the aviation is that their new monoplane Albatross was a wash out and that they have gone back to the old D3 which was so successful. If we have the D3 we know what we're up against.

I've loved all your letters, for they say what's going on really,— not what ought to be going on, if——

May 27.

I've just been up in Paris again and so naturally I'm full of news. Just last week the major called me in and said that he knew I knew a good many French aviation officers, consequently if I could persuade one of their squadron commanders to apply by name for me and Ham (!) he would see that the request was O.K'd. by our headquarters and that we were transferred up there. You can imagine how Ham and I felt! It's just what we've been trying to do for ages. So with the help of Capt. Pelissin, who composed the letter, I wrote to Capt de V who commands a group of 4 Spad squadrons. We asked him to apply for Ham and me at once. Then the major, as he knew of this, sent me up to Paris on Sunday to deliver some important papers that had to go by hand. His idea was that while in Paris I could go to the French aviation H.Q. to arrange about it which I did.

I put in one whole busy day chasing from one office to another soft soaping all sorts of French officers, with "*Oui mon Capitain,*" and "*parfaitement, mon commandant*" until I began to feel rather like a phonograph with only one record. However, I think I got something out of it,—for at least two of them have agreed to inform me the instant any action is taken.

Arch is getting along splendidly. For a while I was quite worried about him, but now he seems to be in very much better spirits, and his wounds are improving right along. I had all kinds of fun with him, for we lunched together both days that I was up there.

Paris is wonderful fun now. Everyone who had left when the bombardment started has returned, and the *boulevards* are crowded. The gun shoots still at intervals but It's a most discouragingly anti-clim—— (It isn't what you think it is!)

Part 3—The Flight

Cablegram

Paris   June 8th.
Mrs Theodore Roosevelt
Moving out at last with Ham very glad love to all

Quentin Roosevelt

June 8, 1918.

I've had so much happening to me, though, in the last ten days, that I have not had time to think even, which is just as well. Ham and I had almost begun to think we were permanently stuck in Issoudun, when with no warning, we were ordered up to Orly, which is just outside of Paris. No one knew anything about the orders, and Ham and I felt sure that it meant our first step out to the front. Once the orders came, though, we only had twelve hours time to settle everything up and leave. You can imagine how we hurried, with all the goodbyes to be said and packing, and paying bills.

I thought we never would get away, but finally it was through, and we got in the truck and started to leave for the main camp to get our clearance papers. Then they did one of the nicest things I've ever had happen. Our truck driver instead of going out the regular way, took us down the line of hangars and as we went past all the mechanics were lined up in front and cheered us goodbye. As we passed the last hangar one of the sergeants yelled, after us, "Let us know if you're captured and we'll come after you." So I left with a big lump in my throat, for it's nice to know that your men have liked you.

June 18, 1918.

At last, almost eleven months after I left the states, I'm doing what I came over here for, out at the front. It's all different from what I thought, too, for I am not with the French at all. You see, while we were down at Chartres telegraphic orders came in for us to report at once to the First Pursuit Group. That is an entirely American outfit, except for the planes of course, Ham and I have been chased about so much that we didn't really believe we'd be put in a squadron when we got here, but there were no two ways about it, and so we started out *via* Paris to comply with our orders.

I had a fairly eventful run out here, chiefly because the motor-cycle developed a passion for punctures. After my third in ten miles, I said just exactly what I thought of the motorcycle as I got to work repairing it. Just as I stopped talking—I had no idea there was a soul within miles, I heard a voice behind me say "Priceless old motorbike,—what!" I looked up and saw one of those long, angular Englishmen, with that thoroughly blank expression which they use to *camoufler* a sense of humour. He had appeared out of a path behind me and had apparently absorbed my comments, anent motorcycles as I talked to it. I had a pleasant discussion on things in general with him, the net result being that I dropped round to his quarters and had a drink of Scotch before moving on. He was a very good sort.

Late in the afternoon I arrived here, to find myself assigned to the 95th Aero Squadron. The one drawback is that Ham is assigned to the 94th. However, we work together and have adjoining barracks, so things aren't as bad as they might be. Otherwise everything is fine. I took a half hour ride yesterday to get used to my plane, and somewhat to the sector. Then later on I went out on a patrol just up along the lines, to, as they put it, get used to being (loathly split infinitive) shot at by the Archies. It is really exciting at first when you see the stuff bursting in great black puffs round you, but you get used to it after fifteen minutes.

Tomorrow I'll be working in Germany as my flight is on for *reglage* planes' protection. So far there are very few Bosche in the air,—but as the B. infantry staged quite an extensive little hate yesterday (The French for hate is a *coup de main*, by the way) we think they may liven things up. There are lots of Americans up here,—and we think they may want to smash them up.

I'll write tomorrow, when I've been over and turn in an official report of my first visit to Germany.

June 25

Its been five weeks since I've heard from any of the family, so I feel sure I must have committed some horrible crime and be in deep disgrace. From my thoroughly black conscience I can find any number of explanations but the one I feel guiltiest about is that this is the first letter I've written in three weeks. There is some excuse though for I have moved all over France in that length of time.

I wish someone who did know something about flying at the front would go back, just to talk for a while with the designers and builders of the Liberty Motor and plane. It's going to be a long time before that thing gets to the front, and though I'm not crazy about the bus I'm flying I'd be much more comfortable in it than I would in a Liberty if I had to go across the lines. They have no right to send the things over here, tell the people in the states how wonderful they are, and then to expect us over here to work with them when each flight shows some new defect to be remedied. Of course they're all minor defects, but still they've been flying the planes over here for a month and yet she's not ready for the front yet.—

My last letter to you was written from the French concentration camp at Chartres, but as I know that mail forwarded to me there never reached me I don't trust the out going mails either. At all events after being ordered from Issoudun to go up with the French, and having put in a week at their concentration camp I was ordered back to the Americans again, this time to go up with the first pursuit group. Of course I was tremendously pleased, for I know all the bunch up here, and anyway It's much nicer to be with Americans.

I am now a member of the 95th Aero Squadron, 1st Pursuit Group. I've been having a most interesting time, too. I've been up on the front now for about two weeks. It's such a change after Issoudun to be out and really doing something. Where we first were it was rather a quiet sector and we generally had to go across the lines before we picked up any Boche, but just yesterday we were moved down into a hot sector quite near Paris, and from all we can gather there are Boche here all the time. I've had about six or seven hours over the lines so far, and I'm just beginning to get an idea of what goes on around; at first you don't see the Boche at all but gradually you begin to get on to them. I can see a certain amount now of what's going on. I've not got any combats as yet and the best I can show for myself is a hole where an Archie went through my wing. The real thing is that I'm on the front—cheers, oh cheers—and I'm very happy.

I'll write again day after tomorrow, after our first patrol of this sector, and tell you what It's like. Lots of love to all the family, and a separate special kind to you.

July 2nd, 1918.

Even though this is an active sector I haven't had much excitement as yet. Yesterday they kept us pretty busy, though. In the morning we went out for a patrol along the ceiling and spent two hours of cruising up and down the line without seeing anything. Then in the afternoon the infantry had a show arranged, in the shape of a 2 x 2 kilometre push on a seven kilometre front. That means of course a great deal of *reglage* and photography work, so there was a lot of *chasse* work to be done, what with protecting our own biplanes and keeping off the Boche. We were scheduled to fly on the low level, at twenty-five hundred metres, to intercept any enemy photographers or *reglage* planes. There were two more patrols above us, one around four thousand and one up along the ceiling, keeping off their *chasse* planes. We didn't run into any of their planes, but there was enough doing down below to make up for it. We were too high to make out any infantry but everywhere the artillery were working. The seven kilometres of attack ran from a wood on past a couple of small villages and ended up in a fair sized town. They were shelling hard all along it and one of the villages was in flames. You could see the white puffs where the shells landed and then when the smoke cleared away, the round crater that they dug in the ground.

Altogether there was lots doing, and I was glad I was comfortably above it all, with no worries but two cold fingers and a bad magneto. When we got in we found that though we hadn't seen any Boche the top flight had—and then some. There were ten of them, and they got into a free for all with nine Fokker biplanes. They had bad luck with machine gun jams, and the Boche made it pretty hot for them. Two of them aren't back—tho they may have landed inside our lines,—and they accounted for two and maybe three Boche.

One man got back here with his plane so shot up that it was nothing short of a miracle that he escaped. He had one centre section shot away, and to hit it the bullet must have gone within an inch of his head. The whole fuselage, and one gas tank are riddled with bullets, and as the Boche use explosive bullets, that fellow can thank his stars. I'm writing this in the hangars as I'm on *alerte*, but so far no Boche have been reported. I go on again from six to nine tonight, and as that's their pet time I have hopes. There's nothing in the world duller than waiting in the hangar for an *alerte* that doesn't come.

July 6, 1918.

Yesterday our flight officer was sent out to patrol at thirty-five hundred metres over about a ten kilometre sector where some sort of straightening the line action was going on. Our orders were not to cross the line, or fight unless forced to. For about fifteen minutes we chased up and down, up and down, with no more excitement than scaring a few *reglage* planes back into Germany. I was busy watching below us—I was flying right—when I saw our leader give the alert signal. I hadn't seen anything below, so I looked ahead and there up about a thousand metres, on the German side I saw a patrol of six Boche.

We started climbing at once, and I was having a horrid time, for while the rest of the formation closed in I dragged farther and farther behind. I have a bad motor, so that when the rest hurry up they leave me. There I was, with only the slim consolation that the leader was probably keeping his eye on me. We climbed on, and I did my darndest to keep up and at the same time keep an eye on the Boche who remained comfortably on top. The next thing I knew, a shadow came across my plane, and there, about two hundred metres above me, and looking as big as all outdoors was a Boche. He was so near I could make out the red stripes around his fuselage. I'm free to confess that I was scared blue. I was behind the rest of the formation, and he had all the altitude. So I pushed on the stick, prayed for motor, and watched out of the corner of my eye to see his elevators go down, and have his tracers shooting by me.

However, for some reason he didn't attack, instead he took a few general shots at the lot and then swung back to his formation. Our only explanation is that he didn't want to fight in our lines,—he had every kind of advantage over us. Lord, but I was glad when he left. When I got back they decided to pull my motor, so I was given another plane for this morning, which belongs to a fellow who's sick.

We went out on patrol again, this time at five thousand and started over across, hunting for trouble. A couple of kilometres inside the line we spotted six of them about a thousand metres below us. We circled and came back between them and the sun, and dove on them. They never saw us until we started shooting so we had them cold. I had miserable luck—I had my man just where I wanted, was piquing down on him, (he was a monoplane) and after getting good and close, set my sight on him and pulled the trigger. My gun shot twice and then jammed. It was really awfully hard luck, for I couldn't fix it. The feed box had slipped, so she only fired one shot at a time, and then quit. I did everything I could, but finally had to give up and come home, as we were about fifteen kilometres their side of the line.

As the papers put it, though, "a successful evening was had by all." We got three of them—They weren't the circus of course. We lost one man, though, and we aren't sure how. We rather think his motor must have gone dead on him, and forced him to land in Germany. So things are looking more interesting around here, and I've had my first real fight. I was doubtful before,—for I thought I might get cold feet, or something, but you don't. You get so excited that you forget everything except getting the other fellow, and trying to dodge the tracers, when they start streaking past you.

July 11, 1918.

There's lots doing in this sector. We lost another fellow from our squadron three days ago. However, you get lots of excitement to make up for it, and nearly every patrol we run into some of them. We've moved again, this time only ten kilometres. It's a much smaller field than the other, but it's nearer the front by those ten kilometres, and the other was really too big for us. Also, I like my quarters much better. I'm billeted in a little French town near the field. I room with Ed Thomas, our transportation officer, in a delightful room. It's in one of those white, plaster houses with tile roofs that sag in between the rafters, and an impossible weather cock on the chimney that doesn't work as there's a sparrow's nest in between its legs. The room is on the ground floor,—with a window on each side, one where you can watch everything that's going on in the street, and the other looking out on a garden that's all in bloom. It's spotlessly clean, with red tiled floor, and a huge grandfather's clock ticking solemnly in the corner.

The old lady who owns the house is equally delightful. She's a little bit of a dried up person, at least as old as the hills, with gold rimmed spectacles, the red cheeks that all these country folk have, and a beard that even —— might be proud of. At first she regarded me with deep suspicion, but I've now succeeded in winning her over. She thawed a little when she found I talked French—but the thing that won her over completely was her dog. When I first came in I was greeted with furious barkings and growlings. By a strong mental effort I succeeded in showing no outward and visible signs of my inward and spiritual doubt, and walked on past him. That night, as I was sitting reading the old lady appeared and with her the dog, who solemnly advanced, wagged his tail, and then put his head on my knee to be patted. After that the old lady and I became fast friends and now I am Monsieur Quentin and a privileged person. Among other things she told me that she had had German officers quartered in her house in 1870 and then again in 1914. Think of it.

I got my first real excitement on the front for I think I got a Boche. The operations officer is trying for confirmation on it now. I was out on high patrol with the rest of my squadron when we got broken up, due to a mistake in formation. I dropped into a turn of a *vrille*—these planes have so little surface that at five thousand you can't do much with them. When I got straightened out I couldn't spot my crowd any where, so, as I had only been up an hour, I decided to fool around a little before going home, as I was just over the lines. I turned and circled for five minutes or so, and then suddenly,—the way planes do come into focus in the air, I saw three planes in formation. At first I thought they were Boche, but as they paid no attention to me I finally decided to chase them, thinking they were part of my crowd, so I started after them full speed. I thought at the time it was a little strange, with the wind blowing the way it was, that they should be going almost straight into Germany, but I had plenty of gas so I kept on.

They had been going absolutely straight and I was nearly in formation when the leader did a turn, and I saw to my horror that they had white tails with black crosses on them. Still I was so near by them that I thought I might pull up a little and take a crack at them. I had altitude on them, and what was more they hadn't seen me, so I pulled up, put my sights on the end man, and let go. I saw my tracers going all around him, but for some reason he never even turned, until all of a sudden his tail came up and he went down in a *vrille*.

I wanted to follow him but the other two had started around after me, so I had to cut and run. However, I could half watch him looking back, and he was still spinning when he hit the clouds three thousand meters below. Of course he may have just been scared, but I think he must have been hit, or he would have come out before he struck the clouds. Three thousand meters is an awfully long spin.

I had a long chase of it for they followed me all the way back to our side of the lines, but our speed was about equal so I got away. The trouble is that it was about twenty kilometres inside their lines, and I am afraid, too far to get confirmation.

At the moment everyone is very much pleased in our squadron for we are getting new planes. We have been using Nieuports, which have the disadvantage of not being particularly reliable and being inclined to catch fire.

The victory recounted in this letter was afterward verified by the French, and duly credited; but the verification was not recorded until after Quentin had fallen.

CHAPTER 3

The Last Patrol

Oyster Bay, July 17, 1918.
Quentin's mother and I are glad that he got to the front and had the chance to render some service to his country, and to show the stuff that was in him before his fate befell him.
On July fourteenth the French were to celebrate and asked us to contribute a number in a theatre in a nearby town, so I appointed Quentin Roosevelt to get up the entertainment. He raked up all the musical talent,—the French are very fond of American ragtime and banjos—and the night before he came into my room and sat on my bed, telling, with a great deal of humour, of what he had done. The next day at noon I called up to arrange about getting his party into town when I heard he was reported missing.

When Quentin failed to turn up, Hamilton Coolidge, who was serving in the 94th Squadron, and Philip Roosevelt, who was Operations Officer of the First Pursuit Group, left no stone unturned to learn his fate. The inevitable crust that hardens one who is daily meeting death was but small protection to them against the blow. Coolidge wrote:

July 16

Dear Mrs. Roosevelt—
In this awful period of suspense when we don't know whether Quentin is dead or alive I feel that the best thing I can do is to tell you in detail the circumstances of his disappearance. On the morning of the Fourteenth a report came in to Quentin's squadron, which was the one on duty at that time, that Boches were crossing the lines in the north eastern part of our sector.

Accordingly a patrol of nine men, Q among them, set off to find the Huns. Just over the lines they encountered a Boche patrol of seven. The wind was blowing into their territory and the air was hazy even above the "ceiling" (a solid layer of clouds) which lay at about two thousand meters altitude. The Boches at once started retreating and a running fight began. This soon developed into a series of individual combats during which the patrols became broken up. The combats did not take place at very close range as the Huns had no desire to fight. They succeeded however in drawing our men further and further into their territory. The combats finally ceased and the men all made for home individually, groping their way through the clouds and mist largely by aid of their compasses.

No one remembers having seen Quentin after the shooting began, but this is entirely natural. Several of the men lost their way or were forced to come down for gasoline soon after recrossing the lines; it is quite likely that one of these things happened to Quentin. Capt. Philip Roosevelt yesterday interviewed an observer who distinctly saw an allied plane descend "piquing sharply, but not in flames and apparently under control." The place and time he gave corresponded exactly to those of Quentin's combat, so it is safe to assume that it was he.

The fact that his plane was neither spinning nor in flames as it came down makes me believe that he landed safely. There are many good reasons why he should have been "piquing sharply"—perhaps to escape from pursuers in superior force, perhaps again, because he was wounded and wished to land before becoming faint. I have talked to the men on his patrol and almost all seem to think that he is a prisoner and was not shot down.

Everything possible is being done to find out news of Quentin, but at this critical time reports do not come through or receive confirmation very rapidly. Of course you will hear through the Associated Press any news that may develop, much more quickly than I could cable it, but you may be sure that I shall forward to you immediately any information which may have escaped the notice of the Associated Press correspondents. I have packed all Quent's things and sent them by truck to Mrs. Ted Roosevelt, 39 Rue Villejust, Paris, where, God grant he may find them again before long.

Affectionate regards to you and Mr. Roosevelt—
                                                    Hamilton Coolidge.

Months later, shortly before his own fate overtook him, he wrote:

> Death is certainly not a black unmentionable thing, and I feel that dead people should be talked of just as though they were alive. At mess and sitting around in our quarters the boys that have been killed are spoken of all the time when any little thing reminds someone of them. To me Quentin is just away somewhere. I know we shall see each again and have a grand old 'hoosh' talking over everything together. I miss him the way I miss mother or the family, for his personality or spirit are just as real and vivid as they ever were.

Lieutenant Edward Buford, Jr., was also reported missing, but landed safely on a French aerodrome. He had seen Quentin's last fight, and described it in a letter to his family, written several months later:

>   Sept. 5th, 1918.
> Father dear:
> You asked me if I knew Quentin Roosevelt. Yes, I knew him very well indeed, and had been associated with him ever since I came to France and he was one of the finest and most courageous boys I ever knew. I was in the fight when he was shot down and saw the whole thing.
> Four of us were out on an early patrol and we had just crossed the lines looking for Boche observation machines, when we ran into seven Fokker Chasse planes. They had the altitude and the advantage of the Sun on us. It was very cloudy and there was a strong wind blowing us farther across the lines all the time. The leader of our formation turned and tried to get back out, but they attacked before we reached the lines, and in a few seconds had completely broken up our formation and the fight developed in a general free-for-all. I tried to keep an eye on all of our fellows but we were hopelessly separated and outnumbered nearly two to one.
> About a half a mile away I saw one of our planes with three Boche on him, and he seemed to be having a pretty hard time with them, so I shook the two I was manoeuvring with and tried to get over to him, but before I could reach them, our machine turned over on its back and plunged down out of

control. I realised it was too late to be of any assistance and as none of our other machines were in sight, I made for a bank of clouds to try and gain altitude on the Huns, and when I came back out, they had reformed, but there were only six of them, so I believe we must have gotten one.

I waited around about ten minutes to see if I could pick up any of our fellows, but they had disappeared, so I came on home, dodging from one cloud to another for fear of running into another Boche formation. Of course, at the time of the fight I did not know who the pilot was I had seen go down, but as Quentin did not come back, it must have been him. His loss was one of the severest blows we have ever had in the squadron, but he certainly died fighting, for any one of us could have gotten away as soon as the scrap started with the clouds as they were that morning. I have tried several times to write to Col. Roosevelt but it is practically impossible for me to write a letter of condolence, but if I am lucky enough to get back to the States, I expect to go to see him.

Two days after Quentin fell the following German *communiqué* was intercepted by our wireless:

On July fourteen seven of our chasing planes were attacked by a superior number of American planes north of Dormans. After a stubborn fight, one of the pilots—Lieutenant Roosevelt,—who had shown conspicuous bravery during the fight by attacking again and again without regard to danger, was shot in the head by his more experienced opponent and fell at Chamery.

Not long afterward a German official bulletin was found on a prisoner:

Group "Jeporen" (name of the general?)
General Command Headquarters.
Ic?—The Intelligence officer, in the name of the General. No. 128185.
Army Corps Headquarters,
the 24th of July, 1918.
Edition including even the Companies, except those which are just now on the first lines, and which will be only mentioned after their relief.
Sheet of Information, No. 10.

from the 21st of July to the 23rd of July, 1918.
THE SON OF FORMER PRESIDENT OF THE UNITED
STATES OF AMERICA, ROOSEVELT, FOUND DEATH
IN AN AERIAL FIGHT ON THE MARNE
At the time of a struggle between a German pursuit squadron of seven machines and twelve American pursuit aviators above the Marne, a fight took place between the German pursuit pilot non-commissioned officer Greper and an American pilot. After a long fight, the German flyer succeeded in bringing down his gallant antagonist.
The hostile airman had been killed by two bullets in the head. He was identified by his papers as Lieutenant Roosevelt, of the U. S. A. Flying Corps.

A clipping from the *Kölnische Zeitung* obtained through the Spanish Embassy gave this account of the fight:

The aviator of the American Squadron, Quentin Roosevelt, in trying to break through the air zone over the Marne, met the death of a hero. A formation of seven German aeroplanes, while crossing the Marne, saw in the neighbourhood of Dormans a group of twelve American fighting aeroplanes and attacked them. A lively air battle began, in which one American in particular persisted in attacking. The principal feature of the battle consisted in an air duel between the American and a German fighting pilot, named Sergeant Greper. After a short struggle Greper succeeded in bringing the brave American just before his gun-sights. After a few shots the plane apparently got out of his control; the American began to fall and struck the ground near the village of Chamery, about ten kilometres north of the Marne. The American flyer was killed by two shots through the head. Papers in his pocket showed him to be Quentin Roosevelt, of the United States army. His effects are being taken care of in order to be sent to his relatives. He was buried by German aviators with military honours.

The German pilot who shot down Quentin Roosevelt told of counting twenty bullet-holes in his machine, when he landed after the fight. He survived the war but was killed in an accident while engaged in delivering German airplanes to the American Forces under the terms of the Armistice.

The funeral services held by the Germans were witnessed on July fifteen by Captain James E. Gee of the 110th Infantry, who had been captured, and was being evacuated to the rear. Captain Gee passed through Chamery, the little village near which the plane crashed to earth. He thus describes the scene:

> In a hollow square about the open grave were assembled approximately one thousand German soldiers, standing stiffly in regular lines. They were dressed in field gray uniforms, wore steel helmets, and carried rifles. Officers stood at attention before the ranks. Near the grave was the smashed plane, and beside it was a small group of officers, one of whom was speaking to the men.
>
> I did not pass close enough to hear what he was saying; we were prisoners and did not have the privilege of lingering, even for such an occasion as this. At the time I did not know who was being buried, but the guards informed me later. The funeral certainly was elaborate. I was told afterward by Germans that they paid Lieut. Roosevelt such honour not only because he was a gallant aviator, who died fighting bravely against odds, but because he was the son of Colonel Roosevelt, whom they esteemed as one of the greatest Americans.

On July 18, in the great allied counter-attack, the village where Quentin fell was retaken from the Germans, and his grave was found by some American soldiers. At It's head was a wooden cross, on which was printed:

> Lieutenant Roosevelt Buried by the Germans.

Following the custom that sprang up in the heroic soil of the air-service, the broken propeller-blades and bent and scarred wheels of the plane were marking his resting-place.

Nearby lay the shattered remains of the airplane, with the seventy-six "wound stripes" which Quentin had painted on it, still to be seen.

The engineer regiment of the division that had retaken Chamery marked the spot where the airplane fell, and raised a cross at the grave with the inscription:

> Here rests on the field of honour
> Quentin Roosevelt
> Air Service U. S. A.
> Killed in action July 1918.

THE GRAVE AT CHAMERY

The French placed an oaken enclosure with a head-board reading:

> Lieutenant
> Quentin Roosevelt
> Escadrille 95
> Tombé glorieusement
> En combat aerien
> Le 14 Juillet 1918
> Pour le droit
> Et la liberté.

A young American officer in a letter to his family thus described the arrival of the tribute from the French:

> Oh yes,—one little episode of the other day might be of interest. I was back of the lines on a truck, in search of kitchen utensils and other things for the men, when down the road came a big open truck loaded with something which looked like a gigantic wooden bed—perhaps twelve feet long and eight feet wide. At the head of it there was a large shield, and above this a carved wooden cross. Did I not know the French idea of homage to the dead, I would not have recognized what it was. As we went by, I looked at the shield—in large carved letters I saw the words 'Quentin Roosevelt.' You see he is buried not far to our rear. It was a bit of French tribute, for, to these people, there is no man like Roosevelt. They still talk about him, and their eyes snap whenever his name is mentioned. He commands their profound respect: they consider him their friend; this was the only way they could show it."

Many very beautiful letters were written to Quentin's father and mother by those who visited the grave; from them three have been selected. The first is from Bishop Brent, the second from a lifelong friend of the family, Doctor Alexander Lambert, and the third from the Reverend C. A. White of Chicago:

> Chamery 14th Aug. 1918.
> I am standing by Quentin's resting place where he lies on the Field of Honour. I came up on duty near Fismes and learned quite by accident that we would pass by the grave. It is at the bottom of a shell scarred slope. The cross is supported by the shaft of his plane, and the twisted wheels are against the brick

fence. There is a reversed rifle at the foot, at the head behind the cross a trench knife. There are some little tributes on the grave—one from Evangeline Booth. It is a month today since Quentin flew to his fate. Dr. Macfarland is with me and we said some prayers for him and for all of you. There are two soldiers of the —— Division here who fought over this very ground and drove the Germans across the river. We are still in the zone of action and the storm of battle is raging, though all is peaceful at this spot. Tonight I am to be with some of our chaplains at a dressing station.

C. H. B.

I do not know if anyone has told you of the kind of country around Chamery, the little village four hundred yards from which he is. It is seven to eight miles North of the Marne directly north of Jaulgonne on the river just above a swinging curve of the road above Cierge. The country is a rolling grassy open hilly place, with only here and there small patches of woods. Last Tuesday I found someone had planted some pansies on the grave and there were other flowers. Evidently someone is looking after the place carefully, because no faded flowers collect there.

Two months ago I went there to find the place and took with me Colonel Elliot of the British Service. We were still fighting in Fismes a few miles north. A Field Hospital stood on a ridge a mile away and troops were going steadily north along the road through Chamery to Fismes. I walked through a harvested oat field with little purple flowers scattered through it. I gathered handfuls and so did Elliot, and as we stood by the stone which marks the place where the machine struck, some fifty feet from the grave, we saw coming up the side road a staff officer on horse back, and along a path worn out across the field from the main road, trudged a line of American soldiers from the battalion halted in the village on their way to Fismes. The boys picked flowers on the way and stood in a group around Quentin's grave, and laid their flowers where we had lain ours. Elliot exclaimed: 'That is the real American spirit, an unconscious and loyal tribute to what both the boy and his father have stood for.'

It must be some comfort to realise for how great a cause Quen-

CHAMERY

tin laid down his splendid personality.

A. L

Chicago Oct 30 1918

I am not sure that I do either of you a kindness in sending you this letter. If it is a mistake on my part charge it to the feelings of a father who has a son "somewhere in France." A few weeks ago I motored some miles from the then Vesle battle front to the grave of your son Quentin. I believe it would be a comfort to you both if you could see his noble resting place in the soil of France as I saw it. The day was beautiful. Sunshine everywhere. A company of boys in khaki march past, eager, active, on their way to the front. There are no other marked graves near. The very isolation and the immediate calmness of the scene seemed to me splendid. Yet the roar of the guns along the Vesle front could be heard. Captive balloons both Boche and Allied floated lazily along the battle line a few miles away. Air planes whirred overhead and now and then one with the sinister black Iron Cross of the Hun on it shot across the sky.

A noble burial place it seemed to me for a brave American like your son. The grave is in the midst of a broad rolling country, at the foot of a gentle slope which beyond the grave drops rather sharply to a more level field. The view in every direction is practically unobstructed for several miles except by the near sloping hillside. As of course you know a simple fence encloses the grave, some simple plants, I think a few faded flowers, all indicative of the loving thoughtfulness of someone. Here where he fell doing his whole duty your son sleeps in the bosom of France. It is a brave place to rest after one's work is done, peaceful now that the battle front has rolled back to the Aisne. Nature is busy making this great battle field beautiful again. She is growing grasses around the edges of shell holes, and scattering some blood red poppies here and there. Your hearts would find a great peace I am sure if you could just see where your boy sleeps.

C. A. W.

Don Martin thus described the scene in a despatch:

> Word that the grave of the young lieutenant had been found spread rapidly. An American division was encamped near by at the time. It would be difficult to estimate the number of

Americans who have made the pilgrimage to the grave since It was located. It is about five hundred feet off a small, slightly used road, on a little ledge of earth overlooking a gorgeous panorama. Paths have been worn to the grave from a half dozen different points—worn by American soldiers, who are still walking sometimes five and six miles just to see the spot and pay reverence to the young American who to serve his country entered the most dangerous branch of the service.

Quentin's death called forth many editorials that flamed forth genuine feeling. Three have been chosen, two American and one French. The first is from the Boston *Transcript*:

LIEUTENANT QUENTIN ROOSEVELT

Not with evil intention, but doubtless in accordance with what they regard as chivalrous, the Germans have dropped upon our advance lines in France what is nevertheless a poisoned dart, for it is the news that Lieutenant Quentin Roosevelt is indeed dead. This word will bring poignant sorrow to millions of Americans. And the sorrow will not be merely sympathy for the distinguished family now bereaved of its youngest son, It's Joseph and It's Absalom; it is sorrow of the people's own, who find in this brave youth the type and representative of their own dearest attachments.

It is the fortune of Theodore Roosevelt to dramatize many sentiments and qualities dear to the people—the home spirit and the home treasure; service and sacrifice for country; and the hopes and aspirations that are common to us all. The people therefore feel the death of young Roosevelt, typical boy of all our boys, in a manner tenser than if they were mourning merely with another.

Just a boy, for he was not yet twenty-one years of age, following or side by side with his brothers, all of them, young Quentin Roosevelt went, seeking the most daring service; and first of them all he has fallen to his death. The country simply stands shoulder to shoulder with the heroic father, who says, 'A great fight and a good death; trust him, he would not fail.' Pride, but a tender pride; a kind of high rejoicing, but with tears in it, especially tears: for the devoted mother; for a thousand bereavements exactly like it march hand in hand with this bereavement, and it is the forerunner of many more thousands yet to come.

All our boyhoods are in Quentin's today; he is the volunteer of all our volunteers:

He leapt to arms unbidden,
Unneeded, over-bold;
His face by earth is hidden,
His heart in earth is cold.

Curse on the reckless daring
That could not wait the call.
The proud fantastic bearing
That would be first to fall!

O tears of human passion,
Blur not the image true;
This was not folly's fashion,
This was the man we knew.'

The second is from Reedy's *Mirror*—St. Louis:

THE ROOSEVELTS

How everybody's heart goes out to Colonel and Mrs. Roosevelt in sympathy over the death of their son Quentin! The outburst of affectionate expression has been finely spontaneous. And the way the colonel takes the blow only intensifies the popular admiration for him. Nothing is in it of theatricality. The parents bow to inexorable fate in a gracious simplicity of proud sorrow or sorrowful pride. The colonel stands out, in the affliction that has befallen him, with a finer glory than ever. He's an American—a man. How cheap and mean the aspersions upon him for criticising the conduct of the war! Well it became General Pershing to send him a special cable about Quentin, and the president to wire his condolences. The colonel would be the last man to say his boy, as such, deserves any more honour than another for doing his duty.

Quentin lived and died his father's creed of sacrificing service. He died fighting with seven enemy planes, fell in the enemy lines—as we all knew a Roosevelt would. And two other sons are among the wounded. What argument such lives and such a death lend to the creed of the true American! The boys justify their father's gospel and career before all the world. And we think of gallant, modest Quentin as typical of all Americans, as the flower and fruit of the patriotism a lax generation first awoke to at his father's call, before war had come and death begun It's revel. He stands for all the fallen upon whom no public glory falls. And the Colonel and Mrs. Roosevelt seem to gather and give off our pity to fathers and mothers all unknown who have made the same sacrifice. They take the blow standing. They say it is well their dear one dies that liberty may live, that force and fraud may be destroyed in world-affairs.

Colonel Roosevelt has been given much by the people in a score of years, but now they give him their tears, their heart of heart; they are drawn into oneness making these parents' grief and pride their own. In these gloom-glory hours the Roosevelts serve their country and their kind in high fashion. And when they prayed, thousands who never prayed before said 'Amen' to their resignation to the Divine Will. Again the Roosevelts bound their people in oneness of spirit about the altar where bled their ewe-lamb. And Quentin rests in Germany by his people's orders, lives in death 'possessed of fame that never shall grow old.'

The last is from *Le Temps*, Paris:

Tel Père, Tels Fils

La mort héroïque du capitaine aviateur Quentin Roosevelt, fils de l'ancien président des Etats-Unis, ajoute une nouvelle page de gloire et de deuil a l'histoire de l'amitié plus que séculaire qui unit l'Amérique et la France, dans une magnifique confraternité d'armes, pour la défense du droit éternel et des libertés du monde.

Le président Roosevelt, dont la vie publique et privée fut toujours un admirable exemple de courage libéralement prodigué au service des plus nobles causes, est un des hommes d'Etat qui ont le plus efficacement contribué au rapprochement de toutes les forces morales de l'humanité sur le champ de bataille où va se décider l'avenir de la conscience humaine. Tout de suite il a protesté contre l'agression qui a déchaîné la guerre et qui, par la violation de la neutralité de la Belgique, a donné, de prime abord, la mesure de l'immoralité de l'agresseur.

Si l'ancien combattant de Cuba n'est pas venu lui-même, comme il le désirait, prendre sa place au milieu du combat et, selon sa coutume, au plus fort du péril, c'est que des obstacles plus puissants que sa volonté l'ont retenu aux Etats-Unis où d'ailleurs il ne cesse de servir, par tous les moyens en son pouvoir, la cause à laquelle il a sacrifié de tout coeur ses plus chères affections. Il nous a donné ses quatre fils, tous engagés volontaires, tous animés de la plus belle émulation d'héroïsme et inspirés des hautes pensées dont la tradition paternelle a illustré leur foyer natal. L'un d'eux, le plus jeune, déjà cité à l'ordre pour une série d'incomparables prouesses, vient de tomber au champ d'honneur. Un autre est blessé. . . .

Puisse la grande âme du président Roosevelt trouver dans cette épreuve la consolation et le réconfort que voudrait lui apporter notre amitié fraternelle! Il sait, il a souvent dit, mieux que personne, combien la beauté du sacrifice librement consenti est féconde en bienfaits pour les générations qui viendront, après nous, recueillir les fruits de nos efforts et de nos souffrances. Ceux qui furent les héros d'une juste cause et les martyrs d'un idéal ne cessent pas d'être présents à la mémoire des siècles et d'agir par une incessante résurrection qui multiplie à l'infini la vertu de leurs actes. Ainsi vivra parmi nous le capitaine Quentin Roosevelt, aimé des frères d'armes qui furent les témoins de ses exploits, honoré des hommages doux et tendres de sa patrie qui le pleure avec fierté, entouré de l'amour de la France qui a recueilli ses reliques sacrées et qui veillera pieusement sur sa tombe glorieuse.—G. D.

It is fitting to close this chapter with these four personal letters:

Paris July 23rd, 1918

My dear Colonel Roosevelt:—

Perhaps you will like to know of a tribute paid you and your son Quentin.

Beside my other work here, I have been going to the Neuilly hospital every morning for two hours to distribute American newspapers to the wounded just arrived from the front. It is a terrible and touching sight. The wards are already so full that all the halls are lined with men on stretchers waiting to have their wounds dressed. They are splendidly brave and uncomplaining and pathetically eager for home news. Yesterday morning I had given away all my New York papers and had only the Paris edition of the New York *Herald* left.

At the end of a long hall I found a man apparently asleep. His head was hanging over the edge of the stretcher and I put a pillow under it to ease his position. When he opened his eyes I asked him "where he had gotten it" as the question is put among them. "Oh! it ain't much I have, lady—" he replied— "just through me hips and somewhere in the back." Then he saw the paper and his eyes lit up. I gave it to him and lighted a cigarette. He said "Gee! but that's swell" and then as his eyes followed the headlines of the paper—"Hell! they got the president's son!" There was no question between us of who *was* or *had* been president, no need to question his or my patriotism.— War, I find, strips the unessential from our lives and speech.

Very sincerely yours,

Laura Kelton Owens.

A deeply appreciated personal letter came from Baltimore:

November 19th.

My dear Colonel and Mrs. Roosevelt:

This is a very old lady writing you, but I feel sure I have that which will be of interest, as it is an incident relating to the dear boy who sleeps on Flanders Field.

We were in a camp up in the White Mountain region, had just been celebrating a reported victory, and as a veteran of the sixties it fell to me to tell some of my experiences, as a northern woman, in the south. We had had a great camp celebration and just finished the national anthem, when someone stepped up on the platform and told us Quentin Roosevelt had made the "supreme sacrifice." There was an instant hush, as though every heart there was lifted in prayer, when out from the back of the hall stepped a young woman bearing a big flag, singing "My Country 'Tis of Thee." All joined in singing it through, then silently with bowed heads passed out into the night, each to his own quarters.

Words cannot convey to you the solemnity of the tribute to the brave young soldier. There were some of us who recalled him as a little laddie in the streets of Washington. There were none who failed in the tribute, or forgot the sad hearts at Oyster Bay.

Most loyally, sympathetically and lovingly,

Mrs. L. B. Lair.

A letter from Captain Philip Roosevelt, Operations Officer of the First Pursuit Group, closed thus:

...and manner of his death, I would rather have died as Quentin did than any other way. It was a critical day in the war. Quentin was taking part in a military mission of an importance which could not be exaggerated, protecting a photographic airplane fifteen kilometres in the enemy lines. This mission was successful and the photographs established beyond a doubt that the enemy must attack within twenty-four hours for one could see the seventy sevens being placed in position in open fields and far back of the lines the reinforcements already marching up to fill the holes which were to be made in the enemy ranks. Quentin lost his life, and it makes his personal loss no less hard to bear to know that he died at a supreme moment, but it does leave behind a tremendous inspiration for the rest of us.

The Reverend John B. Stoudt of Northampton, Pa., wrote:

My brother Lieut. Frederick M. Stoudt served abroad during the war in the Motor Transport Corps, and was stationed most of the time at Verneil, France, at the Reconstruction Park 772, where he had charge of a department in the Sheet Metal and Welding Shop. Towards the end of the war he had upwards of two hundred German prisoners working in his department. He tells of a young German officer, quite intelligent, who delighted in discussing the war, and who would ask many questions about America and our entering into the war.

This young officer told my brother the following in substance, concerning the effect upon the Germans at the falling of your son Quentin. That when he fell the fact was heralded throughout the German army, and throughout the Central powers. That photos of his grave and his wrecked plane were published and exhibited profusedly far and wide. That the German authorities believed it to be good propaganda, with which to hearten both the soldiers and the people at home. But that it had the opposite effect and produced as far as they were concerned a negative effect or result. That no sooner had Quentin fallen but that it was whispered from ear to ear, from trench to trench. That in it one could see how in free America everybody was fighting. That though America was in the war only for a short time, the son of an American President, engaged in one of the most dangerous lines of service, was lying back of the German lines, while their country had been at war three years and that neither the *Kaiser*, nor any of his sons were ever so much as scratched. That it gave the soldiers a vision of the democracy of America, and helped to deepen the feeling that they, the common soldiers, were only cannon fodder for the *Kaiser*. That it made real to them the difference between autocracy and democracy, of which they had heard so much. That this feeling spread like wild fire, not only throughout the army, but also among the people at home. That those elements in Germany that were opposed to the war seized upon it and enlarged the suggestion. This young officer declared that in the judgment of many this was the largest single factor in the breaking of the morale of the German Army.

CHAPTER 4

Official Judgment

American Expeditionary Forces
Office of the Commander-in-Chief
France, July 27th, 1918.
Colonel Theodore Roosevelt, Oyster Bay, Long Island, New York.
My dear Colonel:
Since my cablegram of July 17th, I have delayed writing you in the hope that we might still learn that, through some good fortune, your son Quentin had managed to land safely inside the German lines. Now the telegram from the International Red Cross at Berne, stating that the German Red Cross confirms the newspaper reports of his death, has taken even this hope away. Quentin died as he had lived and served, nobly and unselfishly; in the full strength and vigour of his youth, fighting the enemy in clean combat. You may well be proud of your gift to the nation in his supreme sacrifice.
I realise that time alone can heal the wound, yet I know that at such a time the stumbling words of understanding from one's friends help, and I want to express to you and to Quentin's mother my deepest sympathy and friendship. Perhaps I can come as near to realising what such a loss means as anyone.
Enclosed is a copy of his official record in the Air Service. The brevity and curtness of the official words paint clearly the picture of his service, which was an honour to all of us.
    Believe me.
            Sincerely yours,
                    John J. Pershing.

General Headquarters
American Expeditionary Forces

July 26, 1918.

Memorandum For: The Adjutant General, A. E. F.

Subject: Official Record of 1st Lieutenant Quentin Roosevelt, Air Service.

1. Lieutenant Quentin Roosevelt landed Liverpool August 8th 1917, assigned Issoudun August 17th, assigned School Aerial Gunnery Cazaux March 1st 1918, to duty Officer in charge Training Field seven Issoudun March 24th, to duty Orly May 31st Chartres June 11th Toul June 13th Colombey-les-Belles June 21st, assigned to 95th Aero Squadron Toul June 24th, duty Chartres June 25th Toul July 6th Touquin July 13th, reported missing July 17th, confirmation by German Red Cross of death in aerial combat July 22nd. Confirmed by International Red Cross from Berne, Switzerland, July 24, 1918 as follows:

> International Red Cross wires that German Red Cross confirms newspaper reports Quentin Roosevelt's death in aerial combat further details lacking—King Godson.

2. Lt. Quentin Roosevelt during his whole career in the Air Service both as a cadet and as a flaying officer was a model of the best type of young American manhood. He was most courteous in his conduct, clean in his private life and devoted in his duty. As an officer he had the best interests of the service always at heart, performed his duty no matter what it was, whether agreeable or not, always to the best of his ability and without question or remark.

3. After completion of his training as a pilot he was selected on account of his efficiency as an instructor and had charge of one of the most important flying instruction fields. His great desire and hope was to be allowed to get to the front. This opportunity was not practicable for a comparatively long time on account of his expert services being more needed as an instructor.

4. When the order assigning him to duty with a squadron finally came on June 24th he lost no time in reporting and arrived just in time to take part in the last great enemy offensive where the combat work by his squadron was most strenuous and aided materially in the success of the battle.

5. Lieutenant Roosevelt had already brought down one enemy

plane and had aided the squadron in a number of fights against large enemy air formations where the American units dispersed the enemy and brought down a number of their aircraft. His work during these combats was exceptionally good, his endeavour being the success of the squadron rather than to get individual airplanes to his personnel credit.

6. His loss was deeply felt by his flying comrades in the squadron as well as by all officers and soldiers with whom he had ever come into contact.

R. O. Van Horn,
Colonel, Air Service,
Asst. Chief of Air Service.

American Expeditionary Forces
Office of the Commander-in-Chief.

France, August 23rd, 1918.

Colonel Theodore Roosevelt,
Oyster Bay, L. I.
New York.

My dear Colonel Roosevelt:

Believing that you and Mrs. Roosevelt would want complete information as to where your son rests, I requested that there be prepared an official report, accompanied by photographs. These have just reached me and I am enclosing them to you.

The manner in which Quentin's comrades have marked and sheltered his grave shows how much they loved him, and this must offer you and Mrs. Roosevelt some consolation in the great sacrifice you have made.

Again expressing my regret over the loss of this splendid young soldier, and my sympathy with you, Mrs. Roosevelt and the family, I am, my dear Colonel Roosevelt,

Sincerely yours,

John J. Pershing.

Washington, *le Sept. 21*, 1918.

Ambassade
De La République Française
Aux Etats-Unis.

My dear Colonel:

All those among us, In whatever walk of life, who have lost a son in the present war, receive as a memorial to be preserved in the family, an engraved statement, testifying to the fact that their child gave his life for the great cause.

The President of the French Republic hopes you will permit him to consider that a similar loss has brought you even nearer to our hearts than ever before, and he has instructed me to transmit to you and to Mrs. Roosevelt the same token as is received by the bereft fathers and mothers of France.

In accordance with the directions of President Poincaré, I forward you at the same time as this note, a case containing that document, and I enclose herewith a letter to you from President Poincaré.

As for me, I need not say what I feel in fulfilling this duty; I knew Quentin as a child, and one could easily discover in the child the man that he would be. Millions of long lives will have been forgotten when his memory will still be fresh among us as in his own country.

Believe me, my dear Colonel,
Most sincerely yours,

Jusserand.

*Présidence
de la
République*

Paris 3rd Sept. 1918.

My dear President Roosevelt:

Do you kindly allow me to send you, in memory of your gallant son Quentin, the same diploma as to the parents of the French officers and soldiers who died for freedom? I charge our friend, Mr. Jusserand, to deliver you, with this letter, that token of admiration.

Believe me, sincerely yours,

R. Poincaré.

Q. G. A., le 5 Septembre 1918

*le General Degoutte
Commandant la VI° Armée Française
à Monsieur le Président Roosevelt*

*Monsieur le Président,
Sur le territoire reconquis par la VI° Armée entre la Marne et l'Aisne, avec l'aide des vaillantes troupes des Etats-Unis, nous avons voulu donner aux braves, morts glorieusement pour la défense des Droits de*

l'Humanité, une sépulture qui permettra aux familles qui les pleurent de reconnaître le lieu de leur dernier repos, et à ceux qui recueilleront le fruit de leur héroisme, de venir, dans les années qui suivront la paix victorieuse, leur apporter le tribut de leur reconnaissance profondément émue.

Parmi les plus glorieuses tombes, où se feront ces pieux pélérinages, sera celle de votre fils, le Lieutenant Aviateur Quentin Roosevelt, héroïquement frappé en plein vol, en effectuant une patrouille de protection au-dessus de la Forêt de Ris, le 14 Juillet, le jour même où la France célébrait l'anniversaire de la conquête de ses Libertés.

Elle so trouve près de la Ferme de Reddy, dépendant de la Commune de Coulonges—Je vous envoie la photographie qui en a été prise.

J'ai tenu à y déposer personnellement une couronne pour rendre hommage à la mémoire du jeune héros.

En vous adressant ce pieux souvenir, permettez-moi, Monsieur le Président, de vous exprimer de tout coeur la part que je prends au deuil cruel qui vous frappe.

Le Lieutenant Quentin Roosevelt est héroïquement tombé en terre française pour le triomphe de l'idéal commun de nos deux Pays, dont la vieille amitié devient de jour en jour plus étroite en se scellant du sang si noblement versé, côte à côte, sur les champs de bataille.

Degoutte.

Le Général Pétain

18 Juillet 1918

Monsieur le Président,

J'apprends la mort glorieuse de votre fils, le capitaine aviateur Roosevelt, tombé au front de France en combattant pour la cause de la liberté.

Si votre douleur peut avoir quelque adoucissement, vous le trouverez certainement dans ce fait que votre fils a trouvé une mort héroïque en combattant sous les plis du drapeau Américain que la France entière salue comme le symbole de la victoire certaine.

Veuillez agréer, Monsieur le Président, avec les sincères et vives condoléances de l'Armée Française, l'assurance de toute ma sympathie.

Ch. Petain.

Sg
Grand Quartier General
Des
Armees Francaises de L'est
Etat-Major

Bureau Du Personnel
(Decorations)
   ORDRE No 12,027 "D." (EXTRAIT)
Après approbation du Géneral Commandant en Chef les Forces expéditionnaires Américaines en France, le Maréchal de France, Commandant en Chef les Armées Françaises de l'Est, cite à l'Ordre de L'Armée.
Lieutenant Pilote Quentin Roosevelt, à l'Escadiille Américaine 95:

> *Excellent pilote de chasse, possédant les plus belles qualités de courage et de dévouement, Le 10 Juillet 1918, après un combat contre 5 avions ennemis, a abattu un de ses adversaires. A été tué-glorieusement au cours d'un combat aerien. le 14 Juillet 1918.*

 Au Quartier Général, le 29 Novembre 1918
 Le Maréchal De France,
 Commandant en Chef les Armées Françaises de L'Est,
Pour Extrait Conforme:
Le Lieutenant-Colonel,
Chef du Bureau du Personnel
 (Signature illegible)   Petain.

From the *Naval Institute* of July, 1919:

> The only French war craft named after a citizen other than of France, is the torpedo-boat destroyer *Quentin Roosevelt*, named recently as a mark of respect to the late ex-president and his son. The destroyer is the former Russian *Buiki*, which has been taken over by French naval authorities and renamed. She was rechristened last September. The *Quentin Roosevelt* was turned over by the Russians to the French because their navy was at that time short of men and they were unable to man her.—*Institute.*

CHAPTER 5

"The Judgment of His Peers"

Hdqrs. First Pursuit Group
Air Service—American E. F.
December 21, 1918.

Dear Colonel Roosevelt:
On going through our files preparatory to demobilization of the First Pursuit Group Headquarters, the enclosure (a report locating Quentin's grave) was discovered, having been caught with some other papers and filed away by mistake. As the information requested was later given officially in another letter, it is not necessary for us to forward the enclosed endorsement, and I thought that perhaps you might be interested in having it, as it is signed by one of Quentin's great friends, Lieut. Hamilton Coolidge, who, as you know, was subsequently killed in the Verdun Sector on October 27th.

It is needless for me to say that Quentin's loss was mourned by everybody in the group. He was one of the most popular officers in the organisation, being liked by everyone, officers and men. I know of no one who really enjoyed life more than he did. He always entered into the spirit of everything, whether it was work or pleasure. The day he was killed, he was in charge of an entertainment we were giving to assist in celebrating the French National Holiday, July 14th, and at the rehearsal given the night before, was the life of the party, inspiring everybody with his enthusiasm. That night he came to my room, and I shall always remember his sitting on my bed and describing to me in his inimitable manner, the programme that he had laid out.

He and Captain Coolidge reported to the First Pursuit Group

when we were in the Toul Sector, and both explained that they had been boyhood friends for the past eight years and wished to get into the same squadron. There was a vacancy in two squadrons so the commanding officer assigned Quentin to the 95th and Lt. Coolidge, as he was then, to the 94th. Both became flight commanders in their respective squadrons. Capt. Coolidge felt his loss very deeply, and often spoke to me about him. The day Capt. Coolidge was killed, October 27th, he stopped in my office just as he was leaving on his last patrol, and spoke then of Quentin. I recall now his saying that he wished Quentin could have survived to have been with him at St Mihiel-Verdun offensive, in which this Group had been so successful. Coolidge, as you know, had become an Ace, and had eight official enemy airplanes to his credit. Killed, almost under the shadow of the Armistice as it were, his loss was deeply felt by everyone.

Very sincerely yours,

Henry L. Lyster
Captain, Air Service U. S. A.

July 30, 1918

Dear Mrs. Roosevelt:

It seems almost incomprehensible that Quentin is really gone. At every turn something reminds me of him. This afternoon I walked in a quiet wood where Q. and I walked and chatted together only a few days before his death. I could almost hear his voice but still there is an awful empty feeling inside. Quent was such a complete person—not a mere friend who is interesting in some particular way—he was interesting and lovable in every way. No one I ever knew had so many friends from so many different types and conditions of people.

I am trying to write a little sketch of Quentin since his coming to Prance, in the hope that I may be able to tell you some things about him which you would never have learned from his letters. This will not be finished for a while yet, as it is necessary to write in between times and in the midst of distractions. Also, my ability to express what I feel makes it hopelessly inadequate; still I shall do my best, as I do so want you to know about some of the things that boy has done here.

Quentin's daring has left a profound impression on all of us. I remember once at Issoudun, when after making a bad landing and narrowly missing a ditch, he told me that he had a "horrible sinking feeling," but when it came to facing live Boches in superior number far inside their lines, and each armed with two deadly machine guns, the "sinking feeling" did not figure at all. Too many pilots find a "miss firing motor" or "leaking water connection" an excuse for avoiding proximity to Boche planes.

Quentin, however, found the presence of enemy planes an excuse for temporarily overlooking the inferiority of his own apparatus. His aggressive spirit has made a deep impression throughout our Air Service, and I find in Quentin's death, I won't say a vindication of Mr. Roosevelt's attitude towards our War programme, but a factor which gives his words redoubled force. One heard occasionally, about a year ago, these words, "Yes, the Roosevelt boys are all going across, but you can be sure they'll be given staff jobs." Strangely enough several of the people who made similar remarks have found that they are temperamentally better suited to be instructors at the Aviation Schools, rather than mere pilots at the front.

I am enclosing a letter from one of Quentin's former mechanics. It arrived a few days after his death and is typical of the way every one of those boys felt toward him.

I feel that I share with you and Mr. Roosevelt the thrill of pride that was given us by the circumstances of Quentin's splendid victory, and of his even more splendid death, and I ask you to accept my deepest sympathy at so sacred a loss.

Affectionately yours,
Hamilton Coolidge.

Hamilton Coolidge's Sketch

On the trip across Quentin busied himself most of the time in becoming better acquainted with the officers of his detachment, many of whom he previously knew but slightly. He was thoroughly enthusiastic about the job ahead; his enthusiasm was fundamental, and seemed to me distinct from that of many of his comrades who apparently acquired theirs in the much talking and speculation that accompanied the after dinner smoke. Even his worst spells of homesickness did not dent it, though his natural cheerfulness changed to black gloom on that tedious trip.

Often we walked together in the evenings on the unlighted decks, and always the conversation developed into reminiscences of the events so fresh in our minds.... Never was he sorry for himself. Almost never did he speak of the dangers ahead of him, and then only in a most casual way. Once in a great while he wondered "Shall I ever come back?" but far more often it was "I wonder how long it will be before we come back." His attitude seemed to be fatalistic. He went on the principle that he was on an adventure in which a definite object was to be obtained. When that object was obtained he was coming back. If some accident befell him in the course of it, that was something he could not foresee—then why worry? Quentin did not begrudge the fact that war was going to demand his best efforts, that it would place him in great personal danger. The only thing he begrudged was the inordinate amount of precious time that it would occupy....

Upon arriving in France on August 14th, Quentin was sent directly to Issoudun to take charge of transportation, and for a while supplies also. The camp then consisted of little more than a half dozen army tents, and Cord Meyer was about the only one of his old friends then with him. All I knew of Quentin during the next two months came from his comrades who occasionally had business in Paris. Somehow Transportation and supplies didn't seem to be within the field of Quentin's previous experiences, but everyone spoke of how well he was doing. He successfully conducted several trench trains of supplies from a sea-port town and some of the supplies he obtained occasioned considerable comment because the other men had been unsuccessful in obtaining them.

I later learned that Quentin never needed previous experience to handle a job successfully. His versatility was unlimited. Probably no officer in the air service has had more different jobs than Quentin in the same length of time, and made a real success of each. Yet all the time he was doing these jobs, not because he liked them but because he saw that they were inevitable before flying could really begin. Flying was what he cared about., One day a Frenchman landed at the field in a Caudion. After lunch Quentin was looking over the machine. He had never driven a Caudion before, in fact for over two months he had not flown at all. Neither of those facts disturbed him in the least; he wanted to fly. Two mechanics cranked the engine and a minute later Quentin was circling the field in a machine new to him and controlled in a different manner than any plane he had hitherto been in!

It was during this period that Quentin and Cord Meyer became such good friends. They frequently took motor cycle trips together. Both had some bad smashes, but that seemed only the rather amusing accompaniment of their good times together. It was then, too, that they became acquainted with the delightful Normant family at Romorantin.

On October 15th, when the school opened a new administration took hold. From then on the plan of things and even the personnel, was constantly changing for a while. Quentin always had some job on his hands. One week he went away in charge of a trucking detail. The next saw him in command of a squadron. Often he was called to Paris on questions of accountabilities for supplies. His duties were so many and varied that for a while he had little chance to fly. It really seemed as if his superiors used him for any hard job which required tactful handling. I think of one case in particular in this connection. The cadets at the school in It's early days had undergone some very trying disappointments in regard to their commissions and their pay; they were a demoralised crowd of boys. Quentin was put in charge of them. For several weeks he devoted his entire time to straightening out their difficulties. He had no chance to fly with this work on his shoulders and the strain began to tell.

Coming back from a cross country trip I found him sick and strongly urged him to go to bed. He said that he couldn't leave his work and went right ahead. That is when he really became sick. There were several of us down with grippe at the same time, while Quentin had pneumonia. Under Miss Givenwilson's personal care most of us had soon recovered, but Quentin's sickness had reached a stage where nothing but a complete rest and change could do him good. It was to Bordeaux that he went, if I remember correctly. At any rate he stayed there but two days, after which he returned to Paris. He said it was because during those two days it had snowed and if there was going to be bad weather in Southern France he might as well stay in Paris. I know, however, that what really brought him back to Paris was the persistent devotion to family which was always so marked in him.

Field Seven is where formation flying is taught at Issoudun. It is where Quentin really made his mark at the school. He was sent there after rushing through his acrobatic flying upon returning from Paris, to be the officer in charge of flying. It was the one job he had a chance to hold long enough to organise thoroughly. While anxious to go to the front Quentin realised the futility of that desire for some time to come and therefore settled down to make the best he could out of his work there. He was happy to be there with Cord Meyer for a while, before Cord left. In thinking over those days I always think of Quentin at Field Seven. That is when I knew him best. It is when he had his most permanent job and when he did his best work. It is when he won the devotion of all the mechanics in a way that gave a fine lesson to the "over military" type of officer who tries to impress his authority by an abruptness of manner and speech assumed for the occasion.

Every morning prompt at seven o'clock a gaudily painted plane could be seen circling the camp, sometimes ducking in and out of low hanging clouds, at others diving, twisting and rolling in an extravagant demonstration of nice handling. It was Quentin in his beloved "Dock Yack" plane trying out the weather before sending his pupils off on patrol. In addition to the star cockades and the shield and wing insignia upon the top wing, Quentin had employed a jack-of-all-trades mechanic to paint upon both sides of the fuselage a representation of "Dock Yack" in his auto, as depicted in the Goldberg cartoons. Quentin was extremely pleased with this plane, both as to appearance and flying qualities.

All the time during flying hours he was out upon the field wearing a grimy long leather coat and the traditional silk stocking "*porte bonheur*" as his only head gear. He seemed to be always moving about. Patrols took off and returned with more and more precision as time went on. Planes were ready on time; they were lined carefully to white chalk lines, and the accumulated oil and dust seemed to disappear from their sides and undercarriages. Often I happened to be near when Quentin was criticizing a student flyer. "What were you doing a quarter of a mile behind the formation when it passed over Vatan?", or perhaps "Yes Williams I realise that the Chateauroux hospital possesses a peculiar fascination for you (the nurses) but you know that acrobatics two hundred feet from the ground is poor business, and incidentally weren't you supposed to be in the formation a thousand metres above?" Invariably a puzzled, usually sheepish expression appeared on the face of the victim as he first wondered how his instructor knew of all these things, and then realised that he was not the type of instructor who watches proceedings from a chair on the ground.

Had any of the men on patrol looked carefully above at times they might have seen a small Nieuport circling inquisitively overhead. Indeed the ubiquitousness of their instructor always puzzled the students, for was he not on the ground when they left and then also when they returned, and yet was there any incident of their flight around the country which he did not know about? An instructor who flew himself, who frequently took a student's place in formation, must be a man who took an interest in his work, they figured—and the quality of the flying and hence the reputation of the field gradually but surely adjusted itself accordingly.

At Field Seven there was a supply officer whose duty it was to' secure the many spare parts that are essential in the maintenance of airplanes. There was a construction officer who supervised the building of barracks, the driving of wells, the installation of electric light plants and machine tools in the shop. Sometimes in spite of all their efforts the spare parts were unavailable, the building material could not be had for love or money. "Requisitions had been in for two weeks, but nothing had happened." At supper someone would ask "Where is Quentin?" and another would answer "Oh he has gone over to the main camp on his motorcycle," and the subject would be dismissed. Next morning, however, the needed parts or material would suddenly and mysteriously appear upon a truck.

Once in particular I remember when a long awaited dynamo arrived at the camp. The old one had become inadequate as the demands upon it increased. The new one after being carefully cleaned and assembled by willing mechanics stood ready to supply the much needed current as soon as a suitable foundation should be built for it to rest upon. "But there's not a bit of cement in the supply room; we'll have to wait until they send it from Paris," complained the construction officer. That night it was dark and drizzly so nobody noticed when Quentin disappeared about nine o'clock with two of his men in a truck. About an hour later the truck returned with twenty bags of cement inside. "Where did you get the cement?" someone asked. "Stole it," was Quentin's laconic reply. And let it be remembered that Quentin's official title was "Officer in charge of Flying at Field Seven."

Then there were many rainy days when we couldn't work. We used the room in which Quentin, the doctor and the captain (C. O. of the field) lived as a sitting room; usually the four of us but occasionally several more would wander in. The captain was a Southerner and enjoyed crap games—so dice it was. We sat on Quentin's bed rolling the dice and exchanging francs. Privately we all took our cue from the captain—but after about two games you couldn't tell whether it was he or Quentin who was the veteran "crapshooter." He put his whole heart into everything he did whether it was rolling dice or developing pilots for war. When he did not play in the current game he was sitting in the box wood arm chair reading or writing letters with a concentration that was always a source of wonder to me.

No matter how much noise the phonograph and the gamblers made he never " batted an eye." It seemed to make not the slightest difference to him. He always managed to keep up his reading, but I could never discover whether or not he had a system about it. One minute I would find him reading the *Rhymes of Ironquill*, or Dunsany—the next it would be Boswell's *Life of Johnson*. He nearly always carried a book in his pocket, which reminds me of Archie at Groton. I think Quentin always kept several books going at the same time and read whichever one happened to be handy. He seemed to like queer and obscure things, but probably they were "queer and obscure" only to me! Anyway if he spent time reading them it was only because he had already read every standard and known author.

After an idle day a dinner in town at the "*café de l'Aviation*" usually followed—sometimes with the "Cappy" (he hated the name but wouldn't admit it) and Doc—often with some Frenchmen or other friend at the main camp.

The following are extracts from Lieutenant Coolidge's letters to his family:

> Q. seems to figure In almost everything amusing that happens to me. Last Tuesday I got permission to try the little monoplane again. Thinking to make a big impression (because this monoplane commands attention wherever it goes) I headed straight for here, our outlying field. As I drew near I spotted Q. in his gaudily decorated plane, circling around a toy balloon up over the field, so of course I sailed up to say hello. Just as I got close, however, he turned his attention from the toy balloon flipped over on his back and came diving down on me in attack. That possibility hadn't occurred to me, but one must never refuse a combat, so I hastened to manoeuvre for position. Well it is commonly known that the mono is far superior here to all the other planes in speed, climb and manoeuvre ability, but as it was only my second trip in the little devil and as it is a very sensitive *appareil*, demanding skilful handling, I didn't dare to whisk it around in the slap-dash manner that would have saved the situation, and consequently I was ignominiously defeated in the fight. Now my chances of revenge are poor because another pilot has since wrecked the little plane. It is hard life.
>
> Yesterday Q. and I once more attacked the major on the subject of getting out to the front. Well, a rather discouraging circum-

stance renders it useless just now, so there's obviously nothing to do but wait in patience.

July 11, 1918

Quentin and I were not assigned to the same squadron. We are in the same group, consequently operate from the same base and see each other frequently. Let me tell you of the splendid *coup de main* he sprang today. While on patrol with some eight or nine of his comrades over the lines, the formation became broken up in some quick manoeuvring. Q. suddenly found himself alone. After circling around a few minutes he saw three planes in formation not far away and hastened to rejoin them, falling into place behind them. It seemed a little queer that his leader should be going so far within the enemy lines, but he thought no more about it until the leader made a sudden turn exposing to full view upon his rudder—a large black cross!
"Wrong again" said Q. to himself, but his brain kept right on working. Sneaking close up behind the rear man who either did not see him or supposed him to be one of his friends, Q. took careful aim and let him have a stream of bullets from his machine gun. The plane wavered a second, then toppled over and fell spinning in a spiral like a winged stone. Q. reversed and headed for home at full speed pursued by two bewildered Huns whom he gradually left further behind as his little Nieuport roared along.

A quick backward glance revealed his victim still spinning after a fall of some nine or ten thousand feet; he then disappeared in a cloud bank. Isn't that one of the most remarkable true tales you have ever heard? It's doubtful if this Boche is confirmed—too far inside their lines.

Captain Coolidge became one of America's leading aces; he was killed on October 27, 1918, by a direct hit from an anti-aircraft gun whilst observation planes which were being attacked by six German machines.

The following is the letter Coolidge mentions as having arrived a few days after Quentin's last fight:

On Active Service
July 11, 1918

Dear Lieut. Roosevelt:
I've just read about your victorious tangle with the Huns and

my only regret is that I can not, or rather could not be there to witness it.

Nevertheless I want to congratulate you and wish you all sorts of luck. Everyone of the fellows in the 37th are tickled to death.

There's no use telling you that we miss you, cause we do. Everything is going on the same. No doubt you already know that Lieut. Davis has gone to the front.

I've got a new flivver (exciting news this, no doubt). And this is about all. So again allow me to offer you my heartiest congratulations. Hoping that you'll get 'steen more, I remain as ever, sincerely yours "Dago"

Priv. 1st Cl. D. A. Di Fiore 37th Aero
Squadron Amer. Forces France

O. K. Censored by: A. K. Lowell, Lt. U. S. A.

A. S. S. C.—Yes the boys are all for you and Lt. Coolidge back here. Best of luck. A. K. L.

Mr. W. H. Crawford, President of Allegheny College, gave this account of a meeting with Quentin:

Our truck broke down, and I was too late for the mess, but Lieut. Roosevelt came to see me in the hut, and we had a most interesting interview. It was a wretchedly sloppy night, the lieutenant's rain coat was pretty well spattered with mud, but he was bright, eager and full of life.

As we went out into the rain to his sidecar I said to him: 'Lieutenant there are large numbers of Americans who are very proud of the way the four sons of Theodore Roosevelt are acquitting themselves m this war.' I never shall forget how his face lighted up as he made reply: 'Well you know it's rather up to us to practice what father preaches.'

On all sides I heard only good things about Lieut. Quentin Roosevelt and the devotion of his men to him. I was told that often during the winter months the men would remain out in the storm and train under him, and do it cheerfully, as they did not under any other officer.

The following are extracts from letters written to their relatives or friends by members of the A. E. F. who had come in contact with Quentin:

From A. J. Whaley:

> Young Roosevelt is as modest as a schoolgirl, but as game as they make them in aviation. Keep tabs on this game young chap.

From Lieutenant John F. Wheelock:

> As you know by this time, our hopes that Quentin Roosevelt was only a prisoner were blasted and it is quite certain he is gone. Too bad, because he was a peach. He died in a great scrap it appears, and was buried in German soil with full military honours.

From Banner Shull:

> Quentin Roosevelt is in charge on these trips. We boys would do anything for him. He always sees that his men are taken care of before he thinks of himself.

From Sergeant C. A. Gardiner, Jr.:

> All those bum deals that I spoke of are plum gone now. We have a real man commanding us now, one of Colonel Roosevelt's sons. We have only had him a short while but would do more for him than all the time we knew the other man. You get me—don't you—the minute stuff?

From Corporal Aleck Barlow:

> It hit me pretty hard as I knew him well and used to look after his plane for him quite a little when he was our instructor. He was one of the best and finest men I ever knew. Just a young fellow and full of life. I wonder if his dad is anything like him. If he is I would vote for him if he ever ran for office again. All the boys in the 37th thought a great deal of him and hated to see him go to the front. He was sure a prince.

From a member of Quentin's first "outfit," writing to someone whose son was "missing":

> I guess you feel about the same way we all did when we heard of Lieut. Roosevelt's death. He came over with this squadron, that is the old 29th now the 400th and everybody thought there was nobody like him, and last winter in Issoudun I helped him get his motorcycle started many times when it was so cold.

He was a wonderful fellow and afraid of nothing.

From Mr. R. M. Washburn:

> Yesterday, while an Italian was cutting my hair in a barber shop, he told me that he had served overseas with him, saying, in his own words: 'He was afraid of nothing with his aeroplane; a great operator; was one of us, and could fight, play, box,—do anything; the goodest kid I ever saw.'

From Lieutenant Geo. B. Bailey:

> I had a great week, this last one, flying in formation. Formation flying is in charge of Lieut. Quentin Roosevelt, the son of our famous T. R., and he is a chip off the old block, and a mighty fine and popular fellow.

From Arthur Weirich—Air Service:

> Look at Quentin Roosevelt, one of the finest, cleanest, bravest boys in France—a good flyer; and yet he is one of the first men to get it. Everything in the world waiting for him back in the United States.

From an aviator in the A. E. F. to his parents:

> I am with a fine bunch of boys; one especially—Quentin Roosevelt—is a wonderfully fine chap, and he keeps his father's picture up in his tent at all times—told us it gives him great courage to look at his father's face.

From Guy Bonney, 1st Battalion, 1st Gas Regiment, September 30, 1918:

> Lt. Quentin Roosevelt, the aviator who was killed in the Château Thierry and the son of the former president, was I believe their most talked about and worshiped aviator. It being because he received all of his instruction on this field. They had his old aeroplane, 'Dock Yack,' which he had painted to his fancy with this famous caricature, in a hangar by itself and it was an object of admiration by all. They told us to crawl in and be seated in it so we would have something to remember him by, which we did.
>
> Then, when I made the remark that I had been camped for a length of time up there within a quarter of a mile of his grave, they certainly did crowd around and commence to ask ques-

tions about it. I saw his burial place when the Germans had a cross of theirs and inscribed in German placed over it. They called Roosevelt 'the enlisted man's friend.'

From an officer of the A. E, F.:

A young lieutenant in our Flying Corps who is at present staying here, talked to me about Quentin, and his work at the school. He said that Quentin was a sort of chief among the instructors, that he was a strict disciplinarian but was loved by everybody, and that he was of the greatest use to the fellows who were learning to fly. He stopped for a moment reflecting, and then, half to himself, he muttered 'He was a prince!'

From Miss I. M Givenwilson of the Red Cross, stationed at Issoudun:

Though my heart aches at the loss of him I cannot but feel a joy and pride at having known such a boy. He has done such excellent work since he has been over here. He showed just what could be expected of him all through life. He knew how to handle men, understood them, and was beloved by them. He was so valuable as the officer in charge of training at Field Seven, that he was sent to the Front with great reluctance by the commanding officer here.

This is part of a letter written by Mr. H. A. Maxwell, of Maiden, Massachusetts, to Quentin's father:

As a pioneer Y man for the camp, he was one of the first officers with whom I became acquainted, and his splendid co-operation as an officer in charge of transportation enabled me to make a record in building my first hut. He, with a detail of men, went to Chattereaux, twenty-seven kilometres distant, and got the first piano that came to camp.

He also assisted me in organising two debating clubs, and while he was the commanding officer at the 36th Squadron his personal influence with the men will be long remembered. For a short time they were quarantined, and I recall his taking them on a hike one afternoon. On his return he made a halt in a large field, under a tree, and gave them a good heart-to-heart talk.

In handing him my letters to be censored, I had opportunity for many little chats with him. I recall his putting his hand on my shoulder one day and saying, 'Y man, how could we get along without you.' I replied, 'Ah, go on; you are just like your daddy.' 'Yes, I know,' he said, 'but I've got a great daddy.' I appreciated this frank and tender reference to his father, as I, too, am one.

One day he stopped me in front of the hut prior to It's completion, and said in his way, with which you are familiar, 'Why do you call that a hut? I call it a palace. What a great home for the boys!'

His kind consideration for the interest of others was very marked. I am glad to have known your son, and I assure you that your splendid spirit and your sacrifice for this great struggle to make the world better is a source of inspiration to every true American citizen.

Quentin's family received several touching letters from French parents:

Bizons par Cuzaguet Htes Pyrenées
20 Octobre 1918

Madame:
Nous venons, moi et mon mari, d'avoir un sauf conduit de 48 herues pour aller voir notre pay reconqui, et c'est avec le coeur serrée que nous avons revue notre petit villages. Hélas, de notre interieure tout a été enlevé; il ne nous reste que les yeux pour pleuré. La maison n'a pas trop souffer, elle a été un peut repairé, et l'on peut, je croi, maintenant se metre à l'abrie.

Je me fait donc, Madame, le plaisir de venir vous offrire notre maison, car je me suis fait un devoir de porté un bouquet sur la tombe de votre cher enfant, le capitaine Quentin, qui a été enterré à cote de notre villages. De chez moi il y a 10 minutes pour votre enfant. Il lui a été fait comme il le meritait une jolie tombe, et de tous. C'est pauvre soldats nous avons toujour représente les parents.

Aussitot qu'il arrive un regiment Américains tous von sur la tombe de votre cher enfant. A vous Madame je viens vous offrir notre maison le jour ou vous pouvez venir car il faut esperé que cette maudite guerre finira bientôt, esperons assez de misere et de ruine. Nous restons a Coulonges en Tardenois, Aisne, rue du Poinson N° 1.

Agrée, Madame, mon profond respect

Felicie Fourquet.
refugiees à Bizons.

à Madame et Monsieur Roosevelt.

11 Quiai de Conti
Paris le 17 Juillet 1918

Madame,
Permettez à la mere d'un obscur fantassin Francais de vingt ans de venir vous dire qu'elle partage votre douleur, mêle ses larmes aux votres, et vous remercie de toute son âme de votre sacrifice en la personne de votre cher enfant Quentin.

Madeleine Dornec.

The following letters from Quentin's comrades need no introduction or explanation:

Lovington, Ill.
Easter Sunday

Dear Mrs. Roosevelt:
A mother doesn't need to be told the kind of a man that her boy is, and yet perhaps it would make you just a bit happier should I tell you what his friends thought of him, what a regular lad he was. I'd have written sooner but was a prisoner since July 5th and just arrived home a while ago.

Quentin and I roomed together at Toul when he first came up to the front. One comes to know ones room mate, down deep inside.

There are so many little things that show his measure. I don't need to tell you of his flying, his bravery; words seem inadequate, and others have already tried that. I can only say that he was a brave man and an excellent flyer, a man one liked to have with him when the odds were on the other side, and hope you'll understand what I say so poorly. At night, if I were asleep or he thought that I was, he'd tip toe to his cot, would be just as quiet as possible, he did a thousand little considerate things that do not seem important, yet which really mean much. If I were going out with a partner, just the two, I know no one I'd rather have had than he.

He lived and stepped over the little river as a brave gallant soldier and gentleman, in the way he'd have chosen. We all loved him, the days we had at the front were among the happiest we'll ever know. The lad's only regret was for his family, that I know, and there is the consolation that when the present existence is finished, we all shall see him again on the other side of the little divide.

If I may help in any way please do not hesitate to call upon me.

Sincerely
Carlyle Rhodes.

On Active Service
July 23, 1918.

My dear Mrs. Roosevelt:

Having lived in the same camp with your son Quentin Roosevelt, I can not refrain from telling you that I know he was especially loved by the enlisted men. Of course, he had the respect of his brother officers, but it may be gratifying to you to be told by one who for four months was an intimate observer of his life that he was genuinely popular with the boys.

Only last night a cook in one of the squadrons at this "field" told me of Lieut. Roosevelt dropping in for breakfast. An earlier schedule was in effect and as he had been "night flying," which had kept him up rather late, he missed the regular mess. He dropped in for a cup of coffee. Surely! He got it and whatever else was available. Then he sat down and as he ate he "visited" with the whole kitchen force, "just like a regular fellow" to quote my cook friend exactly.

This sort of thing was typical with him. Among themselves the men called him "Teddy" and many were the remarks that I overheard about him, by the rank and file, full of honest admiration. They knew he was courageous and an intelligent hard worker, but best of all they felt that he had a real interest in them and they loved him for it.

While not an intimate of his, he was in and out of our little hut quite a good deal and I came to like his sturdy person and bright personality.

Believe me, Mrs. Roosevelt, I honour you as the mother of such a son.

Yours respectfully,

Wm. H. Forbes
Y. M. C. A. Sec.

Censored by:
Robert G. Fittnan
1st Lt. A. S. Sig. R. C.

American Aviation Detachment G. D. E.
Aviation Française, Par. B. C. Am. Paris

Dear Colonel and Mrs. Roosevelt:

I wish to express my very sincere sympathy in the death of your son, Quentin. I was at Issoudun with him for six months, and like everyone liked him immensely. The last time I saw him he was doing acrobatics against the moon at night, a feat which requires more than ordinary courage, I left the field before he landed, and had no chance to congratulate him on his performance, but I thought you would like to know of it as it was typical of the young officer I knew—as light heartedly courageous as any man I have ever known.

I know he died as he always flew—gamely, for he certainly was game in every way. He died in the manner all of us in this game would want to "get it," if it is our turn to go—at the front in contact with the enemy. This is the best way of all to go.

Let me express once more my sympathy. The Air Service lost a splendid officer in the death of your son.

Very sincerely yours,

Merian C. Cooper.

Headquarters, 36th Aero Squadron
Cazaux, Base Section No. 2 A. E. F.

From: Enlisted Members of 36th Aero Squadron SC.
To: Hon. Theodore Roosevelt and Family.

We the members of the 36th Aero Squadron SC. U. S. Army having served only recently under your son, Lieut. Quentin Roosevelt, A. S. Sig. R. C. who was in command of the squadron, wish to extend our sympathy and love to his father and mother and family, in the loss of their son and brother. His example shall serve to inspire us in all our trials, and our one ambition is to help avenge his death, which we shall always strive to do.

For and on behalf of the 36th Aero Squadron SC.

Joseph H. Graves,
1st Lt. M. R. C.

400th Aero Squadron, S. C.
Air Service Production Centre No. 2, A. E. F. France
August 1, 1918.

Colonel Theodore Roosevelt,

Oyster Bay, L. I., N.Y.

Dear Colonel Roosevelt:

It is with mingled pride and sorrow that we, the members of the 400th Aero Squadron (formerly the 29th Aero Squadron) write to you on the subject of the sad but glorious death of your son, Lieutenant Quentin Roosevelt.

It was our great privilege to know him as a man and a soldier, for a year past, since the time when he joined our squadron at Fort Wood, New York, early in July, 1917. During the pioneer days of the construction of our immense aviation camp, here in France, he was continuously with our squadron, for a period of several months, during which time he fulfilled the exacting duties of supply officer and of officer in charge of transportation. When he left us a few weeks ago to go to the front, having completed his flying training, we were certain that he would place himself where the fighting was fiercest, for it was his nature to do nothing by halves.

We do not exaggerate when we assure you that he had endeared himself to every man in our organisation, by his manly qualities and his prevailing amiability. He made us feel, to the last man, that he was our friend.

Our admiration for his glorious end rises above our great grief for his loss; and it is in this spirit that we write this small but sincere tribute to his memory.

From: The Enlisted Men of the 400th Aero Squadron
By: Jacob Anderson
                               1st Sgt. 400th Aero Squadron

Among the many accounts of Quentin's activities at Issoudun, the following appeared in the Indianapolis *Star:*

An incident in the short life of Lieut. Quentin Roosevelt, the youngest son of former President Theodore Roosevelt, that recalls the sturdy qualities of manhood of his father and his insistent demand and fearless fighting for right and justice, is related by Lieut. Linton A. Cox of this city, who lately returned from overseas, after serving as an aviator in the 94th Combat Squadron under Capt. Eddie Rickenbacker.

'During the winter of 1918,' said Lieut. Cox, 'when, as flying cadets under the command of Lieut. Quentin Roosevelt, we were receiving training at Issoudun in the art of standing guard in three feet of mud and were serving as saw and hatchet carpenters, building shelters for the 1,200 cadets who were waiting in vain for machines in which to fly, affairs suddenly reached a crisis when it was discovered that the quartermaster refused to issue rubber boots to us, because the regular printed army regulations contained no official mention or recognition of flying cadets.

'Requisition after requisition for boots had been refused by the captain in charge of the quartermaster's depot, in spite of the fact that the boys were wading around in worn-out shoes in slush and mud knee deep. The supply of rubber boots was plentiful, but the captain was a stickler for army red tape, and did not have the courage to exercise common sense, if he had any.' Lieut. Cox stated that so many cadets had become sick because of this needless exposure that Lieut. Roosevelt decided to take matters into his own hands. Going over to the quartermaster's depot and risking court-martial, he demanded of the captain, who was of superior rank, that the boots be issued at once. Again he was refused. Upon being pressed for a satisfactory reason why the requisitions were not honoured, the captain ordered Lieut. Roosevelt out of the office. He refused to go.

'Who do you think you are—what is your name?' asked the captain, who was unacquainted with Quentin. 'I'll tell you my name after you have honoured this requisition, but not before,' answered Lieut. Roosevelt. This led to a hot exchange of words. Suddenly Quentin, being unable longer to control his indignation, stepped up and said, 'If you'll take off your Sam Brown belt and insignia of rank I'll take off mine, and we'll see if you can put me out of the office. I'm going to have those boots for my men if I have to be court-martialled for a breach of military discipline.'

Two other officers who had been attracted to the scene by the loud voices intervened, and the men were separated, whereupon Quentin Roosevelt went to the major in charge of the battalion and refraining from any mention of his recent controversy, related how cadets by the score were being incapacitated for service and were suffering from pneumonia and influenza because requisitions for boots were not being honoured. The major agreed with Quentin that such a situation was absurd and that immediate relief should be granted.

Lieut. Roosevelt had hardly left the major's office when the quartermaster captain came in and stated that there was a certain aviation lieutenant in camp whom he wanted court-martialled.

'Who is this lieutenant?' asked the major.

'I don't know who he is,' replied the captain, 'but I can find out.'

'I know who he is,' said the major. 'His name is Quentin Roosevelt and there is no finer gentleman nor more efficient officer in this camp and from what I know, if any one deserves a court-martial you are the man. From now on you issue rubber boots to every cadet who applies for them, army regulations be d—d.'

The boots were immediately issued and the cadets were loud in their praise of Lieut. Roosevelt.

'This is just one instance of many,' said Lieut. Cox, 'that served to endear Quentin Roosevelt to the men under his command.'

Quentin was billeted in the little town of Mauperthuis during the last few weeks of his life; and inevitably struck up a friendship with the townsfolk, old and young.

Lieutenant Donald Hudson wrote:

> In the little village where Roosevelt lived with his fellow aviators they have renamed the Public Square 'Place Roosevelt,' and written it in big letters on the granite fountain. Quentin Roosevelt was one of the most modest of young men. The few French villagers knew him, and honoured him because of himself, because of his Father, and because of his fighting brothers. "Over his billet he had written the name of Lieutenant Thomas, his roommate, then his own, and then 'God bless our home."

Lieutenant A. B. Sherry, another friend and fellow aviator, tells how

> Q was a great favourite with the inhabitants of Mauperthuis, for he was always chatting with the old men about their affairs, and ever ready to listen to the troubles of their wives, and of the mothers of the boys away at the front.

An account, whose author we have been unable to ascertain, reads as follows:

Quentin, you know, was very young—I know he wasn't twenty-one. He was just a kid, full of life and good spirits. If he had been less peppy, he might not have got killed.

We were all billeted out in cottages in this little village of Mauperthuis, the population of which consisted of old ladies, the average age of whom, judging from appearances, was ninety-three—maybe a little more. Well, Quentin was a great favourite, not only among the members of the squadron, but with the old ladies. He spoke French very well indeed, and with this and his cheery ways he got into their good books, or they got into his, whichever way it was.

They all called him the noble, or the honourable, or the distinguished, or even the great Meestair Roussefel', and he received their greetings very gracefully. Roosevelt was about the only American name the French country people ever had heard until President Wilson became a world figure, and to have a real Roosevelt amongst them was something for these old ladies to talk about.

Young Roosevelt would go about from house to house and gossip with all the old ladies. The rest of us sometimes thought they were a bit of a nuisance. If I were trying to write a letter, for instance, and one of them rushed in with a long story to tell in her rapid, colloquial, quite incomprehensible French, I would feel like asking her to leave me alone for a while. But not Roosevelt. He would lay down his pen, put his paper aside, and chat about the weather or whatever the old lady wanted to chat about.

It would be: 'Ah, Madame Labrosse, and have you heard yet from the husband of your daughter Blanche?'

'But no, Meestair Roussefel', I have received no letter it is two weeks, and I fear that——'

'On the contrary,' Roosevelt would say, 'one should not give up the hope. He will arrive soon.'

'Ah, Meestair Roussefel', I of it hope well.'

The first thing that strikes your eye when you go into one of these French cottages is the framed photograph of the head of the family in uniform. Usually it is the uniform of 1871, and if you make inquiries you will be told all about him. You will be told, too, all about the other photographs in plush frames, and also the framed medals and ribbons. They turn their walls into photograph albums in rural France. A room thus becomes a sort of family history in four big wide-open pages for one who makes inquiries—but most of us didn't make inquiries, for the answer would be only a flow of very rapid French that nobody could understand—except Quentin Roosevelt. Where he learned to speak French I don't know. And he would make the most polite inquiries, and the old ladies would smile sweetly and pour out their stories.

What interested Quentin more than all the photographs, however, was the dancing brevet that hangs above nearly every French mantelpiece. It seems that as soon as you become proficient in anything over there you get either a medal or a brevet, which is a framed certificate. One of the most prized possessions of each of the old ladies of Mauperthuis is a dancing brevet which informs the reader that her son Henri, or Claude or Jean or Paul or Emile, in Anno Domini 1883 or thereabouts has taken so many lessons in dancing and is competent to lead a *cotillion* anywhere from Versailles to Montparnasse. Sometimes you find an old lady who has preserved her own dancing brevet, qualifying her to dance the minuet and the gavotte—for these faded documents date from the days when the new-fangled waltz was not mentioned in polite company.

'Ah, what is it that I see?' Quentin would say. 'A dancing brevet, *en effet*. How it is *gentil, hein?*'

And *Madame* would cross her hands on her lap and smile, and after a '*Je vous en prie*' to express her own unworthiness of such exalted favour, she would explain that her Henri, who is now on the Verdun sector, was a dancer the most unique, the most *magnifique*, the most *charmant*, and a whole lot of adjectives that I don't know, having no French-English dictionary about me.

Roosevelt would go around thus from house to house and the old ladies would beam upon him and after he was gone would exchange gossip about him. He had told them so-and-so, he had done so-and-so, he had praised highly the pictures of the baby of one's niece, had the son of the most great Tedd-ee.

I shall never forget how the news of Quentin's death was received in that little village. Of course, the old lady who kept his billet had considered herself much honoured by the presence of the *gentil* Meestair Rousseffel' beneath her roof. She was one of the oldest ladies in the village—her back was bent almost double, but she was able to get around with a stick and she never missed her round of gossip until the day Quentin was killed. Then she shut herself up in her house for a whole day. When she did come out, she was in deep mourning and her face was very sad.

An editorial of which Quentin's family was unable to learn the authorship was published in the Hartford *Courant*. The writer must have known Quentin intimately.

YOUNG ROOSEVELT'S NATURE

There was something very interesting about Quentin Roosevelt. He was not one of the usual run of boys. He was individual from those first days when boys begin to do things for themselves. Probably things looked to him different from what they do to the ordinary boy.

The ordinary boy sees the world very much as his parents and the older members of the family see it. The regular conventional view takes hold of him early. The mind of no healthy boy is quite standardised, but It's customary processes are in that direction. Little by little he absorbs or accepts the views of the generation into which he is born until these views are his own. It is thus that the judgments and work of the world go forward in an orderly way. One might almost call it the natural way. It is not the business of the usual mind, any more than it is of the usual plant, to originate. The main business of both minds and plants is to transmit, to maintain the good that we have and carry it forward.

Our civil and religious usages have come to us from our ancestors, and the main duty of most of us is to keep these usages alive and hand them forward to our children. This is the ordinary and natural law. It is so with the plants, and it is so with the human mind. The seed of wheat is expected to produce wheat and nothing else, and it habitually does. The human mind is expected to carry forward the ancient struggle against pauperism and ignorance and sin, and it usually does. Most boys are born to do this work, and they do it. They are often a little frisky at times; they disclose tendencies now and then toward new attitudes; but in the end the mass of them are halter-broke and settle down to the job of carrying things forward about as they are.

If most human minds did not work in this methodical and orderly way we would never get anywhere. The gains made in one generation would be frittered away by the next, and we would be continuously fussing with the beginnings. The continuous accumulation of worthwhile improvement would be checked, and the momentum of gains would be shattered into fragments.

Quentin Roosevelt was not built on these usual lines, and apparently he was not designed for this usual duty. He began very early to see for himself. He did not find much to see in human kind, either. He would not have found much in the ordinary man that was new, or especially interesting, if he had looked there. One sample is so much like another that a study of that sort soon exhausts itself. We can see this in the writers of novels and the writers of plays, who have to put strong social spices and sauces into their standardized work to freshen it. This younger Roosevelt turned to the primitive and unadulterated and untrained things, it is related of him that he once managed to get a hive of honey bees into a Washington street car in order to take them home with him to the White House. The ordinary boy learns very early that a bee is an uncertain companion.

Without doubt this Roosevelt youngster had received the same instruction and the same warning. The reason that it did not take was not because he was a bad boy, or a naughty boy, or a foolish boy. It did not take because his own way of looking at things made him sure that there was a method of getting along on safe terms even with bees. The rule about bees is a sound general rule. It fits the ordinary human mind and human sense like a glove. But Quentin Roosevelt's mind and sense were larger than the rule, and he could walk through the rule with a fair degree of safety. It was the same with all the natural things that walk or creep or crawl about the earth. These were the curious and companionable things with him.

One wonders if they understood him as well as he understood them. It is a fair assumption that many of them did. Harm might easily have come to him if they had not. This boy's look at them was different from the look of the usual boy, and upon some mysterious foundation of a common understanding they also knew it. It was his way with them, and his way was not the usual way or the conventional way. It was his own way—original, self-confident, and as honest as unclothed truth herself.

That Quentin Roosevelt took to navigating the clouds was nothing more than a normal unfolding and growth of his singular nature. There is nothing stranger or more unlikely in human history than that man should be able to fly through the air, and yet he is now doing this every day. The originating mind takes to this sort of thing naturally—it is exactly in its line. Unfortunately many of these minds are only half minds. They carry so much of the usual conventional crust that something goes wrong with them, and sooner or later they fall smashing earthward.

We feel sure that Quentin Roosevelt was not of this sort. It took the fierce shock of actual war to knock him out. We do not believe that his nerve broke or quivered for one instant. If his body were hit, or if his machine broke, that would be different. Smitten physically or mechanically, he of course was helpless. The fates had it in for him. But the mind of him went down intact, unshaken, and, so far as was possible in that hurried rush, with the calm outlook of the soul that is unafraid.

It was a great waste, aside from all personal considerations, because human minds that spontaneously and inevitably see things for themselves, outside of the clamps of convention, and almost in honest unconsciousness of such clamps, are too infrequent not to be missed when the human life goes out of them. Bacon quotes one of the fathers as saying that old men go to death, and death comes to young men. It is so, and has been so, all through this great war. Quentin Roosevelt died in the bloom of his youth and with untried powers. By nature he was made for greater things than even the honourable death of a righteous cause.

Chapter 6

Verses

There were many verses written in memory of Quentin, and this book would be incomplete without a short selection from them.

A Group of Poems
(To Quentin Roosevelt)

Spring on Long Island

*You used to think that some day you would hold
Some dear and splendid space
Of shining time to waste
Upon a spring-decked highway's beaten gold;—
Hearing birds sing, and mute and marvelling
Stoop to a harebell's grace—
Free of wind-voices and their breathless urge.
To see a green vine fling
Its brave young sinews upward to the eaves;
Or watch brown brothers soar, and dip, and merge
Dun coats with madder nests among the leaves.*

*And there would be deep noons, and shares of bread.
And water from a brook
Where you could bend and look
Down, at gay clouds that shimmered overhead;—
And from a pool would come the whispering
Of blue flags in a nook . . .
The stream would quaver like an ancient crone
(Hid in It's bubbling spring)
Weaving her magic in the sparkling air—
The feet of water-dancers on the stone*

Or brook-nymphs laughing through their dripping hair . . .
That road would wind like ribbon in the gleam
Of a white moon hung high
Out of your wing-won sky—
And you—a mote upon a silver seam—
While hedgerow blossoms made a bordering
Of moon-lace frilling by.
And a bird's voice, like a violin,
Poignant, would lift and sing
Haunted by 'cello warblings of It's mate;—
There would be night scents, sweet and sharp and thin,
Binding you wordless to that song elate . . .

"Never Before Have the Violets Blown"

Never before have the violets blown
Purple as exquisite;
Seeing they borrow it
From a wide sky his pinions have torn;
Yet must they stand all mute, unquestioning
Where glad green Joy is writ—
Knowing they fold a sleeper who forgets
Against warm pulses of dear violets
His part in vaunt and bacchanal of Spring.

Never before have the poppies flared
Scarlet as radiant;
A pomp as triumphant—
Fire from the stars his wings have dared;
Nor may they glow with brave isouciance
And yet no Vision grant—
Knowing their share in valour . . . they unfold
Their silken banners for heroic mould—
Their crimson badges for the breast of France.

Never before have the wind-voices breathed
In their dim whisperings
Echoes of wings. . . .
Faint from far zones where suns hang unsheathed;
Nor shall they tell but half; adventuresome
For further journeyings—
Knowing him wind's-brother-earth defying.
Gaunt winged, they call him to the flying

Shouting of star-trails and a sapphire dome . . .

THE DARK LEAVES

Oh, Voyager, who swept the blazing gold
Of wheeling planets in immensity:
Whose wing-beats cleft the silences that hold
Their echo yet, in stark serenity:
For you, oh Wreathed! let an altar's light
Flame holily, above the largess heaped—
New corn and grapes that sudden—in a night—
Were reaped. . . .

Glad one! the shining gifts you offered up . . .
Youth's corn in silk, and Youth's longevity:—
The sparkling vintage of Youth's brimming cup—
Youth's broken sword to spell divinity:—
The hushing of Youth's laughter, peal on peal—
The dreams of Youth that garlanded the days—
The wings Youth clapped upon a sandal's heel
The cymbaled measure of Youth's choric ways.

Trailer of stars, a gleaner in the dusk
Lifts the Dark Leaves from red austerity:
Gathers your Arum lilies from the husk
Of trampled wrack;—your lyric purity—
The chaunts you sang to baffle cold and tire—
(Reckon them priceless since Youth's pipe is mute)
The still warm ashes of your sacred fire—
The glowing round of your scarce bitten fruit.

Strange, you should lie a sleeper in high noon . . .
Clothing yourself in wreathed dignity?—
Your hablimental trappings folded: soon
Poppies will trumpet with scarlet clarity:—
(Witness this plumage . . . these, his wings—
Reckon the giving by the dreamless eyes . . .
Are these not meet for altar-gifts—these things?
Seeing the Dark Leaves speak him Heavenwise . . .)

AVENUE QUENTIN

There are no palm trees
Along the way
Holding

Their plumage against the blue.—
Only
The clean voices of the winds.
And the footsteps of Youth,
Call to him
In comradeship from the wide
Highway.
Echo with crisp brittle resonance
Against the frozen rime
Of the sweep,—
Where frosted bitter-sweet scatters
Redly.
But at night—
A slim young shallop moon sails
Boat-wise
Upon his old courses.
Pushes a silver prow through
Cloudrifts—
The lapping gauzes of morning.—
Hailing the veiled houses
Of stars . . .
Nebulous, hushed, and unanswering.—
Here!
Spring will come greenly.
With lush grasses,—
And violets stand in little groups
By the wayside—
Gazing up at you
Out of their deep eyes as if to say
"He is yonder
Where we are bluest!"
But
Only in the spring time is one directed
So unassumingly,—
By small pages in purple smocks.
In July
The field armies in France
Leap
In serried ranks to
The colours!

Scarlet shoulder to scarlet shoulder.
The Avenue Quentin's poppy-guards
Blazon you on with
Chivalry!

Always!
The answer of Youth
To Youth!—
(Glad youth with his laughter
And daring!)
The call
Of one road to another—
Of a slim shallop moon's far sailing.—
Who
May reckon the strange ports she touches?
The way
Of her track through the cloud rifts—
Through the lapping gauzes
Of morning. . . . Speaking shut houses
Of stars . . .—
For in July—
The gleaming zeniths of space
Hurl
Uncharted worlds to the colours!
Flaming planet to flaming planet.
An Avenue Quentin's meteor-hosts—
Blazon you on
With chivalry!

—Lelia Miller Pearce.

YOUNG ROOSEVELT IS DEAD

Young Roosevelt is dead—and I, whose son
Is just a little boy, too young to go.
Read with bewildered eyes the tales recalled
Of pranks the little White House boy had played!

Just such things as ray own does every day
With bugs and beetles, teasing with his snake,
Or startling all about him with his bees—
Exasperating tricks—that win our souls!

Just such things none could think of but a boy.
From blurring page I turn to touch my own,

For somehow he, too, died in that far fall
Of one who typed America's "small boy."

From blurring page I turn to touch my own—
To lift his face unto the lustrous stars
That symbolise the glory of a world—
And once more dedicate my country's son.

From blurring page a sterner nation turns
Because he typed the millions she has borne
Within her fertile womb since long ago
She mated with the freedom of the world.

From blurring page graybeards with palsied hands
May dream again of wondrous youth that flings
All life into a single burning flame
And lives its future in a moment's deed.

Men who, perhaps, have lost the zest for life
May find it in a boy's keen zest for death,
When young life found it sweet to fight and die
If only Liberty in peace might live.

—Eleanor Cochran Reed, in The Times, New York.

The Star of Gold

Quentin Roosevelt, France, July 14, 1918
With the American Army on the Vesle, Wednesday, August 7 (by A. P.).—On a wooden cross at the head of a grave at the edge of a wood at Chamery, east of Fére-en-Tardenois, is this inscription:

Lieutenant Quentin Roosevelt, buried by the Germans.

—Newspaper item.

A Viking of the air was he
Who sailed his fragile plane
Through vast uncharted spaces blue,
As Norsemen sailed the main.
He met the foeman and he fought
Unflinching in the sky,
And died as his brave sire would wish
A soldier-son to die.

The Prussian airmen wrought his grave
And laid him down to rest.

His shroud the leather tunic wrapped
About his gallant breast.
The guns a thunderous requiem
All day above him sound,
America in spirit mourns
Beside his lonely mound.

When twilight over No Man's Land
A veil of purple weaves.
An escadrille of stars appears
Above the hangar's eaves
With one that speeds on wings of light
In ether fast and far;
The Allied aviators say
'Tis Quentin Roosevelt's star.
     —Minna Irving.

The Town Called After Him

The town of Bismarck, Pa., has changed its name to Quentin.—*Vide* Newspapers.

Quentin, young Quentin Roosevelt
Has a town called after him!
Some way, as we read the word
It makes the eyes grow dim.

How brave they were, how young they were!
Our boys who went to die!
Children who played in field and street
So short a time gone by.

Now reach the stature of the stars!
Ah, none of us can say
How many Heavenly places
Are named for such as they.

But romping children here, through years
Secured from horrors grim.
Will speak the name of Quentin
In the town called after him.
     Mary Stewart Cutting.

To Quentin Roosevelt

They sounded taps, young soldier of the free.

CHANGED TO GOLD
From the original cartoon by John T. McCutcheon,
presented to Colonel Roosevelt

And heaped memorial flowers above your breast.
In France across the North Atlantic sea.
Where you are lying quietly at rest.

On soil in bondage to your mortal foe
You fell. Foes laid you in a soldier's grave!
Today above you Yankee bugles blow—
French tears, French flowers, rain upon the brave.

We'd laughed at all your pranks and boyish wit
And scarce could think you grown to man's estate;
The shot that brought you down, the nation hit;
O'er all the land hearts leaped with grief and hate.

But you!—'twas thus, brave heart, you'd choose to go;
If come death must, you'd have him ride a cloud;
And when you went, 'twas gaily, that I know,
As well befits the gallant and the proud.

Above your breast the Yankee bugles blow;
French hands are twining wreaths across the sea;
And somewhere your brave heart is joyed to know
That all about your grave French soil is free.
      —Harry D. Thompson.

A Monsieur Le Président Théodore Roosevelt
Hommage de Respectueuse Admiration d'une Alsacienne de France
Ne pleurez pas l'oiseau qui s'est brisé les ailes
Dans le rude combat des saintes libertés,
Dans l'enthousiasme fier des amitiés fidèles,
Des serments renoués de nos fraternités.

Notre sol que son sang a rougi dans sa chute
Nous en est plus sacré, plus cher peut-être encore,
Et nous avons senti, mieux, à cette minute
Se resserrer nos liens par le don de sa mort.

Ne pleurez pas l'oiseau fauché par la mitraille
Dans l'essor radieux d'un rêve éblouissant,
Qui, tout vibrant encore de l'ardente bataille,
A pris vers l'infini libre son vol puissant.

Votre fils est tombé dans une juste guerre,
Combattant vaillamment un infâme oppresseur,
Dans l'héroïque élan du sacrifice austère,
De son pur idéal sublime défenseur.

Il est des morts pour qui le regret est l'offense,
Ne pleurez pas celui qui fit tout son devoir.
Que votre deuil soit fait de fierté, d'espérance,
Levez plus haut le front, les yeux pour mieux le voir.
Car c'est lui, maintenant, le vrai chef de famille,
Toute sa jeune gloire a rejailli sur vous;
Votre nom, c'est le sien qui sur vos têtes brille,
Etoile au clair éclat, resplendissant et doux.

A votre cœur, pourtant, la blessure est saignante.
Plus grand le vide, hélas, laissé par le départ,
Obstinément, partout, une tombe vous haute.
Que par dessus la mer cherche votre regard.

Dans un sol envahi quelques jours prisonnière.
La voici libre enfin des ennemis chassés,
Et nos drapeaux, baignés dans sa sainte lumière,
Comme un même drapeau s'y tiendront enlacés.

Elle sera fleurie avec des fleurs de France,
Fleurs de notre pays meurtri, mais délivré,
Heureuses de jeter, cri de reconnaissance,
Leur beauté, leurs parfums, sur ce terra sacré.

Et noire âme fervente y veille tout entière.
Car nous gardons, au fond du coeur, fidèlement,
Dans notre souvenir plein de recueillement,
Parmi nos plus chers morts, une place très chère
Au mort que vous aimez, votre fils, notre frère.
           —Charlotte Schnéegans, *14 septembre 1918.*

On the Screen

Within the darkened playhouse as I sat
Sunk in a mood of heavy discontent
Because existence was so difficult:
The things undone—the money I had spent—
And other little, petty, tiresome cares
Weighed on my mind, until I scarce would glance
At all the moving scenes before my eyes,
When suddenly I looked—and there was France:
France! With her scarred and desolated fields,
Sad wastes,—yet piteous poppies blossomed there—
And row on rows of the unnumbered dead

And crosses, crosses, crosses everywhere
And at the last, one solitary cross
Apart, aloof from earthly vanity
And on the cross stood Quentin Roosevelt's name:
Rare sacrifice to crass humanity!

Then did I count myself as nothing worth
And all my little cares so poor and mean—
It must have been a Great Photographer
Who let me see myself upon the screen!
—Elizabeth Jacobi.

The Ongoing

Loose me from tears and make me see aright
How each hath back what once he stayed to weep—
Homer his sight, David his little lad.

He will not come, the gallant flying boy,
Back to his field. Somewhere he wings his way
Where the Immortals keep; where Homer now
Has back his sight, David his little lad;
Where all those are we dully call the dead.
Who have gone greatly on some shining quest.
He takes his way. That which he quested for.
That larger freedom of a larger birth,
Captains him, flying into fields of dawn.

He has gone on where now the soldier-slain
Arise in light. Somewhere he takes his place
And leads his comrades in untrodden fields.
For never can these rest until our earth
Has ceased from travail—never can these take
Their fill of sleep until the Scourge is slain.
And so they keep them sometimes near old ways
In the accustomed fields—now flying low,
Invisible, they cheer the gallant host,
Bidding them be, as they, invincible.

Still he leads on, the gallant flying boy!
Among the "great good Dead" he steers his boundless course.
Now where the soldier-poets pass in light—
Where Brooke and Seeger and the others keep—
The singing Slain, the peerless fighting Dead—

He takes his brilliant way; or where those lately come
Our flying Great, Mitchel and all his men,
Wait him in large, warm-hearted welcoming.

He will come never back! But we who watched
Him take the upper air and steer his boundless path
Firmly against the foe, we know that here
Death could not penetrate. Life only is
Where all is life, and so, before us, keeps
Always the vision of his faring on
To unpathed fields where his great comrades wait,
And, joyful, take him for their captaining—
The brave Adventurer,
The gallant flying Boy!
　　　　　　　　—Mary Siegrist.

Lord Dunsany, in a letter, said:

I was told once before, quite recently, that Captain Quentin Roosevelt had one of my books with him, even sometimes up in the air. It was a touching thing for an author to hear. I don't know what return I can make for that, but I would like to offer the enclosed sonnet to you.

A Dirge of Victory

Lift not thy trumpet, Victory, to the sky.
Nor through battalions, nor by batteries blow.
But over hollows full of old wire go
Where among dregs of war the long-dead lie
With wasted iron that the guns passed by
When they went eastwards like a tide at flow:
There blow thy trumpet that the dead may know
Who waited for thy coming, Victory.

It is not we that have deserved thy wreath:
They waited there among the towering weeds:
The deep mud burned under the thermites' breath
And winter cracked the bones that no man heeds:
Hundreds of nights flamed by: the seasons passed.
And thou hast come to them at last, at last.
　　　　　　　　Dunsany,
　　　　Captain Royal Inniskilling Fusiliers.

ALSO FROM LEONAUR
AVAILABLE IN SOFTCOVER OR HARDCOVER WITH DUST JACKET

WINGED WARFARE *by William A. Bishop*—The Experiences of a Canadian 'Ace' of the R.F.C. During the First World War.

THE STORY OF THE LAFAYETTE ESCADRILLE *by George Thenault*—A famous fighter squadron in the First World War by its commander..

R.F.C.H.Q. *by Maurice Baring*—The command & organisation of the British Air Force during the First World War in Europe.

SIXTY SQUADRON R.A.F. *by A. J. L. Scott*—On the Western Front During the First World War.

THE STRUGGLE IN THE AIR *by Charles C. Turner*—The Air War Over Europe During the First World War.

WITH THE FLYING SQUADRON *by H. Rosher*—Letters of a Pilot of the Royal Naval Air Service During the First World War.

OVER THE WEST FRONT *by "Spin" & "Contact"* —Two Accounts of British Pilots During the First World War in Europe, Short Flights With the Cloud Cavalry by "Spin" and Cavalry of the Clouds by "Contact".

SKYFIGHTERS OF FRANCE *by Henry Farré*—An account of the French War in the Air during the First World War.

THE HIGH ACES *by Laurence la Tourette Driggs*—French, American, British, Italian & Belgian pilots of the First World War 1914-18.

PLANE TALES OF THE SKIES *by Wilfred Theodore Blake*—The experiences of pilots over the Western Front during the Great War.

IN THE CLOUDS ABOVE BAGHDAD *by J. E. Tennant*—Recollections of the R. F. C. in Mesopotamia during the First World War against the Turks.

THE SPIDER WEB *by P. I. X. (Theodore Douglas Hallam)*—Royal Navy Air Service Flying Boat Operations During the First World War by a Flight Commander

EAGLES OVER THE TRENCHES *by James R. McConnell & William B. Perry*—Two First Hand Accounts of the American Escadrille at War in the Air During World War 1-Flying For France: With the American Escadrille at Verdun and Our Pilots in the Air

KNIGHTS OF THE AIR *by Bennett A. Molter*—An American Pilot's View of the Aerial War of the French Squadrons During the First World War.

AVAILABLE ONLINE AT **www.leonaur.com**
AND FROM ALL GOOD BOOK STORES

www.ingramcontent.com/pod-product-compliance
Lightning Source LLC
Chambersburg PA
CBHW030217170426
43201CB00006B/114